# THE CHICAGO SCHOOL

# The Chicago School

How the University of Chicago Assembled
the Thinkers Who Revolutionized
Economics and Business

*Johan Van Overveldt*

**A B2 Book**

# AGATE

CHICAGO

Printed in Canada.

Library of Congress Cataloging-in-Publication Data
Overtveldt, Johan van.
    The Chicago School : how the University of Chicago assembled the
thinkers who revolutionized economics and business / by Johan Van
Overtveldt.
        p. cm.
    Summary: "In-depth history of the Chicago School of Economics, from
its beginnings at the University of Chicago to its global impact on business
and economics"--Provided by publisher.
    Includes bibliographical references and index.
    ISBN-13: 978-1-932841-14-5 (hardcover)
    ISBN-10: 1-932841-14-8 (hardcover)
    1. Chicago school of economics—History. I. Title.
    HB98.3.O87 2007
    330.15'53—dc22

                                                    2005037373


                    10 9 8 7 6 5 4 3 2 1

            B2 Books is an imprint of Agate Publishing.
            Agate books are available in bulk at discount prices.
            For more information, go to agatepublishing.com.

# Table of Contents

# Introduction

IF ADAM SMITH IS THE FATHER OF THAT DISMAL SCIENCE CALLED economics, then Chicago is arguably its capital. It is clearly an understatement to say that economists working at the University of Chicago played an important role in the development of economics as a science during the 20th century, as indicated by the dominance of University of Chicago economists among the laureates of the Nobel Prize in economics, the Francis A. Walker Medal, and the John Bates Clark Medal.

Judging by the way the University of Chicago has dominated the Nobel Prize in economics, one must conclude that Chicago is both a Mecca and a Rome for economic science. The Nobel Prize-winning track record of the University of Chicago is impressive. From 1969, when the prize was first awarded, to 2004, 57 economists have received the honor (in several years, the prize was shared by two or three people). Of those 58 laureates, nine were primarily associated with the University of Chicago: Milton Friedman, Theodore W. Schultz, George Stigler, Merton Miller, Ronald Coase, Gary Becker, Robert Fogel, Robert Lucas Jr., and James Heckman. By this count, Chicago has pocketed more than double the amount of wins of the numbers two and three schools, Harvard University and the University of California at Berkeley. But Chicago's dominance of the Nobel Prize goes further than those 9 out of 57 laureates suggest.

A number of other winners who were not directly affiliated with the University of Chicago were in Chicago when doing their Nobel-winning work. Myron Scholes and Robert Mundell (laureates in 1997 and 1999, respectively) should also be considered Chicago wins. Friedrich Hayek and Tjalling Koopmans, laureates in 1974 and 1975, respectively, spent several years in Chicago, during which time some of their most significant work was done.

To complete the list, one must also mention the winners of the Nobel Prize in Economics who spent time at the University of Chicago as a student and/or a researcher: Paul Samuelson, Kenneth Arrow, Herbert Simon, Lawrence Klein, Gerard Debreu, James Buchanan, Trygve Haavelmo, Harry Markowitz, Vernon Smith, Edward Prescott, and Edmund Phelps.

The argument can even be stretched to the past. Swedish economist Assar Lindbeck, who for many years was closely involved in the Nobel selection process, pointed out that several "important candidates" missed the Nobel Prize because they died shortly after the prize was established; Jacob Viner and Frank Knight, who were among the most prominent economists who ever worked at the University of Chicago, were both singled out by Lindbeck (1985, 52).

The list of Francis A. Walker Medal winners also highlights the importance of Chicago economists. Inaugurated in 1947 by the American Economic Association, this medal was awarded every five years to the living American economist who had made the greatest contribution to the discipline. The award was discontinued in 1981 because of its overlap with the Nobel Prize in economics. In total, seven economists received the Francis A. Walker Award: Wesley Mitchell, John Maurice Clark, Frank Knight, Jacob Viner, Alvin Hansen, Theodore W. Schultz, and Simon Kuznets; most of them had a Chicago connection.

As I hope my analysis will make clear, Knight, Viner, and Schultz are prime examples of "Chicago" economists. Mitchell was educated at the University of Chicago and stayed for a few years as a member of the faculty. Clark was among the leading economists at the University of Chicago from 1915 to 1926, during which time he wrote two of his most important books.

The John Bates Clark Medal, a biennial prize sponsored by the American Economic Association that is awarded to the most promising economist under the age of 40, also lists many Chicago economists among its winners. In 1951, Paul Samuelson was the first laureate. Including the 2005 winner, 29 economists have received the honor, and five of them are undeniably Chicago economists: Friedman, Becker, Heckman, Kevin Murphy, and Steven Levitt. Several other laureates, such as Kenneth Boulding, Zvi Griliches, Marc Nerlove, Sanford Grossman, and Andrei Shleifer, also have strong links to the University of Chicago.

These observations raise a number of questions. What, if anything, is so special about the University of Chicago? Specifically, what was its role in the development of modern economics? What were the major contributions that give Chicago economists a prominent place in the 20th century's history of economic thought? What has made economists working at the University of Chicago so successful in their research work and academic achievements? Was this triumphant century just an incredibly long-lasting coincidence, or is there more to it? Are the scientific merits of Chicago economists real, or are they forced on the rest of the profession by, say, Adam Smith's invisible hand? This book is an attempt to develop some answers to these questions.

## LITERATURE ON CHICAGO

Attention for the University of Chicago and its role in the development of modern economics is not new. Economics at the University of Chicago was different from that which was practiced at other centers of economic research in the last decade of the 19th century. It was James L. Laughlin, the first chairman of Chicago's department of political economy, who created this difference. Laughlin adhered rigidly to the orthodox version of classical economics, and he showed very little appreciation for deviations from this orthodoxy. Under Laughlin's chairmanship, the economics department of the University of Chicago was isolated "as a center of doctrinal orthodoxy and extreme conservatism in matters of policy" (Coats 1963, 490).

Despite his considerable shortcomings as a detached academic, Laughlin assembled a diversified faculty that, through the efforts of such scholars as Wesley Mitchell, Leon C. Marshall, John M. Clark, and Jacob Viner, developed into a strong and much less isolated department. Gordon Tullock (1983, iv) concluded: "Until the 1930s, one could not refer to a Chicago School of Economics. The Chicago department would have been considered simply an extraordinarily strong part of the mainstream of economics." Despite Tullock's observation, A.W. Coats (Coats 1963, 492) speculated in the beginning of the 1960s that "echoes of the past sometimes linger on, and it is conceivable that traces of Chicago's early reputation as a center of economic conservatism have survived until recent times."

The next explicit reference to Chicago as something distinguishable from the rest of the profession came from Aaron Director (1948, v), who referred to Henry Simons as "slowly establishing himself as the head of a 'school' " at the University of Chicago. Although Director did not substantiate the matter further, Jacob Viner wrote the following in a letter to Don Patinkin years later:

> It was not until I left Chicago in 1946 that I began to hear rumors about a "Chicago School" which was engaged in organized battle for laissez faire and the "quantity theory of money" and against "imperfect competition" theorizing and "Keynesianism"... [After attending a conference sponsored by the University of Chicago in 1951] ... I was willing to consider the existence of a "Chicago School" (but one not confined to the economics department and not embracing all of the department) and that this "School" had been in operation, and had won many able disciples, for years before I left Chicago. But at no time was I consciously a member of it, and it is my vague impression that if there was such a school it did not regard me as a member. (Patinkin 1981, 266).

From the late 1950s forward, references to the "Chicago School" became more commonplace. In 1957 Edward Chamberlin of Harvard referred to the "Chicago School of Anti-Monopolistic Competition" (296). Under the leadership of Knight and later Stigler, the University of Chicago did indeed develop into a bastion of rejection of the basic message of Chamberlin's landmark book *The Theory of Monopolistic Competition*, which was first published in 1933.[1] The rejection of Chamberlin's approach coincided with the origin of one of the most important branches of Chicago economics: that is, the Chicago approach to industrial organization and antitrust.[2]

In 1962, the idea of Chicago as something special in the field of economics came into focus in Miller's article "On the 'Chicago School of Economics.'" Miller identified five characteristics by which a "Chicago economist" distinguishes himself or herself from other economists: "the polar position that he occupies among economists as an advocate of an individualistic market economy; the emphasis that he puts on the usefulness and relevance of neo-classical economic theory; the way in which he equates the actual and the ideal market; the way in which he sees and applies economics in and to every nook and cranny of life; and the emphasis that he puts on hypothesis-testing as a neglected element in the development of positive economics" (65).

In the same issue of the *Journal of Political Economy,* Stigler (1962, 71) commented briefly on Miller's article and rejected its claim of the existence of a clearly distinguishable "Chicago School of Economics" on the basis that Miller "has not described either a unifying ethical or political philosophy or an articulate and reasonably specific policy program. Instead, he has merely sketched, less than completely, the views of my friend Milton Friedman ... [Friedman] has not been ignored at Chicago, but I believe that his influence on policy views has been greater elsewhere than here."

Martin Bronfenbrenner, who earned a PhD at the University of Chicago in 1939, also commented on Miller's article. Although Miller had hinted at the distinction, it was Bronfenbrenner (1962, 72–73) who explicitly stated that

> There are not one but two Chicago Schools; the departure
> of Jacob Viner and the passing of Henry Simons are the water-
> sheds between them ... The major differences [between the
> two groups] relate not only ... to attitudes toward monopo-
> lies and unions ... [The older group] involves ... greater con-
> cern with the price level than (the younger group) and less con-
> cern with the money supply. It also involves more concern than
> [the younger group] ... for the ethics and aesthetics of income
> and wealth distribution and redistribution along with, although
> not equal to, concern with economic freedom and allocative
> efficiency.

What is believed to be the first mention of the term "Chicago School" in a widely used handbook on the history of economic thought occurred in 1971.[3] Spiegel (1971) referred to the "Chicago School" in the context of its outright rejection of Chamberlin's theory of monopolistic competition. Furthermore, he notes the "… conservative leanings both in politics and in matters of doctrine [of the members of the Chicago School] … Libertarians all, they preferred rules to authorities and the impersonal forces of the market to their deliberate direction, and they viewed with alarm the increasing scope of governmental activities in the economic sphere." (582, 642).

One year later, Wall (1972, vii) described three basic characteristics of the Chicago School: "First, that theory is of fundamental importance; second, that theory is irrelevant unless set in a definite empirical context; and, third, that in the absence of evidence to the contrary, the market works." This description resembles the one Friedman (1974, 2) gave two years later:

> In discussions of economic science, "Chicago" stands for an approach that takes seriously the use of economic theory as a tool for analyzing a startlingly wide range of concrete problems, rather than as an abstract mathematical structure of great beauty but little power; for an approach that insists on the empirical testing of theoretical generalizations and that rejects alike facts without theory and theory without facts. In discussions of economic policy, "Chicago" stands for belief in the efficacy of the free market as a means of organizing resources, for skepticism about government intervention into economic affairs, and for emphasis on the quantity theory of money as a key factor in producing inflation.

Contrary to Miller and Bronfenbrenner, Friedman saw no distinction between an older and a younger school and emphasized that the 80 years between 1892 and the mid-1970s brought only "minor" changes in what the Chicago School is all about.

In April 1974, the same year that Friedman formulated the aforementioned remarks on the Chicago School, Stigler published a biographical article on Simons in the *Journal of Law and Economics*. In line with Director's 1948 remarks, Stigler (1982b) described Simons as "the Crown Prince of that hypothetical kingdom, the Chicago School of economics" (166). Stigler later comments, "The 'Chicago School' has always been a phrase whose accuracy varied inversely to its content" (170). Stigler defined as a major difference between the older leaders of the school (Knight, Simons, Lloyd Mints, and Viner) and his own generation the fact that for the latter, empirical work was much more important than for the former.

The publication of the book *The Chicago School of Economics,* which explored what was claimed to be the Chicago School from various angles including methodology, libertarianism, law and economics, development economics, industrial organization, and regulation, further distinguished the Chicago School as a significant entity in economics. Samuels (1993, 1,3,4,9) concluded this "constructive critique" by arguing that "... the Chicago School represents the extreme vanguard of neoclassicism. It is the foremost ideological extension of that area of economics ... The ultimate Chicago position is that the market system, whatever its structure of power ... possesses *inherently* more power diffusion than any alternative system." On several occasions in the Samuels volume, attention is drawn to the "self-admitted and intentional propaganda role of Chicago spokesman" (10). As far as could be discovered, this is the first place in which the pursuit of ideological purposes and the use of propaganda are brought forward as characteristics of the Chicago School.

The next landmark contribution on the Chicago School is a 1982 article by Melvin Reder. Whereas Reder described economists at the University of Chicago in the late 1930s as a "mixed bag," he saw the formation of a "Knight affinity group" during the 1940s and 1950s as the focal point of a school at the University of Chicago (2,7). Centered around Knight,[4] this group consisted of members young (Friedman, Stigler, and Allen Wallis) and old (Mints, Director, and Simons). Reder described this Knight-centered group as the "Friends and Members of the Mt. Pelerin Society;" according to him, its approach to economics—in the positive and normative sense—only partially overlaps "Chicago-style" economists' emphasis on the broad applicability of price theory and on empirical verification (32). According to Reder, the dominance of the group around Knight (with Friedman as its towering figure) at the University of Chicago was reinforced by the departure of the Cowles Commission in 1953 and the illness of the Keynesian disciple Lloyd Metzler.

Stigler devoted a chapter of his memoir to the Chicago School; in it, he also painted Friedman as the primary architect of the Chicago School. More specifically, Stigler (1988b, 150–51) identifies three issues that constitute Friedman's "fundamental contributions to the formation of the Chicago School. First, he revived the study of monetary economics … Second, he presented strong defenses of laissez-faire policies … And finally, he developed and employed modern price theory in important ways."

In his own memoirs, Friedman referred to the Chicago School explicitly only once. He argued that the combination of teaching and research in price and monetary theory during his period at the University of Chicago (1948–1976) "gave birth to what came to be known as the Chicago School of Monetary Economics" (Friedman and Friedman 1998, 202).

In the early 1990s, Colin D. Campbell (1994) contributed a four-page piece, "The Chicago School," to the *McGraw-Hill Encyclopedia of Economics*. Stating that "recognition of a distinctive Chicago School arose in [the] 1950s," Campbell described Friedman as "more closely identified with the Chicago School than any other economist," and he indicated that the principal characteristic of the philosophy of the Chicago School is "its emphasis on freedom rather than equality," a characteristic that "stems primarily from the work of Frank H. Knight."

Campbell further defined three important policy positions that are typical for economists of the Chicago School: the belief that "competitive markets are the best way to organize economic activity," the highly critical attitude toward "most types of government regulation of the economy," and the belief that "the kind of monetary system a country has is important" (141, 142). French historians of economic thought Michel Beaud and Gilles Dostaler (1995, 112) described the Chicago School in a similar way: "[It is] the work carried out in very diverse fields of specialization, but united by a solid faith in the neoclassical theory of prices, the conviction that the free market is the most efficient mechanism to allocate resources and a fundamental scepticism about state intervention in the economy."

Baumol (2000) and Lazear (2000), two surveys of modern contributions to economics, do not make any explicit reference to the Chicago School. However, Baumol (2000, 8) argued that as far as microeconomics is concerned, the truly new contributions are to be found in the areas of "human capital theory, the economics of discrimination, moral hazard, principal-agent problems, contract theory, and the Coase theorem." With the exception of moral hazard, scholars from the University of Chicago produced seminal contributions to each of these areas.

In his survey, Lazear focused more on the way in which economics infiltrated neighboring scientific fields such as law, sociology, and political sciences—areas where Chicago scholars such as Becker and Stigler also figure prominently.

The first volume of Ross Emmett's book, *The Chicago Tradition in Economics* (2002, xvii), opens with the following sentence: "The University of Chicago's economists have had a significant impact on the development of the American economics profession and economic policy in the twentieth century." Noting that "the legacy of Chicago economics goes back to the University's earliest days, and is far more diverse than common descriptions of the Chicago School allow," Emmett further argued that "Chicago economics was different by the 1940s, primarily because of the emergence of a contingent of economists committed to developing market-based solutions to social problems" (xvii–xviii).

In a context that is highly critical of what Chicago economics is generally understood to stand for, Philip Mirowski (2002, 203–4) associated the "Chicago School of economics in the postwar period" with three commandments:

Its first commandment is that the market always "works," in the sense that its unimpeded operation maximizes welfare. Its second commandment is that the government is always part of the problem, rather than part of the solution. The third commandment is that the demand curve is the rock-bottom fundamental entity in price theory, and that attempts to "go behind" the demand curve in order to locate its foundations in the laws of utility or "indifference" ... were primarily a waste of time and effort.

Mirowski (2002, 207) criticized the Chicago School for a number of reasons, including the fact that "the economic agent was frequently conflated with a Chicago economist: believing in a partial equilibrium model of the world, the consumer carried out simple inductive statistical exercises to augment the unerringly accurate information provided by the market."

Over the decades, the ideas of the Chicago School have been analyzed as an ideological product. The way in which the Chicago School of economics has come to be identified with the policies of the Pinochet dictatorship in Chile is a good example.[5] The basic doctrine of the Chicago School, Juan Gabriel Valdes (1995, 78) argued, implies a "bias against politics" and hence "an economic reductionism" that makes it a most attractive ideology and policy guide to undemocratic regimes such as Pinochet's. Friedman strongly resisted this line of argument.[6]

I hope this all too brief and hence incomplete overview of the literature on the Chicago School shows that each of the contributions is limited in its approach, either in the time dimension and/or with respect to the topics covered.

I will try to accomplish three goals with this book. First, I will try to give a systematic overview of the contributions made by Chicago economists from the end of the 19th century until the dawn of the 21st century. Second, I hope to bring forward several new insights with respect to the original contributions made by economists working at the University of Chicago. Third, I hope to clearly define and distinguish between the Chicago School and the Chicago Tradition as elements of an explanation for the successes achieved by economists at the University of Chicago.

The focus of this book will be on the work of economists who were members of the University of Chicago's faculty. Although a great deal of interesting research in the spirit of typical Chicago-style economics has been done outside of Chicago, this work will only be mentioned here if it is useful or necessary to better understand Chicago-produced work.

## Overview of the Book

Despite the fact that most research on the characteristics of economics at the University of Chicago focuses on the Chicago School, Chapter 1 will begin with what I define as the Chicago Tradition. The basic characteristics of this Chicago Tradition are: a strong work ethic, an unshakable belief in economics as a true science, academic excellence as the sole criterion for advancement, an intense debating culture focused on sharpening the critical mind, and the University of Chicago's two-dimensional isolation. Much of the credit for the creation of this Chicago Tradition has to go to the University's first president, William Rainey Harper.

Of course, not all of these characteristics of the Chicago Tradition were present when the University of Chicago was founded in 1892. Major parts of that tradition go back to a number of scholars who have been described as the founding fathers of the field of economic study at the University of Chicago, six of whom are standouts. James L. Laughlin and Thorstein Veblen were at the University's Department of Political Economy from day one. Two other important early contributors to the advancement of the University of Chicago as a major center of economic research were John M. Clark and Leon C. Marshall. The fifth founding father is Frank Knight, a man who had a deep influence on many economists at the University of Chicago. I consider Aaron Director to be as a sixth founding father of the Chicago Tradition in economics.

Next to the Chicago Tradition, there is the Chicago School, which is the subject of Chapters 3 and 4. As I define it, the basic characteristic of the Chicago School is the belief that free markets and the price mechanism are the most effective and desirable ways for a society to organize production and economic life in general. The central place of price theory in the teaching of economics at Chicago is embodied in the Economics 301 course for first-year graduate students. That is the reason why I present Viner, Friedman, and Becker—the triumvirate that taught this course during the past three quarters of a century—as the presiding spirits of the Chicago School.

Chapter 3 discusses Viner and Friedman. In his memoirs, Stigler described Viner as the founder of the Chicago School focus on price theory. Viner was that, and much more. He also had a thorough knowledge of the theory of international trade and the history of economic thought, and by the early 1930s, Viner had already written the antidepression prescription that later on came to be identified with John Maynard Keynes. However, Viner rejected Keynes's claim that he had developed a "general" theory, and that the theory of prices was just a special case of that "general" theory.

Friedman challenged the economics of Keynes's General Theory to an even greater degree. Although he is best known for his monetary and macroeconomic research and writings, he was first a price theorist—see, for example, his analysis of the Marshallian demand curve and his permanent income hypothesis. These topics link Friedman to forerunners such as Henry Schultz and Margaret Reid.

Becker is the central figure in Chapter 4. He and Stigler became the champions of the application of basic price theory to a range of areas that were formerly thought to lie outside the reach of traditional economic analysis, including the economics of crime, family, marriage, and discrimination. The strong sociological flavor of much of Becker's work brought him in close contact with James Coleman, a prominent Chicago sociologist.

Chicago economist and Nobel laureate Theodore Schultz was crucial to Becker's work on human capital—the work for which Becker, until today, has earned his highest praise. Schultz established the University of Chicago as an important research center with respect to agricultural economics and development economics. For more than half a century, Schultz's pupil D. Gale Johnson was a pillar of the agricultural economics program and the rest of the economics department at the University of Chicago. Zvi Griliches, Marc Nerlove, Robert Tolley, and Yair Mundlak were also important economists who started in this field of study.

The human capital idea developed by Becker and Schultz became an important part of most modern theories on economic growth, and Chicago's Robert Lucas made fundamental contributions to its development. Human capital also had a substantial influence on labor economics. H. Gregg Lewis played a crucial role in the move away from institutionalism toward more analytical rigor in labor economics. The fact that the University of Chicago gained a worldwide reputation in labor economics has a lot to do with the work of Lewis, Becker, and three other economists who figure prominently in Chapter 4: Albert Rees, Sherwin Rosen, and James Heckman. Chapter 4 concludes with a discussion of the major "youngsters" working in the Beckerian tradition at the University of Chicago: Kevin Murphy, Robert Topel, Tomas Philipson, Steven Levitt, and Casey Mulligan.

The development of monetary analysis at the University of Chicago is the theme of Chapter 5. Most discussions and research on monetary issues at the University of Chicago have been related to the quantity theory of money. The thinking on monetary matters at the University of Chicago will be traced from Laughlin to Simons and Mints and then to Friedman and Lucas.

Any discussion of Chicago and monetary analysis must also touch on the work done by Lloyd Metzler, Harry Johnson, and Robert Mundell, who made the University of Chicago into a pioneering institution of international macroeconomics. Johnson and Mundell are the fathers of the monetary approach to the balance of payments, and Jacob Frenkel and Michael Mussa were among their students. When Frenkel and Mussa left Chicago for the world of policymaking at the beginning of the 1990s, the University of Chicago lost its prominence in the field of international macroeconomics.

Chapter 6 deals with the important role Chicago economists have played in the economic analysis of government intervention, regulation, externalities, and political behavior. In addition to Becker and Stigler, Ronald Coase, who wrote two articles that had an enormous impact on economics and law, figures prominently in this chapter.

Stigler has been one of the most important Chicago economists who also boasts extensive knowledge about the history of economic thought. Much of his pioneering work on regulation is founded on his research in the field of industrial organization. Lester Telser, Reuben Kessel, Yale Brozen, Sam Peltzman, and Dennis Carlton are other Chicago economists whose work is discussed in this chapter.

Chapters 7 and 8 deal with Chicago's business and law schools, two institutions that are also very much part of Chicago's rich tradition in economics. Chicago's Graduate School of Business (GSB), which is the second business school ever established in the United States, went through many ups and downs but finally got on its successful course thanks to the Wallis-Lorie doctrine. A large part of the discussion on the GSB is devoted to the "finance people": Jim Lorie, Merton Miller, Eugene Fama, Fischer Black, and Myron Scholes. All have exhibited a strong belief in the efficiency and rationality of the free-market system. During the 1990s, the Old Guard in finance came to be challenged by a younger generation of economists led by Richard Thaler and Robert Vishny.

At the law school, the influence of economists started with Henry Simons, but only when Director succeeded Simons in 1946 did the law and economics movement really take off. Today, despite much opposition, almost every law school in the United States offers courses in economics. Ronald Coase, Harold Demsetz, Richard Posner, and William Landes were Chicago scholars who contributed to the the development of this law and economics movement. Chicago's Henry Manne and Edmund Kitch brought the law and economics gospel to several other universities. With people like Daniel Fischel, Richard Epstein, Alan Sykes, Randall Picker, and Douglas Baird, and a new generation of youngsters standing by, the Chicago law school remains at the forefront of further developments in law and economics.

Chapter 9 deals with those economists who violated one of the basic rules of the Chicago Tradition: that is, the rule that academic excellence is all-important, and political appointments are not to be pursued. George Shultz and Paul Douglas are major exceptions to that rule. Kenneth Dam and Arthur Laffer are also included here.

Arnold Harberger is another major Chicago economist discussed in this chapter; he is featured not because he launched a political career, but instead because he was the driving force behind the link established between the University of Chicago and Catholic University in Santiago, Chile. The fact that economists trained at these institutions became important policymakers during the Pinochet regime caused a lot of commotion—not only for Harberger, but also for the rest of the university. Friedrich Hayek, who was considered rather ambiguously in Chicago (especially by the economists), is also included in this chapter. Although Hayek was never actively engaged in day-to-day politics, his

*Constitution of Liberty,* which was written in Chicago, is an important political tract.

## METHODOLOGY

A distinction needs to be made among the three different layers of the methodology and sources used to conduct this investigation.

The first layer includes the books, essays, monographs, and articles published in academic journals by Chicago and non-Chicago economists on theories and empirical research developed at the University of Chicago. This information is widely available for anyone who is interested.

The second layer consists of material that is available in the archives of the University of Chicago, in the stacks at the Regenstein Library on the Chicago campus, and in the files of the Communications Department of the University of Chicago. This material includes newspaper and magazine articles, lecture notes, unpublished papers and commentaries, intradepartmental memos, and letters.

The third layer of sources used in the conduct of this investigation is material assembled during more than 100 interviews that were conducted from 1994 to 2003. For the names of the people who were interviewed, refer to the Acknowledgments. Most of these interviews were held on the record, but several people commented off the record on a number of issues. I have respected these requests rigorously. As one might expect, the off-the-record comments produced more controversial statements. When such a statement arose, I tried to obtain at least one other source to confirm it. If a corroborating source was not found, the original statement was dropped. Also, the material that came up during the interviews has whenever possible been linked to information available through the first two layers of information. Interview statements were only used as direct quotes from the subjects involved when the statements contributed to the points that were being made.

When writing about a subject like the development of economics at the University of Chicago, one must be aware of the danger of becoming completely absorbed the subject. I have tried to counter this clear and present danger in two ways: First, I made an exhaustive review of the literature that is mildly to provocatively anti-Chicago School, and second,

I interviewed several economists who know the University of Chicago and its economics well, but whose views and research approaches differ substantially from those typical to the University of Chicago.

## ACKNOWLEDGMENTS

Spread over almost a decade, I spent a total of 10 weeks on the campus of the University of Chicago in Hyde Park. In total, more than 100 interviews were conducted. I especially want to thank those people who put up with me more than once; some of them met with me up to five times.

The major sources of information were Gary Becker, Milton Friedman, James Heckman, D. Gale Johnson, Steven Levitt, Robert Lucas, Casey Mulligan, Tomas Philipson, Sherwin Rosen, Allen Sanderson, Larry Sjaastad, and Lester Telser at the Department of Economics; Robert Aliber, Dennis Carlton, Eugene Fama, Robert Fogel, Claire Friedland, Robert Hamada, Robin Hogarth, John Huizinga, Anil Kashyap, Randall Kroszner, Kevin Murphy, Sam Peltzman, Richard Thaler, Robert Topel, Robert Vishny, and Marvin Zonis at the GSB; and Kenneth Dam, Richard Epstein, Daniel Fischel, William Landes, Eric Posner, Richard Posner, Cass Sunstein, and Alan Sykes at the law school.

In my mind, this project will forever be connected with Merton Miller, who e-mailed me his final comments from his deathbed. Merton died the day I arrived in Chicago for one of my interviewing visits; we had planned to see each other two days later.

I also have to thank several people who were no longer at the University of Chicago when I did my research, but who know the place from the inside: William Baumol, Jagdish Bhagwati, Judith Chevalier, Jacques Drèze, Zvi Griliches, Douglas Irwin, Dale Jorgenson, John Lott, Franco Modigliani, Paul Samuelson, Jose Scheinkman, Robert Solow, Lambert Vanthienen, and Victor Zarnowitz.

Much of the credit for this project must go to Emiel Van Broekhoven and Walter Nonneman, both of whom are professors at the University of Antwerp (UFSIA). I also benefited greatly from remarks made by Ludo Cuyvers, Bruno De Borger, and Wilfried Parys (who also hail from UFSIA); by Jef Vuchelen from Vrije Universiteit Brussel; and by Professor Eric Buyst from the Katholieke Universiteit Leuven.

Special thanks go to Deirdre McCloskey of the University of Illinois, Chicago, who devoted an extraordinary amount of time and energy to this project.

When organizing my trips to Chicago, I got generous support from Allan Friedman and especially Barbara Backe from the communications office of the GSB and from Bill Harms of the University of Chicago's Communication Department. Also extremely helpful were Griet Woedstadt and Lily Deck of the U.S. Information Center in Brussels, who dug up incredible amounts of background material.

Luc and Marc Van Cauwenbergh and Frans Crols deserve, more than anybody else and for reasons that may not be entirely clear to them, their place in these acknowledgments.

Most of my thanks, however, must go to my wife Hilde and my children Matthias, David, Frederik, and Laura. I will need a very long life to make up for the hours that I was not there for them because of this book. However, I know they are even more proud of this book than I am.

# CHAPTER ONE

# The Chicago Tradition
## *"Harper's Bazaar"*

MAX WEBER, THE FOUNDER OF SOCIOLOGY, DEVELOPED THE THE-
sis that the Protestant ethic was instrumental in the development of capitalism in his 1905 book *The Protestant Ethic and the Spirit of Capitalism.*
In his 1935 doctoral dissertation, *Science, Technology, and Society in
Seventeenth-Century England,* the great American sociologist Robert K.
Merton argued that the Puritan ethic typical of 17th-century England
was a major force behind the rise of modern science and hence behind
the Industrial Revolution. Can a similar argument—on a different scale,
of course—be made with respect to the fact that economists working
at the University of Chicago played such a significant role in the development of modern economics? Is there something similar to Weber's
Protestant ethic or Merton's Puritan ethic in Chicago economics?

In my opinion, what I describe as the "Chicago Tradition" is in large
part responsible for the importance of the University of Chicago. Although
some elements of that Chicago Tradition are more typical for the University
of Chicago as a whole, others are unique to its community of economists.
The success of Chicago economists is embedded in that Chicago Tradition,
which is a mixture of historical, institutional, political, sociological, personal, and geographic factors. The broadly defined social context played
a significant role in the development of economics at the University of
Chicago; however, the internal dynamic of scientific inquiry emphasized by
George Stigler[7] must be included as well. The Chicago Tradition, therefore,

is about the social context in which fruitful scientific inquiry was not only able to develop but was inevitable given the setting.

Five characteristics form what will be referred to here as the "Chicago Tradition": a fanatical work attitude, the firm belief in economics as a true science of the highest relevance for daily life, the emphasis on scholastic and academic achievement, the preparedness to put everything continuously into question, and the apparently inspiring isolation of the University of Chicago. The fact that these five characteristics occurred more or less simultaneously at the University of Chicago tends to give the place a somewhat unique character and a distinct intellectual tradition. On occasion, the components of this Chicago Tradition have been the subject of somewhat heated debate on the campus. As Storr (1966, 311) pointed out in his study of the University of Chicago's early years: "From the time when the University opened, professors had disagreed vehemently over the ingredients of the culture upon which true university study should rest. The argument raged right up to the time of the decennial celebration and had not been settled then." Actually, this discussion never went away.[8] The consensus on the exact content of this Chicago Tradition is, in a very typical Chicago way, at once strong and continuously at risk.

## DIVINE SALESMAN

Ernest DeWitt Burton, the University's president from 1923 to 1925, left no doubt about the desirability of a fanatical work attitude, the first characteristic of the Chicago Tradition. In 1923 he stated that the University of Chicago is "primarily a place for hard work. There is no room for the idler here. Amusement is not our principal business" (Murphy and Bruckner 1976, 23). At the University of Chicago, as the saying goes, you "eat, breathe, and sleep economics."

The fanatical attitude to work characteristic may be attributed to William Rainey Harper, the first president of the University of Chicago: "His vision, energy, brilliance, and zeal coupled with a strong religious belief and a continuing commitment to his own research left a lasting mark. He imbued the University with a sense of its own uniqueness, which is essential to understanding the later achievement of the social sciences at Chicago" (Bulmer 1984, 20).

Harper was very much aware that the start-up of the university gave

Chicago a unique chance to realize a visionary project and leave the past behind. A University of Chicago run by a religious organization (the Chicago Baptists) existed from 1858 to 1886.[9] This Old University of Chicago disappeared because of inadequate endowment primarily caused by the financial panics of the 1870s and a lack of vision and sense of purpose among the board of trustees. Harper knew the history of the Old University of Chicago quite well and was determined not to repeat the mistakes that led to its demise (Goodspeed 1916).

In the Midwest, Baptist congregations were growing rapidly, and through the American Baptist Education Society, the Baptist clergy were anxious to create a new university in Chicago.[10] Chicago Baptists succeeded in persuading the wealthiest of all Baptist laymen, John D. Rockefeller, to invest in a Chicago institution rather than one in New York. Rockefeller agreed to contribute $600,000 on two conditions: one, that Harper would become the university's first president, and two, that local Chicago Baptists would have to raise an additional $400,000. Harper came and the Chicago Baptists found the money. The decidedly non-Baptist Marshall Field, Chicago's leading merchant, donated the site for the new university on the Midway Plaisance.

Born in 1856 to a Scottish-Irish family that ran a general store in New Concord, Ohio, Harper soon proved to be a skillful and brilliant salesboy and student. He gave "a new meaning to the term Wunderkind" (Chernow 1998, 307) and finished high school at the age of 14. After earning a PhD at Yale, he taught Hebrew at the Baptist Union Theological Seminary, which was located in the Chicago suburb of Morgan Park. He also showed great talent for finding financial resources for the numerous educational initiatives he developed with seemingly limitless energy: "A vacation was a change of work ... The man's titanic power for toil amazed his colleagues. He never seemed to sleep, he never seemed to rest" (Mayer 1957, 11). The cool and ever-calculating Rockefeller (1909) praised Harper's "extraordinary power of work and his executive and organizing ability" (179) and conceded that he "caught in some degree the contagion of [Harper's] enthusiasm" (178).

From the mid-1880s on, Harper, who had accepted a professorship at Yale's divinity school in 1886, began to dream of a university that focused more on research than teaching. In the 1850s, Henry Philip Tappan had tried to do the same thing at the University of Michigan in Ann Arbor and failed, largely because of political interference. From Tappan's experience, Harper concluded that an orientation toward research was not possible at a state university: "An endowed university was the only hope" (Mayer 1957, 23).

After several meetings in 1887 and 1888, Harper convinced Rockefeller of his notion of a research-oriented university located in Chicago, not New York. When the University of Chicago opened on October 1, 1892, it was "not the first university to pioneer such an emphasis upon research, but Harper was the most effective and enduring institution-builder among the triumvirate of himself, Daniel Coit Gilman at Johns Hopkins University, and G. Stanley Hall at Clark University" (Bulmer 1984,16).

The daring and challenging nature of what Harper tried to achieve with the University of Chicago was aptly described by Edward Levi: "The combination of graduate and undergraduate work, of teaching and research, was regarded as a bold but foolhardy experiment—an attempt to put together the main attributes of the English colleges and of the German centers of learning—and to do so in a most unlikely geographical place. Many of the experts were sure the experiment would fail ... The place would fly apart. The institution was called a veritable monstrosity, 'Harper's Bazaar'" (Murphy and Bruckner 1976, 2).

However chaotic and incoherent the impression created by Harper's initiative was, the new president made sure that all the newly appointed staff and faculty showed the same missionary-like zeal toward the success of the new University of Chicago as he did. Harper strongly identified with the University of Chicago project. Thorstein Veblen (1918, x-xi), one of the first members of Chicago's department of political economy, remarked: "The first president's share in the management of the university was intimate, masterful and pervasive, in a very high degree; so much so that no secure line could be drawn between the administration's policy and the president's personal ruling."

## HESITANT ROCKEFELLER

To Rockefeller, a devout Baptist, the idea of a major university in Chicago was certainly not a case of love at first sight. As a matter of fact, the oil baron had refused to save the Old University of Chicago as it moved into financial ruin. However, the discussions between Harper and Rockefeller helped forge a good relationship between Rockefeller and Thomas Goodspeed, the secretary of Harper's Chicago employer, the Baptist Union Theological Seminary.

Although it had already been on the table from the early 1880s on, Rockefeller became interested in the project only in late 1887, when his business practices came under fire during the debate on the Interstate Commerce Act. Rockefeller instinctively sensed that a major philanthropic enterprise would be a welcome diversion, and the same instinct told him it would be better to locate the university away from New York, his main business center, and Washington, the nation's capital.

Frederick T. Gates, Rockefeller's major adviser in his many philanthropic endeavors, provided the final push to get Rockefeller on board. After significant effort, Gates succeeded in uniting the American Baptist Education Society behind the Chicago university project, as this was the *conditio sine qua non* of Rockefeller's support.

The charter of the University of Chicago was adopted in May 1890, and Harper formally accepted the presidency in February 1891. The University of Chicago opened on October 1, 1892. Clearly, there is something to Barber's claim (1988, 241) that "Rome was not built in one day. The University of Chicago almost was."

Was this "marriage" between Harper, the Biblical scholar, and Rockefeller, the tough businessman, a mere coincidence? Mayer's biographic study of Harper indicates otherwise. Mayer (1957, 3, 63) described Harper as "the professor who met and mastered John D. Rockefeller ... Harper, given his goal, was no less ruthless than Rockefeller, given his." Commenting on the first meetings between Rockefeller and Harper, Mayer wrote: "For the first time in his life, John D. Rockefeller had met a man his own size. And he knew it. He knew all about this earnest young theologian, all about his consuming selflessness, his prodigious powers as an educational organizer, his fanatic success at stirring up the country to the study of Hebrew. He had made up his mind this was the man to spend his money for him" (2).

And spend he did. Harper regularly came up with deficits in the university budget, which put additional pressure on Rockefeller to come up with new grants. An angry Rockefeller demanded a balanced budget for 1905, which Harper promptly delivered; he then immediately cashed in his reward, another million-dollar gift from Rockefeller.[11] By 1910, Rockefeller had spent $35 million building the University of Chicago (Dzuback 1991, 74). In time—primarily because of Harper's spending habits—the relationship between the two men cooled considerably, and Gates became the middleman more and more. Nevertheless, in his memoirs, Rockefeller (1909, 179) remained highly positive about Harper: "As a friend and companion, in daily intercourse, no one could be more delightful than he."

Decades later, Robert Maynard Hutchins, the fifth president of the University, described Rockefeller's attitude toward the University of Chicago as one without precedent: "He must have invented the doctrine that a donor who wishes to advance education and scholarship should leave them to educators and scholars ... Mr. Rockefeller must have had some educational convictions; he may have had some educational eccentricities. He never revealed them ... Mr. Rockefeller's restraint is surely unique in history and surely accounts in large measure for the rapid rise of the University" (Murphy and Bruckner 1976, 240). Harper must have been quite confident of the depth of Rockefeller's commitment to noninterference; in his decennial report presented on July 1, 1902, Harper declared: "A donor has the privilege of ceasing to make his gifts to an institution if, in his opinion, for any reason, the work of the institution is not satisfactory; but *as donor* he has no right to interfere with the administration or the instruction of the university" (Murphy and Bruckner 1976, 82).

This positive evaluation of Rockefeller's relationship with the University of Chicago was not universal.[12] In 1906, Senator J.P. Dolliver of Iowa declared that "the University of Chicago smelled of oil like a Kansas town" (Laughlin 1906a, 43). Richard T. Ely, cofounder of the American Economic Association (AEA), claimed to have refused a job at the University of Chicago because "the institution was supported in part by a monopolist" (Barber 1988, 254). In his biography of Rockefeller, Chernow (1998) wrote that the oil baron "declined to visit Chicago for several years, reluctant to have the university overly identified with his name" (325). Chernow concluded: "Despite intermittent accusations to the contrary, he did not interfere with academic appointments or free expression" (326). However, by selecting Harper as the first president of the new University of Chicago, Rockefeller ensured that his money would not be wasted due to a lack of hard work.

## SERIOUS BUT DIVERSE

Edward Shils (1991a, xi-xii), one of Chicago's foremost scholars on sociology and social thought, described "intellectual gravitas" as "the distinctive mark of the University of Chicago ... scholarly and scientific work was thought of by students and teachers alike not simply as a means of gaining a livelihood or as an agreeable setting for a life of ease and pleasure, but as a matter of the gravest moment." Economists working at the University of Chicago have hewed to Shils's rule of intellectual gravitas, the second characteristic of the Chicago Tradition. Chicago economists have always treated their subject very seriously, even from the beginning,[13] but this does not mean that serious or scientific economics has always been defined in the same way. As is true for so many parts of the story of economics at the University of Chicago, Milton Friedman is the pivotal figure regarding the definition of serious scientific work. Even though any such classification is an oversimplification, in this context a pre-Friedman era, a Friedman era, and a post-Friedman era can be defined.

The pre-Friedman era covers more than a half-century—from the start of the University of Chicago in 1892 to the late 1940s. According to Ross Emmett (2002, xviii), during this period economics at the University of Chicago "reflected the broader movements of American economics." In the words of Morgan and Rutherford (1998a), the essential characteristic of American economics in the interwar period and even before the first World War[14] was "pluralism ... Pluralism meant variety, and that variety was evident in beliefs, in ideology, in methods and in policy advice ... An economist was an investigative scientist whether he or she used the methods of history, statistics, theoretical deduction, empiricism, mathematics, or whatever" (4–5). The same authors argue that the association of objectivity with evenhandedness was very characteristic for this period: "It became the professional ethos of economists of the period to teach both sides of a case: both free trade and protectionism; gold standard and bimetallism; labor unions and capitalism" (8).

The pluralism to which Morgan and Rutherford referred was also characteristic of economics at the University of Chicago in its first half century. James Laughlin, the first head of the department of political economy, stood for orthodox classical economics along the lines of John Stuart Mill. The institutional approach to economics was inspired by Veblen but also by others, including: Harry Millis (labor economics), Chester Wright and John Nef (economic history), James Field (population economics), Hazel Kyrk (consumption economics), and John Maurice Clark. All of them may be considered institutional economists to some extent.

Wesley Mitchell combined institutionalism with an empirical approach, as did Paul Douglas. Henry Schultz worked hard to get mathematical economics off the ground at the University of Chicago, as did socialist Oskar Lange and several members of the Cowles Commission. Last, but not least, there was the work of Jacob Viner, Frank Knight, Henry Simons, and Aaron Director on neoclassical price theory.

Economics at the University of Chicago became less of a "mixed bag" from the 1950s forward (Reder 1982, 2). Scientific economics was increasingly identified with the triad of neoclassical price theory, partial equilibrium analysis, and empirical verification. A consequence of broader influences and more specific Chicago influences, the most important of which was Friedman's return to the University of Chicago in 1946, led to this change in thought. Friedman strongly believed that economics was a science to the extent that neoclassical price theory and empirical verification were combined.[15] Through his imposing personality, legendary intelligence, and extraordinary debating skills Friedman exercised a strong influence on most of the economists working at the University of Chicago.

Moreover, Friedman's reappearance at the University of Chicago in 1946 coincided with several other changes in and around the department that facilitated his rise to dominance. From 1945 to 1946, the landscape changed dramatically: Henry Simons died; Jacob Viner, Oskar Lange, and Simeon Leland left for other universities; Chester Wright retired; and T.W. Schultz became chairman of the department at the relatively young age of 42. Moreover, in 1958 Friedman gained a powerful ally for promoting his brand of scientific economics when Stigler returned to his alma mater on the shores of Lake Michigan. The 30 years between Friedman's return in 1946 and departure in 1976 from the University of Chicago can be labeled the Friedman era without much exaggeration.

Although Friedman and Stigler's contribution to the way in which economics at the University of Chicago developed between the early 1950s and late 1970s is hard to underestimate, broader influences also helped Friedman advance his case that neoclassical price theory, partial equilibrium analysis, and empirical verification are the essence of scientific economics. Analyzing the shift in American economics from the "interwar pluralism" to the "postwar neoclassicism," Morgan and Rutherford (1998a, 9–10) detected two basic "transformation processes"—"the notion of objectivity vested in a particular set of methods, namely, mathematics and statistics ... [and] ... the growing faith in the market solution and the virtues of free competition." Although Friedman was highly critical of sophisticated mathematical modeling, the first of these transformation processes confirmed his belief that "positive economics is, or can be, an 'objective' science, in precisely the same sense as any of the physical sciences" (Friedman 1953, 4).

Crauford Goodwin has made a strong case that the Cold War—"a war of economic ideologies" (Morgan and Rutherford 1998a, 14)—played a pivotal role in the transformation process that shaped postwar neoclassicism. According to Goodwin's analysis, the Cold War led to a situation where "the dangerous heretic was not one who believed in Allah or the Antichrist but one who preached class war, the contradictions of capitalism, and public ownership of the means of production. In the Cold War atmosphere, eccentric ideas could be more than mere apostasy; they could be treachery and even treason" (Morgan and Rutherford 1998, 57). Goodwin noted that by the end of the 1940s, prominent members of the business community backed economists who preached the advantages of free competition and capitalism and "were all associated with the University of Chicago" (Morgan and Rutherford 1998, 69). Friedman strongly denies the relevance of this Cold War argument and the implied patronage of economics—especially at the University of Chicago—by business interests in favor of capitalism and the free-market economy.[16]

In the post-Friedman era, the broad consensus around Friedman's definition of serious scientific economics—neoclassical price theory, partial equilibrium, and empirical verification—gradually evaporated. Two groups were formed. The first continued to work in the Friedman tradition; its major adherents were Gary Becker at the department of economics and most of the economists at the business school and the law school. The second group, which was associated with Robert Lucas, became strongly engaged in the development of "full-fledged general equilibrium mathematics" (Morgan and Rutherford, 1998a, 1). Partial equilibrium analysis was replaced by general equilibrium, and purely theoretical work without empirical content gained a place under the Chicago sun. This division led to heated discussions between the two groups that bore some resemblance to the discussions that took place between the Friedman group of Chicago's department of economics and the economists working at the Cowles Commission during the latter's stay on the Chicago campus.

## HARPER'S LEGACY

A third characteristic of the Chicago Tradition is that the only things that really matter at Chicago are the quality of teaching, one's influence on one's profession, and most of all, scholastic achievement. Charles Max Mason, the University's president from 1925 to 1928, said in 1928: "We in Chicago believe that the skeleton of it all is productive scholarship, and that as that skeleton is clothed with flesh it takes the outlines of a real education, a human education, an education in which through the solution of problems there comes the ability to meet the problems of life" (Murphy and Bruckner, 1976, 32–33). From its very beginnings, the University of Chicago has relentlessly emphasized research as the principal way to achieve scholastic and academic excellence. "A university," according to University President Hutchins, "may be a university without doing any teaching. It cannot be one without doing any research" (Murphy and Bruckner, 1976, 153).

Harper traveled the country in his search for people who excelled at research. With the Rockefeller dollars in his hands, he was "shamelessly robbing Yale, Harvard, Cornell, Hopkins and other schools of their best men" (Mayer 1957, 61).[17] Harper recruited young and talented people with a previously unheard-of combination of promises: reduced teach-

ing loads and thus more time (and money and facilities) available for research; first-rate colleagues; and complete freedom in their intellectual
endeavors. "There were no traditions to restrict him, no trustees attached
to their own image of an old institution, no governors or state legislators
determined to look into what some of them considered a too generous
gift of summer time off and other vacations. Research was a new idea for
many such people and support for it questionable. Unencumbered by inherited restraints, Harper could establish a tradition of his own" (Yoder
1991, 1). Before the project took off, Harper had already decided that the
business of this great new university "would be discovery and the training of discoverers. Every instructor would be an investigator, for," said
Harper, "… it is only the man who has made investigations who may
teach others to investigate'" (Mayer 1957, 22). The relative neglect of undergraduate studies at the University of Chicago has been an indirect
consequence of this strong focus on research.[18]

The way honorary degrees are awarded is a good example of the emphasis on academic achievement. For example, it is out of the question
for a politician, no matter how successful and/or courageous he or she
may have been, to be awarded an honorary degree from the University
of Chicago.[19] Attracting attention in the media or being frequently called
upon to appear before congressional committees are not particularly
valuable assets in Chicago. Even the chairmanship of the president's
Council of Economic Advisers is not considered something to strive
for.[20] According to Reder (1982, 2) "At Chicago, diligent teaching, service in university administration, great distinction—even fame—in government service are at best partial substitutes for continuing research
productivity."

This research productivity does not necessarily have to be "proven" in
print. Chicago has a substantial oral tradition in which research results
are often presented as a part of the teaching. Aaron Director is considered the prime example of this oral tradition, and H. Gregg Lewis can
be placed in the same category.

The Chicago definition of academia makes it easy to understand why
the hiring and promotion decision-makers recruit people who might
make a breakthrough in their discipline. "We look for home runs," as
Robin Hogarth of the business school puts it.[21] Hogarth's remark closely

resembles one made almost half a century earlier by Lawrence Kimpton, the University's president from 1951 to 1960. Kimpton claimed that the University of Chicago's tradition "is one of great men. The criterion of employment or of promotion is not one of length of service or administration favorism. 'Is he good?' is the only relevant question and always will be" (Murphy and Bruckner 1976, 44). In his 1929 farewell address, university president Max Mason stated: "[The University of Chicago] must be outstanding or nothing. There is no reason for its existence as just another university ... There is no excuse for the existence of any mediocre department in the University of Chicago" (Murphy and Bruckner 1976, 31,34).

Yet many of these Nobel laureates were looked upon as eccentrics or nonmainstream scholars when they were doing the very research that drew so much praise, honor, and money —scholars such as Robert Lucas, Gary Becker, Ronald Coase, and Robert Fogel certainly belong in this category.

The search for "home runs" at Chicago is evidenced by a boldness in decision-making that would not be tolerated at most other universities. This boldness has many faces, including giving young people vast responsibility: Robert Hutchins was not yet 30 years old when he became president of the University of Chicago in 1929. This same boldness and relentless search for "home runs" also help explain why papers by University of Chicago economists that were regularly refused for publication in the most renowned journals of the economics profession nevertheless became classics afterwards (Gans 1994). When Lucas was awarded the Nobel Prize in 1995, Harvard economist Robert Barro (1996) wrote of how one of Lucas's ground-breaking papers was initially refused by the editor of the *American Economic Review.*

## FAR AWAY FROM WASHINGTON

The fourth characteristic of the Chicago Tradition is the preparedness to put everything continuously into question—thus, a tendency to disobey the laws of political correctness. The British-born philosopher Alfred North Whitehead (1954, 137) had this intense debating culture in mind when he once remarked: "I think the one place where I have been that is most like ancient Athens is the University of Chicago." Describing the academic environment at the University of Chicago upon his arrival there in the 1920s, Paul Douglas (1972, 43) noted: "There was complete academic freedom, to which ... the faculty ... [was] deeply committed." Arriving in Chicago in 1933, Herbert Simon (1996, 36), winner of the Nobel Prize in Economics in 1978, found out quickly that "nothing was too new, too arcane, or too absurd to excite passionately the bright minds of the students and faculty assembled on the Midway campus."

This fourth characteristic can also be traced back to Harper, who was devoted to the "discipline of the mind" (Mayer 1957, 53). The ultimate purpose of this discipline was higher criticism. The learning of learned men was useless unless they were equipped to analyze it; mere fact-finding, purposeless or repetitious, would not pass for research in Harper's university. The spirit of rigorous criticism already dominated the natural sciences; Harper introduced it into dangerous areas—the social sciences. Recognizing that the emancipation of nature was bringing the enslavement of men with it, Harper declared that "the times are asking not merely for men to harness electricity and sound, but for men to guide us in complex economic and social duties." (Mayer 1957, 54)

Harper was uncompromising on the issue of freedom to ventilate criticism and the more basic issue of freedom of speech. It is instructive in this context to quote again from his 1902 decennial report:

> An instructor in the University has an absolute right to express his opinion. If such an instructor is on appointment for two or three or four years, and if during these years he exercises this right in such a way as to do himself and the institution serious injury, it is, of course, the privilege of the University to allow his appointment to lapse at the end of the term for which it was originally made. If an officer on permanent appointment abuses his privilege as professor, the University must suffer and it is proper that it should suffer. This is only the direct and

inevitable consequence of the lack of foresight and wisdom involved in the original appointment. The injury thus accruing to
the University is, moreover, far less serious than would follow if,
for an expression of opinion differing from that of the majority
of the Faculty, from the Board of Trustees, or from the President
of the University, a permanent officer were asked to present his
resignation. (Murphy and Bruckner 1976, 83)

The relentless questioning of accepted truths makes the University of
Chicago a fertile breeding ground for scientific revolutions. "At Chicago,"
according to the late Rudiger Dornbusch (1996, 82), a professor at the
Massachusetts Institute of Technology (MIT) and a Chicago graduate,
"they do revolution." This remark echoes one made by Kimpton: "A
week without a revolution is a lost week" (Murphy and Bruckner 1976,
48). At the University of Chicago, every argument, no matter how di-
vergent from standard opinion, is taken seriously. Ronald Coase's 1960
entry into Chicago has become legendary in this respect.

Anyone who looks deeply into the often-bewildering variety of
ideas, arguments, and counterarguments flowing around the University
of Chicago campus will be amazed that European and East Coast intellectuals find Chicago economists to be little more than a bunch of
narrow-minded, near-fanatical defenders of capitalism, big business, and
speculative money.

Given the ever-present impulse to be critical of any position taken or
any argument made, it is hardly surprising that the University of Chicago
tends to attract people critical of any establishment or established points
of view. New York and Boston, Chicagoans argue, are psychologically
much closer to Washington than Chicago. A typical example of Chicago
economists' view of the Establishment can be found in Fischer Black's
foreword to the book Merton Miller, the 1990 Nobel Prize winner, wrote
on financial innovations: "Merton Miller is a great economist. He is also
a great warrior. In the 1950's he takes up finance and engineers a stun-
ning campaign that, after a period of years, decisively undermines the
Old Guard and installs Modern Finance. That done, he brings his methods to the Real World, and becomes a strategist for Chicago's commodity

crowd in their battles with New York's establishment and Washington's power brokers" (Miller 1991, vii).

## DISSENTERS WELCOME

A combination of the third and the fourth characteristics of the Chicago Tradition—the quality of research and academic excellence and the obligation to be critical of any accepted truth—makes the atmosphere at the University of Chicago comfortable even for people who are not directly connected to Chicago economists' prevailing mainstream thinking. Veblen, one of Chicago's founding fathers in the field of economics, can be counted as a typical early example of this group. A more recent example is Richard Thaler, who left Cornell University to join the University of Chicago faculty in 1995. Thaler's work focuses on quasi-rational economics and behavioral finance, which has as its premise that investors easily become the victims of their own misjudgments. In contrast, traditional financial research at Chicago is based on the assumption of rationality of market participants—the efficient market hypothesis.

In the 100-plus intervening years between the arrivals of Veblen and Thaler in Chicago, many more examples of dissenters on the campus of the University of Chicago can be found. Consider the case of Lloyd Metzler. Although Friedman and most other macroeconomists at the University of Chicago were becoming increasingly critical of Keynesian economics, the department hired Metzler, a Harvard-educated economist working in the Keynesian tradition, in the late 1940s.

The cases of Polish economist Oskar Lange and several members of the Cowles Commission are also noteworthy examples of the Chicago Tradition. In the late 1920s, Lange left Poland for the United Kingdom and the London School of Economics (LSE). He later received a traveling fellowship from the Rockefeller Foundation and visited several U.S. universities before arriving in Chicago in 1938. Lange was an excellent statistical mathematician and econometrician, but he was also a deeply committed socialist who energetically opposed the attacks of Ludwig von Mises and Friedrich Hayek on the economic efficiency of socialism.

By the time Lange arrived in Chicago, there could not be much doubt about his position as "a strong critic of capitalism" (Emmett 2002, V: viii) and as "the prime defender of planning in the socialist calculation debate, an early interpreter of Keynesianism, and a Marxist" (Mirowski 1998, 268). Again, his academic credentials tilted the balance in his favor.[22] Lange, who was strongly oriented toward quantitative economics, became a natural ally of Henry Schultz, who tried to get mathematical economics and econometrics off the ground at the University of Chicago during the 1930s. When Schultz died in a car accident six months after Lange's arrival, Lange became the senior mathematical economist–econometrician in the department of economics at the University of Chicago.

Reder (1982, 5) describes Lange's time at Chicago as follows: "Lange's influence was due not only to his professional attainments, but also to his great personal charm and broad intellectual interests. In a department where conflicts of very strong personalities exacerbated intellectual differences, Lange's tact and disarming manner enabled him to remain *persona grata* to all ... [His] popularity extended beyond his colleagues to the graduate student body." Evsey Domar took classes taught by Lange in Chicago in 1940 and 1941 and confirmed Reder's description: "Lange was the nicest, the most beloved and the best organized of all my teachers" (Domar 1992, 121).

Lange's departure from the majority of the other economists at the University of Chicago is highlighted in what is generally regarded to be most important book, *Price Flexibility and Employment* (1944). In the book, Lange attacked the neoclassical proposition that if the price of an underemployed factor of production falls, the employment of that factor will increase again. He argued that several indirect effects could frustrate this chain of events. In the passage below, Friedman criticizes Lange's book and contrasts his approach to that which was prevalent in the physical sciences:

> The theorist starts with some set of observed and related
> facts ... He seeks a generalization or theory that will explain
> these facts ... He tests this theory to make sure that it is logi-
> cally consistent, that its elements are susceptible of empirical

determination and that it will explain adequately the facts that he started with. He then seeks to deduce from this theory facts other than those he used to derive it and check these deductions against reality. Typically some deduced "facts" check and others do not; so he revises his theory to take account of the additional facts ... The approach used by Lange, and all too common in economics, is very different. Lange largely dispenses with the initial step—a full and comprehensive set of observed and related facts to be generalized—and in the main reaches conclusions no observed facts can contradict. His emphasis is on the formal structure of the theory...He considers it largely unnecessary to test the validity of his theoretical structure except for conformity to the canons of formal logic ... The theory provides formal models of imaginary worlds, not generalizations about the real world. (Friedman 1953, 282–83)

By the time Friedman's critique of *Price Flexibility and Employment* appeared in the *American Economic Review,* Lange had already left Chicago to join the communist regime that was installed in Poland after World War II. "After World War II," Domar (1992, 121) wrote decades later, "Lange gave up his US citizenship and joined the Polish communist government, which sent him back to the United States as an ambassador. When he addressed the Federal Reserve seminar at that time, I recognized my old teacher, even if more conservatively dressed, whom we all loved so much. He gave an interesting talk. But later, at a presentation at Harvard, he justified every measure undertaken by the Polish regime. For the first and the last time, I felt ashamed for him."

In his memoir, Friedman described Lange as "the rare socialist who had truly mastered economic theory" but he ended his remarks on Lange by going even farther in his condemnation than Domar: "Lange himself did not escape the corruption after he returned to Poland. By all reports, he ended up a tragic figure, a willing puppet of the communist regime, never able to achieve in practice what he had preached in theory. His personal life, also, was devastated. He abandoned his wife, who returned to the US, a sad and lonely figure. When he traveled abroad, it was with another woman, widely suspected of playing a dual role as companion and communist watchdog" (Friedman and Friedman 1998, 55).

## THE COMMISSION

A case can be made that the development of economics at the University of Chicago might have taken a different course had Lange not left for Poland at the end of World War II. "As of 1940-42, Lange often spoke of the kind of Economics Department he would like to have, either at Chicago or elsewhere," wrote Reder, although he does not substantiate the matter further (Reder 1982, 5). Given Lange's work and methodology, the economics department he had in mind would likely have been something quite different than what it later became. There can be little doubt that Lange would have received strong support for his views from the people working at the Cowles Commission for Research in Economics, which had pitched its tents in the Social Science Building at the University of Chicago in the early 1940s.[23]

Alfred Cowles III was a Colorado-based stockbroker and the second-biggest shareholder of the *Chicago Tribune*. By the early 1930s, he was increasingly puzzled by the fact that economic life was so hard to predict. In his search to improve the predictive power of economic analysis, Cowles brought together Harold Davis, a mathematician from the University of Indiana, and Irving Fisher, the well-known mathematical economist from Yale University; the team headed Cowles' Econometric Society. Cowles supported the newly formed society and helped publish its journal, *Econometrica*.

Perhaps most important of all, though, was his founding of the Cowles Commission in 1932. During the 1930s, the Commission limited its activities to an annual two-week summer seminar in the Rocky Mountains; the seminar's emphasis was almost exclusively mathematical economics. Later, Nobel Prize-winners such as Jan Tinbergen and Ragnar Frisch became regular attendees at the Cowles seminars. Cowles was forced to return to Chicago in 1939 to manage his stake in the *Tribune*, and he decided to take the Commission with him. After a short stay in the Tribune Tower in downtown Chicago, it was moved to the facilities of the University of Chicago in Hyde Park.

"The Cowles theoretical econometric work began in earnest with Marschak's arrival," is how Carl Christ (1991, 31) underlines the importance of Jacob Marschak, who became the Commission's research director in 1943. The Kiev-born Marschak was a Russian exile who fled first to Germany because of the Bolsheviks and then to Chicago to escape the Nazis.[24] Better known as "Yasha" to his collaborators, Marschak assembled a group of extraordinarily talented young economists. Among them were no less than eight people who later became Nobel laureates: Tjalling Koopmans, Kenneth Arrow, Lawrence Klein, Herbert Simon, Trygve Haavelmo, James Tobin, Gerard Debreu, and Franco Modigliani. Under Marschak's inspirational leadership, they developed such substantial statistical and econometric techniques that "by 1945 the Cowles Commission had become the Mecca of quantitative economics" (Niehans 1990, 411).

Over time, the Cowles Commission became thoroughly immersed in the Keynesian revolution. Most economists at the Commission were firm believers in the possibilities of elaborate economic planning by the government. For this job to be done, large econometric models had to be developed. Through a system of simultaneous equations, everything was linked to everything. Cowles Commission economists also rejected the typical partial equilibrium analysis or ceteris paribus analysis—"other things being equal"—which were inherited mainly from Alfred Marshall.

The department of economics at the University of Chicago under Friedman was characterized by a firm belief in the use of partial equilibrium models embedded in neoclassical price theory and a high degree of skepticism about the mathematization of economic analysis and the usefulness of advanced econometric techniques. Thus, it was not surprising that quite often the Cowles Commission people and the department of economics people often found themselves entangled in tough arguments. Karl Brunner, who was the first to coin the term "monetarism" in 1968, found himself in the middle of these discussions as a young economist. He later recalled:

There were regular sessions at the Commission with an increasingly mathematical flavor. Beyond the Commission was,

of course, the Department of Economics—a somewhat different world. I became exposed to a group around Aaron Director,
Frank Knight and Milton Friedman. The group met with some
regularity for discussions ranging over a wide array of problems.
The thrust of these differed radically from that of the seminars
at the Cowles Commission. They emphatically advanced the
relevance of economic analysis as an important means of understanding the world, in a manner that I had never encountered
before. (Brunner 1992, 88)

Thus, two groups of people with substantially different attitudes toward and visions of scientific economic analysis—the Marshallian vision
of the Chicagoans versus the Walrasian[25] vision of the Cowles group—
coexisted only yards away from one another in the same building. This
resulted in a heated debate between the two sides: "By 1944, a fairly intense struggle was underway between Knight and his former students on
one side and the Cowles Commission and its adherents on the other. The
struggle had several facets: research methodology, political ideology and
faculty appointments. It continued for almost 10 years, being terminated
only with the departure of the Cowles Commission for Yale in 1953. The
battle engendered a great deal of bitterness which still persists, though
undoubtedly it is diminishing in intensity" (Reder 1982, 10).[26]
     There can be no doubt that relations were strained between some of
the economists from both camps. This antagonism was probably most
personified by Koopmans and Friedman. As Martin Beckman wrote
(1991, 264): "There was tension between Tjalling Koopmans and one
other member of the Department of Economics at the University of
Chicago whose star was just rising and who would later win a Nobel
Prize too." Not only did they disagree on many aspects of economic
analysis and political ideology, but they also had totally different characters. Friedman always sought an intellectual debate and a challenge of
arguments that have been put forward. Koopmans, on the other hand,
couldn't stand the debating culture that was natural to the Chicago environment: once he had made up his mind, there could be no more discussion, as far as he was concerned.

Friedman, however, denies that significant personal animosities ever existed between him and Koopmans—or any other member of the Cowles Commission.[27] However, in his memoir, Friedman recorded that as a regular attendee at the Cowles seminars, "I developed a reputation as something of a hair shirt since I was, and still am, a persistent critic of the approach to the analysis of economic data that became known as the Cowles approach" (Friedman and Friedman 1998, 197).

The following statement from Friedman's memoir addresses the more personal relationship between Friedman, Marschak, and Koopmans: "Marschak and Koopmans had very different personalities. Marschak was a warm, outgoing human being. Koopmans by contrast was rather cold and authoritarian. Marschak was a truly learned person who had wide interests and contributed to different areas of economics ... [Koopmans] specialized very narrowly on theoretical issues ... Unlike Marschak he was much less cooperative in departmental matters" (Friedman and Friedman 1998, 198).

In 1955, the Cowles Commission moved to Yale; it never regained the vitality and creativity that characterized it during its decade in Chicago. This illustrates a clear example of people with a different research agenda thriving in an environment that is sometimes hostile but is nevertheless always stimulating. Undeniably, many people at the Commission produced seminal works during their residency at the University of Chicago. As Martin Beckman (1991, 253) concluded with respect to Koopmans: "He also intimated that on occasions he felt like an outsider in the Department of Economics at the University of Chicago. In the 1950s he had become increasingly unhappy with life in Chicago. It was he who carefully arranged the departure of the Cowles Commission from Chicago to Yale in 1955. But when all is said, it was in Chicago that he did the work for which he received the Nobel Prize in 1975."

## BULLFIGHTS

The first four ingredients of the Chicago Tradition—a fanatical attitude to work, the vision of economics as a true science, the all-dominating importance attached to research and scholarly achievement, and the extreme preparedness to question everything and everyone—come to fruition with Chicago's system of interdisciplinary workshops. Stigler's workshop on industrial organization boasted a platform of intense cross-fertilization between people from the economics faculty, the business school, and the law school; Becker's sociology workshop created something similar for economists and sociologists; and the Economic History Workshop brought together economists and historians. The emphasis on an interdisciplinary approach permeates the history of economics at the University of Chicago.[28]

Becker (1991, 146) remarked: "Chicago's workshop system was a major innovation in conducting economic research and in apprenticing students in research. It has been copied by many other economics departments—often at the instigation of Chicago graduates—and also by business schools and law schools. Although often successful, workshops elsewhere usually do not achieve the intensity of those at Chicago. This is attributable to the faculty commitment at Chicago to the workshop system, and to the extensive discussion of papers read prior to meetings." Becker's remarks notwithstanding, the Chicago-style use of workshops owes a great deal to the history of 19th century university workshops in Germany; there, they formed an integral part of the educational system.[29] Harper was quite familiar with the characteristics of the German university system.

Another major source of inspiration for Chicago's workshop system was the dynamics of the Cowles Commission's research groups. Under the guidance of Theodore Schultz and H. Gregg Lewis, the workshop system blossomed during the 1950s.[30]

The workshops at the University of Chicago have three distinctive characteristics. First, every member of the audience has carefully read the paper presented; second, there is a high degree of attendance by senior members of the faculties; and, third, these happenings are characterized by intellectual bloodthirstiness. This last characteristic of the Chicago Tradition also seems to have been there from the beginning. In 1912, Laughlin wrote: "When the investigator has run the gauntlet of his instructor, and obtained some definite results, then it is good for him and for his fellow-students to lay his performance before the group and stand fire from all quarters" (175). Absolute horror stories circulate on the Chicago campus and other university campuses about how badly some people have been treated in these sessions; they have been referred to as "bullfights" or "the gunfighter's challenge." The British weekly *The Economist* gave the following description of the workshops: "Go to one at Harvard, and you will be treated to a display of collegial information-sharing, as professors listen politely to a visitor's well-rehearsed presentation. At Chicago, however, you will see that same visitor being verbally mauled" (Dornbusch 1996, 82).

George Neumann taught at the University of Chicago for 10 years (1974–84); after he was refused a full professorship, he resigned from the faculty. He declared the workshops to be the distinctive feature of the Chicago system: "They are a bloodbath. People's feelings get hurt, but money can't buy the kind of expertise and input that you get when you give a paper there ... The workshop system there really forces people to confront serious issues. You strip away all the inessential parts of the problem ... The Chicago workshops have turned out some tremendously important work ... Chicago has been accused of being a school that not only believes in survival of the fittest, it practices it."[31]

Friedman strongly objects to comparing the Chicago workshops to bloodbaths. It all depends on what one defines as being aggressive in a discussion. I like to recount an illustrative anecdote that happened during an interview with Friedman on November 1, 1996. "Being 84 years old," Friedman remarked at one point, "I have to make optimal use of the limited time that is left for me." "But, Mr. Friedman," I replied, "it seems to me that your health is still all right and that you have quite a few years to go." Friedman looked me straight in the eye, and in a voice that sent shivers down my spine, he said: "Since you're not a doctor, you cannot in any way say something sensible about my health and about the years still left to me. Let's keep to subjects we're both knowledgeable about." Friedman probably thought he had just made an obvious point and to him, it was not delivered in an aggressive or harsh way.

This experience matches Becker's views on Friedman and his workshop attitude: "Although his comments were not cruel, I believe it would have been better if he permitted more face-saving after it became clear that some research was worthless and had serious flaws. But Friedman has a missionary zeal in the worship of truth" (Becker 1991, 145).

## SPLENDID ISOLATION

The fifth and last characteristic of the Chicago Tradition, as it has been defined here, is rather random: the geographic isolation of the University of Chicago. This isolation must be seen in a two-dimensional way: on the level of the city and on the level of the university. Although it is beyond a doubt the economic center of gravity of the American Midwest, the city of Chicago remains something of an outcast—a kind of "special case" to many people in the leading intellectual centers on the East and West Coasts. Urban sociologist Janet L. Abu-Lughod has placed New York, Chicago, and Los Angeles on an equal footing as America's truly global cities, but the cowboy spirit of the pioneers—the feeling of "us against the rest"—remains very much alive in Chicago.[32] This feeling of isolation and adventure tends to make Chicagoans less reliant on accepted common knowledge and more open-minded toward intellectual innovation and new modes of thought.

The second level of the University of Chicago's isolation has to do with the location of the University's Hyde Park campus. Lake Michigan is east of the campus, and many of the surrounding areas are crime-ridden. Downtown Chicago is about a 20-minute drive away, and Chicago's famous "El" train does not serve the campus directly. All of these factors combine to make the Hyde Park campus something of an enclave. The entirety of the University of Chicago is packed together on a few square miles; this makes for close quarters.

Unlike almost any other major university, many scholars actually live on campus.[33] Eli Shapiro spent years at Chicago, MIT, and Harvard and makes the comparison: "At MIT and Harvard scholars live much less in a community spirit than is the case at the University of Chicago."[34] These physical and geographical characteristics were among the factors Zvi Griliches had in mind shortly before his death, when he reflected on his 1969 transfer from Chicago to Harvard: "I have not been sorry I came to Harvard, though I must say when I came I missed Chicago very dearly. Because Chicago was a department, and Harvard was not" (Krueger and Taylor 2000, 179).[35]

Even in the brave new world of e-connected scholarship, this constant physical proximity forms an integral part of Chicago's intense debating and discussion culture. Deirdre McCloskey recalls from her own experience: "The people from the department, the business school, and the law school often mixed with members of still other departments, talked to each other continuously. There was practically no other place to go to in Hyde Park than the Quadrangle Club. But also elsewhere discussion went on and on: not only in the seminar rooms, offices and hallways but also in the streets, in our homes, everywhere. It never stopped because there was literally nothing else to do."[36] McCloskey's comment is similar to one made decades earlier by Hutchins: "Don't you know that the greatness of the University of Chicago has always rested on the fact that the city of Chicago is so boring that the professors have nothing else to do but to work?" (Shils 1991b, 193).

This two-dimensional isolation has undoubtedly played an important role in the development of several "schools" at the University of Chicago. "A 'school' in the social sciences," sociologist Martin Bulmer wrote, "may be thought of as akin to the term used in art history to designate a group of contemporaries sharing a certain style, technique, or set of symbolic expressions and having at some point or other in time or space a high degree of interaction" (Bulmer 1984, 2). However, as Friedman (1974, 4) has put it, schools of thought developed at the University of Chicago should not be considered "cults ... [or] ... crank outsiders ... [but] ... rather attempts to open up new directions of research and analysis, new ways of looking at phenomena."[37] The ease with which new schools of thought developed at the University of Chicago had nothing to do with "narrowness, homogeneity, and inbreeding" (Friedman 1974, 5).

The list of schools developed at the University of Chicago is long. A few in the social sciences include: the pragmatic philosophy of John Dewey at the beginning of the 20th century; the urban sociology of William Thomas, Robert Park, and Ernest Burgess that flourished during the period 1920–50; the political science approach inspired by Charles

E. Merriam that flowered over the years 1910–40; the school of theology following Charles H. Arnold's work; and the approach of the English department led by Ronald Crane in the 1950s.

The most celebrated—or accursed, depending on who's speaking—of the Chicago Schools is arguably the economics school. Friedman wrote about a "mixture of irritation and pleasure ... at being alternately damned and applauded—and always, as I felt, misunderstood—as a member of the Chicago school" (Friedman 1974, 2).

# CHAPTER TWO

# Chicago's Pioneers
## *The Founding Fathers*

JOHN D. ROCKEFELLER AND WILLIAM RAINEY HARPER SHARED THE vision of creating a university that defied tradition and would revolutionize higher education in the United States. They did indeed bring about something of a revolution in teaching economics, as the University of Chicago became the first North American university to create a separate department of political economy. As Barber (1988, 241) noted: "When Chicago was founded, political economy was linked with history and political science at Johns Hopkins, with political science at Columbia, and with 'social science' ... at Yale." This chapter focuses on the men Harper selected to build this new type of department, such as James L. Laughlin and Thorstein Veblen. John M. Clark also played an important role in the creation of a successful department of economics at the University of Chicago, and it is imperative to focus on Frank Knight and Aaron Director as well. All would play a pivotal role as founding fathers in the creation of the Chicago Tradition in the field of economics.

## THE SECOND MAN

Harper had Richard T. Ely, at that time an unhappy associate professor at Johns Hopkins, in mind for the job of the first chairman of Chicago's department of political economy. Ely was among "the Young Turks who founded the American Economic Association" in 1885 (Coats 1985,

1699). Strongly influenced by the approach and methods of the German Historical School, Ely and the other founding members of the AEA rejected Ricardian economics and the doctrine of laissez-faire as the guiding line for economic policy, and they were very critical of the role of big business in the community. Ely gave Harper his detailed ideas on what his department of political economy at the University of Chicago would look like, but negotiations failed because of Ely's financial demands: "Ely chose to play for higher stakes, and he lost" (Barber 1988, 247).

While his relations with Ely were turning sour, Harper accidentally met James Laughlin,[38] a fierce critic of Ely's economics and a staunch defender of orthodox classical economics. In December 1891, Harper became convinced that Laughlin was the right choice after Laughlin impressed him during a debate on monetary issues in New York. Legend has it that following the debate, Laughlin and Harper spent the whole night walking the streets of New York City, and at five o'clock in the morning Laughlin agreed to start up the department of political economy at the University of Chicago. As head professor at the University of Chicago, Laughlin started with an annual salary of $7,000—"at a time when the senior professors at Harvard or Yale were seldom paid more than $4,000" (Barber 1988, 245). In 1892, Laughlin launched the *Journal of Political Economy*, and it soon became one of the most respected and influential academic journals in the profession.

Laughlin was born in 1850 in the small village of Deerfield, Ohio to parents of Irish-Scottish Presbyterian descent; his father was a successful lawyer. Laughlin attended local schools and starting in 1869, he worked his way through Harvard; he earned a PhD in history there in 1876. Two years later, Charles Dunbar, dean of the faculty at Harvard, appointed Laughlin as an instructor in political economy.

Unhappy about his teaching schedule and Harvard's lecture system in general, Laughlin suffered a nervous breakdown and left Harvard in 1888 (W.C. Mitchell, 1941). After two years outside academia, he joined Cornell as a professor of political economy and finance in 1890.

Although Laughlin took on heavy teaching loads and extensive administrative and organizational responsibilities during his career[39], he managed to publish extensively. Monetary issues occupied a central place in his work, but titles such as "Anglo-Saxon Legal Procedure in Anglo-

Saxon Laws," his doctoral dissertation, and *Industrial America* give a flavor of the broad extent of Laughlin's interests and scholarship.

Laughlin (1906b) can be considered a very early forerunner of the modern insider-outsider theory of unemployment; in 1906, he indicated that if unions push for wages higher than productivity increases allow, nonunion members of society will pay the price in terms of prolonged unemployment. Laughlin's view of monetary economics was atypical of the Chicago view, which focused on the quantity theory of money.[40] He also showed himself to be a staunch supporter of the Federal Reserve System, and he played a minor role in its creation[41] (Laughlin 1914a and 1914b).

Just like Harper, Laughlin had "a great capacity for work" (Nef 1967, 779). Like Harper, he embodied the strong work ethic that is so fundamental to the Chicago Tradition. In 1888, Laughlin joined—first as secretary and shortly afterwards as president—the Manufacturers Mutual Fire Insurance Company of Philadelphia. "He was fond of telling his friends," Nef testified (1967, 780), "that ... never in his life ... had he done so little work as in those two years. Believing that scholarship demanded more time and thought than any other vocation, he could regard the training of scholars with a seriousness which no teacher who feels the slightest need of apologizing for his calling can ever command." Nevertheless, Laughlin did not underestimate the relevance of getting practical business experience, as he argued that "an economist of the first rank" must have "on the one hand ... the power of close, sustained and logical reasoning; but on the other he must have a most thoroughly practical spirit, without vagaries and nonsense. The former he gains chiefly by his academic training; the latter, by general maturity and an intuitive or practical knowledge of the world of business" (Bornemann 1940, 17). Hence, it is no surprise that Wesley Mitchell (1941, 877), one of Laughlin's first and best students, wrote that Laughlin was a man who "cordially approved the business life" and that he energetically fought for the creation of a business school at the University of Chicago.

Nef (1967, 780) highlighted four of Laughlin's qualities that help explain his success with the new department at the University of Chicago: "a genuine interest in his students, passion for scholarships, a gift for recognizing distinction even in persons with whose views he disagreed, and a wide cultural knowledge extending far beyond the frontiers of his subject." Parallel to Nef's view is Barber's (1988, 259) acknowledgment that the "notable achievements" of the department of economics during its first decade "owed much to Laughlin's doggedness and enterprise as an organizer. He took his position as head professor seriously."

## Excellence, Not Conformity

Coats (1963, 491) defined Laughlin as "a rigid thinker, an uncompromising and sometimes unfair polemicist, and an extreme conservative."[42] For example, Laughlin did not hesitate to put the classical economic theory of value and distribution on a par with the Christian faith, referring to "the laws of production and their harmony worth fundamental Christian truths" (Laughlin 1909, 134) "In fact," Laughlin argued, "we find ... that in our efforts to satisfy material wants, the fundamental economic principles are but statements of the form in which Christian ideas take shape" (Laughlin 1909,125). Coats (1963, 491) also remarked that Laughlin was "an unrelenting individualist who genuinely respected the independence of his colleagues and he was as outspoken in his resistance to Harper's encroachment upon his departmental independence as he was toward the encroachment of government upon individual freedom."[43]

Laughlin's foundation of economics were the classical views of Adam Smith, David Ricardo, and above all, John Stuart Mill. Thus, it can be argued that by choosing Laughlin instead of Ely, Harper went from one extreme to the other. Laughlin indeed had "little but contempt for Ely's passion for interventionist solutions to social and economic problems" (Barber 1988, 248), and he wrote sneeringly about "Elyism" (Dorfman 1959, 3:272). Laughlin's hostility to the economics of people like Ely explains to a large extent why Laughlin did not join the AEA until 1904, 19 years after it was founded.[44] By that time, the AEA had become much more mainstream than Ely had intended it to be.

Wesley Mitchell (1941) explicitly referred to Laughlin's lack of originality in his economic thinking.[45] Moreover, a touch of schizophrenia hangs over Laughlin's attitude to economics. He continually stressed the necessity to verify empirically whether existing theories explained the facts or not[46], but at the same time, he dogmatically rejected criticism formulated against the body of classical theory, whatever the empirical evidence may have been. According to Harold G. Moulton, Laughlin's "real shortcoming both as a writer and a teacher lay in the fact that he employed debating tactics which were unfair to those whose theories he was attacking. He never stated the other fellow's case in a genuinely sympathetic way … He usually stated it at its worst and then attacked the logic" (Bornemann 1940, 19). In 1945, Wesley Mitchell concluded: "Despite his limitations, Laughlin was a most effective teacher. He owed his success to his firm faith in the laws of economics, to the zeal with which he sought to make his students accept the truth as he saw it, to his genuine interest in our personal fortunes, and most of all to the fact that we could not accept his hard and fast doctrine" (L.S. Mitchell 1953, 85).

Despite his tendency to declare any deviation from classical economic doctrine to be heresy, Laughlin's major criterion in attracting people for his new department was scientific excellence, not conformity. Laughlin "assembled around him many of the best economists of his day regardless of their political or theoretical leanings" (Emmett 2002, xxi). This characteristic of Laughlin's policy is crucial to a proper understanding of what came to be known as the "Bemis incident."[47]

Edward Bemis was an Ely-like economist who left Vanderbilt University to join the University of Chicago at Harper's behest. Despite the opposition of Laughlin, who on several occasions voiced serious doubts about Bemis's academic competence, Harper pushed through Bemis's appointment. Bemis immediately became involved in several strongly politically and ideologically inspired discussions.

In the summer of 1895, Bemis was forced to leave the University of Chicago by Harper himself. Bemis always claimed that Laughlin went after him for ideological reasons. Commenting on the fact that Bemis sought the support of Ely, Barber wrote: "Between them, Ely and Bemis contrived to present the impression to the public that the University of Chicago was the captive of big business interests … [but] … Bemis and Ely had no evidence to document the claim that outsiders intervened in the university's personnel decisions" (Barber 1988, 253). Bornemann (1940, 26) concluded that "the dispute which arose at the time of [Bemis's] resignation was entirely between Bemis and President Harper."

Laughlin's rule of recruiting excellent men who were not necessarily conformists certainly applied to Thorstein Veblen. Laughlin brought Veblen along to the University of Chicago from Cornell and promptly made him editor of the *Journal of Political Economy*.[48] However, Veblen was not the only economist Laughlin brought from Cornell to the University of Chicago. Adolph C. Miller, a specialist in banking and finance, made the same move in 1892. Ten years later, Miller left for the University of California at Berkeley. Wesley Mitchell describes Miller as the man who "had the finest gift of exposition of any academic I have ever listened to at length … Our minds were not nearly as active while we sat at his feet as when we sat at Laughlin's. We knew that he was the better economist, but we learned less from him" (L.S. Mitchell 1953, 86). Veblen dwarfed Miller's impact at the University of Chicago and in the field of economics.

## VIVISECTIONIST FROM MARS

Veblen, a truly heterodox thinker in the intellectual history of economics, can be considered the intellectual father of the American institutionalist school, which played an important role in the development of economics in the United States duringthe first three decades of the 20th century. The two other major institutionalists were Wesley Mitchell, Veblen's student and colleague at the University of Chicago, and John R. Commons.[49] Born in 1857 to Norwegian immigrants, Thorstein Bundy Veblen grew up in Wisconsin and Minnesota.[50] His father sent him to Carleton College in Northfield, Minnesota, where John Bates Clark, the American father of marginal productivity theory—the cornerstone of neoclassical economics—taught. Although he was a relentless critic of neoclassical economics, Veblen became Clark's favorite student.

Veblen entered Johns Hopkins University but left after just a few months. In 1884, he finally earned a PhD in philosophy from Yale University, which was considered at the time to be "the most conservative center in the country" (Dorfman 1959, 3:435). At Yale, Veblen first came into contact with Darwinism through the writings of the social Darwinist William G. Sumner. He also became strongly influenced there by the work of the psychologist Herbert Spencer and the philosopher Immanuel Kant. Veblen would carry these two influences with him the rest of his life. After he received his PhD, however, he could not obtain a teaching post: "Complaining of ill health, he returned to the family farm, where he passed seven years in loneliness and frustration. That was the Golgotha of his career. He used this enforced and bitter leisure to think down to the roots" (Dorfman 1959, 3:437).

In 1891, he entered Cornell as a graduate student after "family pressure forced [him] out of retreat" (Dorfman 1959, 3:437). At Cornell, Veblen immediately drew the attention of Laughlin, who brought Veblen to the University of Chicago as a fellow one year later.

All of his life, Veblen remained "intellectually homeless" (Dorfman 1959, 3:434). "He was like a man from Mars observing with satirical wit the absurdities of our economic and social order" (Landreth and Colander 1989, 392–93). According to Mitchell, "taking one of Veblen's courses meant undergoing a vivisection without an anesthetic" (L.S. Mitchell 1953, 86).

Veblen's satirical wit regularly translated into vitriolic attacks directed at neoclassical economics and the business community.[51] As John M. Clark remarked in his obituary of Veblen: "His critical essays probably left the majority of readers ... with some bewilderment [regarding] what it was all about ... And Veblen's style resembled a barbed-wire entanglement, difficult to penetrate and with rapier-sharp points to prick the unwary" (J. M. Clark 1929, 743). Veblen's most enduring contribution to economics is his *Theory of the Leisure Class* (1899b), in which he developed the concept of conspicuous consumption.[52] However, Veblen believed that *The Instinct of Workmanship* (1914) was his only important book (Tilman 1992).

Veblen saw no place for economics as a separate science. He wanted to build a single science that fully integrated economics, sociology, anthropology, and psychology.[53] James Loeb, the physiologist who studied the interaction between physiological and psychological elements in the determination of human behavior, and John Dewey, the philosopher and social reformer who paid much attention to Darwin's evolutionary theories, were Veblen's major influences on these issues while he was at the University of Chicago.[54]

Veblen categorically rejected classical and neoclassical economic theory[55]—in fact, there is considerable evidence that Veblen coined the term "neoclassical."[56] He refused to accept neoclassical economics because he rejected abstract deductive reasoning in the social sciences and because he was convinced that the basic assumptions were false.[57] In this sense, Veblen's viewpoint was totally atypical of what would become the basic characteristic of the Chicago School: the use of price theory as the major vehicle for analysis. The basic assumption of neoclassical economic theory is the proposition that in a competitive market environment, individuals and corporations pursuing their own self-interests necessarily promote the best interest of society as a whole. This invisible-hand theorem might have been true in Adam Smith's time, Veblen argued, but times and circumstances had changed. He believed that parenthood, acquisitiveness, workmanship, and idle curiosity are basic human instincts that become totally suppressed in a capitalist society. In 1909, Veblen wrote one of his most powerful critiques of classical and neoclassical doctrine; in it, he condemns as economics a science that is too narrowly based on "hedonistic calculus" with "immutable premises" that are out of touch with reality (622,624). Veblen argued that neoclassical theory was only a theory of distribution that had nothing meaningful to say about, for example, production and economic growth.

Although there was a revival of interest in their work in the decades following World War II, Veblen and the institutionalists were often considered to be uninteresting relics. George Stigler saw a simple reason for this lack of respect for institutionalism: "It had nothing in it except a stance of hostility to the standard theoretical tradition. There was no positive agenda of research, there was no set of problems or new methods they wanted to invoke" (Kitch 1983a, 170). Stigler's negative verdict on Veblen and institutionalism is a typical example of the fundamental disagreement that exists to this day among economists regarding the value of their work. In his obituary of Veblen, John Maurice Clark (1929, 742) noted that Veblen "is rated among the great economists of history or no economist at all; as a great original pioneer or as a critic and satirist without constructive talent or achievement."

The most important point with respect to the subject at hand, however, is that Veblen comes close to personifying exactly the opposite of what the Chicago School represents. It should be emphasized that Laughlin is unanimously described as an uncompromising conservative and fierce defender of classical economics and that Rockefeller, the main financier of the newly established University of Chicago, was the textbook example of a capitalist. But Laughlin brought a man from Cornell—about whom Rockefeller clearly did not object—who vigorously attacked the market economy. In Veblen's opinion, the market economy could not prevent corporations from acquiring monopoly power; therefore, it was more destructive than constructive to society.

Veblen was able to stay and teach at Chicago because Laughlin respected him as an intellectual: "From the time of their first meeting, Laughlin was fascinated by Veblen" (Bornemann 1940, 27).

Veblen was asked to leave the University of Chicago after 14 years because of his lifestyle, which had become more and more eccentric; most of the complications arose from Veblen's romantic life. In his introduction to the 1953 edition of *The Theory of the Leisure Class,* C. Wright Mills of Columbia University wrote: "His wife kept going away and coming back. Girls, we are told, liked Veblen and he did not really object" (Veblen 1899b, ix).

Veblen was asked to resign not because of his intellectual beliefs but because organization and decency, and his already meager appetite for teaching, had slipped away from him. Harper was the driving force behind Veblen's resignation from the University of Chicago, but "Laughlin was sorry to see Veblen go" (Bornemann 1940, 28). That Veblen survived as long as he did at the University of Chicago "was an outcome that owed much to Laughlin's interventions on his behalf" (Barber 1988, 263).

Veblen spent the rest of his career at Stanford University, the University of Missouri, and finally the New School for Social Research in New York. But by and large, as Emmett concludes (2002, xxii), "most of the work Veblen is noted for was written during his tenure at Chicago."

## Gaining Acceptance

In 1907, Harper died unexpectedly, and Harry Pratt Judson succeeded him as president of the University of Chicago Judson, who had "unusual confidence in Laughlin" (Bornemann 1940, 33), gave the latter much more freedom with respect to new appointments. Soon,

Laughlin attracted several new men to his department of political economy, the most noteworthy of whom are Chester W. Wright and Leon C. Marshall.[58]

Laughlin recruited Marshall from Ohio Wesleyan University, where he had proven himself as an able and innovative administrator of its library. Although Marshall had a solid reputation as a teacher, his main long-term influence was as "an outstanding administrator ... Laughlin soon entrusted to Marshall a good share of the administrative burdens of the Department. In Laughlin's absence ... Marshall appeared to have been the acting head of the Department" (Bornemann 1940, 33).

When Laughlin retired in 1916, Leon Marshall became chairman of the department of economics, a job he kept until leaving for Johns Hopkins University in 1928. In his memoir, Paul Douglas (1972, 36) referred to Marshall as "that inspiring leader of men." Marshall contributed much to the organization and institutional development of the department of economics. "Marshall," according to Emmett (1998, 139), "pointed the way toward what modernist education in economics was to become during the 1930s ... In his vision of graduate education at Chicago, then, Marshall encapsulated the radical transformation of social scientific education: a broadening of the economics education offered to develop informed citizens, coupled with a narrowing of the economics education offered in advanced and graduate work."

As far as scientific endeavors are concerned, the most important contributor during Marshall's chairmanship was undoubtedly John Maurice Clark, son of John Bates Clark, who came to the University of Chicago in 1915; needless to say, John M. Clark's father had a tremendous impact on his work. As Dorfman noted (1959, 5:440): "Throughout his career [John M.] Clark proclaimed his debt to his father. Even in his sharpest advances beyond the frontier of tradition he insisted that the seeds were to be found in his father's work."

John M. Clark was born in 1884, and he graduated from Amherst College in 1905 and earned a PhD at Columbia University in 1910 with a dissertation on railroad economics.[59] After short teaching spells at Colorado College and Amherst, he arrived at the University of Chicago in 1915, where he stayed for the next 10 years. Given his father's fame, his East Coast background, and his own solid reputation, John M.

Clark brought prestige and respect to Chicago's department of political economy.

Laughlin's presence and his rigid view of economics had maneuvered the department of political economy at the University of Chicago into a kind of intellectual isolation. After the rigorous, inflexible Laughlin, the gentle, diplomatic John M. Clark was exactly what economics at the University of Chicago needed. John M. Clark returned to Columbia in 1926, and he retired from there as a professor in 1953.[60] He died in 1963.

During his Chicago period, John M. Clark proved to be both a student of his father and a product of his times. He emphasized the relevance of orthodoxy and of the neoclassical, Marshallian heritage. However, his thinking was also strongly influenced by Veblenian institutionalism and an accompanying distrust of neoclassical economics, the market economy, and big business.

John M. Clark (1919, 281) stressed that for a "solid economic theory," one needed "price theory" as well as "social economics." Like Veblen, he argued that "consistent economic man has long been known to be a sheer abstraction" (Clark 1918, 29). Dorfman (1959, 5:461) summarized it well: "The great value of his contribution lies in its synthesis of neo-classical economics and institutionalism, its presentation as an integrated whole." Friedman took a course from John M. Clark during his stay at Columbia University and commented: "J.M. Clark was painfully shy in personal contacts ... Despite his hesitant lecturing style ... I regard his course as second only to [Harold] Hotelling's as the most rewarding of those I took at Columbia. It was theory with a different approach and in a different context from what I had been exposed to at Chicago, yet no less rigorous or relevant" (Friedman and Friedman 1998, 45–46).

However, John M. Clark's first major contribution to economics had nothing to do with the debate between neoclassicists and institutionalists. Instead, it was about the business cycle and more specifically the role the acceleration principle plays in it: changes in consumption and output bring about magnified changes in investment expenditures and the whole process leads to fluctuations in economic activity, income, and employment.[61]

The impact of institutionalist thinking and the fear of degradation of the competitive process are present in the two books John M. Clark published during his Chicago years. In the first of these books, *Studies in the Economics of Overhead Costs* (1923), he focused on the overhead costs of large-scale industrial enterprises as a major incentive for these corporations to go for discriminatory, even monopolistic strategies.[62] In the second book, *Social Control of Business* (1926), he described how social control of business activities had increased spectacularly in the United States since the 1870s, in large part because of the shortcomings of the system he described in the previous book. Therefore, John M. Clark concluded (1926, 521), pure laissez-faire is simply impossible and the country should move "cautiously towards a program of social-liberal planning."

## WATERED-DOWN INSTITUTIONALISM

By the time John M. Clark left the University of Chicago, institutionalism was still very much around, but it was much less radical than what Veblen had championed. Five economists contributed to the later institutionalism movement: Wesley Mitchell, Robert Hoxie, Chester Wright, Simeon E. Leland, and John Nef (the latter two belong to a later generation).

Born in Rushville, Illinois, Wesley Mitchell counted himself among "the aborigines," the moniker given to the University's first students when it opened in 1892 (L.S. Mitchell, 1953, 85). Mitchell's doctoral dissertation was completed under Laughlin's supervision, and this work led Mitchell to focus on the quantity theory of money during his Chicago years.[63] In 1903, Mitchell left the University of Chicago for the University of California at Berkeley, and his later work focused on purely empirical research on the business cycle.[64] Over the years, he became increasingly critical of neoclassical economics, which is among the most important reasons why Dorfman (1959, 3:455) describes Mitchell as "the foremost heir of Veblen."[65]

Robert Hoxie did his undergraduate work at Cornell and followed Laughlin to the University of Chicago, where he earned a PhD. Hoxie taught at the University of Chicago until committing suicide in 1916. Hoxie's relationship with Laughlin seems was comparable to that of Laughlin and Veblen: "Hoxie and Laughlin were as far apart as East and West, but it speaks for Laughlin's tolerance that he brought Hoxie to, and kept him in, his Department" (Bornemann 1940, 29).

Hoxie was first and foremost a labor economist who "gradually found it difficult to reconcile the static equilibrium model of Marshallian economics with the structure of modern industrial labor" (Emmett 2002, 2: viii), and he focused on the effects of trade unions.[66] His posthumously-published book *Trade Unionism in the United States* (1917) was described 40 years later as "one of the few permanent contributions to the theory of labor organization by an American economist" (Dorfman 1959, 3:451). Although Hoxie's work has many institutional characteristics, he was much more than a pure institutionalist. As far as economic theory is concerned, one of Hoxie's two papers on demand, supply, and the market prize (Hoxie 1906) are interesting contributions to economic theory.

The three other post-Veblen institutionalists—Wright, Leland, and Nef—are better described as historians focused on economic institutions rather than as true institutionalists. Chester Wright was a product of Harvard who began his teaching career at Cornell. Laughlin recruited him away from Cornell, and he remained in Chicago from 1907 to 1944. His major publication was an economic history of the United States (Wright 1941). Leland, a specialist in public finance, was born in 1897, received a master's degree at the University of Kentucky, and had a postgraduate year at Harvard. He came to Chicago in 1928 and was president of the department from 1939 to 1945. In 1946, he moved on to Northwestern University. In the early 1940s, Leland served as chairman of the board of the Federal Reserve Bank of Chicago. However, neither Wright nor Leland can be considered really important scholars for the development of economics at the University of Chicago.

Nef, who was born in Chicago in 1899, was the son of John Nef, Sr., the first professor of chemistry at the University of Chicago. Nef attended Harvard for his undergraduate studies and earned a PhD from Washington's Robert Brookings Graduate School, the forerunner of the Brookings Institution, in 1927. In 1929, he returned to the University of Chicago with a joint appointment in the departments of history and economics.

Like John M. Clark, Nef occupied a position somewhere halfway between a price theorist and an institutionalist. He stayed in Chicago until moving to Washington, DC, in 1962; he died there in 1988.[67]

Nef's first publication (1932), about the rise of the British coal

industry, became a classic almost immediately, but his later work tended
to focus on broader issues regarding the future of mankind. An important initiative of Nef's at the University of Chicago was the 1941 creation
of the Committee on Social Thought, which brought Friedrich Hayek
to the university in 1950. Just as with Wright and Leland, it is fair to say
that Nef's impact on the subsequent development of economics at the
University of Chicago was rather limited.

## TAKING ON GOD

A Chicago economist who boasted a critical attitude toward any kind
of dogma or accepted truth—one of the essential characteristics of the
Chicago Tradition—to an almost pathological degree was Frank H.
Knight. Born in McLean County, Illinois, Knight was the oldest of 11
children raised in religious orthodoxy: His parents were adherents of the
Plymouth Brethren, "an intellectually narrow sect" (Shils 1997, 36).

He received his basic education in Tennessee at the American University, Milligan College, and the University of Tennessee. There, he
studied philosophy, theology, social sciences, history, literature, German,
French, and chemistry. At Cornell University, he switched the focus of
his studies from philosophy to economics[68] under the influence of Alvin
Johnson and Allyn Young and earned a PhD in 1916 with a dissertation
entitled "A Theory of Business Profits." At Cornell, he was also strongly
influenced by Herbert Davenport; later, he made Davenport's *Economics
of Enterprise* (1913) required reading for his courses at Chicago.

After spending two years at the University of Chicago, Knight became an associate professor at the University of Iowa in 1919. Nine years
later, he returned to Chicago and filled John M. Clark's vacant chair in
economic theory. Knight stayed at the University of Chicago for the rest
of his life.

Shortly after Knight's death, the following lines appeared in the
*Chicago Tribune:* "His skepticism, one of the trademarks of his brilliance
in economic analysis, also carried over into other fields. Former students
recall that his two great whipping boys were medical doctors and the
clergy. He considered the clergy a form of quackery as bad as he regarded
doctors. Both of them, Knight considered, pretended to know things
that couldn't be known."[69] One of Knight's students, Don Patinkin, re-

called the following quote from Knight about medicine: "I once asked a historian of medicine when he thought doctors began curing more people than they killed. 'Well,' he answered, 'I think that that will be in another generation or so'" (Patinkin 1981, 35). This statement is typical of Knight's anticlericalism: "In Christianity, surely, we find the supreme 'irony of history': that an original teaching centered ethically in humility, meekness, self-denial, and self-sacrifice became organized into corporations whose dignitaries have hardly been matched for arrogant grasping, using and flaunting of power and wealth and for insistence on prerogative to the borderline of worship" (Knight 1956, 277).

In his memoir, George Stigler, who was one of Knight's best-known students, wrote that Knight was "an irreverent critic of scholars and institutions, and it was indicative of both his skepticism of all authority and his intellectual vigor that sometimes he could not read *his* copies of important books: they were literally filled with (even between the printed lines) his written comments" (Stigler 1988b, 16).[70] James Buchanan, the Nobel Prize–winning economist, recalled the following from his student days at the University of Chicago: "To Frank Knight, nothing was sacrosanct, not the dogmas of religion, not the laws and institutions of social order, not the prevailing moral norms, not the accepted interpretations of sacred or profane texts. Anything and everything was a potential subject for critical scrutiny" (Buchanan 1991, 244). Buchanan believed that Knight's religious upbringing was a major source of his critical spirit: "Only through an early experience of having wrestled with God, the source of the ultimate putative authority, and having at least held his own in the encounter, Frank Knight had no difficulty at all in taking on any or all of the lesser gods, as variously represented in the many small dogmas of science, art, politics and history" (Buchanan 1991, 247,248).

Knight rejected blind faith in any "ism"—including communism, socialism, and capitalism. In 1932, he gave a speech to the National Student League entitled "The Case for Communism: From the Standpoint of an Ex-Liberal" (Knight 1932a). This pamphlet is not so much a case for a communist regime as it is an expression of profound desperation by an intellectual who saw no future for 19th-century liberalism based on economic laissez-faire and political democracy. Indeed, Knight's speech did not a single word that truly endorsed communism.

Almost 20 years later, Knight's condemnation of communism went even farther with the following remarks about Marx and Engels's *Communist Manifesto:* "[it] called on the workers of the world to unite for the violent overthrow of all pre-existing social order, because of 'you have nothing to lose but your chains.' Madness, criminal madness, of course; but how many of the bright and educated have fallen for and preached it" (Knight 1956, 273). In line with his condemnation of communism, Knight rejected central economic planning and any attempt to improve public policy, because he was convinced that political decision-making—in a democracy or a dictatorship—was fundamentally unreasonable. "All talk of social control is nonsense," Knight wrote in his review of Harvard economist Sumner H. Slichter's *Modern Economic Society* (1931) (Knight 1932b, 458).

Knight's suspicion of politicians and their motives was deep-seated. He once said, "The probability of the people in power being individuals who would dislike the possession and exercise of power is on a level with the probability that an extremely tender-hearted person would get the job of whipping master in a slave plantation."[71] Not surprisingly, Knight fundamentally mistrusted political reformers: "When a man or group asks for power to do good, my impulse is to say: Oh, yeah, who ever wanted power for any other reason, and what have they done when they got it? So I instinctively want to cancel the last three words, leaving simply, 'I want power'; that is easy to believe ... I am reluctant to believe in doing good with power anyhow" (Knight 1956, 281).

Knight was indeed "an incurable cynic about human nature" (Bernstein 1996, 218); however, he showed "not the cynicism of the embittered man, but the cynicism of one who looked with understanding—and, though he would probably have denied it, even compassion—on the limitations of man and society" (Patinkin 1981, 48).

## FREEDOM FIRST

Knight considered himself a classical liberal who gave overall importance to true individual freedom. To Knight, freedom itself was a primary goal: "Wealth and poverty are terribly important things, but ... their significance seems to me an absurd oversimplification. Freedom itself, as a value per se, is far more important" (Knight 1956, 269). Here an important difference emerges between Knight and the classical economists: Utilitarianism led the classicists to focus on the free-market organization as a means to an end—the achievement of the greatest possible aggregate of consumer welfare—but Knight defended the competitive system because to him, a market working under the conditions of perfect competition is the embodiment of true freedom. He was more interested in the maximization of freedom than consumer satisfaction. Furthermore, Knight consistently argued that economic freedom is essential to the existence of all other forms of freedom, including religious, political and intellectual freedom.

Although he always defended the free competitive market as the best form of economic organization, Knight never engaged in a blind defense of capitalism and the free-market system. In fact, all his life Knight struggled with the ethical basis of a competitive economy. Bernstein (1996, 219) remarked: "Knight's cynicism and concern for moral values made it hard for him to come to terms with the selfishness, and frequently, the violence of capitalism ... Yet he stuck with capitalism because he considered the alternatives unacceptable." Allen Wallis, one of Knight's students, agreed: "It should be noted that Knight himself never accepted the kind of views that Friedman put forward in, for instance, *Capitalism and Freedom* which Knight regarded as an ultrasimplistic work that ignored many subtle problems. On the other hand, Knight was even more devastating in his analyses of social policies that differ from those advocated by Friedman."[72]

In 1923, Knight published a paper called *The Ethics of Competition;* in it, he put forward three reasons why the competitive system can hardly be considered just.

First, the competitive system distributes income on the basis of luck and inheritance rather than effort: "The luck element is so large ... that capacity and effort may count for nothing ... the luck element works cumulatively, as in gambling games generally" (Knight 1956, 56).

Second, the competitive system is more of a gamble, and thus it is a poorly equipped mechanism to meet widely acceptable standards of fairness (e.g., give an even start-up opportunity to every person).

Third, the competitive system cannot be considered an exemplary tool for satisfying demands, as it molds itself to the tastes of its members and neglects important aspects of the quality of life: "In a social order where all values are reduced to the money measure in the degree that this is true of modern industrial nations, a considerable fraction of the most noble and sensitive characters will lead unhappy and even futile lives. Everyone is compelled to play the economic game and be judged by his success in playing it, whatever his field of activity or type of interest, and has to squeeze in as a side line any other competition, or non-competitive activity, which may have for him a greater intrinsic appeal" (Knight 1956, 58).

Knight's views also align with another characteristic of the Chicago Tradition—the importance of scholarship. Stigler wrote: "His devotion to knowledge was exemplified and its message reinforced by Knight's way of life. He was not a consultant to great bodies or small, whether public or private; he did not ride the lecture circuit; he did not seek a place in the popular press ... A major source of his influence was the strength of his devotion to the pursuit of knowledge. Frank Knight transmitted, to a degree I have seldom seen equaled, a sense of unreserved commitment to *truth*" (Stigler 1988b, 17–18). Knight was personally even more outspoken on this issue: "The pursuit of truth ... is the ideal type of ethical association, which is to say of all true society" (Knight 1956, 132). "What impressed me," Shils (1997, 34) wrote about Knight, "was a man so honest that he could reason himself into paralyzing uncertainties, an idealist so lofty in his aspirations that anything that fell short of them was oppressive disappointment."

## THE CRUSADING ECONOMIST

It is virtually impossible to put a specific label on Knight as an economist. Well-argued attempts have been made to describe Knight as, respectively, a neoclassical, an Austrian, and an institutional economist. Take the following two quotes. Hodgson argued that "there were both neoclassical and Austrian elements in Knight's thinking, and these played no small part. But also, in a strong and theoretically meaningful sense, he was an institutionalist" (Hodgson 2001, 69). Malcolm Rutherford emphasized that "Knight subjected the ideas of institutionalists to sustained criticism ... and consistently maintained the central importance of standard price theory in any economic analysis, whether theoretical or historical in nature."[73]

Knight's best-known tract on economics is *Risk, Uncertainty and Profit* (1921), which is based on his doctoral dissertation. It is considered to be "one of the most important economics monographs of the 20th century" (Hodgson 2001, 68) and "the first work of any importance, and in any field of study, that deals explicitly with decision-making under conditions of uncertainty" (Bernstein 1996, 219).

The purpose of his analysis was to explain the existence of profits in a regime of perfect competition. Indeed, classical economic theory concluded that in such an environment, profits eventually disappear. Knight made a distinction between insurable (fire, theft, and so on) and uninsurable risks. The first type of risk cannot give rise to profit, because it is insurable. If one assumes that perfect competition exists, companies face continuous change in the marketplace and it is not possible to insure against these changes. The way that these uncertainties are handled can give rise to profit. According to his analysis, even under perfect competition profits will only disappear when the economy arrives at some abstract stationary state at which all uncertainty has vanished.

Although the most basic insight Knight develops in *Risk, Uncertainty and Profit* concerns the concept of uncertainty,[74] it is not the only remarkable theme in this book. As Nobel Prize-winner Gerard Debreu used to say during his days at the Cowles Commission in Chicago, Knight's tract has all the basic ingredients of the concept of general equilibrium.[75] In *Risk, Uncertainty and Profit,* Knight devised the first complete formulation of the concept of perfect competition.

The lesser-known work *The Economic Organization* originated from Knight's (1933) lecture notes from his time in Iowa. "The price system" plays an absolutely crucial role in Knight's description of "the social organization of economic activity" (4): "On a general understanding of the fundamental laws of price relations, and on their thoughtful application in measures of public policy, rests all hope for prosperity under democratic institutions, all hope for efficiency in industry and a progressively more equitable distribution of the burdens and benefits of social cooperation in economic life" (32).[76]

In *The Economic Organization,* Knight presented the wheel of wealth diagram that would become standard in textbooks on economics for the first time. His meticulous analysis of the role of time in the economic process brought him to the conclusion that the traditional classification of the factors of production into land, labor, and capital is seriously misleading. According to Knight, "the ultimate elements or sources of productive power are *nature, man* and *time* or *waiting*" (61). These notions it clear that Knight was a forerunner of Becker's seminal analysis on the issue of the allocation of time.

As an economist, Knight engaged in several intellectual battles that sometimes took the form of crusades. Three issues stand out: capital and interest theory, monopolistic competition, and welfare economics.

Knight became a fierce critic of the Austrian capital and interest theory that was dominant in the last decades of the 19th century.[77] Eugen Böhm-Bawerk and his Austrian School largely worked within the classical framework that distinguished between the various factors of production and the returns these factors earn: wage, rent, interest, and profit. For each of these four types of income, a specific theory had to be developed. With Irving Fisher of Yale University, among others, Knight rejected this Austrian approach. In the two articles in which he developed his theory of interest, Knight (1936a, 1936b) related the economic explanation of the interest rate to the productivity of capital and came very close to defining all factors of production as capital goods.[78] "Interest," Knight concluded, "is a form in which the yield of a capital good (or some part of it) is paid and received, rather than a distinct share in distribution coming from a distinct source" (Knight 1956, 25).

It should be noted that Knight's articles on interest rates appeared in the same year as Keynes's General Theory. One of the elements on which Knight based his criticism of Keynes's analysis was the fact that Keynes related the interest rate to the flow of current investment.

Knight's second crusade concerned the concept of monopolistic or imperfect competition. The real analytical content of a competitive system had been left undefined, even by Alfred Marshall; most of the time, it was presented as the opposite of a pure monopoly. In 1933 Joan Robinson and Edward Chamberlin published respective classic books in which they argued that this view of market structures was far too simplistic.[79] In *The Theory of Monopolistic Competition,* Chamberlin presented monopolistic competition as the dominant market structure in a free-enterprise system; he defined it as a situation where a firm becomes a quasi-monopolist for its own product(s) via product differentiation.

The Chamberlin theory attracted considerable support in the profession, but Knight (1938) was, not surprisingly, a critic. Chamberlin (1957, 296) eventually wrote about the "Chicago School of anti-monopolistic competition" that was characterized by "the zeal with which the theory of monopolistic competition has been attacked." Ironically, both Knight and Chamberlin were deeply influenced by the same economist—Allyn Young, who taught both at Cornell, where Knight studied, and Harvard, where Chamberlin studied.

Knight's third primary intellectual battle was about welfare economics. In 1924, he published a famous paper on social costs, "Fallacies in the Interpretation of Social Cost" (Knight 1997). His work was a clear forerunner of Ronald Coase's (1960) famous paper on the same subject and a fundamental criticism of some elements of *Wealth and Welfare* (1912) and *Economics of Welfare* (1918), two books in which Arthur C. Pigou made seminal contributions to the development of welfare economics. Pigou, who hailed from England's Cambridge University, was the first to explicitly make the distinction between private and social marginal costs. If the two coincide, according to Pigou, the competitive system takes care of an efficient allocation of resources, and if they diverge, the system produces market failures and the government should intervene with taxes and/or subsidies. By 1913, Allyn Young had already brought forward flaws in Pigou's reasoning.[80]

Knight furthered Young's efforts and criticized the logic of Pigou's famous example of the two roads. Knight proved that "if the roads are assumed to be subject to private appropriation and exploitation, precisely the ideal situation which would be established by the imaginary tax will be brought about through the operation of ordinary economic motives" (Knight 1997, 213). As a result of Knight's criticism, Pigou dropped the road congestion example from subsequent editions of his book. Knight's analysis "rehabilitated the neoclassical view that under competitive conditions, efficient allocation of resources would prevail ... The market failure which Pigou and his disciples thought they had demonstrated was precisely the opposite of market failure. It was the failure of government

to establish property rights in scarce resources that caused the congestion" (Breit and Ransom 1998, 197).

Almost 40 years later, the generalization of the intimate relationship
between clearly specified property rights and the efficient functioning of
a free market economy was developed more explicitly by Coase, who acknowledged that he had known of Knight's argument when he wrote his
famous article on social cost and even added: "I would say that the title
of my paper came from Frank Knight" (Kitch 1983a, 215).

## Eternal Doubt

Knight had at least as much impact on the development of economic
thought through his influence on other scholars as he did through his
publications. Blaug (1985, 116) argues that Knight's "teaching at the
Chicago University in the interwar years inspired generations of students and many famous economists have testified to the stimulus they
received in their youth from Knight's skeptical, rambling and discur-
sive lectures." Reder (1982, 6) identifies Knight's main contribution to
the Chicago Tradition as that "of sage and oracle, rather than initiator
of research programs ... Like the profession at large, Knight's students
absorbed his ideas, but did not use them as point of departure for their
own work. Knight contributed to the formation of their minds but did
not influence the direction of their research programs."

A case can be made that the widening gap that developed between
Knight's economics and those of even his closest students, such as Friedman, Stigler, Director, and Wallis, was due to Knight's disdain for and
open hostility to quantitative methods. Knight's take (1956) on the
Kelvin Dictum ("When you cannot measure, your knowledge is meager and unsatisfactory") has become legendary in Chicago: "[This say-
ing] ... very largely means in practice: If you cannot measure, measure
anyhow!" (166). Knight also dismissed the increasing prevalence of statistical data for economists by saying, "This does not mean ... that economics will be or can be purely statistical" (26).

Knight was no less harsh in his judgment of mathematical economics. In 1923, he wrote: "The mathematical economists have commonly
been mathematicians first and economists afterward, disposed to over-

simplify the data and underestimate the divergence between their premises and the facts of life. In consequence they have not been successful in getting their presentation into such a form that it could be understood, and its relationship to real problems recognized by practical economists" (Knight 1997, 41). However, he wrote this passage 28 years later:

> Only by the use of mathematics is it possible to bring together into a single comprehensible system the variety, the complexity, and most of all the interdependence, of the factors which determine prices, costs, output, and demand and the wages or hire of productive agents ... The principle value of such elaborate and abstract systems lies in forcibly reminding the inquirer that a change in practically any economic variable has direct or indirect effects on innumerable other magnitudes, thus preventing him from fatally oversimplifying conceptions of economic cause and effect. (Knight 1956, 27)

Knight's reservations, or at least his doubts, about the tendency to turn economics into a quantitative, empirical, and mathematical science arguably have much to do with his deep-rooted ambiguity toward economics. The opening sentence of *The Economic Organization* is characteristic of this ambiguity: "It is somewhat unusual to begin the treatment of a subject with a warning against attaching too much importance to it; but in the case of economics, such an injunction is quite as much needed as explanation and emphasis of the importance it really has" (Knight 1933, 1).

In 1941, he wrote about "the fallacy ... that social science is a science in the same sense as the natural sciences" (Knight 1956, 121), but 10 years later he argued that "there is a science of economics, a true, even exact, science, which reaches laws as universal as those of mathematics or mechanics" (Knight 1956, 135). Another remark from the same work echoes these statements: "The growing accumulation of numerical information covering a wide variety of economic facts, coupled with the advance of statistical technique, has been working a notable change in the character and content of economics as a whole; without nullifying any of its established principles, it has given more knowledge of the actual degree of stability or variability in the relationships in real life" (Knight 1956, 26).

Knight's attitude about quantitative economics played an important role in the bitter relationship that existed between him and his more mathematically and empirically orientated contemporaries at the University of Chicago, including Henry Schultz and Paul Douglas. The friction between Knight and Douglas became so tense at one point that the two men practically stopped talking to each other and only maintained communication through letters. Stigler quotes extensively from these letters in his memoir; in one of them, Douglas writes to Knight: "It has been quite evident from your personal conversations and your public speeches and what you have said to many others that you regard me as something of a charlatan and a demagogue" (Stigler 1988b, 184).

## SOCRATES

In his review of *Chicago Economics,* Reder (1982, 7) wrote: "In preparing this essay, I have been struck by the many strong expressions of intellectual indebtedness both of Chicago economists and legal scholars (such as Edward Levi and Robert Bork) to Aaron Director. Despite Stigler's repeated admonitions about the difficulty of communicating "influence," Director appears to have exercised a great deal of influence on the principal figures in Chicago economics from the 1930s to the present."

Although he is less well known than Knight or Veblen, Director also had a pivotal role in the creation of the Chicago Tradition and the Chicago School. Most contemporary Chicago economists who knew Director, whether they were in the business or law school or the economics department, speak highly of him and readily admit that he had a tremendous influence on the development of economics at the University of Chicago. James Heckman believes that Director is the "absolute master of price theory."[81] According to Sam Peltzman, Director's adage was, "Don't jump to conclusions. If you see something that is at odds with the competitive model, don't say immediately something like 'this is monopoly' but investigate it carefully and then draw your conclusions."[82]

Although their style and personal approach were totally different, Director proved to be a real intellectual catalyst on the order of Knight.

As Bernard Meltzer (1966, 5) of the University of Chicago's law school acknowledged: "[Director] has been a superb teacher not only of students but also of their instructors ... he has been conducting one of the most successful programs of adult education in the United States." Wesley Liebeler of the University of California at Los Angeles (UCLA) pointed out that Director made fundamental contributions in the field of antitrust, but "to me his most important contribution by far is much less tangible ... He developed and reinforced in his students a state of mind without which much of what they have done would not have been done or would have been done less well" (Kitch 1983a, 184). Director's prominence as an intellectual catalyst establishes him as one of the founding fathers of the Chicago Tradition. "In forming most present day policy views of Chicago economists, Director and Friedman have been the main intellectual forces," Stigler said (Stigler 1982b, 170).

Director was born in 1901 in the Ukrainian town of Cherterisk, but he and his parents came to the United States when he was 12. He received a bachelor's degree from Yale University in 1924. His sister Rose, who married Milton Friedman in 1938, wrote in her memoir: "Aaron spent the year after he graduated from Yale hitchhiking, first around this country and then Europe ... At that period of his life, he was a socialist—an example of the old adage, 'If one is not a socialist before age 30, one has no heart; if one remains a socialist after 30, one has no head'" (Friedman and Friedman 1998, 14). During his period of self-discovery, Director worked in a coal mine and a textile factory. He visited England, France, and Czechoslovakia to learn about their workers' movements. His socialist sympathies explain the fact that, on his return to the United States, he became director of workers' education for the Oregon State Federation of Labor and head of Portland Labor College.[83]

In 1927, he enrolled at the University of Chicago as a graduate student. After three years at the University of Chicago, Director got a job there as an instructor in economics and a research assistant to Paul Douglas, with whom he wrote the book *The Problem of Unemployment*. From 1937 to 1938, Director visited the London School of Economics (LSE). Knight, who was by that time suspicious of anyone who was close to Douglas, asked LSE's Lionel Robbins to give his opinion on Director.

Robbins referred to Director's "quite unique balance of qualities—a perfectly civilized man" and praised "his judgment, his scholarship, his analytical ability" (Coase 1993b, 244). Director went from London to Washington, where he served in different government positions until he was recalled to Chicago in 1946 to take over Henry Simons' position as the economist in the Chicago Law School after Simons' death.

When Paul Samuelson came to the University of Chicago in 1932, Director was teaching the course in elementary economics. Samuelson told Leonard Silk that he took to the course "as a cat takes to catnip, or as my first daughter took to ice cream at the age of nine months when ice cream was put on her tongue. She went wild—there were things she had never heard of! I took to economics that way … He [Director] had a very cold, sardonic sense of humor. He was an iconoclast. This was at the bottom of the Great Depression, and to have a member of the Chicago School casting scorn upon so many of the panaceas being offered at that time was titillating" (Silk 1976, 8). Silk described Director as "a mordant critic of governmental and social institutions" (Silk 1976, 46).

During a 1985 lecture, Stigler characterized Director as follows: "He has a strong, independent mind and he has thought deeply on many questions, dissecting widely accepted and comfortable ideas to reveal their essential superficiality and frequent inconsistencies … I cannot recount the number of times in which Director's always courteous questioning led me either to change my views or to seek evidence to reinforce their relevance and weight. If we had been in Greece, I'm sure I would have called him Socrates" (Breit and Spencer 1995, 102–103).

The first topics Director tackled were unemployment, economic stagnation, and the policies needed to fight these evils—not surprising for someone who started his career during the Great Depression. In the government policy arena, Director favored financing public works through direct money creation instead of higher taxation. In depression times, he saw real possibilities in increasing the demand for labor through planned public works (Director 1930).

As he developed these arguments further, Director came to the conclusion that traditional policies of monetary expansion such as open-market operations would be inadequate in a climate of depression. He reasoned that the lack of confidence among businessmen during a depression tends to be so overwhelming that even if banks were willing to extent credit at low rates of interest, their market—businessmen—would be reluctant to seek it.

Amidst the disorientation of the Depression, Director persuasively argued against the then fashionable idea that technical progress that led to widespread unemployment. In a response to the engineer-led movement of the 1920s and early 1930s pleading for more national economic planning, Director masterfully analyzed the dynamics of technical change, advances in prosperity, job destruction in declining sectors, and job creation in expanding sectors:

> It is clear, therefore, that the decline of employment in the mechanized industries, on the railroads, in mining, and agriculture, must be set off against increases in the number of actors, teachers, barbers, cleaning, dyeing, and pressing-shop workers, cooks, chauffeurs, truck drivers, building-trade craftsmen, and laundry workers, to mention but a few of the growing occupations—occupations that may not meet the standards of an engineer's utopia but which apparently satisfied the 'wants' of the human beings as they are. This past development is one which is likely to continue. First, there was a decline in the numbers required to produce the nation's food; we shall soon witness a decline in the numbers required to man the nation's industries—and it will be the service occupations which will take up the slack. (Director 1933, 14)

## THE GODFATHER OF LAW AND ECONOMICS

At this point, it seems appropriate to ask why such a gifted economist as Director has such a short publication record. According to his brother-in-law Friedman, Knight was a major reason:

> Aaron Director was, just as men like Homer Jones and George Stigler; a true disciple of Knight's. Although much influenced by Knight, I do not consider myself to be such a disciple. I was much more interested in the scientific aspects of economics than

in the philosophical ones. Those close to Knight like Aaron, Homer and to a somewhat lesser extent George, tended to become inhibited in their writings because Knight always sought for absolute perfection. Although Frank Knight himself was prolific, people like Aaron Director were always afraid of being debunked. Knight's specialty was debunking.[84]

Sometimes others had to hold the pen to get Director's view across. "Almost a decade ago," Stigler wrote in 1970, "Aaron Director proposed a law of public expenditures: public expenditures are made for the primary benefit of the middle classes and financed with taxes which are borne in considerable part by the poor and the rich" (1). The rest of Stigler's article is concerned with the illustration of and an explanation for Director's Law—"which its inventor refuses to do" (1).

In fact, Director stood at the cradle of the research program concerned with the clash between general welfare and the actions of pressure groups. "By inculcating the idea that the government must manage things," Director stated in 1951, "are we not encouraging the growth of organized minority groups among workers and employers which will divide the country into warring camps?"[85] With such statements, Director proved to be a distant forerunner of the theory of public choice and of Chicago's theory of regulation posed by George Stigler, Sam Peltzman, Gary Becker, and Richard Posner.

In 1964, Director published a remarkable article on the markets for goods and ideas; in it, he devised a paradox: Why is it that the people who insist on the necessity of freedom in the market of ideas are the same folk who plead against free markets and for government intervention in the market for goods? Director's explanation is especially telling about his own gentle nature: "Everybody tends to magnify the importance of his own occupation and to minimize that of his neighbor. Intellectuals are engaged in the pursuit of truth, while others are merely engaged in earning a livelihood … It may be asserted with some confidence that among intellectuals there is an inverse correlation between the appreciation of the merits of civil liberty—including freedom of speech—and the merits of economic freedom" (Director 1964, 6,5).

Coase (1994, 67) dropped the polished wording in his comments about Director's article: "The market for ideas is the market in which the intellectual conducts his trade. The explanation of the paradox is self-interest and self-esteem. Self-esteem leads the intellectuals to magnify the importance of their own market. That others should be regulated seems natural, particularly as many of the intellectuals see themselves as doing the regulating. But self-interest combines with self-esteem to ensure that, while others are regulated, regulation should not apply to them."

Director's analysis of monopoly is arguably his most important contribution to modern economics; through it, he became one of the founding fathers of the field of law and economics. During the first part of the 20th century, it was generally recognized at the University of Chicago that monopoly was a widespread phenomenon that threatened society's well being and economic and social progress. Both Veblen and Knight often wrote about the importance of monopoly, and Henry Simons was obsessed with it. "In 1950," Stigler (1988b, 99) says, "I believed that monopoly posed a major problem in public policy in the United States, and that it should be dealt with boldly by breaking up dominant firms and severely punishing businesses that engaged in collusion."[86]

Director helped change the thinking about monopoly—first at the University of Chicago and later in broader circles. The course in antitrust law that Director taught with Edward Levi at the Chicago law school was the place where this change took shape. Director's major innovation was to look at monopoly and antitrust legislation through the lens of price theory, and his work stimulated related research by others, including Ward Bowman, Robert Bork, John McGee, and Lester Telser.[87] Director concluded that important efficiencies were frequently realized through these practices, that the exercise of monopolistic power should not be exaggerated, and that often-assumed practices of monopoly, such as predatory price cutting, simply did not occur in real life.

These new insights on monopoly and its policy consequences soon led Chicago economists to formulate a fundamental critique of U.S. antitrust legislation. Stigler (1988b, 165) made the point as follows: "The combination of the shift in attention to efficiency, and the restoration of the powerful role of competition, has done much to weaken the arguments for an antitrust policy that seeks to deal with minor or transitory or (as in the case of vertical integration) erroneously identified monopolistic practices … Antitrust remedies should be reserved for important and persistent monopoly problems, many or most of which are created by government regulations." The reforms of antitrust enforcement in the United States in the 1970s and 1980s illustrate importance of the work done at the University of Chicago. These reforms clearly bear the imprint of Chicago-style economics, and Director's role in this evolution was pivotal and undeniable.

# CHAPTER THREE

# The Chicago School Part 1
## *Stern Taskmasters*

THE LATE BRITISH ECONOMIST LIONEL ROBBINS (1962, 16) DE-
scribed economics as "the science which studies human behavior as a relationship between ends and scarce means which have alternative uses."
Robbins's definition can be built upon by adding that the three basic
ingredients of any economic problem are human behavior, alternative
uses, and scarce means. In his book *The Economic Organization* (1933),
Frank Knight subdivided the economic problem into five interrelated
subproblems.

The first subproblem concerns how a society decides which goods
and services will be produced and in what proportions they will be produced. The second subproblem deals with the organization of production; Knight divides this subproblem into "the allocation of the available
productive forces and materials among the various lines of industry" (3)
and "the effective coordination of the various means of production in
each industry into such groupings as will produce the greatest result" (9).
The third subproblem concerns distributing what is produced among
the members of society, and the need for a system that brings consumption into line with production is the core of the fourth subproblem. The
fifth subproblem, which is considerably more of a long-term problem,
concerns the issues of economic progress and the maintenance and improvement of the social structure of society.

All five of these subproblems involve making choices. Essentially, there are two mechanisms for making these choices: At one extreme is central planning based on the command principle, and at the other extreme is the free-market system, with its voluntary exchange. Strict central planning tends to be inevitably linked to political dictatorship, and free-market economies tend to go hand-in-hand with political democracy.

In a democracy based on the principles of decentralization, competition, and free markets, prices express the desires and needs of all of the economic agents. Given a situation where certain well-defined conditions are met, the price mechanism (that is, the movement of relative prices) leads to an optimal solution for each of the five subproblems outlined above.

After World War II, neoclassical price theory gradually came to monopolize the approach of University of Chicago economists. This conversion began with Jacob Viner and was carried to its highest point by Milton Friedman and Gary Becker. Friedman and Becker consistently argued that neoclassical price theory—combined with empirical verification—is true economic science. This particular approach to and analysis of the economic problem is typical for the Chicago School. This chapter deals with Viner and Friedman and the Chicago economists who followed in their work.

## STERN TASKMASTERS

As it is defined in this book, the Chicago School is about a belief that the price mechanism is the key element in successfully solving economic problems and a belief in using this concept to understand and explain broad range of societal phenomena.[88] Although it permeates the entire curriculum, Graduate Course 301 on price theory really hammers this Chicago School approach into the students. Melvin Reder, a former Chicago graduate student and professor in the GSB, wrote:

> The teaching of 301 has always been the prerogative of the department's *big guns* and over the years has been identified successively with Viner, Friedman and Becker. Different though these economists have been in the foci of their research interests,

they have had a certain commonality of pedagogical style that has given a continuing character to 301 and to the training program as a whole. The common element is a combination of well organized presentation, seriousness of purpose and strictness of standards. Course 301 has always been tough and its teachers have been stern taskmasters. (Reder 1982, 8–9)

However, it is not entirely correct to state that Chicago's emphasis on price theory started with Viner's 1916 arrival. Knight also continuously stressed neoclassical price theory as an indispensable part of any framework to get a proper understanding of economic issues, and before Viner and Knight, Herbert J. Davenport focused strongly on neoclassical price theory in his classes.

Davenport, whose parents left him a substantial fortune, was born in 1861 in Burlington, Vermont. He received a diverse education, as he studied at the Harvard Law School, the University of Leipzig, l'Ecole des Sciences Politiques in Paris, the University of South Dakota, and finally the University of Chicago, where he earned a PhD in economics in 1898. After a few years as a high school principal in Lincoln, Nebraska, Davenport taught at the University of Chicago from 1900 to 1908, when he left to become head of the department of economics and dean of the business school at the University of Missouri.[89] In 1916, Davenport departed for Cornell University. Like his close friend Thorstein Veblen, who strongly influenced him during his time at the University of Chicago, Davenport was "by nature a controversialist" but one who rather closely adhered to the "economic theory of the classic line" (Homan 1931, 696). In this last sense, Davenport rejected Veblen's institutionalist approach and was on the same wavelength as James L. Laughlin regarding free trade (Davenport 1897). Knight considered Davenport to be one of the "most important and original thinkers of his time"[90] (Patinkin 1973, 791). Wesley Mitchell described Davenport as "one of the best trainers in technical economic theory in the United States" (W.C. Mitchell 1967, 301).

Davenport wrote several books, and basic price theory is a part of each of them: "All economic purposes and methods take on the price emphasis. Price becomes the central and pivotal fact in all industry and business. The theory of price is thus the core of all economic theory" (Davenport 1914, 31). Although mathematical ability was not his long suit, Davenport saw the theory of prices in the context of general equilibrium analysis:

> Prices have their setting in a great moving equilibrium, all the parts of which are related to all the other parts, and are in close interdependence with them. As one part changes, others and then still others change ... We start with the entirely correct assumption that the market price of any commodity is determined by the demand for it and the supply of it, and that this price is the equating point between the demand and supply. But note that this way of formulating the price problem concerns itself with only one commodity at a time. Prices are tacitly taken for granted as already fixed for all other lines of production. (Dorfman 1959, 3:385)

Like Veblen and the other institutionalists, Davenport pleaded for a restricted interpretation of the applicability of economics. "To him," Paul Homan noted in his obituary of Davenport, "the economic process was strictly the process by which men attempted to achieve gain for themselves; the science of economics was an analysis of the manner in which this end was sought and attained in the modern world; the organization of the process centered upon the entrepreneur, actuated by the profit motive and upon the outcome of whose activities and choices depended the remuneration of all the contributory agents" (Homan 1931, 697).

Although he allowed for a somewhat larger role for the state than Laughlin did, for example, Davenport was generally unsympathetic toward government interference.[91] He rejected socialism and was opposed to most forms of labor reform. He favored an income tax—provided it was based on expenditure.

His analysis of depressions was also noteworthy. The credit mechanism and the rigidity of wages played a crucial role in the dynamics of commercial crises. Davenport favored public works during periods of high unemployment.

Davenport's role notwithstanding, Chicago's reputation in teaching price theory largely rests with the names of Viner, Friedman, and Becker. These stern taskmasters have more in common than just teaching Economics 301, however. Viner was Friedman's teacher at Chicago, and he taught Becker as an undergraduate at Princeton; Becker was one of Friedman's students at Chicago. Friedman succinctly summarized Viner's pivotal role: "Professionally, Viner's course in theory opened a new world. He made me realize that economic theory was a coherent, logical whole that held together, that didn't consist simply of a set of disjointed propositions" (Breit and Spencer 1995, 85). George Stigler describes Viner as "immensely erudite, rigorous and systematic in instruction ... [and] ... the founder of the Chicago tradition of detailed training in neoclassical microeconomics" (Breit and Spencer 1995, 99).

## A GREAT BULLY

Assar Lindbeck identified Jacob Viner as one of four economists who most likely would have been awarded the Nobel Prize if they had lived longer (Lindbeck 1985). There is no doubt Viner was held in high esteem by his fellow economists. Mark Blaug (1985, 256) wrote that he was "quite simply the greatest historian of economic thought that ever lived."[92] On the occasion of the centenary of Viner's birthday, Arthur Bloomfield (1992) of the University of Pennsylvania, one of Viner's former students, quoted many other prominent economists who praised Viner.

When Viner was awarded the Francis A. Walker Medal in December 1962, the Committee on Honors and Awards of the AEA characterized him as follows: "He represents the greatest combination of theoretical keenness (with no need for fancy techniques), alertness to policy issues, and historical scholarship in both economic institutions and economic ideas. In all the fields to which he has contributed, including his specialty, international economics, his name will survive brightly as a deflator of pretentious nonsense as well as an original creator."[93]

Viner, whose parents had emigrated from Romania, was born in Montreal in 1892. He first studied at McGill University under Stephen Leacock, who had earned his PhD at the University of Chicago. In 1915, Viner went to Harvard, where he was strongly influenced by Frank W. Taussig, the leading international trade economist of the time. After a short stay at the University of Chicago in 1916, Viner followed Taussig to Washington and worked with him at the U.S. Tariff Commission from 1917 to 1919. In 1919, he returned to the University of Chicago; he became a full professor there in 1925. In 1946, he left Chicago for Princeton; he retired from there in 1960 and died 10 years later.[94]

Three factors prompted Viner to leave the University of Chicago. There appears to have been important differences of opinion between him and Robert Hutchins, who was then president of the University of Chicago—although Viner explicitly denied this.[95] He also wanted to be closer to his children, who had settled on the East Coast. Last, after three decades in Chicago, Viner was attracted to the East Coast because of its intense economics academic community.

Paul Douglas, a major Chicago economist who studied at Harvard around the same time as Viner, recalled how Taussig used to bully his students (Douglas 1972), and Viner apparently copied Taussig's merciless classroom manners to a considerable extent. As Paul Samuelson testifies (1972, 6): "Viner was a student, *the* prize student of Frank Taussig, that master of the Socratic method. Taussig played on his classes as Pablo Casals plays on his cello. He knew which idiot would botch up Ricardo's trade-off between profit and the real wage; he knew which cantankerous student had to be kept out of the classroom's verbal interaction lest he short-circuit the dialogue. Viner added one new ingredient: terror." Bloomfield's (1992, 2057) recollection runs parallel with Samuelson's: "To be called up to the blackboard in the front of class and bombarded with a string of tricky questions until one made an error, to be followed by a contemptuous stare, was indeed a terrifying and humiliating experience, as I know well from one such experience myself."

Stigler (1988b, 20) tells the story of the student who made a mistake at the end of an otherwise reasonable enumeration of the factors determining the elasticity of demand for a product: "Viner turned red and said: 'Mr. X, you do not belong in this class.' My spine, and probably all of those in the class, began to tingle." However, Stigler also admits: "Yet, outside the classroom he was kind and helpful" (Breit and Spencer 1995, 99). Bloomfield (1992, 2057) adds: "Jacob Viner was simply a great teacher. The 'ferociousness' of Viner seems to have been confined to Economics 301. In the other courses I took with him, he was a quite different man: formidable, yes, but without the rough handling of students." Along similar lines, Martin Bronfenbrenner described Viner as "a strutting Talmudic Napoleon [with] facial expression alternating at express-train speed between joviality, challenge and utter contempt." (D. Goodwin 1998, 1776).

Viner's ambivalent approach to teaching is perhaps best expressed by Evsey Domar, who took Viner's course in economic theory in 1940: "Viner was superb because he was extremely nasty. He would write a statement on the board, challenge us to comment on it, and then make fools of those who tried. To fight him back became my greatest ambition. I spent hours getting ready for the fight; fortunately, I knew some math. Did I ever win an argument? Perhaps a couple of times during that summer quarter. But what a joy that was, that sweet feeling of revenge! Can you think of a more effective teaching method? But can you be as nasty as Viner?" (Szenberg 1992, 121). Samuelson (1991, 543) adds another perspective: "Years later when I discussed with Jack Viner the legend of his ferocity, he said that the department had given him the function of screening the candidates for higher degrees. It was not work for which he was ill-equipped."

Underlining Knight's educational importance, James Buchanan has fewer nice things to say about Viner and Friedman:

> Had my Chicago exposure been limited to the likes of Jacob Viner and Milton Friedman, both of whom were also my teachers there, I doubt that I should have ever emerged from the familiar ranks of PhDs with no or few publications. Jacob Viner, the classical erudite scholar whose self-appointed task in life seemed to be that of destroying confidence in students, and Milton Friedman, whose dominating intellectual brilliance in argument and analysis relegated the student to the role of fourth-best imitation—these were not the persons who encouraged students to believe that they too might eventually have ideas worthy of merit. (Breit and Spencer 1995, 173–4)

Viner initiated the systematic teaching of neoclassical price theory as the backbone of all education in economics at the University of Chicago.

In the profession at large, Viner was well known as an outstanding historian of economic thought. What is generally less known is the fact that Viner was among the first to criticize John Maynard Keynes's general theory. This is initially surprising because Viner's analysis of the Great Depression was not much different from Keynes's.[96]

## DEALING WITH KEYNES

It is obvious that an event like the Great Depression of the 1930s left an indelible mark on the work of the economists who lived through it. Viner was no exception.

In 1931, five years before the publication of Keynes's general theory, Viner had already pointed to the use of fiscal policy to counter a depression; in that same year, Keynes had visited the University of Chicago to participate in the Harris Foundation Lectures (Patinkin 1981). Three decades later, Viner (1963, 263) rejected any suggestion that he somehow got that depression-policy mix from Keynes: "I used it at least as early as the summer of 1931, and I don't think I derived it from Keynes, with whose journalistic writings I then had little acquaintance." Viner immediately recognized the political problem of reversing an expansionary fiscal policy when business conditions improved.

Two publications from 1933 summarize Viner's thinking on the Depression and the policies needed to fight it. First, he argued that the decline in profit margins caused by product prices falling faster than business costs was the origin of the Great Depression. As long as the United States remained on the gold standard, he saw no other solution to the profit-margin problem than to reduce wages. When United States subsequently abandoned the gold standard, Viner advocated policies that relied on cost compression and also pushed up the price level. For this to be achieved, an increase in the money supply in circulation was a necessary precondition. Given the pessimism that was then rampant among businessmen and ordinary people, he did not believe attempts to induce the banks to expand their loan volumes would bear fruit. His conclusion was that a policy aimed at creating a budget deficit financed by borrowing from the banking system or by direct money creation should do the trick.

Viner's views on how to fight the Depression were largely reflected in the first issue of the Public Policy Pamphlets of the University of Chicago. The first of these pamphlets was signed by 11 Chicago economists, of whom Viner was "probably the most articulate" (Bloomfield 1992, 2073). Henry Simons and Paul Douglas were the best-known of the other signatories; Frank Knight was certainly the best-known absentee.[97]

Although the title of the pamphlet was "Balancing the Budget," Viner and his colleagues argued that the federal government should *not* balance the budget during a depression. They identified such items as emergency outlays, public debt retirements, and expenditures for investments and public works as expenditures that should not be financed from current taxation: "In a deep depression the injury inflicted upon taxpayers by requiring them to defray the cost of every governmental activity by current taxation in order to avoid increasing the public debt appears to be greater than can be justified. Of course, it is necessary to avoid borrowing to such an extent that the credit of government becomes seriously impaired" (Viner et al, 1933, 5,6).

Viner clearly realized that the Great Depression was a socioeconomic and financial crisis of an extraordinary nature. Logically, the analysis of that situation could not be expected to lead to a general theory of the movements in the main macroeconomic aggregates, nor could the consequent policy prescriptions be regarded as sensibly applicable in less extraordinary times.

This basic insight made Viner a critic of Keynes's *General Theory of Employment, Interest and Money* the moment it was published in 1936. In the first paragraph of his review of Keynes's book, Viner (1936, 147) already sets the tone: "It brings much new light, but its display of dialectical skill is so overwhelming that it will have probably more persuasive power than it deserves." The only relevance Viner saw in Keynes's arguments was in the analysis of the (very) short term of the business cycle. The three fundamental issues on which Viner rejected Keynes's analysis were the remedies for unemployment, the determination of the interest rate, and especially the consumption function.[98]

Although Keynes (1936, 17) recognized that "real wages and the volume of output (and hence of employment) are uniquely correlated, so that, in general, an increase in employment can only occur to the accompaniment of a decline in the rate of real wages," he thought it would be impossible to reduce wage rates as a solution for involuntary unemployment. Viner (1936, 149) counterargued: "Keynes's reasoning points obviously to the superiority of inflationary remedies for unemployment over money wage reductions. In a world organized in accordance with Keynes's specifications there would be a constant race between the printing press and the business agents of the trade unions, with the problem of unemployment largely solved if the printing press could maintain a constant lead and if only volume of employment, irrespective of quality, is considered important."

Keynes (1936) leaves no doubt about his view of the determination of the interest rate: "The rate of interest obviously measures … the premium which has to be offered to induce people to hold their wealth in some form other than hoarded money" (216). At the heart of his reasoning lies the assumption that people generally tend to display liquidity preferences—they wish to retain part of their resources in the form of money. The neglect of these liquidity preferences, Keynes argued, led the classical economists to the belief that the desire to save and the desire to invest would always be equal.

However, Viner argued that "Keynes has grossly exaggerated the extent to which liquidity preferences have operated in the past and are likely to operate in the future as a barrier to full employment" (153).[99] Keynes's explanation of the determination of the interest rate is, according to Viner, "the most vulnerable part of his analysis" (157). Viner found no reason in Keynes's general theory to abandon the classical doctrine that "interest is the reward for saving and is directly determined by the supply schedule of savings with respect to the interest rate and the investment demand schedule for capital" (157). Keynes's monetary theory of interest was also strongly attacked by Knight (1937).

The third element of Viner's critique concerned the consumption function, which Keynes wrote as $C_w = cY_w$, with c as the propensity to consume out of income. Keynes assumed that this consumption function and the propensity to consume were relatively stable because measuring consumption and income in wage units allows for changes in expenditures resulting from changes in real wages. Viner (1936, 164) challenged this proposition: "The response of consumption to a reduction in real income may be, for a time, substantially different if the reduction takes the form of a decrease in money income, prices remaining the same, from what it would be if money income remained the same but prices increased."

Viner also criticized Keynes's consumption function for the omission of wealth ("accumulated resources") as an explanatory variable of observed consumption patterns.

## The Propensity to Be Hostile

Viner reviewed his 1936 review of Keynes's general theory 27 years later (1963, 255) and saw no reason to change his opinion about Keynes's major work: "Within the boundaries of short-run analysis, and especially of short-run depression analysis, I regard the claim made for its having achieved a 'Keynesian Revolution' in economics as a permissible manifestation of an enthusiasm for which there is substantial justification … On its adequacy as long-run analysis, and especially on its denial that [in a truly competitive economy] there exist powerful automatic forces which in the long run, if not counteracted by perverse governmental intervention, will restore 'equilibrium,' I still remain skeptical at least with some propensity to be hostile."

Next to the overemphasis on short-termism, Viner reproached Keynes for his lack of objectivity and judiciousness, particularly for his virulent attacks on orthodox English economics from Ricardo to Marshall and Pigou. Viner wrote:

> I had myself been trained in that tradition, but by 1930 or 1931 I had realized that to an appreciable extent it gave no light, or misleading light, on the nature and origins of major economic fluctuations. I took it for granted, however, that the unsuitability of its standard analytical procedures for analysis of 'depression' and 'boom' was the result not of general stupidity or perverse bias on their part but a lack of professional interest in and dedication to short-run analysis … Keynes, however, was writing in a white heat of revolt from the English classical tradition, and treated its neglect of or deliberate abstraction from short-run

phenomena as deliberate and stupid denial of their existence, while himself abstaining from acknowledging or exploring the possibility that in the short-run phenomena there were inherent forces which tended to produce quite different long-run than short-run consequences. (Viner 1963, 254–5)

Despite his critical attitude towards *The General Theory*, Viner qualifies Keynes as a "heroic figure" whose personality and intellect he much admired, but he saw him more as a prophet and a politician:

Keynes, I am sure, often interpreted his role as that of the prophet and the politician, and it was in such a period, I presume, that he once wrote: 'Words are to be a little wild, for they are the assaults of thoughts on the unthinking.' I do not challenge this for prophets and politicians, for they have special occupational license to promote their objectives free from stodgy inhibitions on the exercise of all their rhetorical resources for persuasion. I believe in the virtues of professional division of labor, however, and I am troubled, therefore, when economists adopt the role and the tactics of the prophet or the politician, especially when there is any ground for suspicion that what is involved is false prophecy. (Viner 1963, 265)

Nevertheless, Viner showed a great deal of respect for Keynes as an economist. Viner agreed with Keynes on the shape of the postwar international monetary system.

Viner's respect for Keynes also explains why he was the driving force behind the attempt to offer Keynes an honorary degree from the University of Chicago in 1940. However, Knight strongly protested against it. Knight did recognize Keynes as someone of "unusual intelligence," but at the same time stated: "I regard Mr. Keynes's (views) with respect to money and monetary theory in particular … as, figuratively speaking, passing the keys of the citadel out of the window to the Philistines hammering at the gates" (Bernstein 1996, 222).

Like Simons, Knight's attitude toward Keynes was much more hostile than Viner's. Don Patinkin had the privilege of examining Knight's own copy of *The General Theory of Employment, Interest, and Money*. Among the penciled notes that were to be found all over the book, " … the expletive 'Nonsense!'— replaced on occasions by even stronger terms—makes a frequent appearance in these margins" (Patinkin 1981, 299). In his presidential address to the 1950 annual meeting of the AEA, Knight commented on "movements—I will not say fads—in economic writing and teaching," and declared: "The latest 'new economics,' and in my opinion rather the worst for fallacious doctrine and pernicious consequences, is that launched by the late John Maynard (Lord) Keynes, who for a decade succeeded in carrying economic thinking well back to the Dark Age" (Knight 1956, 252). In reviewing *The General Theory of Employment, Interest, and Money*, Simons (1936a) declared that given his analysis and ensuing policy prescriptions, Keynes may "succeed in becoming the academic idol of our worst cranks and charlatans—not to mention the possibilities of the book as the economic bible of a fascist movement."

More than half a century later, Friedman (1997) closely echoed Simons with the following verdict on Keynes: "Keynes's bequest to technical economics was strongly positive. His bequest to politics, in my opinion, was not … In particular, it has contributed greatly to the proliferation of overgrown governments increasingly concerned with every phase of their citizens' daily lives … Keynes was exceedingly effective in persuading a broad group—economists, policymakers, governments officials, and interested citizens—of … two concepts … first, the public interest concept of government; second, the benevolent dictatorship concept that all will be well if only good men are in power" (20). Friedman continues, saying this political bequest has done much harm for two reasons: "First, whatever the economic analysis, benevolent dictatorship is likely sooner or later to lead to a totalitarian society. Second, Keynes's economic theories appealed to a group far broader than economists primarily because of their link to his political approach" (22).

It is remarkable that Friedman's judgment on Keynes is almost the reverse of Viner's. Viner held a rather negative opinion of Keynes as an economist but a more positive view of Keynes in the broader context.[100]

## "THE OUTSTANDING ALL-ROUNDER"

Viner's comments on Keynes's General Theory and his analysis of the Great Depression prove that he was a macroeconomist of considerable skill and ability—an "outstanding all-rounder,"[101] as he was described. However, his real specialization was in three other domains of economics: the theory of international trade, the history of economic thought, and neoclassical price theory.

With respect to international trade, he closely investigated various arguments for protection and sometimes found theoretical justification in those arguments; nonetheless, he rejected them for historical and practical reasons (Viner 1937, 1952). In the introduction to a collection of his essays on international economics, he wrote: "I remained throughout a free trader, unsympathetic to the new protectionism" (Viner 1951, 9). Viner's vision on the doctrine of free trade and its desirability as the cornerstone of trade policy was not fundamentally different from Taussig's position half a century earlier: Taussig recognized that the pure doctrine of free trade could be amended on several grounds and that its application was not as easy and simple as economists thought up to the end of the 19th century.[102] Nevertheless, Taussig emphasized that the core of the classical theory of international trade remained without a serious rival.

In the intellectual battle fought in the 1930s regarding the explanation of the patterns of international trade specialization, however, Viner ultimately lost.[103] Viner's approach, which was generally known as the "real-cost approach," was based on the assumption that trade flows are governed by prices and that these prices are proportional to quantities of factors of production used and their real costs. The real-cost approach lost the battle to the Heckscher-Ohlin model, in which trade flows are based on differences in factor endowments. His real-cost position placed Viner in opposition to Knight.[104]

Viner's other important contributions to the field of international trade policy were concerned with dumping (1923), balance of payments adjustment (1924), and customs unions (1950). In his book *The Customs Union Issue*, Viner produced the first rigorous analysis of customs unions; this work served as the basis for James Meade's (1956) standard work in this field. Viner went against the dominant view among economists of that period that the creation of customs unions inevitably represented a movement toward freer trade.

Viner's argument rested on the distinction that he made between trade creation and trade diversion. Trade creation is the replacement of the high-cost domestic production of a customs union member by the lower-cost production of other members, and trade diversion is the replacement of low-cost nonmember production by higher-cost member production. The conclusion Viner drew was that from a general welfare point of view, customs unions would be beneficial or not depending on the relation between these two tendencies.

In his doctoral dissertation, Viner studied the balance of payment adjustments under the fixed exchange rates that his homeland, Canada, had experienced from 1900 to 1913. He carefully analyzed the mechanisms set in motion by capital imports into Canada and concluded that the results were consistent with the predictions of classical price-specie-flow theory. Viner argued that imports of capital led to price increases of exports relative to imports, and the prices of the purely domestically traded commodities rose relative to both. These changes in relative prices made people readjust their expenditures (less domestic goods, more imports); the final result was a deficit on the current account of the balance of payments. Viner's analysis received a lot of criticism.[105]

The theory of international trade played an important role in Viner's work on the history of economic thought as well. His *Studies in the Theory of International Trade* (1937) outlined in detail the intellectual history of the free-trade doctrine. Douglas Irwin summarized: "According to Jacob Viner, in its best expressions the doctrine uniquely combines four distinct elements of thought. First, it embraces the stoic-cosmopolitan belief in the universal brotherhood of man. Second, it describes the benefits to mankind arising from the trade and exchange of goods. Third, it embodies the notion that economic resources are distributed unequally around the world. Finally, it attributes this entire arrangement to the divine intervention of a God who acted with the deliberate intention of promoting commerce and peaceful cooperation among men" (Irwin 1996, 15).

As a student of the history of economic thought, Viner also focused on utility theory (1937), methods of economic analysis (1925b), mercantilism, and Adam Smith. Viner was one of the first to draw attention to the fact that one had to be familiar with both the famous *Wealth of Nations* and *The Theory of Moral Sentiments*, written 19 years earlier, to get a real understanding of Smith's world. "Smith was *the* great eclectic ... Science, philosophy, theology, psychology, history, contemporary observation of facts—all of them were made to produce, under Smith's capable management, an abundance of evidence of the existence of an order in nature in which beneficent intentions towards mankind could be discerned" (Viner 1927, 199,200).

However, Viner was also among the first to stress that "Adam Smith was not a doctrinaire advocate of laissez faire … He had little trust in the competence or good faith of government. He knew who controlled it, and whose purposes they tried to serve … He saw, nevertheless, that it was necessary, in the absence of a better instrument, to rely upon government for the performance of many tasks which individuals as such would not do, or could not do, or could only do badly" (Viner 1927, 231–2).

Viner was also the first to challenge the idea that mercantilism was a doctrine that regarded power as the only end of foreign policy. In the second of five lectures on economics and freedom delivered at Wabash College in June 1959, Viner stated (1991, 45): "Although modern scholars, under German influence, commonly interpret mercantilist policy as having had as its sole ultimate goal the building up of national power, this seems to me basically wrong. The mercantilists sought for their nations, as ultimate ends, both power and plenty, and believed that each was a prerequisite for the attainment of the other."

Viner's famous 1931 article, "Cost and Supply Curves" (Viner 1958), must be mentioned when discussing microeconomics and price theory. The article became famous for its incorrect presentation of the long-run and the short-run cost curves in the case of a firm with internal economies. Another interesting publication by Viner in the field of price theory addressed the question of how one can know whether a certain market price is a competitive one or not,[106] and a third contribution was his 1921 article on pricing policies, "Price Policies: The Determination of Market Price" (1958). In it, Viner refers to different market structures that can occur in the real world. More than 10 years before the classic contributions of Edward Chamberlin and Joan Robinson, Viner distinguished between perfect competition, monopoly, and some intermediate sets of market forms.

## SMITH'S DISTINGUISHED SPIRITUAL SON OR …

"I have tried to influence public policy. I have spoken and written about issues of policy. In so doing, however, I have not been acting in my scientific capacity but in my capacity as a citizen, an informed one, I hope. I believe that what I know as an economist helps me to form better judgments about some issues than I could without that knowledge. But fundamentally, my scientific work should not be judged by my activities in public policy," said Friedman, in a lecture on March 21, 1985 (Breit and Spencer 1995, 92).

The background to Friedman's remark is that to many, Friedman is more a political activist with a right-wing agenda than an excellent academic economist. His friend Stigler had his own opinion about Friedman's lack of popularity among professional economists: "His *de facto* presidency of the unorganized Friends of Private Enterprise has not endeared him to the majority of professional economists ... Friedman's role as the leading friend of private enterprise would be viewed a good deal more sympathetically by economists if only he did it less well."[107]

The following characterization by Edward Herman, emeritus professor at the University of Pennsylvania, maintains the same negative view. "Friedman," according to Herman (1995, 36), "was considered an extremist and something of a nut in the early post war years ... Friedman is an ideologue of the right, whose intellectual opportunism in pursuit of his political agenda has often been heavy-handed and sometimes even laughable." Samuelson, who is also not a follower of Friedman's, sees Friedman in much more mellow light: "I don't think Milton is a charlatan ... He believes what he says at any time he says it. But he also has a very healthy respect for his audience. If you are a yokel, he gives you a hokum answer. If he is giving his presidential address, he states it more guardedly and more carefully" (Silk 1976, 48).[108]

Friedman is probably one of the most enthusiastic and articulate supporters of a free-market economy that has ever lived. "Adam Smith is generally hailed as the father of modern economics and Milton Friedman as his most distinguished spiritual son," as *New York Times* economist Leonard Silk (1976, 43) put it.

The metaphor of Friedman as the "most distinguished spiritual son of Adam Smith" makes it all the more fascinating to imagine, considering that Friedman was nearly a citizen of the former Soviet Union. His father and mother were born in Carpatho-Ruthenia, emigrated separately to the United States, married there, and settled in Brooklyn, New York.

Shortly after Friedman's birth in 1912, they moved to New Jersey, and his father died when Friedman was 15 years old.

In high school, Friedman did extremely well in mathematics, and he received a partial scholarship to Rutgers University. As he attended school there, he supplemented his income by working as a waiter and department store clerk. At Rutgers, he planned to major in math, but two teachers made Friedman change his mind: Arthur Burns, who later became the chairman of the Federal Reserve System and the U.S. ambassador to West Germany, and Homer Jones, who later became the vice president of the Federal Reserve Bank of St. Louis. In his memoir, Friedman wrote that "my greatest indebtedness, aside from my parents, was unquestionably to Arthur Burns, who was my teacher at Rutgers, and thereafter my mentor, guide, and surrogate father for much of my adult life" (Friedman and Friedman 1998, xi).

By the time he graduated from Rutgers, Friedman had two offers for full-tuition scholarships: one in applied mathematics from Brown University and one in economics from the University of Chicago. Under the influence of Burns and Jones, Friedman chose Chicago and economics. At Chicago, he was taught by Knight, Viner, Simons, Lloyd Mints, Douglas, and Henry Schultz, and Rose Director, the sister of Aaron Director, was a classmate. Rose Director and Friedman became lifelong companions—as husband and wife.

Other fellow students at Chicago included George Stigler and Allen Wallis. Reder (1982, 7–6) identified Friedman, Aaron and Rose Director, Simons, Stigler, and Wallis as the "principal members" of Knight's "affinity group"—who, according to Douglas (1972, 128), "seemed to be everywhere." Years later, Friedman expressed second thoughts about Knight's influence, claiming that "Knight's attitude and natural contrariness too often led to a stifling of scholarly productivity of others."[109] After a year in Chicago, Friedman left for Columbia University in 1933, where he worked with Harold Hotelling, the well-known mathematical economist and statistician, and Wesley Clair Mitchell.

Before he obtained his PhD from Columbia University in 1946 (the year in which his 30-year professorship at the University of Chicago began), Friedman assumed three jobs that would also have a considerable impact on his further career.

Simon Kuznets, a 1971 Nobel laureate, hired Friedman to help him at the National Bureau of Economic Research on a project concerning professional incomes (Friedman and Kuznets, 1945). In 1985, Friedman claimed that the book was finished "just before World War II, but was not published until after the war because of a controversy about one of its findings. That finding has to do with the effect of the monopolistic position of the American Medical Association on the incomes of physicians—not exactly a subject that has lost interest over the subsequent forty-odd years" (Breit and Spencer 1995, 87). The Kuznets and Friedman analysis introduced the distinction between permanent and transitory components of income, a distinction that became the backbone of Friedman's study of the consumption function and also (partly) earned him the Nobel Prize in 1976.

His second and third jobs concerned the war. Friedman spent 1941 to 1943 at the U.S. Treasury tax division. The innovation of withholding income tax immediately at the source was one of the projects he worked on. "There is no doubt," he said more than 40 years later, "that it would not have been possible to collect the amount of taxes imposed during World War II without withholding taxes at source. But it is also true that the existence of withholding has made it possible for taxes to be higher after the war than they otherwise would have been" (Breit and Spencer 1995, 88).

From 1943 to 1945, he worked as a mathematical statistician at the Statistical Research Group of the Division of War Research at Columbia University.[110] There, Friedman became suspicious of econometric forecasts based on multiple regressions and sophisticated mathematical economic models. This skepticism grew as the years went by; eventually, it would obscure the fact that the first important scientific contribution Friedman made was in the field of pure statistics.

## ... Or Marshall's?

At the end of World War II, the Cowles Commission for Research in Economics was installed at the University of Chicago. The fact that leading members of this Commission—such as Jacob Marschak, Trygve Haavelmo, Lawrence Klein, and Tjalling Koopmans—were heavily involved in the development of Walrasian general equilibrium economics and building sophisticated econometric models was a constant source of friction between them and the group around Friedman at the University of Chicago's department of economics. Although he had the mathematical skills to do it, Friedman never went into sophisticated model building. His trademark in economic research was always the use of simple models based on neoclassical price theory and empirical verification of the model presented. It was largely because of Friedman's work and influence that, in the decades after the World War II, the combination of Marshallian, partial equilibrium economics with empirical verification became "scientific economics" at the University of Chicago.

Economists working at the Cowles Commission were among those who fought the hardest against Friedman's writings on methodological issues in economics.[111] Although his 1952 paper on "The Methodology of Positive Economics" is generally best known, Friedman had already developed the major elements of his methodology by the early 1940s.[112] Friedman viewed the methodological issues facing economic researchers not from the high grounds of philosophy of science but instead from a pragmatic point of view—that is, "as an economist who came upon [these issues] in the process of doing economics" (Hirsch and de Marchi 1990, 66). Friedman (1953, 8) stated that "theory is to be judged by its predictive power."

Friedman rejected the idea that relevant theories need to have realistic assumptions. He even argued that "truly important and significant hypotheses will be found to have 'assumptions' that are wildly inaccurate descriptive representations of reality, and, in general, the more significant the theory, the more unrealistic the assumptions" (Friedman 1953, 14).

Friedman closely linked the search for realism in assumptions with major developments in economics that he did not find useful: Walrasian general equilibrium economics, monopolistic competition analysis, and institutionalism. More than 40 years later, Hirsch and de Marchi (1990, 2) concluded that "Friedman's views deviate so markedly from those which have been dominant in economics from Senior, Cairnes and Mill to J.N. Keynes and Lionel Robbins that it would not be an exaggeration to call them revolutionary."

There is a close link between Friedman's views on methodology and his further work in the field of neoclassical price theory: for the latter to be an operational tool of analysis, strong assumptions must be made. With the statistician Leonard Savage, he made a significant contribution to the individual's utility function for choices involving risk (Friedman and Savage 1948), and with his student buddy Allen Wallis, he also contributed to the derivation of indifference curves.[113] In addition, he did landmark work on his Marshallian demand curve; the permanent income hypothesis he developed while analyzing consumption; and his critique of the Phillips curve—one of the cornerstones of Keynesian macroeconomics.

In 1949, Friedman published a paper called "The Marshallian Demand Curve" (1953). In the paper, he argued that the traditional way of presenting a demand curve was not what its spiritual father, Alfred Marshall, had in mind when introducing the concept in his *Principles of Economics* (1890).[114] Friedman's basic point was that in demand analysis (as it was applied in those days), money or nominal income was supposed to be constant when moving along a demand curve. According to Friedman, what Marshall had in mind was that real income should be held constant in the analysis, which would result in movement of the demand curve. In Friedman's view, the fact that this Marshallian or income-compensated demand curve had largely disappeared from economic analysis was most unfortunate. He saw this "mistake" as a symptom of the fact that the general equilibrium approach was, at the time of his paper, on the verge of taking precedence over Marshall's partial equilibrium analysis. The former "has arisen out of, and reflects, an essentially arithmetical and descriptive approach to economic analysis," while the latter represents "an analytical and problem-solving approach." The Walrasian approach was "in consequence less useful for most purposes" (Friedman 1953, 100). For Friedman, much more was at stake here than purely technical aspects— instead, this concerned "alternative conceptions of economic theory," where, in the Marshallian vision, "the test of the theory is its value in explaining facts, in predicting the consequences of changes in the economic environment. Abstractness, generality, mathematical elegance— these are all secondary, themselves to be judged by the test of application" (Friedman 1953, 89,91). In the Walrasian vision, "abstractness, generality and mathematical elegance have in some measure become ends in themselves, criteria by which to judge economic theory. Facts are to be described, not explained" (Friedman 1953, 91).

## A Pioneer Lacking In Brilliance

Friedman engaged in research on demand issues in large part because he got a job as a research assistant to Henry Schultz upon returning from Columbia to the University of Chicago in 1934. In spite of the considerable opposition to the type of research work he was doing (particularly from Knight), Schultz was among the pioneers in the use of quantitative methods at the department of economics at the University of Chicago. Schultz produced his major contribution to economics in 1938: *The Theory and Measurement of Demand.*

Milton and Rose Friedman describe Schultz as "a highly pedantic teacher and scholar, not original or profound, who had qualities of tenacity, patience and industry ... Sheer analytical ability was not his forte" (Friedman and Friedman 1998, 38,52). Stigler, another student of Schultz's, writes about "Schultz's pretentious teaching style" (Stigler 1988b, 27).

Others who knew Schultz very well do not share Friedman and Stigler's harsh verdict of Henry Schultz as an economic researcher and a person. Samuelson described Schultz as "an earnest pioneer who lacked in self-confidence and brilliance" (Shils 1991, 536). Simon was "fond of this shy, dedicated man" (Simon 1996, 53). According to his Chicago colleague Douglas, Henry Schultz was "at once amazingly thorough, precise, and kindly ... He was the truest seeker of truth I have ever known" (Douglas 1939, 105). Reder refers to Bronfenbrenner and Marschak as students of Henry Schultz's "who always spoke very highly of [him]" (Reder 1982, 4). Hotelling refers to Schultz's "warm-hearted interest in individual students" and quotes from a letter from H. Gregg Lewis: "Mr. Schultz was to us an unselfish friend and adviser. He was always interested in all aspects of our personal well-being and never in a patronizing way" (Hotelling 1939, 100–101).

Under the supervision of Henry Moore, Schultz earned a PhD at Columbia University in 1925.[115] By that time, Henry Schultz, who was born in what was then Russian Poland in 1893, had come a long way. In

1907, his family immigrated to the United States and lived in very poor circumstances on the Lower East Side of New York City. Schultz worked evenings to finance his bachelor's degree from the College of the City of New York in 1916. From there, he went to Columbia University where Edwin Seligman, Wesley Mitchell, and John Dewey were also major influences. Wounded in action in France during World War I, he returned to the United States in 1919 after a brief stay at the LSE and took up different government jobs, including posts with the Department of Labor and the U.S. Tariff Commission.[116]

Henry Schultz received an appointment at the University of Chicago in 1926. With Douglas, who arrived in 1920, Schultz laid the groundwork for empirical verification of economic theory to become a basic component of the Chicago Tradition. As Schultz's student Ted Yntema (1939, 159) noted: "Schultz undertook to bridge the gap between factless theory and theoryless fact."

From the beginning, Schultz was intrigued by mathematical economics.[117] In this respect, he was "a disciple of Cournot, Walras and Pareto" (Yntema 1939, 155). James Heckman, the Henry Schultz Distinguished Service Professor at the University of Chicago, wrote: "Schultz united three previously disconnected branches of knowledge: (a) the theory of consumer demand; (b) the statistical theory of regression and time series analysis; and (c) the empirical analysis of economic data," with this last element being "the most original aspect of his work" (Heckman 1997, 2).

This description fits well with a recollection of one of Henry Schultz's students, Kenneth Boulding: "I recall him once coming around the stat lab where we were grinding out coefficients of correlation on mechanical calculators. He sympathized with us and said, 'I know this is very boring, but you *are* getting familiar with the data.' Today, of course, a computer gets familiar with the data and nobody else does" (Boulding 1992, 71). Schultz also played an important role in the dissemination of Eugene Slutsky's seminal 1915 paper on consumer theory, "On the Theory of the Budget of the Consumer."

Friedman rendered "invaluable assistance," as Schultz himself put it, in the creation of *The Theory and Measurement of Demand* (Schultz 1938, xi). As a matter of fact, Chapters XVIII and XIX on the theory of related demands were largely written by Friedman. In the book, Henry Schultz makes no references to Knight, but there are several to "my friend and colleague" Viner (Schultz 1938, 52). *The Theory and Measurement of Demand* is dedicated to Henry L. Moore, one of the American pioneers in econometrics.

Along with his wife and two daughters, Henry Schultz died in a car accident in September 1938, about the same time as the first publication of his magnum opus.

## REVOLUTION IN CONSUMPTION

Friedman, the neoclassical price theorist, also devoted intense focus to consumption. He worked on the subject from 1935 to 1937, when he was connected with the Study of Consumer Purchases at the National Resources Committee. Friedman's work in consumption analysis must be seen as part of his increasingly critical attitude toward Keynesian macro-economics, which analyzed consumption an aggregative way. Friedman's consumption analysis was true to the Chicago Tradition of emphasizing price theory as the building block of sound economic analysis, as it started from a microeconomic point of view.

Keynes wrote his consumption function as $C_w = cY_w$, with c being the propensity to consume out of current income. He seems to have been very sure of this relationship: "The fundamental law, upon which we are entitled to depend with great confidence both a priori from our knowledge of human nature and from the detailed facts of experience, is that men are disposed, as a rule and on the average, to increase their consumption as their income increases, but not by as much as the increase in their income" (Keynes 1936, 96). The logical consequence of Keynes's proposition is that one would expect the rate of savings to go up when a country gets richer.

Kuznets investigated this concept over a century-long period in the United States and found that the savings rate had *not* risen. These findings and work Friedman did as Kuznets's partner provided the background for Friedman's book *Theory of the Consumption Function* (1937), which he considered to be "my best purely scientific contribution" (Friedman and Friedman 1998, 222).[118] Like Franco Modigliani and

David Blumberg's groundbreaking 1954 work on the life cycle theory of consumption and saving, this book revolutionized consumption theory by paying attention to the intertemporal factor.

Friedman developed his theory from the distinction "between income as recorded—which we term measured income—and the income to which consumers adapt their behavior—which we term permanent income—and, similarly, between measured consumption and permanent consumption" (Friedman 1957, 221). The permanent component of income is "to be interpreted as reflecting the effect of those factors that the [consumer's] unit regards as determining its capital value or wealth: the nonhuman wealth it owns; the personal attributes of the earners in the unit, such as their training, ability, personality; the attributes of the economic activity of the earners, such as the occupation followed, the location of the economic activity, and so on" (Friedman 1957, 21).

Friedman concluded that there exists "a ratio between permanent consumption and income that is the same for all levels of permanent income but depends on other variables, such as the interest rate, the ratio of wealth to income, and so on ... the transitory components of a consumer's unit's income have no effect on his consumption except as they are translated into effects beyond his horizon. His consumption is determined by longer-range income considerations plus transitory factors affecting consumption directly" (Friedman 1957, 221).

Friedman's permanent income analysis resolved the paradox of the Keynesian consumption function pointed out by Kuznets. Indeed, Friedman's model implies that increases in the saving rate that occur when income rises are to be viewed as mainly transitory. Friedman's permanent income hypothesis also played a crucial role in his monetary analysis—the centerpiece of which is the quantity theory.

The interpretation of this quantity theory addresses the question: What determines the velocity of money? Or, to put the same question in another way: What determines the demand for money? One of the major findings of the empirical research done by Friedman and his students at the University of Chicago was that velocity is a stable function of long-term or permanent income. On the basis of these findings, Friedman concluded that the best thing the monetary authorities could do to achieve price stability was to follow a fixed rule of increase in the money supply.

With respect to their consumption theories, Friedman and Modigliani fully acknowledged the intellectual debt they owed to Margaret G. Reid, who was a rarity in her generation: an extremely successful woman in the field of academic economics.[119] In his Nobel lecture, Modigliani pointed to Reid's highly imaginative analysis as a major source of inspiration (Maler 1992). In the introduction to his *Theory of the Consumption Function*, Friedman acknowledges Reid as the person who "with characteristic enthusiasm, persistence, and ingenuity ... pressed me to write up the underlying theory" (Friedman 1957, ix).

In the early 1950s, Reid wrote several papers with the basic objective of trying to understand consumption patterns that are typical for different income categories. She studied the relationship between income and consumption for farm and for urban families in four U.S. states and found out that linking income to consumption expenditures was much more difficult for farm families. She offered as a tentative explanation for this phenomenon the fact that their income behaved more erratically over time (Reid 1952). Reid tried to develop different concepts of income in an attempt to distinguish which parts of income could be considered permanent and which were transitory (Reid 1953; Reid 1962; Dunsing and Reid 1958).

## Distinguished Women

Margaret Reid was born to a large Scottish family in Cardale, a small town in the rural state of Manitoba, Canada, in 1896. She obtained her bachelor's degree in home economics from the University of Manitoba. Reid started teaching in a local high school but was thrown out after she had dared to go to a dance party—something the local head teacher had strictly forbidden. "This was very typical for Margaret. She was a gutsy lady with a good sense of humor. However, she also had a very strong sense of purpose and a willpower that was truly extraordinary. Margaret easily broke through all the anti-women-in-academics-stuff that was so typical for those days," remembers Mary Jean Bowman, who knew Reid well at Iowa State College and the University of Chicago.[120]

Shortly after the party incident in 1921, Reid left Canada for the United States and became a citizen in 1939. Reid never married and died in 1991 at the age of 95 with the University of Chicago as her sole heir.

Reid did her graduate studies at the University of Chicago, where Knight was a major influence on her development. The same was true for Hazel Kyrk, under whose supervision Reid wrote her doctoral dissertation. The dissertation was the backbone of her first book, *The Economics of Household Production* (1934). In the book, Reid defined household production as unpaid activities performed by and for the members of the household. To estimate in dollar terms the market value of household production, Reid developed the opportunity cost method (in this case, the earnings foregone because of household production). In later work (Reid 1943), she worked out several other methods for valuation, such as the comparison with the retail price of market substitutes and the cost of hiring people to do the same work. In 1947, she concluded that household production had a value ranging between 20 and 22 percent of U.S. gross national product (GNP) (Reid 1947).

Encouraged by Kyrk, Reid moved to Iowa State College to continue her research. She remained at Iowa State College from 1930 until 1943, which means her stay there largely coincided with that of T. W. Schultz. According to Bowman, "T.W. Schultz played an important role in getting us women the academic recognition that certainly Margaret Reid deserved."[121] From 1945 to 1948, Reid served as head of the family economics division of the U.S. Department of Agriculture. After three years at the University of Illinois, she returned to the University of Chicago in 1952. She officially retired in 1961, but remained active until she was nearly 90 years old. "She had her tables in the library that were used only by Margaret. As a sole exception to their usual procedure, the library staff left her tables and everything on them always untouched," recalls Claire Friedland of Chicago's GSB.[122]

In 1980, the AEA made Reid a Distinguished Fellow. She was the first female economist ever to receive this honor. The AEA's motivation for granting her this honor speaks for itself: "Her high standards and her single-minded devotion to her science have influenced generations of students and colleagues ... Margaret Reid was one of the pioneers in several areas of research on consumer and household behavior ... The empirical tradition at the University of Chicago owes much to Margaret Reid's example and teaching. She was a famous taskmaster in the art of applying critical thinking to data."[123] Indeed, Reid was first an empirically oriented economist.

It is hardly an exaggeration to state that, with her PhD supervisor Kyrk, Reid created the field of household economics, which led to important new insights on such issues as consumption economics.[124] Kyrk and Reid were the first among the early generation of excellent female economists at the University of Chicago.

Hazel Kyrk entered Ohio Wesleyan University in 1904 and served as domestic help in the home of Leon C. Marshall, who was at that time an economics professor at Ohio Wesleyan. When Marshall moved to the University of Chicago, Kyrk followed and earned her PhD there in 1920. After holding positions at several other institutions, Kyrk returned to the University of Chicago in 1925 and remained there until her retirement in 1952. Kyrk focused her entire academic career on empirical research of household expenditures[125] and also served on several government bodies, including the Bureau of Home Economics and, during the World War II, the Office of Price Administration.

Rose Director Friedman, who was born in 1911, studied at the University of Chicago. There, she worked as Knight's research assistant but never finished her PhD. During the 1930s, she worked for the Natural Resources Committee in Washington and joined the National Bureau of Economic Research in New York.

Her major contribution to economic research was the report she published in 1947 with Dorothy Brady.[126] Brady and Director-Friedman formulated what came to be known as the relative income hypothesis, which was the proposition that a family's consumption depends on its relative position in the income distribution of its community and not so much on its absolute level of income (Brady and Director-Friedman 1947).

Mary Jean Bowman was born in New York City in 1908 and earned a PhD in economics from Harvard in 1938. After holding several other positions, she joined the University of Chicago in 1958 as professor of economics and education. Although the economics of education were a prime area of Bowman's research, she also devoted attention to the issue of expectations and decision-making under uncertainty.

## Fighting Keynesian Dogma

The consumption analysis initiated by Reid and furthered by Friedman and Modigliani became a standard branch of modern macroeconomics. Friedman made another major contribution to macroeconomic theory with his critique of the Phillips curve.

Samuelson and Robert Solow, who were both Nobel Prize-winning economists from MIT, introduced the Phillips curve in 1960 as an operational tool for short-term macroeconomic management with a trade-off to be made by policymakers between inflation and unemployment (Samuelson and Solow 1960). Also in 1960, Reuben Kessel, a young Chicago economist, and Armen Alchian found evidence that contradicted the then-prevailing view that prices usually rise faster than wages. For Keynesian economics and the Phillips curve to work, the existence of this wage lag was essential. Reviewing a wide range of empirical evidence, Alchian and Kessel concluded that "unwarranted validity has been assigned to the wage-lag hypothesis" (64).

Friedman conceded that the Phillips curve, which fundamentally concerns wage determination and unemployment, "rests uneasily between price theory and monetary theory" (Friedman 1976a, 213). Nevertheless, he devotes a whole chapter to it in his book *Price Theory*. The Phillips curve linked the rate of change of nominal wages to the unemployment rate by stating that inflation was supposed to go up when unemployment came down, and vice versa. Against this background, the aftermath of the OPEC-reinforced recession of 1974–75 came as a shock: inflation and unemployment were going up simultaneously. More than five years before the term *stagflation* (*stag*nation + in*flation*) surfaced, both Friedman and Edmund Phelps of Columbia University had developed the theoretical arguments against the Phillips curve and its policy implications (Friedman 1966; Friedman 1968; and Phelps 1967). Friedman and Phelps argued that in the long run, the Phillips curve was vertical.

In 1976, Friedman (1976a, 215) wrote: "The discussion of the Phillips curve started with truth in 1926, proceeded through error some 30 years later, and by now has returned back to 1926 and to the original truth. That is about 50 years for a complete circuit." Indeed, 32 years before A.W. Phillips of the LSE published his famous paper on the relationship between unemployment and the rate of change of money wages (Phillips 1958), Irving Fisher had undertaken a similar investigation (Fisher 1926).

However, Friedman pointed out, there were two major differences between Phillips and Fisher: Fisher analyzed price changes and Phillips analyzed wage changes, and Fisher and Phillips differed fundamentally on the direction of causation. For Fisher, the rate of change in prices sets the process in motion—given that all their other expenses do not directly change in line with the change in the price level, businesspeople find their profit margins increasing and therefore have an incentive to expand production, which leads to a temporary increase in employment. Instead, Phillips saw the process starting with a change in the level of employment that led to variations in the rate of change in nominal wages, and hence, inflation.

Friedman described Phillips's analysis as utterly fallacious, because any serious analysis of the demand for and the supply of labor should focus on real wages and not on nominal wages. Constant real wages can occur with any kind of inflation rate. Phillips made this error because one of the essential elements of the Keynesian revolution "was the assumption that prices are highly rigid relative to output, so that a change in demand ... would be reflected almost entirely in output and very little in prices ... [Phillips] was therefore assuming the change in nominal wages to be equal to the change in real wages" (Friedman 1976a, 219). Another characteristic of the Keynesian analysis was that "real wages *ex post* could be altered by *unanticipated* inflation. Indeed, the whole Keynesian argument for the possibility of a full employment policy arose out of the supposition that it was possible to get workers (at least in the 1930s when Keynes wrote *The General Theory*) to accept lower real wages produced by inflation that they would not have accepted in the direct form of a reduction in nominal wages" (Friedman 1976a, 220).

As far as macroeconomic stabilization policy was concerned, "only surprises matter," Friedman told the audience during his Nobel lecture (Friedman 1976b, 352) in reference to the difference between anticipated and unanticipated changes. "If everyone anticipated that prices would rise at, say, 20 percent a year, then this anticipation would be embodied in future wage (and other) contracts, real wages would then behave precisely as they would if everyone anticipated no price rise, and there would be no reason for the 20 percent rate of inflation to be associated with a different level of unemployment than a zero rate" (Friedman 1976b, 352).

Unanticipated changes, however, are an entirely different matter:

> Start from an initial stable position and let there be, for example, an unanticipated acceleration of aggregate nominal demand. This will come to each producer as an unexpectedly favorable demand for his product ... It will be rational for him to interpret it as at least partly special and to react to it, by seeking to produce more ... He will be willing to pay higher nominal wages than he had been willing to pay before in order to attract additional workers. The real wage that matters to him is the wage in terms of the price of his product and he perceives that price as higher than before. (Friedman 1976b, 352–53)

To the workers, however, the new situation presents itself quite differently.

> What matters to them is the purchasing power of wages not over the particular good they produce but over all goods in general. Both they and their employers are likely to adjust more slowly their perception of prices in general—because it is more costly to acquire information about that—than their perception of the price of the particular good they produce. As a result, a rise in nominal wages may be perceived by workers as a rise in real wages and hence calls forth an increased supply, at the same time that it is perceived by employers as a fall in real wages and hence calls forth an increased offer of jobs. (Friedman 1976b, 353)

Workers and employers, of course, adjust to reality, and when this happens, the initial employment-creating effect will disappear.

When Friedman presented this analysis in Stockholm at the end of 1976, it was on its way to becoming part of mainstream macroeconomic theory. When he made essentially the same argument when addressing the AEA nine years earlier (Friedman 1968),[127] it had created quite a bit of controversy. As the Friedman-Phelps analysis implies, the vertical Phillips curve is located at the level of unemployment that came to be described as the nonaccelerating, or natural, rate of unemployment. This natural rate is not an eternally constant number, but instead it refers to that rate of employment "which is consistent with the existing real conditions in the labor market. It can be lowered by removing obstacles in the labor market, by reducing friction. It can be raised by introducing additional obstacles. The purpose of the concept is to separate the monetary from the nonmonetary aspects of the employment situation" (Friedman 1976a, 228).

## Too Long a Shadow?

Friedman made seminal contributions to price theory as well as to monetary economics. Some argue that "he challenges Keynes as the twentieth century's most influential economist" (Breit and Ransom 1998, 226). In the words of Deirdre McCloskey (2003, 143): "The 30 years 1935-1965 were dominated by the very English, Eton-graduate son of an English academic; the next 30 years were dominated by the very American, Rutgers-graduate son of Ashkenazi garment workers. Most people thought in the 30 years after 1935 that socialism was inevitable, or at least good, partly because Maynard said so; since 1965 more and more people have thought that capitalism is inevitable, or at least good, partly because Milton has said so" (McCloskey 2003, 143).

Friedman had strong opinions on issues that were not directly related to price theory and monetary economics and usually voiced them with his wife, Rose.[128]

First, the Friedmans became ardent defenders of parental freedom in educational choice through the use of a voucher system.[129] Second, they favored a volunteer army.[130] Third, Friedman did not hesitate to describe a firm's social responsibility as restricted to using its resources and engaging in activities designed to increase its profits within the rules of the game of fair competition (Friedman 1970). Fourth, convinced that most welfare programs further impoverish the poor, Friedman pleaded strongly for the introduction of a negative income tax (Friedman 1962).

Friedman's influence on economists at the University of Chicago and the way they do their jobs is enormous. Even at the start of the 21st century, people often openly wondered in discussions, "What would Milton have thought about this?"

However, some on the Chicago campus raise the question of whether Friedman's effect went too far. According to Gary Becker, Friedman's student, "some students found the intensity of the course, the high standards demanded and the bluntness of Friedman's comments on questions and written work too difficult to absorb psychologically ... Most students, however, found Friedman's approach an eye-opener, and were willing to put up with pressures and low grades to be exposed to his brilliant insights about price theory" (Becker 1991, 141).

Did Friedman regularly cross the thin line between having—through his formidable intellect and brilliance as an economist—a pervasive and stimulating impact on other people's views and work and reducing others to run on autopilot, strictly flying according to the instructions of Friedman's plan?[131]

Becker remarked: "I believed at the same time that some top students shied away from working with Friedman because they could not take the heat: they could not handle psychologically his sharp and blunt criticisms and his quick insights. In essence, they feared being overwhelmed intellectually. I also had those fears but managed to control them enough to recognize how much I could learn from him" (Becker 1991, 144). It's hard to avoid the conclusion that Becker's temporary departure from the University of Chicago in 1957 was at least partially caused by a desire to escape Friedman's overpowering intellectual impact. "If you disagree with Milton, it becomes very difficult to face him daily," according to Lester Telser, who graduated from Chicago in 1956 and stayed there for practically his entire career.[132] His intense discussions with several people from the Cowles Commission—especially Koopmans—are legendary to the people who witnessed them. Friedman was assisted tremendously in these and other discussions by his extreme self-confidence.[133]

Friedman stopped teaching Economics 301 in 1976. He was succeeded by Becker, who would continue the rigorous teaching of price theory—or simply *economic theory*, as he prefers to define it—for the next 20 years. Although teaching Economics 301 at the University of

Chicago must be considered a strong link between Viner, Friedman, and Becker, major differences can be detected.

Eugene Rotwein documented the way in which Viner differed from the two others. (Rotwein 1983). Bronfenbrenner argued that such early Chicagoans as Viner and Knight showed "more concern with the ethics and aesthetics of income distribution along with, although not equal to, concern with economic freedom and allocative efficiency" (Bronfenbrenner 1962, 73). Ross Emmett brought an additional perspective by pointing out that the University of Chicago became different by from mainstream economics "by the 1940s because of the emergence of a contingent of economists committed to developing market-based solutions to social problems" (Emmett 2002, 1:xviii).

Viner, Friedman, and Becker also differ greatly in their fields of concentration. Viner focused on issues of international trade and the history of economic thought, and Friedman (except for his younger years) devoted his attention mainly to monetary and macroeconomic matters. Becker will be looked upon as one of the major innovators of the 20th century for his application of economic analysis to a broad range of societal phenomena including discrimination, crime, and the family.

# CHAPTER FOUR

# The Chicago School Part 2
## *Getting Beckerized*

THE BACKBONE OF THE CHICAGO SCHOOL IS A BELIEF IN THE analytical power and predictive capabilities of neoclassical price theory. However, this is not the same thing as saying that price theory is a set of dogmas written in stone. According to Milton Friedman, the only unalterable concept is that "there is a coherent theory dealing with the adaptation of resources to wants by individuals who can be regarded as having fairly well defined tastes and preferences. Basic price theory fundamentally deals with one question: why do people do what they do?"[134] It is hard to find any economist who has focused more thoroughly and consistently on that single issue than Gary Becker. Over the years, Becker has become identified with the economic analysis of such issues as discrimination against minorities, crime and punishment, addiction, family, and marriage.

The nontraditional orientation of Becker's research has regularly stirred up emotions and given rise to comments such as this one from Robert Solow: "There are some things that should not be analyzed as if they were subject to being bought and sold. Let's be philosophical. Call them primary things, things that are intrinsic to themselves. There are all kinds of social circumstances that are fundamentally different from economic circumstances" (Warsh 1993, 138). George Stigler's judgment stands in sharp contrast to Solow's implicit moral condemnation of the Beckerian type of economic analysis: "It requires courage to deal with emotional commitments as racial discriminations. One is certain to be accused by some readers (and even more by many nonreaders) of moral insensitivity if not downright prejudice. Yet the social value of Becker's scarce combination of courage and great analytical power is immense" (Stigler 1988b, 196).

As Becker readily admits,[135] of all the work he has done, so far his work in the field of human capital has produced the largest impact on economic science. However, Theodore W. Schultz and Jacob Mincer must be acknowledged as the real initiators of this research program.

The links between Becker, Mincer, and Schultz are more than just close. Mincer received a PhD from Columbia University in 1957 and spent the next two years as a postdoctoral fellow at the University of Chicago. Schultz was chairman of Chicago's department of economics from 1945 to 1961 and continued as one of its most outstanding and influential members long after that. Becker earned a PhD from the University of Chicago in 1955; he stayed there as an assistant professor until he moved to Columbia.

## FARMER'S WISDOM

T.W. Schultz was born to German settlers in Arlington, South Dakota in 1902. Rural life and agriculture dominated his youth and early adult years, and poverty was not alien to him. In 1924, he entered the agricultural economics program at South Dakota State College and proceeded to the University of Wisconsin in 1927. After he obtained a PhD there in 1930, Schultz moved to Iowa State College, where he served as head of the department of economics and sociology from 1935 until 1943. He successfully revitalized the small and sleepy department despite adverse external circumstances such as the Great Depression.

Some of the many young male economists he brought to Iowa included Kenneth Boulding, Gerhard Tintner, Albert Hart, and George Stigler. Schultz also brought a group of outstanding young female economists—most notably, Margaret Reid—to Iowa State. He left Iowa State in 1944 and joined the faculty of the University of Chicago, where he stayed for the rest of his life; he died in February 1998.

As an economist, Schultz was characterized by his former student

Mary Jean Bowman (1980, 81) as follows: "He has constructed no formalized models of growth; he has little interest in esoteric models (or what Assar Lindbeck described as 'Samuelson's tail'). Such models are not in his style and he sees them as too remote from realistic confrontation with issues in public policies and their understanding." Marc Nerlove (1999, 728), another of Schultz's students, observed: "Although he never really mastered these subjects in a technical sense, he knew good theory and good econometrics when he saw it … His keen economic intuition and often profound insight proved more reliable in the end than any technical expertise." The directness, openness, and accessibility that characterized the economic research he produced could also be found in his lectures and work with students. In the words of D. Gale Johnson, "Working with T.W. was a two-way traffic lane: you not only learned immensely from him but he himself was always eager to learn from you, too."[136] Bowman (1980, 82) agreed: "Schultz has been outstandingly effective as an intellectual catalyst."

During his time at Iowa State, Schultz became linked to the Chicago School when he began to apply the apparatus of price theory to agricultural economics. In his first major book, *Redirecting Farm Policy,* he wrote: "Farm production involves the decisions of literally millions of entrepreneurs, each confronted with a different set of resources, and consumption involves the decisions of even more millions of consumers with widely different needs, tastes, and purchasing power. The decisions and actions can be effectively coordinated through prices" (Schultz 1943, 8–9). Later, Schultz (1979, 640) applied the apparatus of price theory to the problems of poor countries: "The major mistake has been the presumption that standard economic theory is inadequate for understanding low-income countries and that a separate economic theory is needed." It is hardly an exaggeration to say that Schultz's contribution to agricultural economics and the economics of developing countries is equitable to that of H. Gregg Lewis for labor economics and Aaron Director for the study of law and economics. In 1979, Schultz and Arthur Lewis received the Nobel Prize in economics.

Schultz did not hesitate to draw strong policy conclusions. He became very critical of government policies toward agriculture[137] and in a 1977 essay entitled "Economics, Agriculture, and the Political Economy," he wrote: "When imports and exports are controlled, agricultural prices do strange things. When marketing boards have a monopoly, farmers and consumers are well advised to beware. When governments authorize the procurement of agricultural products from farmers, the agricultural economy is placed in receivership. When the ministers of agriculture treat agricultural scientists as clerks, the agricultural research enterprise becomes stagnant" (Schultz 1993, 227). Johnson explained: "One of his major points was that governmental policies that increased output prices or distributed subsidies that were highly correlated with inputs or output would do little or nothing to improve the economic position of low-income groups in agriculture. He argued that the primary function of prices was to direct the use of resources, and that their use to increase, or modify the distribution of, income resulted in a waste of resources and had little or no effect on income" (D.G. Johnson, 1979, 549B).

Schultz's insistence on objectivity and intellectual integrity led to his departure from Iowa State in 1944. Schultz had started a series of war-time farm and food policy pamphlets with funding from the Rockefeller Foundation. The fifth pamphlet, which was written by Oswald Brownlee, argued that an acre of land could produce more margarine than butter. As a result of this statement, Schultz and his young economists became the victims of attacks from, among others, the *Des Moines Register*, the leading newspaper in Iowa; the powerful Iowa dairy producers' lobby even tried to block the Brownlee pamphlet's publication. Schultz resigned from Iowa State, and the best of the younger economists—including Reid, Johnson, and Albert Hart—departed as well.[138] Reid and Johnson followed Schultz to the University of Chicago.

At the University of Chicago, Schultz moved from agricultural economics to the then-new area of human capital: "In my work here and with my graduate students we were discovering that most of the increases in agricultural production during the 1940s and 1950s were occurring with no corresponding increases in land and physical inputs, and with literally fewer people … 30-40% of the total increases in production was unexplained. It turned out that the quality of people was increasing; so, too, for physical inputs. If you stepped back, you saw it: skills were increasing and health was improving, although we weren't able to measure it in the beginning."[139]

Schultz first touched on this discovery in the late 1940s when, as director of research for a Latin American mission of the National Planning Association, he investigated the rapid economic progress that was being made in Latin American countries such as Mexico and Brazil.[140] This led Schultz to rather optimistic conclusions about mankind's prospects of escaping from hunger and poverty.

He liked to contrast his own insights with the doctrines put forward by the leading 18th-century economists David Ricardo and Thomas Robert Malthus. Ricardo proposed the law of diminishing returns, which implied that an increase in inputs leads to less than proportionate increases in output. Malthus held that population would always tend to rise faster than food production. Schultz (1979, 641) counterargued that "… Man has the ability and intelligence to lessen his dependence on cropland, on traditional agriculture, and on depleting sources of energy and can reduce the real costs of producing food for the growing world population. By means of research we discover substitutes for cropland, which Ricardo could not have anticipated, and as incomes rise parents reveal a preference for fewer children, substituting quality for quantity of children, which Malthus could not have foreseen."

The policy conclusions of the research that Schultz, his colleagues, and his students were doing at the University of Chicago in the 1940s and 1950s were at odds with some of the popular theories of the time. One of these popular views held that for the poorer countries to catch up with the richer ones as soon as possible, they had to direct their savings—and the foreign aid they received—toward investments in steel mills, huge industrial complexes, urban expansion, and other types of tangible assets. Schultz (1961, 16) argued that this was the wrong track to follow: "Some growth of course can be had from the increase in conventional capital even though the labor that is available is lacking both in skills and knowledge. But the rate of growth will be seriously limited."

## TRUE TO HIS ROOTS

There can be no doubt that T.W. Schultz was the founder of a strong Chicago tradition in agricultural economics. "But perhaps," Chicago graduate Daniel Sumner notes (1996, 14), "his most enduring contribution to agricultural economics at Chicago was encouraging his student D. Gale Johnson to join him in the move from Iowa State." Although

Thorstein Veblen and Henry Schultz, among others, had previously done some work in this field, it was with T.W. Schultz and Johnson that agricultural economics at the University of Chicago really flourished. In 1948 they obtained funding from the Rockefeller Foundation for their research program in agricultural economics. During the 1950s Schultz and Johnson succeeded in increasing the number of foreign students, mostly from Israel, Latin America, and Asia, trained as agricultural economists at the University of Chicago. Schultz-Johnson graduates also set up programs in agricultural economics along Chicago lines in such American universities as Yale, Minnesota, Purdue, and North Carolina State.

D. Gale Johnson was born in 1916 on a family farm in the small town of Vinton, Iowa. He earned a bachelor's degree from Iowa State College in 1938 and a master's degree a year later from the University of Wisconsin. After spending two years at the University of Chicago, Johnson returned to his alma mater in Iowa and earned a PhD in 1944 under the supervision of T.W. Schultz. He joined Schultz in his move to the University of Chicago, although during the second half of the 1940s he spent one year at the State Department and another at the Department of the Army. In 1954 Johnson obtained a full professorship at Chicago. From 1960 to 1970 he served as Dean of the Division of the Social Sciences, and he twice acted as Chairman of the Department of Economics: 1971–75 and 1980–84. Between them, T.W. Schultz and Johnson chaired Chicago's department of economics for more than half of the period 1945–85. Johnson died in April 2003.

Johnson focused his research on the economics of agriculture. In an elaboration of his doctoral dissertation, Johnson (1944) made a strong case for strict separation in government policy vis à vis agriculture between resource allocation and possible measures to support the income of farmers. The fact that these two issues were usually not separated made Johnson a consistent critic of farm policies.[141] In his 1947 book, Johnson worked out one of Schultz's ideas—the use of forward prices instead of direct government intervention as a means to reduce uncertainty for farmers and hence increase their access to credit.

Despite his many administrative and organizational duties, Johnson was a prolific writer. In particular, he researched the agricultural labor market and the agricultural sector in centrally planned economies intensively, and his opinion of socialized agriculture was very negative. He described it as having caused more human suffering, hardship, and exploitation than any other human institution except slavery and war. Johnson even argued that "the deaths that can be attributed to socialized agriculture as, for example, in Stalin's Soviet Union and Mao's China, may well equal those of World War II, including Hitler's attempts at extermination of Jews and others."[142]

He wrote a book with Karen Brooks on Soviet agriculture that carefully analyzed how food subsidies, budget deficits, and the monetary overhang were linked and how price distortions would ultimately destabilize the entire economy (Brooks and Johnson 1983). Johnson was also an attentive observer of China's agricultural system and the enormous change it underwent in the 1980s.[143]

Farm labor analysis was a topic that he kept returning to in his research.[144] In one early paper, Johnson reported that farmers were earning only about two-thirds as much as factory workers in the late 1930s, and that to equalize earnings, 4 million farm residents would need to migrate out of agriculture (Johnson 1948a). He also produced evidence of high returns to capital in agriculture (Johnson 1948b).

Johnson ended his full-time career as teacher and researcher with a sweeping apologia for agriculture and farmers, the subject that he had studied for six decades. In his Richard T. Ely Lecture at the 1996 AEA annual meeting, he claimed: "It was only because farmers could produce a surplus over and above their own consumption that cities were possible and resources were released to support those who studied nature and learned some of its important secrets. The Industrial Revolution was made possible by two significant agricultural improvements: rapid increases in labor productivity, which permitted labor to be released from agriculture to produce other useful things; and simultaneous increases in food production to provide for the growing population" (Johnson 1997, 1).

## Tool Builders

One of Johnson's major contributions concerned the aggregate supply function of the agricultural sector (Johnson 1950), an analysis that was a forerunner of later work by Zvi Griliches and Marc Nerlove.

Born in the Lithuanian city of Kaunas in 1930, Griliches lost his whole family in Hitler's camps. In 1945, he left for Palestine; there, he was captured by the British and sent to an internment camp in Cyprus. Two years later, he finally managed to enter Israel, where he studied history and languages at Hebrew University. His first choice as a field of study at Hebrew University was agricultural economics, but Griliches was not allowed to sit for the department's entrance exams because of his lack of formal education.

Griliches came to the United States in 1951 and was naturalized eight years later. By 1954, he earned bachelor's and master's degrees in agricultural economics from the University of California at Berkeley alongside fellow students such as Yair Mundlak and Arnold Zellner. At Berkeley, he was influenced by Ivan Lee, who had a PhD in statistics from Iowa State, and George Kuznets, brother of Simon Kuznets, who specialized in psychometrics. It was Lee in particular who encouraged Griliches to go to the University of Chicago for his PhD work.[145]

Griliches arrived in Chicago in 1955 and earned a PhD in 1957. "The most important teachers for me at Chicago," Griliches commented much later, "were [T.W.] Schultz and [Arnold] Harberger. Schultz in the sense of being a mentor ... And Al because you could sort of see that you could implement things" (Krueger and Taylor 2000, 178). Griliches became a full professor at the University of Chicago in 1964, and one year later he was awarded the John Bates Clark Medal.

In 1969, he left for Harvard University, where he stayed for the remainder of his career. Shortly before his death in November 1999, Griliches declared: "When I [arrived at Harvard] I missed Chicago very dearly. Because Chicago was a department, and Harvard not" (Krueger and Taylor 2000, 179).[146]

Writing on the subject of agricultural economics at the University of Chicago during the years 1956–65, Sumner notes (1996, 21): "The most important addition to Chicago during this period was Zvi Griliches, as a student, and shortly thereafter as a faculty member. The Griliches contribution was pervasive." Griliches's most pervasive impact on Chicago— and economics in general—was his work building usable research tools. In his own words: "I started in agricultural economics, a field that took both data and econometrics seriously and used it to attack substantive problems. Econometrics was a tool, not an end in itself, and this became also my attitude to it" (Griliches 1998, xi). Griliches's contribution to the solution of distributed-lag models is an excellent example of his practical orientation to tool building.[147] In his first major publication on agricultural economics, which emerged from his PhD dissertation, he demonstrated that new hybrids are first adopted where they are most profitable with respect to market size, weather, soil, and other conditions (Griliches 1957). Griliches was among the first to calculate returns on spending on research and development. He concluded that "*at least* 700 per cent per year was being earned, as of 1955, on the average dollar invested in hybrid-corn research" (Griliches 1958, 419).

Griliches's hybrid corn papers were also important with respect to the methodology of measuring total factor productivity in the agricultural sector—a subject Griliches himself developed further in later research.[148] He was also one of the first to try to estimate the quality change of labor input.[149] Later, his research reached the conclusion that approximately one-third of the calculated total factor productivity was attributable to improvements in the education of the U.S. labor force (Jorgenson and Griliches 1967).

Even in his earlier research, Griliches did not limit himself to the agricultural sector. For example, he analyzed the demand for cars in terms of the implicit demand for such characteristics as horsepower and automatic transmission (Griliches 1961a). This paper started off the research on the concept of hedonic prices that inspired many, including Sherwin Rosen. A year later, Griliches coauthored a paper on restyling costs in the auto industry (Fisher, Griliches, and Kaysen 1962). In his post-Chicago period, Griliches focused on growth accounting, the impact of product quality on price level indicators, research and development, productivity, and economic growth.

Marc Nerlove was another major tool-builder with roots in the agricultural economics program at the University of Chicago. Nerlove, who was born in Chicago in 1933 and educated as an undergraduate at the University of Chicago, became an academic nomad. He got a master's degree and a PhD from Johns Hopkins University. After short spells at the U.S. Department of Agriculture, Johns Hopkins, and the University of Minnesota, he was at Stanford (1960–65) and Yale (1965–69) before returning to the University of Chicago in 1969. He stayed at the University of Chicago as a professor of economics for five years.

In 1974, he joined the faculty of Northwestern University, where he stayed for eight years. After 1982, Nerlove worked at the University of Pennsylvania, the University of Maryland, and the International Food Policy Research Institute. He adapted his PhD research into a book on agricultural supply that put great emphasis on the responsiveness of farmers to price changes (Nerlove 1958b). In his efforts to construct an agricultural supply function, Nerlove was the first to incorporate the adaptive expectations hypothesis into the model (Nerlove 1958a). In his later work, Nerlove continued working on econometric and statistical tools for economists and on issues related to agricultural and population economics.

Yair Mundlak, who joined the University of Chicago's department of economics on a part-time basis in 1978, has made significant contributions in the field of agricultural economics in more recent years. Mundlak was born in Poland in 1927, but his parents immigrated to Israel that same year. Mundlak earned a bachelor's degree in agricultural economics at the University of California at Davis and a master's degree in statistics at the University of California at Berkeley. At Berkeley, he also earned his PhD in agricultural economics in 1957. He returned to Israel, where he became a professor at the Hebrew University in Jerusalem and a driving intellectual force behind Israeli agricultural development.

George Tolley is another valued contributor to the field of agricultural economics.[150] Tolley earned a master's degree in economics in 1950 and a PhD in 1955 from the University of Chicago. From 1955 to 1966, he taught at North Carolina State University in Raleigh, and in 1966, he returned to Chicago.

Tolley's work focused on urban economics, environmental economics, and natural resource economics. In his research on agricultural economics, Tolley focused heavily on the impact of pricing policies.[151] Tolley, like Nerlove and Mundlak, remained more of a background figure in the story of the Chicago School.

## IMMORAL

The three themes on which T.W. Schultz worked intensively as an academic researcher—agriculture, poverty, and human capital—are clearly interwoven. Schultz himself expressed it as follows in his Nobel lecture:

> Most of the people in the world are poor, so if we knew the economics of being poor we would know much of the economics that really matter. Most of the world's poor people earn their living from agriculture, so if we knew the economics of agriculture we would know much about the economics of being poor ... [A]griculture in many low-income countries has the potential economic capacity to produce enough food for the still-growing population and in so doing can improve significantly the income and welfare of poor people. The decisive factors of production in improving the welfare of poor people are not space, energy and cropland: the decisive factor is the improvement in population quality. (Schultz 1979, 639–40).

Although Mincer (1958) is generally believed to be the economist who was the first to use the term "human capital," Schultz was actually the first. In his 1953 paper "Land in Economic Growth," Schultz (1993, 142) wrote about the conventional factors of production land, labor, and capital and referred to "a new set of resources which counts the improvements in the quality of resources. In the main they are in the nature of human capital. The stock of these new resources has been increasing relative to the conventional set and the return has been relatively high." A few years later, he defined human capital or human wealth as "improvements in human effectiveness arising from the fact that man has developed capacities that result from investments in man" (Schultz 1959b, 75). Schultz's first systematic treatment of investment in human capital was his 1960 presidential address to the AEA (Schultz 1961).

In the 1950s and early 1960s, "human capital" was not a familiar or comfortable concept. Three decades after he published his book on human capital, Becker remarked: "To approach schooling as an investment rather than a cultural experience was considered unfeeling and extremely narrow. As a result, I hesitated a long time before deciding to call my book *Human Capital* (1964) ... Only gradually did economists, let alone others, accept the concept of human capital as a valuable tool in the analysis of various economic and social issues" (Becker 1993b, 392).

Opposition to human capital as a concept came first from the sentiment that it was unsavory for scholars to treat people like machines and to write papers and books about such things as the rate of return on investment in people and the incentive for man to invest in himself. "Why are we so reluctant to acknowledge the role of human wealth?" T.W. Schultz asked himself by the end of the 1950s, "The mere thought of doing so seems to offend us; to discuss it openly appears to rub many people the wrong way. Why is it in bad taste? The answer is that we cannot easily rise above our values and beliefs; we are strongly inhibited from looking upon men as an investment, except in slavery, and this we abhor" (Schultz 1959a, 110).

Opposition came from the ideological side as well. In the Marxist view of the world, it was (and still is) asserted that the exploitation of labor by capital is a basic problem for humanity. This concept starts shaking on its foundations the moment human capital is accepted as a reality. Did part of what is traditionally considered to be labor in fact become capital? If there is capital embodied in labor, then what capital is exploiting what labor?

Opposition to the concept of human capital also came from economists themselves. Most, if not all, economists are trained in economic theories that divide the factors of production into three homogeneous categories: land, labor, and capital. Human capital broke down this straightforward analytical framework and forced economists to adopt a more sophisticated approach.

Opposition to the human capital theory became particularly strong in the early 1970s when Kenneth Arrow and Joseph Stiglitz almost simultaneously developed the theory of screening and Michael Spence developed the theory of signaling.[152] In short, these theories argued that education is not primarily an investment made to build up an income-earning capacity, as the human capital approach claims; instead, it is merely a screening device to select more able persons or a mechanism to send signals to the market about skills and capacities. "Even if schooling also works in this way," Becker replied, "the significance of private rates of return to education is not affected. Moreover, it should be noted that virtually no effort has been made to determine the empirical importance of screening ... Furthermore ... college would be a horrendously expensive 'employment agency'" (Becker 1993, 8).

## MAGNUM OPUS

Naming Schultz, Mincer, and Becker as pioneers of the introduction of human capital in mainstream economics is not the same as saying that they were the first who touched on the subject.[153] "Among the few who have looked upon human beings as capital," Schultz noted (1961, 2–3), "there are three distinguished names. The philosopher-economist Adam Smith boldly included all of the acquired and useful abilities of all of the inhabitants of a country as a part of capital. So did Heinrich von Thünen, who went on to argue that the concept of capital applied to man did not degrade him or impair his freedom and dignity ... Irving Fisher also clearly and cogently presented an all-inconclusive concept of capital." Schultz also acknowledged his Chicago colleagues Friedman and Harry Johnson for their early contributions on human capital.[154]

However, it was Gary Becker who would become the leading economist in the field of human capital. Becker was born in 1930 in Pottsville, Pennsylvania, and did his undergraduate work at Princeton University; Viner was among his professors there. Becker almost turned his back on the economics profession: "Ever since my undergraduate days at Princeton, I was more interested in social issues than in those traditionally considered by economists. I almost changed to sociology when a senior because economics seemed too narrow. Fortunately, I went to Chicago for graduate studies, and the stimulus from Milton Friedman, H. Gregg Lewis, T.W. Schultz and others then at Chicago convinced me that economics could be used to study 'social' problems as well" (Becker 1995, xvi). Those issues "traditionally considered by economists" were of a more monetary or macroeconomic nature. Becker tried his hand at them,[155] but these topics couldn't really get him going as a researcher.

Becker's doctoral dissertation resulted in his first major publication, *The Economics of Discrimination* (1957). In it, Becker applied price theory to the phenomenon of discrimination, the prejudice and hostility toward members of particular groups of society inspired by such factors as race, religion, and sex. Using a simple model of international trade, Becker introduces the so-called discrimination coefficients that, like trade tariffs, measure the intensity of discriminatory actions and feelings.[156] The reaction to Becker's analysis set the tone for how Becker's work has been perceived for the rest of his career—it had previously been unheard of to apply the toolbox of a materialistic science like economics to such deeply "human" ethical issues as discrimination. As Rosen recalled (1993, 33): "It is hard to describe what a daring work this was back then, given the tenor of the times in the United States, and the general scepticism of economists and other social scientists for work that strayed too far from familiar turf." It is noteworthy that the University of Chicago Press only agreed to publish Becker's manuscript after Stigler and others intervened (Stigler 1988b).

Becker left the University of Chicago in 1957 for New York's Columbia University, where collaboration with Mincer furthered his interest in human capital. Becker published the first edition of his magnum opus, *Human Capital*, in 1964. In 1993, Becker's Chicago colleague Rosen (1993, 26) had the following remarks about Becker's book: "Practically every thought in it has been pursued in the research community. Upon rereading today, the work stands the test of time extremely well." The basic assumption embodied in the book is that the decision to invest in human capital (e.g., education, training, and health) can be analyzed in the same way as any other investment. People engage in that investment when the benefits outweigh the costs. One of the most important conclusions was the calculation of rates on return on education and the finding that elementary school education yields higher returns than high school education, which in turn shows higher returns than college education (Becker 1993a).

In *Human Capital*, Becker also seriously questioned a theorem that had become the cornerstone of government policy on the training of people. According to Arthur Pigou's analysis of externalities, training was an externality. The Pigouvian argument is that a company that invests in the development of a person's abilities always faces the risk that this person may be tempted away by another company, which will then reap the benefits of the human-capital investment. This analysis led to the conclusion that the market mechanism will lead to underinvestment in training and government should instead be responsible for investing in training.

Becker introduced the distinction between general and firm-specific training and knowledge. He proved the Pigouvian argument to be wrong as far as general training is concerned—people who get training will pay for it themselves by accepting wages that are beneath the value of the work they perform during their training periods.

As already indicated by Rosen, the analytical framework of Becker's theory of human capital ignited a wide variety of research activities that yielded some important insights. Rents to be earned on firm-specific skills explain "why workers with highly specific skills are less likely to quit their jobs and are the last to be laid off during business downturns" (Becker 1993a, 393). Young people tend to be more mobile than older people because, given more or less the same costs involved in moving, younger people have a longer period left in which they can recoup these costs through higher earnings.[157] The wage gap between men and women—the so-called gender gap—is linked to the fact that "traditionally, women have been far more likely than men to work part-time and intermittently, partly because they usually withdrew from the labor force for a while after having children. As a result, they had fewer incentives to invest in education and training that improved earnings and job skills" (Becker 1993b, 394).

Becker's theory of human capital also shed new light on the famous Leontief paradox (Leontief 1953). Nobel Prize winner Wassily Leontief concluded that the United States, the most developed economy in the world, was in fact exporting labor-intensive products. Traditional international trade theory postulated that the United States should be exporting capital-intensive products and that specialization in labor-intensive activities should be performed in less-developed countries. A possible resolution to this paradox is that "the United States is in fact particularly well endowed with human capital, which is embodied in the labor force but not taken into account in econometric studies based on national accounts data" (Sandmo 1993, 11). Another interesting finding that arose from the human-capital theory is that the continuing (and even increasing) lack of development throughout large parts of the African continent may be connected with high death rates among young Africans (many of which are attributable to the spread of AIDS), which discourages investment in human capital.

Human capital theory forced Becker to address touchy issues such as the attitudes of various ethnic groups about investments in human capital: "Differences among ethnic groups in the United States are fascinating. Groups with small families spend a lot on each child's education and training, while those with big families spend much less. The Japanese, Chinese, Jews, and Cubans have small families and the children become well educated, while Mexicans, Puerto Ricans, and blacks have big families and the education of the children suffers ... It should come as no surprise that children from the ethnic groups with small families and large investments in human capital typically rise faster and further in the United States' income/occupation hierarchy than do children of other groups." (Becker, 1993a).

## CHICAGO GOES ENDOGENOUS

Human capital led to a fundamental revision of the theory of economic growth. At the time Schultz, Mincer, and Becker developed human capital theory, the neoclassical growth model principally developed by Solow dominated the agenda. A basic characteristic of Solow's model was that in a steady state, the growth rate of output (or income) per person is determined by technological change; this is often defined as the Solow residual.

Two major problems remained unsolved in the neoclassical growth model. The conclusion that convergence of economic growth among countries was inevitable: If two countries have the same rate of population growth, the same savings rate, and access to the same production function, they will eventually reach the same level of income. The evidence on this convergence hypothesis, however, is mixed.[158] Another flaw of the Solow-based models is that economic growth is mainly driven by "something"— the Solow residual, technological change, factor productivity, etc.—that seems to fall outside the explanatory power of traditional economic theory. But, as Schultz lamented in 1961, to define this "something" as "'resource productivity' gives a name to our ignorance but does not dispel it" (T.W. Schultz 1961, 6).

The University of Chicago was home to research that explored both of these weaknesses of the neoclassical growth model; among those pioneering this research were Robert Lucas and Paul Romer, who earned his PhD at the University of Chicago in 1983. The idea Romer developed in his doctoral dissertation and subsequent papers was that the neoclassical assumption of diminishing returns on investment and on accumulated capital per capita need not be true at all (Romer 1986). Romer traces this idea back to the work of Arrow and Alfred Marshall, but it was also present in a paper Frank Knight wrote in 1944.[159] The key elements for arriving at increasing returns on capital accumulation are knowledge and spillover effects: "[In] the model [Romer worked out] ... growth is driven primarily by the accumulation of knowledge by forward-looking, profit-maximizing agents ... Investment in knowledge suggests a natural externality. The creation of new knowledge by one firm is assumed to have a positive external effect on the production possibilities of other firms because knowledge cannot be perfectly patented or kept secret" (Romer 1986, 1003).

Lucas (1988a) worked out his basic ideas and models in his 1985 Marshall Lectures at Cambridge University. He considers human capital to be a nonrival or a positive externality in the sense that one worker's human capital raises his own productivity and also that of other workers. One of Lucas's related research efforts started from the question: "Why doesn't capital flow from rich to poor countries?" (Lucas 1990a). The starting point is a logical consequence of the neoclassical theory of trade and growth—capital flows to where the marginal product of that capital is highest (i.e., the economies with less capital, which usually means the poorer countries). Lucas concluded that this theory was clearly not in accordance with the available evidence. The reason for this, Lucas argued, is the huge differences in the quality of labor across the globe: "Correcting for human capital differentials reduces the predicted (capital) return ratios between the very rich and very poor countries from about 58 at least to about 5, and possibly, if knowledge spillovers are local enough, to unity" (Lucas 1990a, 94).

In his 1991 Fisher-Schultze Lecture to the Econometric Society, Lucas (1993, 270) concluded, "the main engine of growth is the accumulation of human capital—of knowledge—and the main source of differences in living standards among nations is differences in human capital. Physical capital accumulation plays an essential but decidedly subsidiary role."

Several issues raised by Lucas's Marshall Lectures were further developed by Nancy Stokey, who joined the faculty of the University of Chicago in 1990. Stokey earned a bachelor's degree in economics from the University of Pennsylvania in 1972 and a PhD from Harvard University six years later. From 1976 to 1990, she taught at Northwestern University. By the time she moved to Chicago's department of economics, Stokey had become Lucas's life partner. In several papers that clearly belong to the research program on endogenous growth, Stokey examined concepts such as the process of learning by doing (1988) and the interaction between investment in human capital and the openness of countries (1991).

Becker collaborated with Kevin Murphy and Robert Tamura to build an interesting model of endogenous growth (1990). In particular, the model threw new light on the observation that some countries or regions persistently grow more slowly than others. This model is embedded in both the theory of human capital and the Beckerian analysis of the family.[160] A major conclusion of this model is that there is more than one steady state of the economy. One is characterized by large families, little human capital, and slow growth, and the other is characterized by small families, large and growing human capital resources, and relatively fast economic growth. The reason for this divergence is that "when human capital is abundant, rates of return on human capital investment are high relative to rates of return on children, whereas when human capital is scarce, rates of return on human capital are low relative to those on children. As a result, societies with limited human capital choose large families and invest little in each member; those with abundant human capital do the opposite" (Becker, Murphy, and Tamura 1990, S35). In the early 1970s, Becker published a paper on the interaction between the quantity and quality of children with H. Gregg Lewis, one of his Chicago mentors (Becker and Lewis, 1973).

Does the analysis of Becker, Murphy, and Tamura inevitably lead to the conclusion that poor countries are trapped forever in a no-growth scenario? No, as "a country may switch from the first 'Malthusian' equilibrium to the second 'development' equilibrium if it has reasonably prolonged good fortune and policies that favor investment" (Becker, Murphy, and Tamura 1990, S35–S36). These switching points are characterized by rapid accumulation of human and physical capital and declines in birth rates and family sizes. The authors highlight some of the changes that helped to trigger the early growth of the West: "… improved methods to use coal, better rail and ocean transports and decreased regulation of prices and foreign trade" (Becker, Murphy, and Tamura 1990, S34). The Becker, Murphy, and Tamura model served as a basic building block for the Kuznets Lectures that Lucas delivered in 1997 (Lucas 2002).

## REVERSING THE BALKANIZATION

Several economists at the University of Chicago played an important role in Becker's development into one of the leading economists of the second half of the 20th century. One of the lesser-known people who had a major influence on Gary Becker was H. Gregg Lewis, under whose supervision Becker wrote his doctoral dissertation on discrimination. Lewis was a pioneer in the development of modern labor economics. Following in Lewis's footsteps, Becker and other Chicago economists, including Albert Rees, Sherwin Rosen, and James Heckman, became prominent labor economists.

Lewis was born in 1914 in Homer, Michigan, and spent, either as a student and a faculty member, more than 40 years at the University of Chicago. He earned a bachelor's degree in 1936 and a PhD in 1947,[161] thereby receiving his education from an extraordinary generation of teachers headed by Frank Knight, Jacob Viner, and Henry Simons. From these men, he learned price theory, and from Paul Douglas, to whom he was research assistant for a while, Lewis developed an appetite for quantitative economics. An able mathematician and statistician himself, Lewis was also professionally close to Henry Schultz. After Henry Schultz's unexpected death in 1938, Lewis was the department's first choice to teach statistics. He declined because he more interested in the application of quantitative techniques in applied economic research rather than the quantitative techniques themselves.

Lewis pioneered the application of basic price theory to the workings of the labor market.[162] In the words of his student Albert Rees, Lewis can be regarded as the father of "analytical labor economics, in contrast to institutional labor economics," where the former means "the application of economic theory and econometrics to problems of the formation of human capital, the allocation of time between market and nonmarket activities, the allocation of labor among alternative uses, and the compensation of labor" (Rees 1976, S3). Rosen paints the historical context:

> When Lewis entered the field in the early 1940's, he hardly was recognized as a labor economist, and his work remained outside the main thrusts of the field until the 1960s. Institutional approaches dominated labor economics prior to the 1930s and the mass unemployment of the Great Depression and the rise of trade unionism made a thoroughgoing economic approach to labor unattractive to most economists. Rational models were ridiculed, marginal productivity and the theory of the firm were considered irrelevant by labor economists and wage determination was thought to be largely immune from competitive forces. Labor markets were "balkanized" (Ashenfelter 1994, 143).

A scholar who typified the more institutional approach to labor economics was Harry Alvin Millis, who earned bachelor's and master's degrees from Indiana University (Brown et al 1949). In 1899, he earned a PhD at the University of Chicago; Wesley Mitchell and Herbert Davenport were among his fellow students. After spells at the universities of Arkansas, Stanford, and Kansas, he returned to the University of Chicago in 1916. In 1928 he became chairman of the department of economics, a post he held for ten years. Millis continuously combined his academic work with public service; he was a member of the U.S. Immigration Commission and the National Labor Relations Board, and he earned a nationwide reputation as an arbitrator in labor disputes.

Lewis earned his PhD the year before Millis died. Richard Freeman, a Harvard labor economist who studied at the University of Chicago, refers to Lewis's work as a "creative synthesis ... his encyclopedic analysis went far beyond literature reviews or mechanical calculation of meta-statistics" (Ashenfelter 1994, 143). His two major publications contain groundbreaking material on the demand for labor and the impact of unions on wage differentials (Lewis 1963 and 1986). As for his work with students, Freeman describes Lewis as the "ideal reader" who "checked what you did and more often than not found some error. By analyzing statistical studies with Kuznetsian care, Lewis influenced the way a generation of labor economists did empirical work. Lewis was the conscience of labor economics ... he had an extraordinary devotion to getting things right" (Ashenfelter 1994, 144, 147).[163]

The attention and time Lewis devoted to his students didn't mean he made life easy for them, as Rees testified (1976, S4): "A dissertation was not acceptable if it could be improved, no matter how long it had been in progress." Jeff Biddle (1996, 174) credits Lewis with "a strong sense of duty—duty to his department, to his students, to his fellow economists, and to the ideal of the careful and impartial scholar."

Lewis left the University of Chicago in 1975 to become a professor of economics at Duke University in North Carolina, where he stayed until his death in 1992. Although Lewis attributed his departure from Chicago to "the desire of himself and his wife to put down roots in a warmer climate in which they could eventually retire" (Biddle 1996, 183), there is considerable evidence that he left Chicago at least partially out of disappointment.[164] Rees (1976, S8) wrote as much between the lines: "He was long denied the recognition he has so richly earned. His promotions came very slowly; his salary lagged behind that of colleagues with less solid but more conspicuous achievements. If he was ever discouraged by this, he gave no outward sign of it." It took Lewis 18 years to complete the route from instructor to full professor.

## THE LEWIS HERITAGE

One of Lewis's most remarkable students was Albert Rees, who was born in New York City in 1921 and died in 1992 in Princeton, New Jersey. After earning a bachelor's degree at Oberlin College, Rees moved to the University of Chicago, where he earned a master's degree in 1947 and a PhD three years later with a dissertation on the effects of unions in the basic steel industry.[165] Rees taught at the University of Chicago for almost 20 years (1948–1966) and served as chairman of the department of economics during the years 1961–64. In 1966, he left for Princeton University, and in 1979, he assumed the presidency of the Sloan Foundation. Like Lewis, his teacher, Rees focused his research on the impact of trade unions.[166] Although he recognized that unionism may increase the downward rigidity of wages, he concluded on the basis of empirical research that "the degree of competition on the product market may be as important as, or more important than, the degree of unionization in explaining interindustry differences in wage movements during depressions" (Rees 1951, 153).

Rees rejected the "unions-cause-wage-price-spiral" theory that was popular in the 1950s.[167] In the early 1960s, he demonstrated that "inflation can be brought to a halt, even in an economy with strong unions, if we are willing to use the brakes of tight money policy and high marginal rates of taxation and to suffer the consequences of a rate of unemployment appreciably above the frictional level" (Rees and Hamilton 1963, 64).

From the 1970s forward, two new labor economists surfaced at the University of Chicago: Sherwin Rosen and James Heckman. Although their work follows the spirit of Lewis's approach to labor economics, Lewis's direct impact on the work of Rosen and Heckman was less than that of Rees, as Lewis had already left the University of Chicago by the time Rosen and Heckman joined the department of economics.

Rosen was born in Chicago in 1938 and began his undergraduate studies at Purdue University. Rosen left engineering for economics at the behest of Purdue economist Thomas Denberg.[168] After being refused at Yale, Rosen enrolled at the University of Chicago in 1962. His class included an unusually high number of people who were to become celebrated economists themselves—Robert Lucas, Eugene Fama, Sam Peltzman, Neil Wallace, and Finnis Welch. Under Lewis's supervision, Rosen earned a PhD in 1966 with a dissertation on employment in railroads (Rosen 1968).

In 1964, Rosen went to the University of Rochester and spent time there with Robert Fogel, who would become another major Chicago economist. Two years before Rosen's arrival in Rochester, W. Allen Wallis had become the president of the University of Rochester. Like Rosen, several other Chicago graduates came to Rochester in Wallis's wake, including Rudiger Dornbusch, Michael Mussa, and Robert Barro.

In 1977, Rosen returned to the University of Chicago, but not before he supervised Richard Thaler's doctoral dissertation at the University of Rochester.[169] By the mid-1990s, Thaler came to the University of Chicago and used his theories of quasi-rational economics and behavioral finance to challenge the efficient-market hypothesis, the cornerstone of the GSB's worldwide reputation in the field of finance. Rosen died in March 2001.

Analysis of labor market-related issues was the most important topic in Rosen's research. Like Lewis, Rosen published different papers on the economic effects of trade union behavior.[170] In the spirit of Ronald Coase's seminal contribution on the nature of the firm, Rosen analyzed the impact of transaction costs on the working of labor markets (Rosen 1988).

The fact that he returned to the University of Chicago seven years after Becker's return clearly left its mark on Rosen's research topics. Although he had already touched on them while still at Rochester, issues related to human capital became a focal point of his publications.[171] In his analysis of what went wrong with the Swedish model—the type of socio-economic organization that was long seen as the "third way" between raw capitalism and inefficient socialism—Rosen mingled human-capital theory with labor and household economics (Rosen 1996). During his career, Rosen built a reputation as a meticulous model builder. Accordingly, his 1974 paper on product differentiation is among his best work (Rosen 1974).

Another example of Rosen as exemplary craftsman is his analysis of the economics of superstars (Rosen 1981, 1983b). He found two elements to be crucial for modern superstardom to exist: "One element is that the technology of consumption or use of the services provided by the activity must be such that poor talent is an inadequate substitute for superior talent ... The other element has to do with certain peculiarities in the technology of the production of the services through the use of audiences" (Rosen 1983b, 454). The importance of the modern media lies in the fact that they "represent technologies that, in effect, allow a person to clone himself at little cost ... Most economic activities are far more constrained in this respect" (Rosen 1983b, 456).

The first element Rosen advances in his superstar paper as an explanation for the existence of this phenomenon—poor talent is an inadequate substitute for superior talent—also played a crucial role in his analysis of the market for lawyers in the United States. Rosen made the following remark about the law's superstars, a small, elite group of lawyers that enjoy huge earnings (1992, 243): "Such concentration in earnings is the natural outcome of the economically efficient assignment of large legal claims to the most talented practitioners." Rosen concludes with his own answer to the question of whether the social product of the lawyers' services is worth having or not: "Economic efficiency in a market economy based on private property requires an orderly way of resolving differences over what are property rights in specific cases. The legal profession is easy to pick on because virtually all civil disputes and litigation merely transfer resources from one party to another ... To answer the normative question, one must assess whether the ex ante effects of prospective disputes promote efficient economic and social behavior that otherwise would not occur. This is what makes the ex post costs worth bearing" (Rosen 1992, 243–44).

## HENRY'S HEIR

James Heckman was born in Chicago in 1944. Heckman earned a bachelor's degree in mathematics from Colorado College in 1965 and a master's degree in economics from Princeton University three years later. In 1971, he obtained a doctoral degree in economics at Princeton with the dissertation, "Three Essays on the Supply of Labor and the Demand for Goods." According to Heckman, "At Princeton, Albert Rees, my PhD supervisor, had a major impact on my development. However, at least as much influence came from Gary Becker and Jacob Mincer."[172] Heckman spent 1970 to 1974 at Columbia University, but from 1974 forward he was a member of Chicago's department of economics.

Heckman became an applied tool builder in econometrics. In 1985, he became the Henry Schultz Professor, which underscored Heckman's own perception of himself as the heir to the type of work Schultz was doing several decades earlier at the University of Chicago.[173] A year earlier, the AEA had awarded Heckman its John Bates Clark Medal. In its citation, the AEA emphasized Heckman's work in econometrics and statistics.[174]

The Royal Swedish Academy of Sciences also recognized Heckman's important contributions to economics by awarding him and Daniel McFadden of the University of California at Berkeley the Nobel Prize in economics in 2000. In its citation, the Academy referred to the contributions of both laureates in "the field of microeconometrics"—that is, "the empirical analysis of the economic behavior of individuals and households, such as decisions on labor supply, consumption, migration or occupational choice."[175] The Academy also specifically referred to Heckman as "the world's foremost researcher in econometric policy evaluation ... [whose] ... most influential work deals with problems that arise when data are generated by a non-random selection process." Furthermore, the Academy stressed that "Heckman's contributions to microeconomic theory have been developed in conjunction with applied empirical research, especially in labor economics."

Heckman's major contribution to labor economics concerned the analysis of labor supply, with special attention paid to the role of women in this supply.[176] Traditional labor economics examined labor supply purely in terms of hours worked. A change in the real wage rate was supposed to generate income and substitution effects—the balance of which determined what happened to the hours worked. In this analysis, the decision to participate or not in the work process was simply ignored. In 1993, Heckman concluded that one of the major discoveries of the research on labor supply is the "crucial distinction with important empirical payoff ... between labor supply choices at the extensive margin (i.e., labor force participation and employment choices) and choices at the intensive margin (i.e., choices about hours of work or weeks of work for workers)" (116). Almost 20 years earlier, Heckman (1974a, 1974b, 1974c) published three papers related to issues of labor supply in one year.

Just like Rosen and so many others, Heckman was also captivated by the human-capital revolution. He made an interesting contribution by developing a cycle model of labor supply, earnings, consumption, and nonmarket benefits of education (Heckman 1976). One of the topics studied in this paper was the differences in age-consumption profiles between blacks and whites. The economic progress of black Americans was to become another major issue in Heckman's research. Becker's work—particularly his seminal research on the economics of discrimination—is clearly an influence here. Heckman argued against some researchers' claims that affirmative action's positive effect on the relative wage position of the black population was at best limited.[177] A crucial point in Heckman's counterargument was the distinction between the progress of American blacks in the north and in the south. "The record from the South," Heckman (1990, 235) concluded, "indicates that labor markets shifted favorably toward blacks in a fashion that can most economically be accounted for by assigning a major role to a federal civil rights policy ... However, it is incorrect to attribute all of the black improvement in the South to civil rights laws ... Social activism combined with improvements in schooling quality and industrial development were also important contributors." By 1998, Heckman was able to conclude that "a careful reading of the entire body of available evidence confirms that most of the disparity in earnings between blacks and whites in the labor market of the 1990s is due to differences in skills they bring to the market, and not to discrimination within the labor market" (101).

Heckman is best known to a broader public for his labor-market policy work. He was extremely critical of the popular belief that the U.S.'s labor market and educational system were unable to equip workers with the necessary skills required in the modern economy and that because of these shortcomings, the wage situation of less-skilled workers had deteriorated considerably from the mid-1970s forward.[178] A huge need for investment in human capital was demanded by the defenders of this new consensus, so he and his colleagues calculated that "it would take a human capital investment of 1.66 trillion (in 1989 dollars) to restore the 1979 earnings ratios of less-skilled workers to workers with some college education" (Heckman, Roselius, and Smith 1994, 84). Apart from the mind-boggling aspect of that figure, "... the evidence on the effectiveness of training programs reveals that publicly provided training is ineffective. Returns from private training programs are much greater. However, private training programs typically exclude disadvantaged workers because the private returns to their training is low" (Heckman, Roselius, and Smith 1994, 117). To Heckman and his colleagues, there was only one sensible way out of this difficult situation: "economically efficient programs would focus on early training and education at the primary and secondary schooling level rather than on postsecondary education and training" (Heckman, Roselius, and Smith 1994, 117–118).

## FAMILY TIME

Lewis, Rees, Rosen, and Heckman are all Chicago economists who have produced important research in the field of labor economics.[179] Of course, the same can be said of Becker—and not simply because of his seminal contributions to the theory of human capital. Becker's analysis of time as an economic factor also belongs to the field of labor economics.[180] In his Nobel lecture, Becker (1993b, 386) remarked, "different constraints are decisive for different situations, but the most fundamental constraint is limited time. Economic and medical progress have greatly increased length of life, but not the physical flow of time itself, which always restricts everyone to 24 hours per day. So while goods and services have expanded enormously in rich countries, the total time available to consume has not."

A major source of inspiration for Becker's analysis of time was Jacob Mincer (1963), who concluded that the analysis of the demand for several commodities is seriously flawed if the factor of time is left out. Becker's basic point runs parallel to Mincer's observation: To obtain the full cost of any activity or product, one must include the time used in production or consumption. This modified the traditional outlook of choice theory—the heart of the new theory was the "assumption that households are producers as well as consumers; they produce commodities by combining inputs of goods and time according to the cost-minimization rules of the traditional theory of the firm" (Becker 1965, 516).

Becker's research on the time factor and other topics came together in 1981's *A Treatise on the Family*, a book that almost instantly became as influential as it was controversial. In his Nobel lecture, he described the effort he had invested in this work:

> Writing *A Treatise on the Family* is the most difficult sustained intellectual effort I have undertaken … Trying to cover this broad subject required a degree of mental commitment over more than 6 years, during many nighttime as well as daytime hours, that left me intellectually and emotionally exhausted.

In his autobiography, Bertrand Russell says that writing the
*Principia Mathematica* used up so much of his mental powers
that he was never again fit for really hard intellectual work. It
took about two years after writing the *Treatise* to regain my intellectual zest. (Becker 1993b, 395)

Becker presented many issues related to the family as investment decisions that should be made with the objective of welfare maximization.
In Becker's analysis, welfare maximization was not confined to materialistic elements. When people marry, decide to have children, divide the
work to be done among family members, make plans to leave bequests,
or decide to divorce, they make these decisions on the basis of the costs
and the benefits involved. This analytical framework and the conclusions
it produced were completely contrary to the ways people in the Western
world are used to thinking about family structures and relations; therefore, it is easy to appreciate that the thought process of his *Treatise* must
have been extremely demanding and exhausting. Given the resistance his
earlier research had faced, Becker must have known beforehand that his
approach would encounter fierce opposition. For example, Becker's theory of fertility, a crucial element in his broader theory of the family, was
sharply attacked by Paul Samuelson (1976).

One of the most significant conclusions of Becker's analysis is that
in a modern society time becomes more expensive—including the time
spent raising children. Moreover, children need more education and
training to get the skills they need, which further accelerates the cost of
raising children. Thus, it is no surprise that birth rates have declined in
modern societies and that married people make a conscious choice to
have smaller families.

Another interesting implication concerns divorce. Contrary to common belief, wealthier people divorce less often than poorer people. For
Becker, this empirical evidence fits in well with his theory, because the
wealthier a couple is, the more both partners will gain by staying together. In a poor family, either party forfeits little in a divorce.

The Rotten Kid Theorem is generally the best-known part of Becker's
treatise on the family. This theorem shows that selfish children with altruistic parents can exhibit behavior that gives the impression of being

altruistic—but that is actually selfish. These "Rotten Kids" realize it is in their own best interest to act in a way that pleases their benefactors and that disguises their real motives.

Becker's *Treatise on the Family* bears much resemblance to his *Human Capital*. Both books set the agenda for a research program that would attract many economists. In reviewing the book, Yoram Ben-Porath (1982) wrote the following: "What Becker has given us is first of all a set of analytical concepts and a taxonomy ... If (the framework) were to be judged in isolation, then indeed the risk of merely having produced an empty and sterile semantic exercise could not be dismissed ... Its usefulness does not consist in being right or wrong in terms of one substantive hypothesis, but in the fact that it charts a reasonable strategy, makes it possible to derive new hypotheses and relate them to a broad set of other findings."

As Becker readily acknowledges,[181] a major influence on the analysis developed in *A Treatise on the Family* came from James Coleman, the man who introduced the concept of the *Homo economicus* into sociology.[182] Coleman's most influential book is probably *Foundations of Social Theory* (1990). In it, Coleman develops the theory of rational choice, which implies that social structures, group norms, and so on result from the purposeful actions of rational individuals. However, it works both ways: social standards and institutions are important for the understanding and explanation of individual behavior.

Coleman was born in 1926 in Bedford, Indiana, and received a bachelor's degree in chemical engineering from Purdue University. He switched to sociology while in graduate school and earned a PhD in 1955 from Columbia University. While Coleman was at Columbia, he studied price theory under Stigler. However, this course didn't affect young Coleman too much.[183] The attractiveness of the economic approach or the application of rational choice theory to sociology came to him in the late 1950s when he left Chicago's department of sociology for Johns Hopkins University, where he stayed from 1956 to 1973. In 1961, he wrote his first major book, *The Adolescent Society,* in which the economic approach is already clearly present. Coleman returned to the University of Chicago in 1973 and remained there for the rest of his career until his death in 1995.

Becker described Coleman as "a better analyst of real economic problems than most economists who know far more economic theory" (Clark 1996, 379). The Johns Hopkins sociologist Edward McDill rates Coleman "as the pre-eminent sociologist of his generation, both as theoretician and empirical researcher" (Clark 1996, 368). Daniel Patrick Moynihan wrote that "Coleman became one of the first of the politically incorrect scholars of our time" and that he "was viciously attacked in the mode that Hannah Arendt had observed among the totalitarian elites in Europe—the ability to immediately dissolve every statement of fact into a question of motive."[184]

Schooling and education were the major elements in Coleman's research. In a study for the U.S. Congress, he and his fellow researchers concluded that black children obtained better school results in integrated classes.[185] On the basis of new research that was published nine years later, Coleman and his team concluded that desegregation efforts (such as busing) had backfired because they had led to the flight of white children from schools where blacks had arrived in large numbers.[186] These conclusions made Coleman the target of some vicious attacks. The outburst of indignation that Coleman faced was comparable to that he experienced in 1982, when he found evidence that the performance of students in private and Catholic schools were systematically better than those of their counterparts in public schools.[187] A few years later, Coleman commented as follows on this systematic difference: "... the fundamental assumption on which publicly supported education in the United States is based, is wrong for the social structure in which we found ourselves today. Perhaps the school should not be an agent of the state or of the larger society but of the community of families closest to the child" (Coleman 1985, 17).

## RATIONALIZING CRIME

Coleman was always very hesitant about drawing firm policy conclusions and proposals from his research.[188] The same can be said of Becker. Most serious economic research allows researchers to reach some conclusions while bringing new questions to the forefront. As Becker argued, "... it is most of the time not up to the economic scientist to draw up policy agendas."[189] Becker was mainly interested in positive economics and much less interested (at least in his academic publications)[190] in normative aspects of public policy. Becker's own work is one long testimony to this attitude, with one major exception—his analysis of the economics behind crime and punishment.

Once again, Becker shocked most of the intellectual community with his first publication on the issue of crime (Becker 1968). Becker's book went squarely against the basic message of psychiatrist Karl Menninger's 1966 book *The Crime of Punishment*. At the time Becker published his analysis of crime, Menninger's book was quite influential in policy circles. Menninger's basic message was that criminals are more often than not victims themselves—of the family situation they came from, of the education they got (or didn't get at all), or of some other circumstance completely outside their own will or personality. The obvious conclusion of this way of looking at crime in society is that the harder you punish criminals, the more you miss the roots of and the solution to this problem.

Becker's basic point was that crime only happens because it "does pay." In his Nobel lecture, Becker characterized his work on crime as follows:

> I explored ... the theoretical and empirical implications of the assumption that criminal behavior is rational ... but again 'rationality' did not imply narrow materialism. It recognized that many people were constrained by moral and ethical considerations, and they did not commit crimes even when these were profitable and there was no danger of detection. However, police and jails would be unnecessary if such attitudes always prevailed. Rationality implied that some individuals become criminals because of the financial and other rewards from crime compared to legal work, taking account of the likelihood of apprehension and conviction, and the severity of punishment. The amount of crime is determined not only by rationality and preferences of would-be criminals but also by the economic and social environment created by public policies, including expenditures on police, punishments for different crimes, and

opportunities for employment, schooling, and training programs. (Becker, 1993b, 390)

The basic setup of Becker's analysis is that crime produces a social loss
in income, which an optimal policy should try to minimize. "This loss
is the sum of damages, cost of apprehension and conviction, and costs
of carrying out the punishments imposed ... Vengeance, deterrence,
safety, rehabilitation, and compensation are perhaps the most important of the many desiderata proposed throughout history. Next to these,
minimizing the social loss in income may seem narrow, bland, and even
quaint ... Yet one should not lose sight of the fact that it is more general
and powerful than it may seem and actually includes more dramatic desiderata as special cases" (Becker 1968, 207–208).

As the likelihood of apprehension and the severity of punishment are
two of the major determinants of crime, authorities can strike different
types of balance between the two in their policies. Among criminolo-
gists, this type of analysis tended to receive a mixed or negative reaction.
The pure economics of Becker's approach toward crime and punishment
was also criticized.[191] Empirical studies on the effect of different determinants on the crime rate nevertheless revealed results that supported
Becker's approach.[192]

Becker's analysis of crime launched a research project in which his
student Isaac Ehrlich was prominently involved. "The basic thesis,"
Ehrlich (1973, 559) concluded, "underlying our theory of participation
in illegitimate activities is that offenders, as a group, respond to incentives in much the same way that those that engage in strictly legitimate
activities do as a group."

Two other interesting contributions to the economics of crime are
worthy of mention. The first, which is also linked to Becker's work on social interactions, looked for an explanation of the high variance of crime
rates across time and space. "Social interaction," the authors claimed,
plays an important role here, because "one agent's decision to become a
criminal [is] positively [affecting] his neighbor's decision to enter a life
of crime" (Glaeser, Sacerdote, and Scheinkman 1996, 508).

One of the authors of that work, Jose Scheinkman, was born in 1948 in
Rio de Janeiro, Brazil, and earned degrees in economics and mathematics

in his homeland. In 1974, he earned a PhD in economics at Rochester University. Scheinkman was a member of Chicago's department of economics for 25 years until his 1999 departure for Princeton University. Scheinkman's research focused on a wide range of topics including the random-walk hypothesis (Scheinkman and LeBaron 1989), the relationship between economic growth and the development of cities (Glaeser et al. 1992), and privatization (Glaeser and Scheinkman 1996).

The second noteworthy contribution originated at Chicago's law school where, during his relatively short stay there (1995–99), John Lott Jr. created a huge controversy with his book *More Guns, Less Crime*. In line with Becker's basic thesis, Lott (1998) argued, "when crime becomes more difficult, less crime is committed" (19). The basic conclusion of Lott's empirical analysis was that the legalization of concealed handguns for law-abiding citizens is "the most cost-effective means of reducing crime" (20). Furthermore, "women and blacks ... obtain the largest benefits from discretionary concealed handgun-laws" (160). Mark Duggan (2001) seriously questioned Lott's conclusions during his short spell at the University of Chicago.

## UP TO A HIGHER LEVEL?

Almost 30 years after his controversial analysis of crime and criminal behavior was published, Becker wrote *Accounting for Tastes* (1996), which contained several previously published papers and three new chapters. The most important of these new sections was the one entitled "Preferences and Values."

In it, Becker made two primary points. First, the hypothesis of stable preferences was no longer tenable. With the article *"De Gustibus Non Est Disputandum,"* Becker and his coauthor, Stigler (1977), had made this hypothesis into a cornerstone of standard economic analysis. Second, he indicated how the economic analysis of preference formation and change could proceed. "This is not, as some claim, a question of turning my back on earlier work," Becker explained, "but a further development in my thinking on economics. It is also not a refutation of basic price theory. Quite on the contrary, because in using price theory in the analysis of preferences it can be argued that price theory is brought to a higher level of explanative and predictive power. It is, however, evident that treating preferences as endogenous increases the danger of circular reasoning. Hence the importance of developing our theoretical arguments in such a way that we end up with empirically verifiable hypotheses."[193]

Becker described the essence of his new approach to economic analysis as retaining "the assumption that individuals behave so as to maximize utility while extending the definition of individual preferences to include personal habits and addictions, peer pressure, parental influences on the tastes of children, advertising, love and sympathy, and other neglected behavior" (Becker 1996, 4). The incorporation of experiences and social forces into preferences happens through two capital stocks—personal and social capital—which Becker regarded as part of the total stock of human capital of a person: "Initial stocks of personal and social capital, along with technologies and government policies, do help determine economic outcomes. But the economy also changes tastes and preferences by changing personal and social capital" (19). Personal capital "includes the relevant past consumption and other personal experiences that affect current and future utilities" (4).

A crucial element in the development of personal capital is the way in which individuals discount the future. This allowed Becker to introduce a third type of capital, imagination capital, which is an ability to judge the future. Of course, the discounting of future utilities is strongly influenced by the degree of time preference.[194]

Social capital "incorporates the influence of past actions by peers and others in an individual's social network and control system" (Becker 1996, 4). Becker noted that individuals had very little direct influence over their social capital because "once a social network is given ... the production of their social capital ... is mainly determined by the actions of peers and relevant others" (Becker 1996, 13). However, the indirect influence people have over their social capital is enormous "since they try to become part of social networks that benefit rather than hurt them" (Becker 1996, 13). Like personal capital, a basic element of Becker's analysis of social capital is that "an increase in a person's social capital increases her demand for goods and activities that are complements to the capital and reduces the demand for those that are substitutes" (Becker 1996, 13).

Becker's analysis—especially with respect to social capital—owes much to the pioneering work done by Chicago sociologist Coleman. With *Social Economics*, which he wrote with Kevin Murphy, Becker further developed the idea of the unified social science that Veblen had dreamed about a century before and that Coleman had been obsessed with as well. In the introduction, the authors crystallize what the book is about: "Modern economics," Becker and Murphy (1999, 3) state, "typically assumes that individual behavior is not *directly* influenced by the actions of others. Of course, it is understood that every individual is greatly affected *indirectly* since the behavior of other individuals and firms determine the relative prices of different goods, the rewards to different kinds of labor and capital, marital prospects, political programs, and most other aspects of economic, social, and political life." The remainder of the book uses the economist's toolbox to analyze the impact of culture, norms, and social structure on a broad range of issues.

## THE UCLA GANG

As the coauthor of *Social Economics,* Kevin Murphy established himself beyond the Hyde Park campus as one of the main heirs to the Becker legacy at the University of Chicago. From the 1996–97 academic year forward, Becker began teaching Economics 301 with Murphy, who is now the George Pratt Shultz Professor of Business Economics and Industrial Relations. In 1997, Murphy received the John Bates Clark Medal. In its citation, the AEA described Murphy as "brilliant economist whose skills span the full range of the discipline. He is a superb data analyst and econometrician … he is a gifted and original theorist."[195]

Born in Los Angeles in 1958, Murphy received his undergraduate education at UCLA, where he earned his bachelor's degree in economics in 1981. Mike Ward, a PhD from the University of Chicago who taught the intermediate course in microeconomics at UCLA, aroused Murphy's interest in Chicago-style economics and also introduced him to Finnis Welch, who initiated him into the field of labor economics.

Welch was born in 1939 in Olney, Texas, and earned a PhD in 1965 from the University of Chicago. Under the influence of H. Gregg Lewis and T.W. Schultz at Chicago, he focused on the returns to schooling.

After two years (1964–66) at the University of Chicago, he spent some time at different universities before settling down at UCLA from 1978 forward.

The fact that UCLA is often referred to as the University of Chicago at Los Angeles underscores the close link between the two institutions' approaches to economics. Murphy and Welch are both clear exponents of this link; another is Edward Lazear.

Lazear was born in 1948 in New York City, but grew up in Los Altos, California. He received bachelor's and master's degrees from UCLA, and in 1974, he earned a PhD in economics from Harvard University. That same year, he joined the University of Chicago's GSB, where he taught until he left for Stanford University's business school in 1992.

Labor economics has always been Lazear's field of specialization; in fact, he cofounded the *Journal of Labor Economics*. As the coauthor of an influential textbook on microeconomic theory,[196] Lazear covered a wide range of subjects in labor economics, such as schooling, wage differentials, unionization, productivity, and industrial politics.[197]

Murphy came to Chicago in 1982; in less than seven years, he rose from a teaching assistant to a full professor at the GSB. An academic career almost eluded him: "After earning my BA, I contemplated launching myself in the liquor business. The choice between business and academics was a hard one. It was especially Finnis Welch who in the end pulled me over," Murphy recalls.[198]

Two other UCLA teachers who had a major influence on Murphy were Benjamin Klein and Armen Alchian, but the two teachers who influenced Murphy most at Chicago were Becker and Rosen: "In the hands of Gary, economics becomes an art. Gary Becker is among the greatest inventors in the history of economics. Sherwin Rosen on the other hand was a real craftsman who is very strong in modelling."[199] Under Rosen's supervision, Murphy earned a PhD in 1986 with specialization in the labor market as his topic.

One can divide Murphy's research into three main areas: labor economics, economic growth, and *ad hoc* issues such as advertising and addiction. Murphy's first major paper in the field of labor economics was a detailed analysis of the evolution of unemployment in the United States from 1968 to 1985 (Murphy and Topel 1987).

The paper's coauthor, Robert Topel, was another proponent of the close links between UCLA and the University of Chicago. Topel, who was born in 1952 in Los Angeles, earned a bachelor's degree in 1974 and a PhD in economics six years later at UCLA, so the sources of influence on his training as an economist are similar to Murphy's. He came to Chicago's department of economics in 1980, returned to UCLA in 1985, but came back to Chicago one year later—this time to the GSB.

Topel was among the first to empirically investigate the relationship between the way unemployment insurance is financed and the occurrence of unemployment.[200] He also focused on different aspects of specific (as opposed to general) human capital.[201]

His analysis of job mobility and wage changes was closely related to this work on human capital (Topel and Ward, 1992). Rising wage inequality in the United States and other countries, Topel concluded, "is driven by a steady increase in the relative demand for skilled labor which has outrun the increasing supply of such labor ... The 'solution' to the economic and social problem of rising inequality is that changes in the supply of skills must, through investments in human capital, catch up with the rise in demand for skilled labor" (Topel 1997, 55–56).

Topel teamed with Murphy to produce several other papers on labor economics. In 1991, along with Chinhui Juhn of the University of Houston, they searched for an explanation of why the natural rate of unemployment increased substantially between the early 1970s and the late 1980s. "Standard macroeconomic models, which have focused mainly on the cyclical behavior of wages and unemployment," the three argued, "are clearly inappropriate for the longer run, when wages are demonstrably flexible and labor markets are more likely to clear" (Juhn, Murphy, and Topel 1991, 124). Their analysis led to the conclusion that "the natural rate varies with labor market conditions" (125) and that "significant secular increases in unemployment, nonparticipation, and nonemployment are heavily concentrated among less skilled individuals" (76).

In the paper, Juhn, Murphy, and Topel point out the existence of a perverse demand and supply interaction: less demand for low-skilled workers reduces their wages and increases their unemployment, which increases the tendency toward withdrawal from the labor market. The same theme surfaced in a 1997 paper by Murphy and Topel focused on the concept of nonemployment, meaning not only those people who are without a job and actively seeking one but also the "potential workers who choose not to seek employment" (Murphy and Topel 1997, 295). According to Murphy and Topel, nonemployment is highest among the lesser skilled, who are usually the main victims of technological change.

## MORE BREEDS MORE

Human capital links Murphy's work in labor economics to the second major theme in his research: the determinants of economic growth. In 1991, Kevin Murphy, Andrei Shleifer, and Robert Vishny published a paper in which they outlined how the allocation of ability across occupations influences economic growth.[202] Murphy, Shleifer, and Vishny came to be known as "the Trio" because they attended graduate school in Chicago simultaneously[203] and also because of their frequent collaboration on papers. In 1994, Shleifer left the University of Chicago for Harvard, and he received the John Bates Clark Medal in 1999. In the award citation, the AEA describes Shleifer as a "superb economist, working in the old Chicago tradition of building simple models, emphasizing basic economic mechanism, and carefully looking at the evidence."[204]

In 1988, Murphy, Shleifer, and Vishny asked: "Virtually every country that experienced rapid growth of productivity and living standards over the last 200 years has done so by industrializing ... Yet despite the evident gain from industrialization, and the success of many countries in achieving it, numerous other countries remain unindustrialized and poor. What is it that allows some but not other countries to industrialize?" (1). Their answer was that to get industrialization going, a country needs a "big push" through the "simultaneous industrialization of many sectors" with "industrialization of one sector ... enlarging the size of the market in other sectors" (1). Governments, the Trio argued, have a crucial role to play in this development process: "First, a program that encourages industrialization in many sectors simultaneously can substantially boost income and welfare even when investment in any sector appears unprofitable. This is especially true for a country whose access to foreign markets is limited through high transportation costs or trade restrictions" (28–29).

There is a striking similarity between the "big push" paper of the Trio and one Murphy published two years later with Becker and Robert Tamura. Both papers fundamentally rely on a factor-intensity argument. In the "big push" paper, industrialization breeds more industrialization because there are positive scale effects. Becker, Murphy, and Tamura (1990) made a similar argument regarding the stock of human capital in the process of economic growth.

In a third paper, Murphy, Shleifer, and Vishny (1993) used the same concept to analyze the effect of rent-seeking on economic growth. Rent-seeking, defined as "any redistributive activity that takes up resources" (408), reduces economic growth because rent-seeking activities exhibit increasing returns to scale (among other reasons). Murphy, Shleifer, and Vishny saw three mechanisms at work: "First, there may be a fixed cost to setting up a rent-seeking system, such as a legal code. Once it is set up, however, lawyers can cheaply sue each other's clients ... Second, rent-seeking may be self-generating in that offense creates a demand for defense ... Third, rent-seekers have a 'strength in numbers.' If only a few people steal or loot, they will get caught; but if many do, the probability of any one of them getting caught is much lower" (408).

Public rent-seeking (rent-seeking by government officials and bureaucrats) is particularly ponderous for the innovative sector and is a second channel through which rent-seeking reduces growth: "To start a new firm, an innovator must get business, building, water and fire permits, tax documents ... and often dozens of other documents ... Innovators' demand for these government-produced goods is high and inelastic, and hence they become primary targets of corruption" (Murphy, Shleifer, and Vishny 1993, 412–13).

Four additional factors make new producers more vulnerable than established ones: "First, innovators have no established lobbies ... Second, innovators are often credit-constrained and cannot easily find the cash to pay the bribes ... Third, innovative projects are typically long-term ... This provides rent-seekers plenty of opportunities for future expropriation ... Fourth, innovative projects are typically risky, which makes them particularly vulnerable to rent-seeking. For if a project succeeds, the returns are expropriated, whereas if it fails, the innovator bears the cost" (413).

As to the determinants of economic growth, Murphy also pointed to an interesting interaction between social status, education, and growth.[205] This analysis combined two earlier research findings: the Trio's conclusions on the importance of ability distribution across occupations, and the recognition that the quest for social status is an important factor in the allocation of workers in occupations.

Becker, Murphy, and Harvard's Glaeser published a related piece of research on the origins of economic growth in 1999. They observed:

> ... Over the majority of historical time, minimal increases in world population went together with negligible growth in per capita incomes. And both 'took off' in the 19th century ... Population may reduce productivity because of traditional diminishing returns from more intensive use of land and other natural resources. However, larger specializations encourage greater specialization and increased investments in knowledge, mediated in part through bigger and more important cities. Therefore, the net relation between greater population and per capita incomes depends on whether inducements to human capital and expansion on knowledge are stronger than diminishing returns to natural resources. (Becker, Glaeser, and Murphy 1999, 145,149)

## THE BECKER LEGACY

Three other younger economists at the University of Chicago are clearly working in the Beckerian tradition of economics: Tomas Philipson, Steven Levitt, and Casey Mulligan.

Born in Sweden in 1962, Tomas Philipson earned a bachelor degree in mathematics in his home country and, after a stay at the Claremont Graduate School, moved to the University of Pennsylvania, where he earned his Ph.D. in economics in 1989. Hearing Gary Becker give a seminar at the University of Pennsylvania opened up a whole new world for the young Philipson. Becker saw a lot of potential in the young Swede and got him a post-doctoral fellowship at the University of Chicago. "The first two years at Chicago, I spent on my re-education as an economist", said Philipson[206]. In 1990, Philipson joined the department of economics at the University of Chicago. In addition to serving as a faculty member at the department and at Chicago's law school in the late 1990s, Philipson became a tenured professor at Chicago's Irving B. Harris Graduate School of Public Policies.

Over the years, Philipson earned a reputation as an authority in health economics—especially in the branch of economic epidemiology. This branch studies the occurrence of any kind of disease, but "differs from other approaches by attempting to determine the underlying forces leading to the transmittive choices made by individuals"[207]. His prominence in the field of health economics was underscored by his appointments as the senior economic advisor to the Commissioner of the Food and Drug Administration (FDA) during 2003-2004 and as the senior economic advisor to the administrator of the Centers for Medicare and Medicaid Services (CMS) in 2004-2005. One of his most remarkable publications in health economics is the book Philipson and Richard Posner published in 1993[208] on the HIV/AIDS epidemic. In the book, they analyze the epidemic with an economist's toolbox: "Individuals who are contemplating sexual relations or other interactions that can transmit the AIDS virus compare the probability adjusted costs and benefits of alternative practices, notably safe sex (for example sex with condoms) and risky (unprotected) sex. Because safe sex implies costs ... because the expected cost of risky sex depends on the probability of infection, which is low for many people, rational behavior in the face of the risk of AIDS does not imply the elimination of all risky sex" (Posner & Philipson 1993, 218).

At least two other Philipson publications merit mention. A paper he prepared with John Cawley on insurance markets challenged the standard argument for government intervention in insurance markets. This argument is based on the postulate of asymmetric information (i.e., well-informed demanders facing poorly informed suppliers). Asymmetric information leads to adverse selection, the underprovision of insurance, and higher unit prices. After examining the available evidence for the U.S. life insurance market, Philipson and Cawley concluded that "the standard arguments about adverse selection in insurance greatly exaggerate the superiority of the information on the demand side" (Philipson & Cawley 1999, 842).

A 2005 paper prepared with Gary Becker and Rodrigo Soares of the University of Maryland dealt with longevity and world inequality. The paper's three authors argue that if one adds the quantity of life (represented by longevity) to the traditional measure of the quality of life (represented by GDP per capita), a kind of "full" income measure is obtained that gives a better idea of the evolution of world inequality. They computed that this full income measure increased between 1965 and 1995 by 140% for developed countries and by 192% for developing countries, thus concluding that over that period, world income inequality declined on average[209].

In the fall of 1997, Steven Levitt joined the faculty of the department of economics as an assistant professor. He had earned his B.A. in economics from Harvard in 1989 and his Ph.D. from MIT five years later, and from 1994 until June 1997, he worked as a junior fellow at the Harvard Society of Fellows.

Levitt came to Chicago for two reasons: "First, for most people at the East Coast universities, Chicago is the enemy. I wanted to know more about this enemy. Second, at Cambridge I arrived at a point where in seminars I knew in advance what everybody was going to say. That's a kind of 'comfort' one never has in Chicago seminars"[210]. In the spring of 2003, Levitt received the John Bates Clark Medal for his largely empirical work on the economics of crime and the effects of alternative criminal justice policies.

In 2005, Levitt became something of a celebrity as author of the best-selling book *Freakonomics*, which is subtitled, "A rogue economist explores the hidden side of everything". In this book, which was co-authored by journalist Stephen Dubner, Levitt employs "the best analytical tools that economics can offer" and allows for "whatever freakish curiosities may occur" (Levitt & Dubner 2005, 14).

In one of his most noteworthy papers, Levitt examined the relationship between the numbers of police officers in a given area and that area's crime rate. Most studies that had previously investigated this relationship concluded that there was either no relationship or possibly a positive relationship between the two variables. However, Levitt argued that "… you have to be very careful with this kind of correlation. It doesn't tell you much by way of causation. Isn't it possible that because of an increasing crime rate, the demand for police increases?"[211] He also found

that increases in the size of police forces in large cities are disproportionately concentrated during mayoral and gubernatorial election races.
After this "unusual" increase in the police force, a clearly negative relationship between the number of police and crime emerges: "The elasticity of violent crime with respect to sworn officers is estimated to be −1.0;
for property crime the elasticity is around −0.3" (Levitt 1997, 271). Levitt
also found—again contrary to widely held opinion—a negative relationship between juvenile crime and the severity with which juvenile criminals are punished[212]. According to another empirical study, bad prison
conditions seemed to play a very significant deterrent role for potential
criminals—much more so than capital punishment.

Levitt has also worked on several research projects with John Donohue
III of the Stanford Law School. The most notorious of these resulted in
a 2001 paper with a provocative conclusion about the link between the
legalization of abortion in the U.S. and falling crime rates. Since the
early 1990s, the U.S. experienced the sharpest drop in crime since Prohibition's end in 1933. Many reasons have been put forward to explain
this drop, including increases in imprisonment, growth in the number
of police, "zero-tolerance" policies, declines in the crack and cocaine
trade, and full employment. "While acknowledging that all of these factors may have also served to dampen crime," Donohue and Levitt offer
another explanation: "The decision to legalize abortion over a quarter-
century ago" (Donohue & Levitt 2001(a), 380]. Three pieces of evidence
underpin the link between abortion and crime reduction: "First, ... a
broad consistency with the timing of legalization of abortion and the
subsequent drop in crime ... Second, ... the five states that legalized
abortion in 1970 saw drops in crime before the other 45 states and the
District of Columbia, which did not allow abortions until the Supreme
Court decision in 1973 ... Third, [we show] that higher rates of abortion
in a state in the 1970s and early 1980s are strongly linked to lower crime
over the period 1985 to 1997" (381,382).

Like Levitt, Casey Mulligan also has a Harvard background; he
earned his B.A. in economics there in 1991. "Xavier Sala-i-Martin had a
major influence on me during my Harvard period. It was Bob Lucas and
Nancy Stokey who convinced me in April 1991 to come to the University
of Chicago to do my graduate work. What makes this place so attractive for me is the fact that economics here is a unified body of theory

and analysis with many applications. The basic ingredients of this approach are price theory, general equilibrium, and optimization," said Mulligan[213]. Mulligan's research is characterized by its wide variety, with topics including preference formation, altruism, economic growth, labor economics, and social security. According to Mulligan, "The University of Chicago offers a truly unique chance to learn from outstanding senior scholars. I try to maximize my learning from them. Inevitably this forces me to shift my research focus regularly"[214].

Mulligan earned a Ph.D. at the University of Chicago in 1993 with a dissertation entitled *Intergenerational Altruism, Fertility, and the Persistence of Economic Status*. The dissertation argued that the degree of altruism is an object of choice and hence can be analyzed using the economist's toolbox. In a very recognizable Beckerian tradition, this approach received some hostile reactions: "When I distributed drafts of my dissertation to major research universities in an effort to obtain a faculty position, I learned that mainstream reactions ranged from outrage and loud disapproval to polite indifference" (Mulligan 1997, xvi). Four years later, his doctoral dissertation resulted in the book *Parental Priorities and Economic Inequality*. This book deals with "a potential source of inequality, the transmission of economic status from one generation to the next" (Mulligan 1997, 1).

Mulligan's book asks why parents behave altruistically toward their children, and what determines the degree of altruism that they show. "I suppose that, for the most part," Mulligan wrote, "parental choices are altruistically motivated. Parents devote some of their resources to children because they want their children to be happy and successful. Parents do not devote all of their resources to their children because their children's success is not their only concern. This concern must be balanced with others, especially the desire of parents to spend on themselves. [This book] examines how parents balance their priorities and shows how the balancing, through its effects on the transfer of resources to children, affects the economic success of children" (2). Mulligan concludes that, "Altruism is a complement with the success of children. A decline in the price of either of those two goods therefore increases the demand for both. A low parental value of time, a determinant of the cost of accumulating altruism, therefore encourages both altruism and consumption by children. Divorce, a low interest rate, or high estate and income tax rates, determinants of the relative price of a child's consumption, also discourage altruism and consumption by children" (333).

With Becker, Mulligan investigated the relationship between efficient taxes and big government. They showed that for a sample of countries, more efficient tax systems—i.e., systems that rely on broad-based taxes with fairly flat rate structures—are associated with bigger government. Becker and Mulligan argued that inefficient taxes can improve the taxpayers' welfare because the political system then creates additional pressure for suppressing the growth of government.[215]

# CHAPTER FIVE

# The Monetary Side of Chicago
## *Quantity Country*

IN HIS DECEMBER 1995 NOBEL LECTURE, ROBERT LUCAS EXPRESSED a belief in the quantity theory of money in its purest form or, to put it as he did for the lecture's title, in the "Neutrality of Money." Money is said to be neutral when changes in the money stock do not affect variables in the real economy (e.g., production and employment) and instead lead only to proportional changes in the price level.

Lucas is one of a long line of economists who believed in the quantity theory of money. John Locke, Richard Cantillon, David Hume, and Per Nicolas Christiernin were early contributors to this work. The 1776 publication of Adam Smith's *An Inquiry into the Nature and Causes of the Wealth of Nations,* which marked the start of economics as a modern science, is another milestone in quantity theory. To a large extent, Hume's synthesis served as the model on which Adam Smith and David Ricardo based their monetary analyses.[216]

The two basic quantity theory equations are the Cambridge equation and the Fisher equation. The Cambridge equation is named for the University of Cambridge, the alma mater of Alfred Marshall and John Maynard Keynes. Marshall (1923) analyzed the demand for money in the same way as the demand for any other commodity; he concluded that the people's demand for money tends to be a constant fraction of nominal income.

Illustrated mathematically, the Cambridge equation is: $M = kPY$.

With real activity (Y) determined outside the monetary sphere in accordance with Say's Law (the claim that supply creates its own demand), Marshall concluded that increases in the money supply (M) feed directly into the price level (P). Irving Fisher's (1911) equation of exchange is MV = PT, with V being the velocity of money and T the volume of transactions.[217] In later versions of the quantity equation, T was often replaced by Y, a measure of real income or production. Fisher also believed that in the long run, changes in the quantity of money are reflected in proportionate increases in the price level. In the short run, however, Fisher thought real effects of monetary changes were possible, and even probable.

Much of 20th-century monetary analysis can be understood in terms of the quantity theory. This rule certainly holds for monetary analysis at the University of Chicago. The major players in this part of the story of Chicago and economics are James Laughlin, Henry Simons, Lloyd Mints, Milton Friedman, Robert Lucas, Lloyd Metzler, Harry Johnson, Robert Mundell, Jacob Frenkel, and Michael Mussa.

## "Certainly Incorrect"

At first, it seemed that the University of Chicago would not offer a fertile breeding ground for the quantity theory. James Laughlin repeatedly claimed that the quantity theory did not conform to the facts. In Laughlin's view (1903, 317), increases in the price level had everything to do with increases in the costs of producing goods, which in turn resulted from the monopolistic practices of trade unions and big companies: "The circulating medium is not a cause of prices: it is only a convenient means of exchanging goods after the price has already been fixed." Laughlin even argued in favor of reversed causality: the demand for money creates its own supply. In 1902, he declared the quantity theory to be "certainly incorrect" (Laughlin 1902, 514), and more than 20 years later, he wrote: "A heavy responsibility rests on the advocates of the quantity theory. By giving academic support to the belief that an increase in money and credit raises prices, they have given support to innumerable fallacious schemes for relieving debtors by issuing more money" (Laughlin 1924, 280). His rejection of the quantity theory diametrically opposed Laughlin to many of his contemporaries, including Francis Walker at MIT, Frank Taussig at Harvard, and certainly Irving Fisher at Yale.

Laughlin's opposition to the quantity theory of money must be seen in its historical context. In the last decades of the 19th century, the United States had experienced price declines and severe debtor problems that led to increasingly forceful calls for a relaxation of the gold standard. A free coinage measure passed by the U.S. Senate in 1892 led to much unrest and, eventually, to the banking panic of May 1893.[218] The controversy over which monetary policy to follow was one of the main issues in the 1896 presidential campaign. Laughlin (1903, 407) was on the hard-money side of this debate: "A rise of prices by a depreciation of the standard would cause a disruption of ordinary industry comparable only with an attempt of a man to pull down his house upon himself and his family."[219]

Laughlin continually encouraged his students to do empirical research. Sara McLean Hardy (1895) investigated the period 1860–1891 and found no evidence to support the quantity theory. H. Parker Willis (1986) concluded that the quantity theory was gradually losing its credibility among economists.

Laughlin's most brilliant student on monetary issues was Wesley Clair Mitchell. Mitchell did his doctoral dissertation work under Laughlin's supervision and received a PhD in 1899. He expanded his dissertation on Civil War inflation into his first book (Mitchell 1903). With respect to the quantity theory, Mitchell (1896, 165) concluded, "… the course of prices in the United States, then, presents a case which cannot be explained by the quantity theory." But he could not agree with Laughlin's basic view of the major reason behind an increase in the price level: "As soon as values of commodities are expressed in terms of money, those values are dependent, not on the demand and supply of money alone, nor on the cost of producing the commodities alone; but upon the combined action of supply and demand for money and the cost of producing the commodities" (Mitchell 1896, 145). In 1903, Mitchell moved to the University of California at Berkeley; a year later, he proclaimed the whole debate on the quantity theory to be futile (Mitchell 1904).

Harold G. Moulton was another important Chicago economist who was working on monetary analysis in the first two decades of the 20th century. Moulton, who was born in LeRoy, Michigan, in 1883, came to the University of Chicago for his graduate studies and earned a PhD in economics in 1914. He later joined the faculty of Chicago's department of political economy. In 1922, he moved to Washington, DC, to become the first director of the Institute of Economics. Under his guidance, the Institute of Economics merged with the Institute for Government Research and the Robert Brookings Graduate School in 1927 to form the Brookings Institution, and Moulton remained as its president until 1952. During his Chicago years, however, Moulton published several books on monetary and banking affairs.[220]

As far as the quantity theory is concerned, he seems to have been close to Mitchell's position: the quantity of money was certainly not the only determinant of the inflation rate. For example, he concluded, "... a mere curtailment in the volume of bank currency will not *necessarily* reduce prices" (Moulton 1920, 157).

## GETTING SIMONIZED

In the late 1920s at the University of Chicago, Henry C. Simons brought the quantity theory of money back to the forefront. George Stigler described Simons as "the Crown Prince of that hypothetical kingdom, the Chicago school of economics" (Stigler 1982b, 166). Herbert Simon acknowledged that it was Simons who, for the first time, "gave me a glimpse of the applications of rigor and mathematics to economics" (Simon 1996, 39). Don Patinkin (1982, 246) described Simons's effect on his students as being "Simonized to some degree or other."

Simons was born in 1899 in Virden, Illinois. He ran away from home when he was 17; nevertheless, he earned a bachelor's degree in economics at the University of Michigan in 1920. The next year, he became one of Frank Knight's leading students at the University of Iowa. From 1923 forward, he began to visit the University of Chicago regularly and finally followed Knight to Chicago in 1927. After a stay in Germany during the first half of 1928, Simons spent the rest of his life in Chicago. According to the official story, he died of a heart attack at the age of 47, but several Chicago sources confirmed that Simons actually committed suicide.

Simons, a protégé of Knight, was the object of a bitter fight between Knight and Douglas. Douglas did not think much of Simons as an intellectual or as a teacher, and he was opposed to the renewal of Simons's appointment in 1932. Douglas complained about Simons's lack of academic output, among other things. By that time, Simons had indeed only published three book reviews, but 40 years later, Stigler (1982b, 167), one of his students, defended him: "The actual facts concerning his industry were different: by 1933, Simons had worked out the main elements of his position in virtually every respect. A famous unpublished memorandum 'Banking and Currency Reform' (of which he was the main author) has the fundamental elements of his monetary theory and hints of much of the remainder and in the *Positive Program for Laissez-Faire* (1934) all the elements are present. The success of this pamphlet presumably ensured his continuance at Chicago although Douglas' last effort to terminate the appointment came in 1935."

Stigler (1982b, 167) describes the major difference between Simons and Knight: "Simons was a strong believer in the possibility of purposive, disinterested reform, with the intellectual playing a great role in such reform, whereas Knight believed that social life was basically non-rational and hence not improvable." That Simons, in the end, did not achieve much with his zeal for reform is explained by a contemporary, Charles O. Hardy (1948, 314): "Simons was a brilliant and logical thinker ... He was, however, an ivory-tower economist; he drew his inspiration from economists, and his influence was chiefly on economists. He was too independent in his thinking and too little regardful of the obstacles to public acceptance of the ideas to make much progress in changing the world."

In 1933, Simons became the first economist to teach at the University of Chicago's law school. However, again in the words of Stigler (1982b, 168), "Simons' primary interest was in macroeconomic policy, not allocative price theory, and the reciprocal relevances of monetary policy to the law and of the law to monetary policy are severely limited." The cross-fertilization between law and economics really got under way under Aaron Director, who succeeded Simons as the economist at the law school in 1947. There is a touch of irony to this; Director initiated the idea that monopoly was much less of a problem for society than was previously thought, and Simons was obsessed with monopoly.

As a macroeconomist, Simons was not unaffected by the monetary upheaval of the 1930s. Stigler identified Simons as the major force behind the famous Chicago Plan on banking and currency reform. Simons's Chicago contemporary Lloyd Mints "credited Simons (for policy proposals) and Knight (for philosophical inspiration) as key architects of the Chicago position" (Peterson and Phillips 1991, 80). The Chicago Plan for banking reform is a document sent to Henry A. Wallace, President Franklin Roosevelt's Secretary of Agriculture, on March 16, 1933, when the country was in the midst of a severe financial crisis.[221] It was signed by eight Chicago economists: Frank Knight, Lloyd Mints, Henry Simons, Henry Schultz, Garfield Cox, Aaron Director, Paul Douglas, and Albert Hart. Although he was in agreement with the economics of the plan for the most part, Jacob Viner did not sign because he thought it was politically impossible to realize. In a note to President Roosevelt, Wallace described the Chicago Plan as "awfully good" (Phillips 1995, 49).

The main elements of the Chicago Plan were twofold: First, there was the demand to separate investment and commercial banking, and second, the plan called for checkable deposits of the commercial banks to be 100 percent covered by reserves. This 100 percent coverage was presented as the alternative to deposit insurance. The Banking Act of 1933 ordered the separation of investment and commercial banking but did not take up the idea of 100 percent reserve coverage. A new Chicago memorandum that emphasized the need to use monetary policy to get the economy growing again was published at the end of 1933. The Chicago economists also pleaded for a more centralized Federal Reserve System. Ronnie Phillips (1995, 64) argued: "... this document was evidently written by Henry Simons."

## A CHICAGO TRADITION

Friedman and Patinkin both identify Simons as "undoubtedly the dominant figure in discussions of monetary and fiscal policy" at Chicago in the 1930s and 1940s (Patinkin 1981, 246) with "Frank Knight and Jacob Viner at one remove" (Friedman 1956, 52). Mints also focused on monetary issues, but his approach was from the banking perspective.[222] George Tavlas (1997, 156) defines the "Chicago core monetary group" as consisting of "Simons, Knight, Viner, and Mints," but Douglas and Director also deserve mention. In 1927, Douglas had already written an analysis of the Great Depression in terms of the quantity theory. Increasing the money supply by financing public works was Douglas's remedy; Director made similar arguments in various publications. More than 40 years later, Rose and Milton Friedman seemed to have changed their minds about the relative importance of Simons and Mints. "Lloyd Mints, though less brilliant and exciting than Viner," wrote Rose Friedman, "served the same function for us in monetary theory that Viner did in price theory ... Like Viner, Mints concentrated on the fundamentals, not on institutional arrangements. He was thorough and meticulous in his presentations and, again, like Viner, assigned us readings ranging over a wide variety of views" (Friedman and Friedman 1998, 38).[223] The Friedmans do not even mention Simons in this context.

Simons's (1934, 24) basic principle of monetary policy was that it should be guided by "an explicit, simple rule or principle" that is "definite, intelligible and inflexible." "To establish," Simons (1934, 24) commented, "as part of a free-enterprise economy, a monetary authority with power to alter vitally and arbitrarily the position of parties to financial contracts, would seem fantastic."[224] Simons (1934, 24) left different options open about what that rule should be, but "two observations may be submitted dogmatically: (1) that the adoption of one among the several definite and unambiguous rules proposed by competent students is more important than the choice among them; (2) that rigid stabilization of exchange rates on other [gold standard] countries is totally inadequate and undesirable as rule of national currency policy." He also saw two basic possibilities with respect to the rule to follow for monetary policy: one is "fixing the quantity (M) or the total turnover (MV)," and the other is "the rule of stabilizing some index of commodity prices" (Simons 1934, 24–25). According to Simons, both possibilities had major weaknesses. On the possibility of following a fixed rule on the quantity of money, he wrote: "The obvious weakness of fixed quantity, as a sole rule of monetary policy, lies in the danger of sharp changes on the velocity side for no monetary system can function effectively or survive politically in the face of extreme alternations of hoarding and dishoarding" (Simons 1936, 5).

Friedman claimed that Simons's one-time rejection of a fixed-quantity rule for the guidance of monetary policy was based on a faulty analysis. According to Friedman (1967a), Simons's fear of large fluctuations in the velocity of money (V) rested to a large extent on a misunderstanding of the causes of the economic and monetary collapse of the 1930s. In fact, Friedman argued (1968, 3), Simons made the same fundamental mistake as Keynes in thinking that the Great Depression occurred despite aggressive expansionary policies by the monetary authorities: "The Great Contraction is tragic testimony to the power of monetary policy—not, as Keynes and so many of his contemporaries believed, evidence of its impotence." Friedman's argument is similar to those developed by Douglas (1927) and Viner (1933b). It also corresponds to the argument posed by a group of Chicago economists in a famous pamphlet on the Great Depression (Viner et al. 1933). One of Friedman's basic points was that velocity was quite stable; therefore, monetary policy could be based on a fixed-growth rule for the quantity of money and not, as Simons had advocated in 1936, on stabilizing the price level. On this issue, Patinkin was right to reject Friedman's claim that his presentation of the quantity theory was uniquely representative of the Chicago monetary tradition.

Patinkin (1981, 245) also claimed that an integral part of the Chicago monetary tradition of the 1930s and 1940s was the thought that "the government has an obligation to undertake a countercyclical policy. The guiding principle of this policy is to change M so as to offset changes in V, and thus generate the full-employment level of aggregate demand MV." As late as 1951, Mints (1951, 191) wrote that "discretionary monetary power ... robs policy of the very thing which is most needed in monetary matters; namely certainty with respect to monetary conditions ... We need not weapons to combat developed booms or depressions but stable monetary conditions maintained in accordance with some one, announced rule of action." Like Mints, Simons (1934, 14) wrote that "we should characterize as insane a governmental policy of alternately expanding rapidly and contracting precipitously the quantity of paper money in circulation—as a malevolent dictator easily could do, first issuing currency to cover fiscal deficits, and then retiring currency from surplus revenues." Viner (1931) and Douglas and Director (1934) also expressed a preference for fixed rules.[225]

In 1969, Patinkin published a paper that criticized Friedman's restatement of the quantity theory.[226] Two years later, Patinkin was joined by Harry Johnson (1971, 11), who indirectly referred to Friedman's version of the Chicago oral tradition as "scholarly chicanery used to promote a revolution or a counterrevolution in economic theory." In an effort to figure out why it took Patinkin and Johnson so long to come out with their critique of Friedman, Robert Leeson (2000, 738) wrote: "The disputants [Patinkin and Johnson] played for higher stakes than the subject matter of their essays might suggest ... From the late 1960s [until their deaths] both were highly agitated about a one-page section in a 1956 essay: this can only adequately be explained by Friedman's increasing influence over the policy, their jealousy, the competition for Nobel Prizes, and their sense of being oppressed by the shadow of Friedman" (Leeson 2000, 738).

## QUANTITY THEORY AND EMPIRICS

The 100 percent reserve requirement central to the Chicago proposals of the 1930s became an integral part of Friedman's own monetary and fiscal framework for economic stability; Friedman's first comprehensive statement of his views on macroeconomic policy, "A Monetary and Fiscal Framework for Economic Stability," was published in 1948. In it, he argued that a fully automatic stabilization policy would have shorter time lags than a discretionary policy.

Friedman further explored this theme in a paper that was first published in the French journal *Economie Appliquée* (July 1951) and then found its way into his *Essays in Positive Economics* (1953) under the title "The Effects of a Full-Employment Policy on Economic Stability: A Formal Analysis." Edmund Phelps (1990, 30) identified this 1951 paper as "the veritable magna carta of Monetarism." According to Phelps, Friedman's paper showed that "a continuously activist policy ... may actually be *destabilizing*" (30).

Neither paper focuses explicitly on the quantity theory of money. Friedman didn't present his version of quantity theory until a few years later. Friedman's (1956, 52) quantity theory was "in the first instance a theory of the demand for money. It is not a theory of output, or of money income, or of the price level." It was self-evident for Friedman, a price theorist, to go back to the Cambridge cash-balance approach, which focused on the demand for money. He positively related money demand to permanent income and negatively related it to the expected interest rate on bonds, the expected rate of return on equity, and expected inflation. Writing this money demand function as f(.) and equilibrating money supply M/P with money demand, one obtains the following equation: M/P = f(.). To bring this latter expression into the Fisher equation MV=PY, one can write V=Y/f(.). Because "the quantity theorist accepts the empirical hypothesis that the demand for money is highly stable," and because output is dependent on real factors, this automatically leads to the conclusion that V too is highly stable, although it need not "be regarded as numerically constant over time" (Friedman 1956, 62). Friedman and his student David Meiselman (1963) argued that his version of the quantity theory was a more powerful instrument of analysis than Keynesian instruments such as the consumption function and autonomous spending.[227]

Friedman's theoretical work on the quantity theory led him to empirically verify the theory. Most of this empirical work was done with Anna Schwartz of the National Bureau of Economic Research. Thirty years after the publication of *A Monetary History of the United States 1867-1960* (Friedman and Schwartz 1963), several re-reviews of this classic were published in the *Journal of Monetary Economics*.[228] In his review, Lucas claimed that " ... if I ever go to Washington for some other reason than viewing cherry blossoms, I will pack my copy of *A Monetary History* and leave the rest of my library—well, most of it— at home." Boston University's Jeffrey Miron recalled the following incident that took place during an MIT graduate course in monetary economics taught by the Keynesian macroeconomist Stanley Fischer: "Midway through the course, Fischer asked the class how we knew that money played an independent causal role in determining the fluctuations in output. The class was, as usual, dumbfounded. It was also shocked to learn that, according to Fischer, the best evidence in support of a causal role for money was that contained in *A Monetary History of the United States, 1867-1960* by Milton Friedman and Anna J. Schwartz" (17).

*A Monetary History* began in 1948, when Arthur Burns, then chairman of the National Bureau of Economic Research, asked Friedman to direct a broad study of monetary factors in the business cycle. Schwartz, who unlike Friedman had a very thorough knowledge of the history of American banking, had joined the staff of the National Bureau in 1941.[229] Moses Abramovitz, a close friend of Friedman's since their graduate days at Columbia, brought the two together.

Friedman and Schwartz's work on the monetary history of the United States developed under a cloud of professional doubt.[230] First, Friedman and Schwartz used simple statistical methods without much of a detailed theoretical model; this led Paul Samuelson (1970, 43) to conclude that *A Monetary History* represents "black box theory."[231] Second, their economic methodology was much more Marshallian (partial equilibrium) than Walrasian (general equilibrium). Third, their main conclusions were completely at odds with the "money doesn't matter" attitude that was typical of the Keynesian approach of the period.[232]

"Of the relationships revealed by our evidence," Friedman and Schwartz concluded in *A Monetary History* (1963), "the closest are between, on the one hand, secular and cyclical movements in the stock of money and, on the other, corresponding movements in money income and prices ... Apparently, the forces determining the long-run rate of growth of real income are largely independent of the long-run rate of growth of the money stock" (678). As far as the stability of the velocity of money was concerned, their conclusion was that "the numerical value of velocity ... changed considerably. However, the change occurred rather steadily ... Velocity has shown a systematic and stable movement about its trend, rising during expansion and falling during contraction" (682). Friedman and Schwartz's *A Monetary History* offered that the roughly one-third reduction in the stock of money was the key element explaining the severity of the Great Depression of the 1930s. The work of MIT's Peter Temin (1976) can be considered typical of the Keynesian counterarguments.[233] Several other economists argued that the monetary and nonmonetary explanations of the Great Depression can be reconciled.[234]

In parallel with his National Bureau of Economic Research work with Anna Schwartz, Friedman started his Workshop in Money and Banking in 1954. Some of the best research presented in this workshop found its way into a book edited by Friedman: *Studies in the Quantity Theory of Money* (1956).

Philip Cagan's contribution to this volume, "The Monetary Dynamics of Hyperinflation," was an instant classic.[235] Cagan received a master's degree in 1951 and a PhD in 1954 from the University of Chicago, where he was an associate professor from 1955 to 1958.[236] For a long time, Cagan remained closely connected to the Friedman-Schwartz project on monetary research, including making several contributions to it.[237]

Martin Bailey, who earned a PhD in economics from Johns Hopkins University in 1956, also worked on the Friedman research project and was a part of Chicago's department of economics until 1965. Bailey published several notable papers on monetary issues.[238]

Miguel Sidrauski, a very promising Argentinian economist who died in 1968 at the age of 28, is another contributor who is also worthy of mention. Sidrauski had earned his PhD at the University of Chicago in 1967 with a dissertation on monetary growth theory.[239]

Twenty years after the publication of *A Monetary History*, Friedman and Schwartz (1982, 5) regarded the results of their further empirical work as a solid confirmation of the quantity theory: "The simplest of quantity theories, which supposes that the ratio of nominal money to nominal income is a numerical constant … turns out to be an impressive first approximation." A decade later, Friedman (1992, 39,48) showed an unshaken belief in the validity of the quantity equation of money: "Fisher's equation [$MV = PT$] plays the same foundation-stone role in monetary theory that Einstein's $E = mc^2$ does in physics … The rate of monetary growth affects primarily prices. What happens to output depends on real factors: the enterprise, ingenuity, and industry of the people; the extent of thrift; the structure of industry and government; the relations among nations."

## LIVING BY THE RULE

Friedman's conviction that a sensible macroeconomic stabilization policy could only focus on one element, a constant money-growth rule, grew out of his theoretical and empirical work on the quantity theory. His first clear statement of this rule is to be found in his "Program for Monetary Stability" (Friedman 1960).[240] In his 1967 presidential address to the AEA, Friedman closely echoed Simons when he stated: "The precise rate of growth, like the precise monetary total, is less important than the adoption of some stated and known rate." Other than the money supply, Friedman claimed, no other variable can be taken as *the* criterion for the conduct of monetary policy: "If, as the authority has often done, it takes interest rates or the current unemployment percentage as the immediate criterion for policy, it will be like a space vehicle that has taken a fix on the wrong star" (Friedman 1968, 14).

Friedman made the case for a constant money-growth rule not only on the basis of economic and monetary analysis but also on constitutional grounds. The constitutional aspect had everything to do with the fact that uninhibited money creation makes it possible for a government to obtain resources from its citizens through an invisible, creeping tax mechanism. In the context of the American constitutional system of limited government, Friedman argued, it is important to take money creation completely out of the realm of daily politics.[241]

His insistence on the money supply as the only sensible criterion for the conduct of monetary policy earned Friedman his reputation as a fanatical monetarist. Leading Keynesians such as Paul Samuelson (1970, 43–44) disagreed vigorously with Friedman: "I knowingly commit that most atrocious of sins in the penal code of the monetarists—I pay a great deal of attention to all dimensions of 'credit conditions' rather than keeping my eye on the solely important variable [money growth] ... Often, I believe, the prudent man or the prudent committee can look ahead six months to a year and with some confidence predict that the economy will be in another than an average or 'ergodic' state. Unless this assertion of mine can be demolished, the case for a fixed growth rate for M, or for confining M to narrow channels around such a rate, melts away."

But is Friedman really the monetary extremist he was and is still often described as? Rudiger Dornbusch and Stanley Fischer, two more Keynesian-oriented former students of Friedman's at Chicago, make the following point:

> Friedman and other monetarists make an important distinction
> between the short- and long-run effects of changes in money. They
> argue that in the long run money is more or less neutral. Changes
> in the money stock, after they have worked their way through the
> economy, have no real effects and only change prices; the quantity

theory and the neutrality of money are, from this long-run perspective, not just theoretical possibilities, but instead a reasonable
description of the way the world works. But in the short run, they
argue, monetary policy and changes in the money stock can and
do have important real effects. (Dornbusch and Fischer 1994, 210)

Harvard's Lawrence Summers, another new Keynesian, argued: "As for
Milton Friedman, he was the devil figure in my youth. Only with time have
I come to have large amounts of grudging respect. And with time, even in-
creasingly, ungrudging respect" (Yergin and Stanislaw 1998, 151).

J. Bradford DeLong of the University of California at Berkeley, takes
the argument one step further. DeLong, who is not exactly a monetarist
either, makes five propositions about the key ideas of the New Keynesian
research program:

1) The frictions that prevent rapid and instantaneous price adjustment to nominal shocks are the key cause of business fluctuations
in employment and output. 2) Under normal circumstances,
monetary policy is a more potent and useful tool for stabilization
than is fiscal policy. 3) Business cycle fluctuations in production
are best analyzed from a starting point that sees them as fluctuations around the sustainable long-run trend (rather than as declines below some level of potential output). 4) The right way to
analyze macroeconomic policy is to consider the implications for
the economy of a policy *rule*, not to analyze each one- or two-year
episode in isolation as requiring a unique and idiosyncratic policy response. 5) Any sound approach to stabilization policy must
recognize the limits of stabilization policy, including the long lags
and low multipliers associated with fiscal policy and the long and
variable lags and uncertain magnitude of the effects of monetary
policy. (DeLong 2000, 84)

DeLong continued:

All five of the planks of the New Keynesian research program
had much of their development inside the 20th-century monetarist tradition, and all are associated with the name of Milton

Friedman. It is hard to find prominent Keynesian analysts in the 1950's, 1960's, or early 1970's who gave these five planks as much prominence in their work as Milton Friedman did in his. For example, the importance of analyzing policy in an explicit, stochastic context and the limits on stabilization policy that result comes from Friedman (Friedman 1953).[242] The importance of thinking, not only about what policy would be best in response to *this* particular shock but also what policy *rule* would be best in general—and would withstand economists' errors in understanding the structure of the economy and policymakers' errors in implementing policy—comes from (Friedman 1960). The proposition that the most policy can aim for is stabilization rather than gap-closing was the principal message from (Friedman 1968). The power of monetary policy is a result of the lines of research developed from (Friedman and Schwartz 1963) and (Friedman and Meiselman 1963). Finally, a large chunk of the way the New Keynesians think about aggregate supply found its origins in Friedman's discussion of the 'missing equation' in (Gordon, 1974). (DeLong 2000, 84)

## LUCAS'S NEW GOSPEL

One of Friedman's most powerful Keynesian challengers was Italian-born Franco Modigliani, who spent most of his academic life at MIT and was awarded the Nobel Prize in economics in 1985. In 1977, Modigliani wrote (1977, 1):

> Milton Friedman was once quoted as saying "we're all Keynesians now" and I'm quite prepared to reciprocate that "we're all monetarists"—if by monetarism is meant assigning to the stock of money a major role in determining output and prices ... The distinguishing feature of the monetarist school and the real issues of disagreement with non-monetarists is not monetarism, but rather the role that should probably be assigned to stabilization policy. Non-monetarists accept what I regard to be the fundamental practical message of the *General Theory*: that a private enterprise economy using an intangible money *needs* to be stabilized, *can* be

stabilized and therefore *should* be stabilized by appropriate monetary and fiscal policies. Monetarists by contrast take the view that there is no serious need to stabilize the economy; that even if there were a need, it could not be done, for stabilization policies would be more likely to increase than to decrease instability.[243]

Those Modigliani described as monetarists would be described as the new classical economists in the jargon of the 1980s and beyond. The generally recognized leader of this group of economists that revolutionized macroeconomics is Robert Lucas, and Thomas Sargent and Robert Barro were two of Lucas's major partners in the development of new classical macroeconomics. Barro spent the years 1972 to 1975 and 1982 to 1984 at the University of Chicago. Sargent is sometimes assigned a role in the development of new classical economics almost as important as that of Lucas, but he rejects this honor, seeing himself, as far as importance for economic theory is concerned, as "a dwarf in relation to Bob."[244] Sargent cannot really be considered a Chicago economist in the sense discussed in this book, however, as his time there was short; he spent one year (1973–74) visiting at the University of Chicago and joined the department of economics in 1994, leaving again in 1998. He spent 17 years (1971 to 1987) at the University of Minnesota, during which time he helped turn the Federal Reserve Bank of Minneapolis into a major stronghold of the new classical approach (P.J. Miller 1994).

Lucas was born in Yakima, Washington, in 1937, one of four children in a family where "politics were always the leading topic of discussion" (Breit and Hirsch 2004, 277). He did his undergraduate studies at the University of Chicago and went to the University of California at Berkeley for his graduate studies in history, but he returned to the University of Chicago while still a graduate student. "I was fascinated by economic history," Lucas explains, "but quickly realized I didn't know enough economics to really grasp the important issues. Several people advised me the best place to learn economics was the University of Chicago."[245] Lucas earned a PhD in economics at the University of Chicago and refers to Friedman, Arnold Harberger (his dissertation supervisor), Zvi Griliches, and H. Gregg Lewis as the faculty members who influenced him most.[246] During the first months of his graduate education, Lucas worked through Samuelson's *Foundation of Economic Analysis* (1947), an experience he later described as "exhilarating." This led him to the position that "mathematical analysis is not one of many ways of doing economic theory: it is the only way. Economic theory *is* mathematical analysis" (Breit and Hirsch, 2004, 279). From 1963 to 1974, he taught at the Carnegie Institute of Technology and at Carnegie-Mellon University; afterward, he returned to his alma mater.

Following the groundbreaking work of John Muth, who was a colleague of Lucas's at Carnegie, the new classical model is based on three essential building blocks.[247] First, it is assumed that the expectations of economic agents are rational and forward-looking.[248] The two other essential building blocks of the model are the assumptions that economic agents behave as utility maximizers and that market forces always work toward equilibrium of supply and demand. Unlike their Keynesian forerunners, new classical economists focused on the supply side of the economy. The Lucas supply function, which dictates that the supply process is driven mainly by price changes, had already been worked out by the end of the 1960s (Lucas and Rapping 1969).[249]

A basic ingredient of this supply function was the so-called intertemporal elasticity of labor supply, which refers to the fact that households work more when wages are high and less when wages are lower. Friedman and his generation of monetarists easily agree with the above characteristics of new classical economics, except for one key element: whereas Lucas and his followers insist that markets clear rapidly, most monetarists argue that if disturbances occur, markets will react slowly most of the time and with variable lags, depending on the circumstances.

The new classical approach led Lucas and Sargent to express strong criticism of Keynesian economics: "That the predictions [of Keynesian economics] were wildly incorrect and that the doctrine on which they were based was fundamentally flawed, are now simple matters of fact, involving no subtleties in economic theory" (Lucas and Sargent, 1994, 6).

However, the Keynesians fought back. Particularly outspoken among them was Robert Solow: "Suppose someone sits down ... and tells me he is Napoleon Bonaparte. The last thing I want to do is to get involved with him in a technical discussion of cavalry tactics at the battle of Austerlitz ... Now Bob Lucas and Tom Sargent like nothing better than to get drawn into technical discussions, because then you have tacitly gone along with their fundamental assumptions; your attention is attracted away from the basic weakness of the whole story. Since I find that fundamental framework ludicrous, I respond by treating it as ludicrous—that is by, laughing at it" (Klamer 1983, 146).

Alan Blinder, another leading Keynesian economist, is at least as acerbic: "Some of the new classical economists are extremely ideological. If you give them evidence, for example, that fully anticipated money matters, evidence counter to their world view, they say that you're wrong" (Klamer 1983, 159). Barro is the most ideological of the new classical economists according to Blinder, who adds: "Sargent is much more serious ... I think Lucas is a blend of those two" (Klamer 1983, 159).

## Sophisticating The Tradition

Lucas saw no contradiction between the new classical approach and the Chicago tradition of basing monetary analysis on the quantity theory: "We tried to rewrite the monetarist analysis with more rigor."[250] Lucas produced two largely empirical papers on the quantity theory. In the first, he concluded that "a given change in the rate of change in the quantity of money induces (i) an equal change in the rate of price inflation; and (ii) an equal change in nominal interest rates" (Lucas 1980, 1005). In the second paper, Lucas builds on the work of Allan Meltzer for the period 1900 to 1957 by creating an estimate of a money demand function for the United States for the period 1957 to 1985. This analysis led to the confirmation of one of Friedman's basic points with respect to the quantity theory: "real money demand is a stable function of permanent income (or wealth)" (Lucas 1988b, 158).

Lucas pushed the quantity theory beyond the point where Friedman had left it. In his Nobel lecture, Lucas referred extensively to Hume, who was one of the first to write systematically about the quantity theory of money.[251] Like Friedman, Hume confirmed the neutrality of money in the long run, recognizing that monetary expansions or contractions can have short-term effects on output and employment. "If everyone understands that prices will ultimately increase in proportion to the increase in money," Lucas asked in his Nobel lecture, "what force stops this from happening right away? Are people committed, perhaps even contractually, to confine to offer goods at the old price for a time? If so, Hume does not mention it. Are sellers ignorant of the fact that money has increased and a general inflation is inevitable? But Hume claims that the real consequences of money changes are 'easy to trace' and 'easily foreseen.' If so, why do these consequences occur at all?" (Persson 1997, 248).

Lucas believed that the fact that these questions had few answers was mostly attributable to the fact that economists formerly did not have the technical-mathematical equipment to work through the dynamics of the adjustment process in a detailed way. He goes on to say:

> Patinkin interprets all of monetary theory from Wicksell's
> *Interest and Prices* (1898) through his own *Money, Interest and*
> *Prices* (1965) as concerned with processes of adjustment between
> one quantity-theoretic equilibrium position and another …
> The passages on dynamics [in] Hume … could be slipped into
> Keynes' *Treatise on Money* (1930) or Hayek's *Monetary Theory*
> *and the Trade Cycle* (1933) without inducing any sense of anach-
> ronism. Yet all of these theorists *want* to think in general equi-
> librium terms, to think of people as maximizing over time, as
> substituting intertemporally. They resort to disequilibrium dy-
> namics only because the analytical equipment available to them
> offers no alternative … The intelligence of these attempts to
> deal theoretically with the real effects of changes in money is
> still impressive to the modern reader but only serves to under-
> score the futility of attempting to talk through hard dynamic
> problems without any of the equipment of modern mathe-
> matical economics. (Persson 1997, 252–53)

General equilibrium macroeconomics is the vehicle that allows modern economists to make up for the deficiencies of the older analyses. Lucas systematically incorporates rational expectations in his general equilibrium models. In a clear methodological break with what his teacher Friedman regarded as valuable economic analysis, much of Lucas's work can be placed in this general equilibrium perspective. Friedman always claimed that partial equilibrium was the more useful tool for economic analysis. Lucas also endorsed the usefulness and the revolutionary character of general equilibrium theory: "This new ability

to incorporate dynamic and probabilistic elements into economic theory ... has already had a deep, permanent influence on virtually every
branch of applied economics. What people refer to as the 'rational expectations revolution' in macroeconomics is mainly the manifestation,
in one field of application, of a development that is affecting *all* fields of
application" (Lucas 1987, 2). Sargent had no doubt: "Bob Lucas has altered the science of economics fundamentally."[252]

Lars Peter Hansen, an important partner in Lucas's attempts to
achieve a more dynamic and probabilistic economic theory, received
a PhD from the University of Minnesota and was at Carnegie-Mellon
(1978–82) before joining the University of Chicago.

General equilibrium research led to major new insights on the concept of money neutrality. In his Nobel lecture, Lucas said:

> The main finding that emerged from the research of the 1970s is
> that anticipated changes in money growth have very different ef-
> fects from unanticipated changes. Anticipated monetary expan-
> sions have inflation tax effects and induce an inflation premium
> on nominal interest rates, but they are not associated with the
> kind of stimulus to employment and production that Hume de-
> scribed. Unanticipated monetary expansions, on the other hand,
> can stimulate production as, symmetrically, unanticipated con-
> tractions can induce depression. The importance
> of this distinction between anticipated and unanticipated mone-
> tary changes is an implication of every one of the many differ-
> ent models, all using rational expectations, that were developed
> during the 1970's to account for short-term trade-offs (Persson
> 1997, 263).

Lucas first worked out this framework in his 1972 seminal contribution to economic theory, "Expectations and the Neutrality of Money".[253]

## Top Modeler

The general equilibrium approach also made Lucas an innovator in the
field of business cycle research. In the 1970s, Lucas published several pa-

pers about a business cycle model that could explain the Phillips curve (that is, the positive relationship between the inflation rate and the level of output). In his basic model, "information conveyed to traders by market prices is inadequate to permit them to distinguish real from monetary disturbances" (Lucas 1972, 121). This analysis leads to the conclusion that unanticipated changes in the growth rate of money will cause economic agents to confuse purely nominal changes in prices with changes in relative prices. Hence, mistakes in production and employment decisions are made.

This approach directly led to what came to be known as the real business cycle theory.[254] The basic claim of this school of thought is that the business cycle is not driven by monetary (or demand) shocks; instead, it is driven by real (or supply) shocks arising from random fluctuations in the rate of technological progress. One of the major policy implications arrived at by theorists exploring the real business cycle was that "efforts at stabilization [of the business cycle] are likely to be counterproductive" (Prescott 1997, 385). Lucas arrived at a similar conclusion in 1977: "Insofar as fluctuations are induced by gratuitous monetary instability, serving no social purpose, then increased monetary stability promises to reduce aggregate, real variability and increase welfare. There is no doubt, however, that *some* real variability would remain even under the smoothest monetary and fiscal policies. There is no *prima facie* case that this residual variability would be better dealt with by centralized, governmental policies than by individual, decentralized responses" (Lucas 1977, 25–26). He is also on the same page as his teacher, Friedman: "Basically, I tend to agree with Milton's proposal that a fixed rule for the growth of the money supply is the least harmful type of policy."[255] As a more general remark, Lucas adds: "I don't like labels but if I really have to have one I still go for monetarist. On basic macroeconomic policy issues I still feel myself most comfortable with people like Milton Friedman and Allan Meltzer."[256]

As far as the phenomenon of the business cycle is concerned, Lucas argued in *Models of Business Cycles* that "the post-war business cycle is just not a very important problem in terms of individual welfare. The gains from removing *all* existing variability from aggregate consumption—even if this could be done with *no* evil side effects (which it could not)—are surely well below 1 percent of national income. Policies that deal with the very real problems of society's less fortunate—wealth redistribution and social insurance—can be designed in total ignorance of the nature of business cycle dynamics ... and the discovery of better business cycle theories will contribute little or nothing to improved design" (Lucas 1987, 105). In late 2002, Lucas further elaborated on these issues in his presidential address to the AEA: "the potential for welfare gains from better long-run supply side policies exceeds *by far* the potential from further improvements in short-run demand management" (Lucas 2003, 1). Lucas's fascination with fundamental, longer-term issues is also evident from his analysis of world income dynamics: "The growth rate of world production per person peaked at around 1970, at something like 3.3%, and can be expected to decline thereafter ... [The inequality of world income] rose at an increasing rate until well into the 20th century, and peaked sometime in the 1970s. It, too, is now declining" (Lucas 2000, 163).

Another significant Lucas contribution is his critique of the theory of economic policy based on large-scale econometric models. One of the fundamental characteristics of these mainly Keynesian-inspired models is that the parameters linking monetary, fiscal, and other policy instruments to policy targets (e.g., inflation and unemployment) are treated as remaining relatively stable over time. Lucas showed that when authorities change their policies, people act in accordance with the rational expectations hypothesis, take these changes into account when making decisions, and otherwise alter their behavior accordingly. The old parameters linking policy to targets are then no longer valid or, as Lucas himself concluded: "Given that the structure of an econometric model consists of optimal decision rules of economic agents and that optimal decision rules vary systematically with changes in the structure of series relevant to the decision maker, it follows that any change in policy will systematically alter the structure of econometric models" (Lucas 1976, 41). A quarter of a century earlier, Friedman criticized large-scale econometric models for not being able to represent complex reality with sufficient accuracy.[257]

By the time Lucas had formulated his critique of econometric policy evaluation,[258] he had already rejected the traditional Phillips curve as a policy tool that offered a trade-off between inflation on the one hand and real output and employment on the other. Lucas rejected the standard explanation of the conventional Phillips curve—that movements in the same direction by output and inflation arise "from relatively stable structural features of the economy, and are thus independent of the nature of the aggregate demand policy pursued. The alternative explanation of the same observed tradeoff is that the positive association of price changes and output arises because suppliers misinterpret general price movements for relative price changes. It follows from this view, first, that changes in average inflation rates will not increase average output, and, secondly, that the higher the *variance* in average prices, the less 'favorable' will be the observed tradeoff" (Lucas 1973, 333). Lucas's analysis followed in the footsteps of Friedman and Edmund Phelps.

On the basis of the research cited above, Lucas also came to conclusions about unemployment diametrically opposed to those of the Keynesians. He rejects Keynes's typical distinction between voluntary and involuntary unemployment:

> The worker who loses a good job in prosperous times does not *volunteer* to be in this situation: he has suffered a capital loss. Similarly, the firm which loses an experienced employee in depressed times suffers an undesired capital loss. Nevertheless the unemployed worker at any time can always find *some* job at once, and a firm can always fill a vacancy instantaneously. That neither typically does so *by choice* is not difficult to understand given the quality of the jobs and the employees which are easiest to find. Thus there is an involuntary element in *all* unemployment, in the sense that no one chooses bad luck over good: there is also a voluntary element in all unemployment, in the sense that however miserable one's current work options, one can always choose to accept them." (Lucas 1978, 354)

## GOING INTERNATIONAL

Lucas, Friedman, Mints, Simons, Laughlin, and the other Chicago economists introduced in this chapter paid only passing attention to the international aspects of monetary theory. This characteristic of the monetary work done at the University of Chicago changed dramatically with the arrival of Harry Johnson and Robert Mundell in the late 1950s and early

1960s. Both men acknowledged that the work of Lloyd Metzler formed a major source of inspiration for their own research.[259]

Metzler, who was born in Lost Springs, Kansas, earned a PhD from Harvard in 1942. He stayed at Harvard until 1946. Afterward, he spent a year at Yale and then succeeded Viner in the field of international trade at the University of Chicago. Metzler was offered the position at Chicago when Samuelson refused to return to his alma mater.[260]

From 1943 to 1944, Metzler served as an economist at the Office of Strategic Services in Washington. From 1944 to 1946, he joined the research staff of the Federal Reserve Board. Up to the time Metzler arrived in Chicago, his main work other than issues of international trade had been in the field of business cycles—specifically, the role of inventory fluctuation in those cycles.[261]

When Lloyd Metzler arrived in 1947, the University of Chicago was in turmoil. Oskar Lange left for Poland, Jacob Viner left for Princeton, and Simeon Leland left for Northwestern. Simons died in 1946, and in that same year, a relatively young T.W. Schultz became chairman of the department of economics and Friedman returned to Chicago. Last but not least, the intellectual culture shock going on between Chicago economists (Knight, Friedman, Allen Wallis, and Director) and the Cowles Commission leaders (Marschak and Koopmans) was gathering steam.

Metzler was thoroughly educated in Harvard's Keynesian tradition. The famous fiscal policy seminar given by Alvin Hansen and John Williams played an important role in Harvard's Keynesian domination: "How to overcome the depression through expansionary fiscal policy offered a startling challenge. Alvin Hansen's Fiscal Policy Seminar was the center of the new economics ... Many of the great names which led the profession in later years, from Paul Samuelson and Lloyd Metzler on, were members of our group and it will indeed be hard to find so ideal an environment for enthusiastic graduate work" (Musgrave 1992, 193).

For Chicago graduate Martin Bronfenbrenner, the appointment of the Keynesian Metzler was proof of the fact that anyone could become a member of the Chicago faculty, given solid scholarship, sufficient research productivity, and good performance as a teacher: "The Chicago teaching staff was never monolithic ... although the same might not always be said of the intellectual leaders among Chicago graduate students.

In the thirties, dissent was concentrated among the labor economists (Paul Douglas, Harry Millis), in the neo-Thomist John Nef and in the socialist Oskar Lange. In the postwar period, it was concentrated in the Cowles Commission (Tjalling Koopmans, Jacob Marschak), in Nef as before and in the Keynesian Lloyd Metzler" (Bronfenbrenner 1962, 73).

By the late 1940s, it was clear that Metzler indeed preferred Keynes to the quantity theory. Metzler showed the same preference regarding the international aspects of monetary theory:

> Contemporary ideas about the way in which an even balance of payments is achieved have always been closely related to prevailing theories of money and prices. In the pre-Keynesian era, when the quantity theory of money was the accepted version, the balancing process was described largely in terms of movements in money and the level of prices. Later, under the influence of Lord Keynes's *General Theory of Employment, Interest, and Money*, these monetary variables were replaced by changes in the circular flow of income or by movements in the level of output and employment. To some extent the *General Theory* reflected a condition of deep depression and widely fluctuating output; it was therefore not applicable to the prosperous conditions which prevail today. Nevertheless, in modifying his concepts of monetary theory to allow for conditions of depression and fluctuating output, Keynes made a contribution to the traditional theory which will have a profound influence on the theory of international adjustment even when full employment prevails. Specifically, he introduced the concept of a monetary rate of interest which altered the foundation upon which the traditional quantity theory of money was based (Bourneuf, Domar, and Samuelson 1973, 209).

Metzler produced several interesting contributions to the theory of international trade. In a 1949 survey of international trade theory, he pointed out that what became known in economics as the Robinson-Metzler condition or Marshall-Lerner condition (the economists involved were Joan Robinson, Lloyd Metzler, Alfred Marshall, and Abba Lerner) of stability in foreign exchange markets really had origins in the work of the British economist C.F Bickerdike (1920). In short, the Bickerdike condition says that for a devaluation to improve the trade balance of a country, the sum of the demand elasticity for exports and the demand elasticity for imports must be greater than unity. The algebraic condition Metzler formulated shows that "even if this sum (of demand elasticities) is smaller than unity, the elasticity of the trade balance may still be positive if the supply elasticities are sufficiently small" (Bourneuf, Domar, and Samuelson 1973, 20).

Another remarkable contribution is the Metzler-Laursen effect (developed with Svend Laursen). Metzler and Laursen argued that a flexible exchange rate did not necessarily insulate a country against foreign shocks to real income, employment, and prices. It is somewhat surprising that Friedman never openly reacted to this amendment to the advantages of flexible exchange rates. The most probable explanation is that the Metzler-Laursen effect empirically proved to be a rather insignificant phenomenon, even though it is a considerable intellectual achievement. Despite a successful surgery for a brain tumor, Metzler's creative output slowed after 1952.

## Canadian Colossi

In 1981, David Warsh introduced the readers of the *Boston Globe* to Harry Johnson and Robert Mundell: "Mundell became a professor there [Chicago], lured by the legendary Harry Johnson. Together, building on Lloyd Metzler's work, Mundell and Johnson trained today's generation of leaders in tools unknown to orthodox Keynesian analysis: the monetary approach to balance of payments problems. [Rudiger] Dornbusch says the fruits of their work—formal models of money creation, deficit finance, external imbalance, monetary interdependence and inflation— became available just in time for their use in the analysis of the collapse of the Bretton Woods international monetary system at the end of the 1960s" (Warsh 1993, 194). In addition to common Canadian roots, they both shared important links with the University of Chicago and brought a distinct international touch to its department of economics.

In 1956–57, Mundell was a postdoctoral fellow at Chicago, and he returned in 1965 for six years. Johnson arrived in Chicago in 1959 and served there full-time until 1966 and part-time until his death in 1977. In a chronological sense, it is more logical to start this exposition with Johnson. Although Johnson put forward the proposition that the core of the development of the monetary approach is to be found in the work of Mundell,[262] it was Johnson who launched this research project.

In 1958, Johnson wrote: "balance-of-payments deficits and difficulties are essentially monetary phenomena" (Johnson 1976c, 51). In the same paper, Johnson made the link with the quantity theory of money: "A balance-of-payments deficit implies *either* dishoarding by residents, *or* credit creation by the monetary authorities—either an increase in V, or the maintenance of M" (51).

Johnson and Mundell's collaboration is comparable to that of T.W. Schultz and Gary Becker; Schultz initiated the research program on human capital, and Becker worked through the issue on a technical level. With respect to the monetary approach to the balance of payments, Schultz's role was played by Johnson, and Becker's by Mundell.

Johnson was very skillful with geometric and mathematical tools in the classroom,[263] but he should be remembered as "a synthesizer and a user of theory to probe 'real world' policy issues ... He did his best to *appear* unoriginal ... He was not a deliberate maximizer of his own reputation" (Corden 1984, 568). Blaug (1985, 101) points to quantitative and qualitative aspects: "Harry Johnson was notorious in his lifetime as a living machine for producing economic literature: during a relatively short career of twenty-seven years, he produced over five hundred academic papers, one hundred and fifty book reviews, thirty-five books and pamphlets, and hundreds of newspaper articles ... Moreover, almost nothing that he wrote was tossed off. On the contrary, the average quality of his output was astonishingly high."

It is impossible to neatly fit Johnson into a traditional category for macroeconomists. Although he began his career as a Keynesian, Johnson soon distanced himself from Keynes's disciples. He considered Keynesian economics to be a special case of neoclassical theory.[264]

On the occasion of the 25th anniversary of the publication of the General Theory, Johnson argued that Keynes "drastically overgeneralized a particularly bad depression" and that his followers "[had turned] a theory in which money is important into the theory that money is unimportant" (Johnson 1961, 13,15). Johnson took a strong stand against "vulgar Keynesians ... ignoring the monetary analysis as an irrelevant complication" (Johnson 1961, 15). Johnson's 1962 review article on monetary theory and policy (Johnson 1962), his review of Friedman and Schwartz's *Monetary History of the United States* (Johnson 1965), and his book on macroeconomics (Johnson 1976b) all underline the importance he attached to the quantity of money.

Johnson will certainly be remembered as the person who initiated the modern monetary approach to the balance of payments, which he immediately connected with the two mainstream approaches to the balance of payments of the time: elasticities and absorption.[265] Both are concerned with the current account, whereas the balance of payments consists not only of this current account but also of the capital account and the "bottom line" (i.e., the change in the international reserve position of the country).

The elasticities approach stresses the importance of changes in relative prices (e.g., brought about by a devaluation) for the current account. Absorption emphasizes the national income accounting-based idea that a current account deficit necessarily implies an excess of expenditures on home and foreign goods (i.e., absorption) over income or production (a surplus implies income or production larger than expenditures).

The monetary approach to the balance of payments relaunched by Johnson starts from the identity $M = D + R$, where M stands for nominal money supply, D for domestic credit, and R for international reserves. The factor M is, of course, the same M that shows up in the quantity theory equations. Because a deficit on the balance of payments (which is the combined result of current and capital accounts) necessarily means a loss of international reserves, it is obvious that this must have a counterpart in either an increase in domestic credit creation or a decrease in the money supply (the "dishoarding of residents" Johnson referred to). Johnson immediately added (1976c, 51): "To conclude that balance of payments problems are essentially monetary is not, of course, to assert that they are attributable to monetary mismanagement—they may be, or they may not be the result of 'real' forces in the face of which the monetary authorities play a passive role" (Johnson 1976c, 51).

Johnson (1976c, 52) then goes on to make a distinction between a balance of payments deficit resulting from stock or flow decisions: a stock decision alters "the composition of the community's assets by substituting other assets for domestic money," but in a flow decision, the deficit results from spending "in excess of current receipts." This distinction is relevant both theoretically and for policy purposes, because "a 'stock' deficit is inherently temporary and implies no real worsening of the country's economic position, whereas a 'flow' deficit is not inherently temporary and may imply a worsening of the country's economic position" (Johnson 1976c, 52). To correct a flow deficit, a country can try two types of policy: "those which aim at (or rely on) increasing output, and those which aim at reducing expenditure" (Johnson 1976c, 55). With this reasoning, Johnson (1976b, 56) falls in line with the absorption approach, as he replaces the distinction between output-increasing and expenditure-reducing policies with the distinction between "expenditure-switching and expenditure-reducing policies" in his further analysis. For the first category of policies, devaluation and trade controls are the main instruments; for the second, "monetary restriction, budgetary policy, or even a sufficiently comprehensive battery of direct controls" (Johnson 1976b, 56) are the main instruments.

## TRADING PLACES

When he was 20 years old, Harry Johnson graduated from the University of Toronto with a degree in political economy. After a short stay at St. Francis Xavier University in Antigonish, Nova Scotia, Johnson began a term of military service that brought him to England; he spent 1944 to 1945 at the University of Cambridge. On his return to North America, Johnson enrolled in the PhD program at Harvard.

In 1948, Dennis H. Robertson offered him a job as an assistant lecturer at Cambridge University. Johnson enthusiastically accepted and returned to Cambridge for eight years. In *The Shadow of Keynes*, which he wrote with his wife, Elizabeth,[266] Johnson painted the University of Cambridge as "a self-satisfied example of the virtually inexorable operation of the 'law of diminishing disciples' in the wake of the genius of John Maynard Keynes" (Johnson and Johnson 1978, 151). In the degeneration into ideology at Cambridge, "the intellectual leadership ... was provided by Joan Robinson, who was supported by continual discussion with Richard Kahn, Piero Sraffa and Nicholas Kaldor" (155). Michael Kalecki, "who had developed a Marxist version of Keynes' theory" (158), was a decisive influence on Robinson. One of their main activities was "making fun of [Dennis] Robertson," one of the last "classical" economists remaining at the University of Cambridge.[267]

Under Robinson's leadership, these economists were, according to the Johnsons, "perverting economics ... for furthering left-wing politics" (Johnson and Johnson 1978, 150). Harry and Elizabeth Johnson summarized post-Keynesian economics at the University of Cambridge, and for the English establishment of that period in general, in five propositions:

> The first ... is that all economics in the main tradition of scientific economics is mere "orthodoxy", and as such is to be despised and turned on its head ... A second proposition is that money cannot possibly matter ... The third ... is that "full employment" is ... to be pursued at any cost ... The fourth proposition ... is that the workers ought to be so grateful for the efforts of their intellectual and political superiors to give them the benefits of full employment that they will refrain from any embarrassingly inflationary demands ... The final proposition ... is that faster economic growth is the panacea for all England's economic and for that matter political problems and that faster growth can be easily achieved by a combination of generally inflationary demand-management policies and politically appealing fiscal gimmickry. (Johnson and Johnson 1978, 222–25)

Johnson's unhappy experience with economics at Cambridge resulted in a near-obsession to reform British graduate studies in economics that would make them scientifically oriented rather than ideologically oriented. His efforts toward this objective at Cambridge and the University of Manchester, to which he moved in 1956, failed. He also failed to accomplish these goals in 1966 at LSE, where he was a visiting professor. Deeply disappointed, he left Great Britain and the LSE in 1974.

In his resignation letter, which was published in *The Times* and the cause of much public debate, Johnson argued that he had no choice but to leave because by that time, the prospects had become bleak "in terms both of the development of graduate work and of the economic position and rewards of the academic career in Britain."[268] Despite an intellectual climate that he thoroughly disliked, his years in Cambridge and Manchester were immensely productive. A series of his often pioneering articles on international trade were collected in *International Trade and Economic Growth*, which earned Johnson a PhD from Harvard in 1958.

In 1959, Johnson left England for the University of Chicago. There, he found a community of economists committed to serious teaching and research activity that was unthinkable in the country he'd left behind. Even compared to Harvard and Yale, the American universities he knew best, Johnson considered the University of Chicago to be the ideal environment for someone focused on the advancement of economic analysis. One of the things that pleased Johnson most about economics at the University of Chicago was the ever-present push to back up theory with empirical evidence (Tobin 1978). Chicago remained Johnson's home base until his death, but he did lecture at the Graduate Institute for International Studies in Geneva in 1976 and 1977.

According to James Tobin (1978), Johnson's already extraordinary pace of writing accelerated during his period at the University of Chicago. In the same work, Tobin referred to difficulties that resulted from Johnson's disagreement with Friedman's analyses and propositions.[269] On different occasions, Johnson was very critical of the monetarist policy agenda, but at other times, he was just as critical of Keynesian propositions.[270] Johnson had a constant urge to be contrarian in the hope of stimulating scientific discussion. In this respect, he was more of a monetarist outside Chicago and more of a Keynesian in Chicago.[271]

It would have been rather surprising if two great economists like Friedman and Johnson had not disagreed on certain issues, and it is quite obvious that these difficulties never drove Johnson to consider leaving Chicago. The differences must have been enormously stimulating because, as Tobin remarked, Johnson was never as productive as he was in his Chicago years. Nevertheless, when Friedman received the Nobel Prize in 1976, Johnson praised the laureate's many accomplishments but also complained that Friedman "has frequently trapped and sandbagged critics of reputation and integrity by the technique of under-disclosure of analysis and evidence and apparent overstatements of the strength of his results" (Johnson 1976b, 95).

Jagdish Bhagwati offers the following insight about the relationship between the two economists: "If you are pragmatic and argue with an ideologue as bright as yourself, you will win some and lose some. Every time you lose, you will change your views because you are pragmatic. But every time the ideologue loses, he is shielded from perceiving this and will hold on to his assertions. Over time, therefore, you will move closer to the ideologue. Harry, the pragmatic scientist, who appeared to us to be mildly centrist during his years at Cambridge, moved increasingly closer therefore to a Friedmanesque worldview: this was inevitable" (Bhagwati 1982, 9). Bhagwati's argument seems flawed, however; if Bhagwati is correct, Johnson would have moved gradually to the position of the Keynesian "ideologues" during his years at Cambridge. That did not happen.

## Free Marketeer

There can be little doubt that during his years at the Chicago, Johnson became a convinced free marketeer who was very critical of government intervention. Johnson's article celebrating the 200th anniversary of the publication of Adam Smith's *Wealth of Nations* is an excellent illustration:

> In espousing competition as the best policy, Smith was building on extensive observation of the incompetence of governments, and of the moral unreliability of man. It is true, and relevant, that he suffered from no idealistic view of the competence and wisdom of private individuals pursuing their own self-interests; but it is not I think true, as some would have us believe, that it was only the governments of his own day that he distrusted, and that if reincarnated he would have given his approval to, or at least not withheld his approval from, the welfare state and governmental control by the meritocracy.[272]

His growing criticism of government intervention resulted from his research in the field of international economics—Johnson's first area of research as an academic economist. In one of his best-known papers, he wrote, "... when a country is following a protective policy, improved efficiency in the protected industry will actually reduce the country's real income" (Johnson 1967a, 152). With these remarks, Johnson became one of the originators of the concept of immiserizing growth.

He also reached an interesting conclusion on protectionism: "It is an interesting reflection on policy that protectionists usually demand increased protection when comparative advantage shifts against the protected industries, in effect claiming that part of the increased productive potential inherent in such a shift should be spent on the increased support of these industries" (Johnson 1967a, 153). By the early 1970s, Johnson concluded that "the proposition that freedom of [international] trade is on the whole economically more beneficial than protection, is one of the most fundamental propositions economic theory has to offer for the guidance of economic policy" (Johnson 1971, 187).

In 1967, Johnson published *Economic Policies Toward Less Developed Countries*, in which he analyzed methods of stimulating economic development in Third World countries. Johnson concluded that the Prebisch doctrine could not work.

The Argentinian economist Raul Prebisch, who dominated the Economic Commission for Latin America, also strongly influenced the prevailing ideas about development issues in the 1960s and 1970s. Prebisch's doctrine had two essential arguments. He believed that long-run price development of primary products versus finished products works unavoidably against developing countries, and that import substitution, with infant-industry protection as a corollary, is the only possible path to development (Prebisch 1959). Tight national government planning of the economy was needed to achieve these objectives. The Prebisch doctrine delivered the blueprint for decades of development policy, and Johnson (1967b) was among the very first to argue that it was destined to fail.

A year and a half before his death, Johnson delivered a speech at a conference on developing countries held at the University of Chicago. This speech contains a good summary of his perspective toward the end of his life:

Growth and development are primarily a matter of intranational rather than international relationships and change ... One is necessarily led to wonder about the essentially mythical view that international trade and also investment, as practiced over the past two centuries or so, have worked to prevent or inhibit the development of the new nations ... One suspects that the habit of laying the blame for lack of development, and current poverty, on the system of competitive international trade is a form of role transference that serves the useful political purpose in the new nation of exculpating the past and present cultures from responsibility for lack of development, and permitting the politically mythological possibility of achieving development by political effort not requiring fundamental social change (Johnson, 75, 7).

## SENIOR AT THIRTY

Robert Mundell was born on October 24, 1932 in Kingston, a town in the Canadian province of Ontario, and received a bachelor's degree in economics and Slavonic studies from the University of British Columbia in 1953. Less than three years later, he earned his doctoral degree at MIT, and there Charles Kindleberger introduced him to the world of international economics. In a way that suggests some degree of restlessness, Mundell moved on from one institution to another: LSE, University of Chicago, University of British Columbia, Stanford University, Johns Hopkins University in Bologna, the IMF (where he became senior economist before the age of 30), George Washington University, Georgetown University, McGill University, the Brookings Institution, and the Geneva Graduate Institute of International Studies.

By the time Johnson brought Mundell back to the University of Chicago in 1965, Mundell had published a collection of papers that had firmly established him as a leading scholar in the field of international macroeconomics.[273] British economist James Meade, who shared the 1977 Nobel Prize in economics, had sowed the seeds of this branch of economics with his book *The Balance of Payments* (1951). Regarding Meade's contribution, Jurg Niehans remarked: "Though full of excellent economics, the book is virtually unreadable. It was left for Robert Mundell to provide for the turgid prose of his former teacher the same service Hicks had provided for the glittering prose of Keynes, namely a translation into an elegant and manageable model" (Niehans 1990, 342). The "service" John Hicks had provided for John Maynard Keynes was developing the famous IS-LM diagram that became the workhorse of Keynesian economics (Hicks 1937); the "elegant and manageable model" Niehans refers to is the Mundell-Fleming model.

In 1962, a paper by Mundell and another by Marcus Fleming appeared in the same issue of the IMF's Staff Papers.[274] At that time, both Mundell and Fleming were working for the IMF's research department. They essentially opened up the closed-economy macromodels by introducing such phenomena as capital mobility, flexible versus fixed exchange rates, and balance of payments crises. The major policy conclusion of the Mundell-Fleming model was that under flexible exchange rates, monetary policy is a very powerful policy instrument and fiscal policy is powerless. Under a regime of fixed exchange rates, the power of these two types of policy instruments is completely reversed.

The mechanics of the Mundell-Fleming model were euphorically received by the Keynesian macroeconomists. The model reinforced their conclusion that, through the appropriate choice of policy instruments, authorities could steer the economy and the level of income, production, and employment. As was obvious from the mid-1970s forward, this conclusion was wrong—essentially because the Mundell-Fleming model, like any other model, is based on a number of assumptions. The world—and especially the field of economics—forged ahead and largely forgot about those assumptions. Again and again, Mundell warned that his models required careful interpretation; two of the basic assumptions of the Mundell-Fleming model are constant prices and almost perfect capital mobility. Furthermore, Mundell warned, "… it should be apparent that the analysis is short-run in character and this neglects long-run consideration of changes in the capital stock and the level of indebtedness" (Mundell 1968a, 271).

Mundell became increasingly unhappy with how his basic model of international macroeconomics and its numerous derivations came to be misused by fellow economists and policymakers.[275] Thus, in 1968, Mundell published *Man and Economics,* a treatment of subjects radically different from those he had focused on before. In this book, Mundell is revealed to be a true Chicago-style economist: "Economics seems to apply to every nook and cranny of human experience. It is an aspect of conscious action. Whenever decisions are made, the law of economy is called into play. Whenever alternatives exist, life takes on an economic aspect. It has always been so. But how can it be? It can be because economics is more than just the most developed of the sciences of control. It is a way of looking at things, an ordering principle, a complete part of everything" (Mundell 1968b, preface). On the topics of incentives, human behavior, and a critical assessment of the policies concerned, he remarked: "It is one thing for society to arrange to help out the crippled, the handicapped, and the deprived who have suffered from ill luck, misfortune, or great initial handicaps. It is quite another thing to create in healthy individuals the expectation that the government has the responsibility to compensate them for personal actions that have actually turned out bad" (Mundell 1968b, 193). Mundell's book clearly relates to the work of Stigler and Becker, among others.

The story of Mundell and his Chicago-related publications on international macroeconomic affairs must include a mention of his seminal contribution on the theory of optimal currency areas, "A Theory of Optimal Currency Areas" (Mundell 1968a). In it, Mundell discusses the cost (in terms of unemployment and inflation) of being in the currency area when it is hit by an external shock. Mundell concluded that the higher the degree of internal factor mobility, the smaller this cost would be.

Ten years later, Fleming (1971), Mundell's former partner at the IMF, stressed that it is important to make a distinction between labor and capital mobility. It is interesting to note that Meade (1957) had earlier published a paper that pointed to factor mobility as an important element in making a common currency area economically efficient. To Meade, a central fiscal authority with extensive redistributive powers is essential for an optimal currency area.

At the time of this writing, the Economic and Monetary Union in Europe is characterized by neither a high degree of labor mobility nor the existence of a powerful central fiscal authority. Therefore, one would think, Mundell would not be found among the strong supporters of the Economic and Monetary Union. However, this is not the case; on several occasions, Mundell wrote favorably about the single European currency. In two important but largely unnoticed papers published in 1973,[276] Mundell showed that a common currency leads to reserve pooling and portfolio diversification, which in turn leads to a better spread of the effects of an asymmetric shock.

## ANOTHER WATERLOO

The marriage between Mundell and the University of Chicago began to sour by the end of the 1960s. Two major factors played a role in the eventual divorce. First, as documented by David Warsh, Mundell started to neglect his teaching, scholarly, and professional obligations more and more: "Elected a fellow of the Econometric Society, he neglected to open the envelope that contained the news. As president of the hemispherical economic society, he failed to show up to deliver his presidential address. A stormy, imperious man, his stint as editor at the *Journal of Political Economy* nearly ruined that prestigious journal" (Warsh 1993, 195).

Mundell's economic work continued to be extraordinary, despite what struck some who knew him at the time as a turbulent demeanor. Arthur Laffer, one of Mundell's students at the University of Chicago, illustrated this point strikingly:

> I remember my first encounter with him, at a University of
> Chicago workshop. It was winter 1967 ... To me, the university
> workshop looked like a set from "The Addams Family"—a stark,
> dimly lit room, sparsely furnished with dusty oak table and chairs,
> soot-covered windows and a clanging steam radiator. In walked
> a sallow, tousle-headed, pipe-smoking figure wearing a faded
> trenchcoat belted with a clothesline cord. Bob Mundell's odd ap-
> pearance was exacerbated by his painfully slurred speech. After
> the workshop we went to the Quad Club for martinis, where-
> upon his speech went from bad to worse. But however slurred the
> delivery, his economics had never been sharper or more lucid."[277]

The second problem had to do with Mundell's approach to econom-ics. Although empirical verification is an integral part of what makes up the Chicago Tradition, Mundell was much more interested in pure economic theory than in empirical work, and this attitude brought him increasingly into conflict with other members of the department of economics. A reference to this situation is found in the preface to *The Monetary Approach to the Balance of Payments*:

> In 1971, Mundell left the University of Chicago for the University of Waterloo, leaving behind him a group of graduate students working on the pure monetary theory of the balance of payments, whose supervision through the final stages fell to Johnson. Johnson was convinced, partly on the basis of encounters in policy debates with policy makers stubbornly committed to the elasticity approach to balance of payments policy prescription and analysis, that continued concentration on the refinement and elaboration of the pure theory would yield rapidly diminishing returns in terms of theoretical insight, and that to challenge the theories accepted in policy-making circles—mostly based on a crude elasticity analysis if not an even more unsophisticated purely arithmetical exercise—the theory would have to be backed up by solidly based empirical evidence. This emphasis fitted the "Chicago" approach to economics. (Frenkel and Johnson 1976, 11,12)

In the year he left Chicago, Mundell wrote a paper in which he proposed fighting stagflation with an unusual policy recommendation: "The correct policy mix is based on *fiscal ease* to get more production out of the economy and *monetary restraint* to stop inflation" (Mundell 1971b, 24). Ten years later, this paper earned him an amusing nickname: "the odd genius behind 'supply-side' economics" (Warsh 1993, 192). As to fiscal easing, Mundell argued that "tax reduction is the appropriate method" (Mundell 1971b, 25). It is not a coincidence that Mundell prepared this paper while Laffer was also at the University of Chicago, as Laffer later became a major adviser in the Reagan administration. Then-Federal Reserve Board Chairman Paul Volcker saw to it that tight money, combined with huge tax cuts, was the hallmark of the first term of the Reagan presidency.

From the University of Waterloo, Mundell moved on to Columbia

University in 1974. His creative research output slumped and he began to spend more and more of his time in the Italian region of Tuscany. Nevertheless, Mundell received the Nobel Prize in economics in 1999. In its justification of Mundell's award, the Royal Swedish Academy of Sciences noted: "Robert Mundell has established the foundation for the theory that still dominates in practical considerations of monetary and fiscal policy in open economies ... Although dating back several decades, Mundell's contributions remain outstanding and constitute the core of teaching in international macroeconomics ... Mundell's contributions serve as an excellent illustration of the value of basic research. At a given point in time, academic achievements may seem rather esoteric; not long afterward, however, they make take on great practical importance."[278] Mundell received the Nobel Prize work dating from the 1960s. Therefore, it is clear that Mundell's win constitutes another clear win for the University of Chicago. Or, in the words of the Royal Swedish Academy of Sciences: "Robert Mundell's most important contributions were made in the 1960s. During the latter half of this decade, Mundell was among the intellectual leaders in the creative research environment at the University of Chicago."[279]

## CLOSE COMPANIONS

During the second half of the 1960s, three of Harry Johnson and Robert Mundell's students began their careers as international macroeconomists: Rudiger Dornbusch, Jacob Frenkel, and Michael Mussa. Dornbusch earned his PhD at the University of Chicago in 1971, taught for two years at the University of Rochester, returned to Chicago's GSB for one year, and then went on to MIT's department of economics.[280] Frenkel and Mussa spent more time in Chicago than Dornbusch, and the parallels between their careers have some symmetry.[281]

Jacob Frenkel was born in Israel in 1943. He received a bachelor's degree in economics and political science from Hebrew University in 1966 and then moved to the University of Chicago, where he earned a master's degree in economics in 1969 and a PhD in 1970. Between 1973 and 1979, Frenkel rose from assistant professor to full professor at the Chicago's department of economics. From 1982 forward, Frenkel was the David Rockefeller Professor of International Economics.

Mussa was born in Los Angeles in 1944 and earned a bachelor's degree in economics and mathematics at UCLA in 1966. He then moved to the University of Chicago, where he received a master's degree in economics in 1970 and a PhD four years later. Afterward, he taught at the University of Rochester from 1971 to 1975. In 1976, Mussa returned to Chicago as an associate professor of economics at the GSB, and four years later, he became the William H. Abbott Professor of International Business at the GSB.

In 1987, Frenkel became economic counselor and director of research at the International Monetary Fund. Mussa took a leave of absence from 1986 to 1988 to join President Reagan's Council of Economic Advisers. In 1991, Frenkel was asked to become governor of the central bank of his homeland, Israel, which was plagued by high inflation.

At the end of 1999, Frenkel became vice-chairman of Merrill Lynch International. Frenkel's position at the International Monetary Fund (IMF) was taken over by Michael Mussa, who left the IMF at the end of 2001. Frenkel and Mussa became involved in the policymaking process, which was not surprising considering their research and writings. Although they respected high academic standards, their work was always related to topics that were close to the agenda of economic policymakers.[282]

Frenkel and Mussa's most important contributions are in the fields of analysis of the balance of payments and exchange rate determination. The development of the monetary approach to the balance of payments[283] and of the Mundell-Fleming model for analysis of the open economy dominated the environment in which Frenkel and Mussa received their graduate education and started their careers as young economists. This Mundell-Fleming model had several limitations, including the fact that it did not contain a coherent theory of exchange rate determination. Frenkel and Mussa played a major role in developing the monetary approach to the exchange rate.[284]

The monetary approach to the exchange rate, which became part of the broader asset-market approach to the exchange rate, emphasizes the exchange rate as the adjustment mechanism that equilibrates domestic and foreign markets for money rather than the exchange rate as the price that clears international flows of goods and services. Models that use the monetary approach to the exchange rate include supply and demand equations that describe domestic and foreign money-market equilibrium and impose continuous purchasing power parity. This purchasing power parity condition implies that the exchange rate between two currencies equalizes price levels in the currencies' countries. Frenkel found strong evidence that purchasing power parity held during the 1920s (1978) but collapsed in the 1970s (1981). Moreover, expectations were introduced explicitly in the models (Mussa 1982). Much of Mussa and Frenkel's work contributed to upgrading the Mundell-Fleming model into a useful tool for macroanalysis of the open economy (Frenkel and Razin 1987).

Frenkel and Mussa became staunch defenders of a regime of floating exchange rates; to do so, they teamed up with the proponents of a major element of Chicago economics (i.e., the efficiency of markets that are allowed to operate without government intervention). This efficient-market hypothesis became strongly identified with such Chicago scholars as Harry Roberts, Eugene Fama, and Merton Miller.

Frenkel and Mussa's defense of the floating-rate approach was based on several arguments. They established that the claim that free-floating exchange rates are excessively turbulent was not applicable in the 1970s: exchange rates fluctuated less than the prices of other assets, such as common stocks, interest rates, gold, and other commodities. Their conclusion about government actions to reduce exchange-rate turbulence were similar to Friedman's fixed money growth rule: "government policy can make a positive contribution to reducing costly and unnecessary turbulence of foreign exchange rates … by reducing high and variable rates of monetary expansion which, for example, result from misguided attempts to stabilize nominal interest rates" (Frenkel and Mussa 1980, 379).

Another of their arguments in favor of floating exchange rates is that exchange-rate overshooting is hard to empirically substantiate and must be carefully interpreted if and when it occurs. Most importantly, Frenkel and Mussa claimed that floating exchange rates contribute to the efficient functioning of the economic system: "Changes in real economic conditions requiring adjustments in the *relative* prices of different national outputs occur continuously. Under the system of pegged rates, relative price adjustments are achieved through the slow changes of national price levels and through occasional changes of parity. Under the floating rates, adjustments in the relative price of different national

outputs occur rapidly and in anticipation of changes in economic conditions rather than after the need for adjustment has become apparent."
(Frenkel and Mussa 1980, 378).

When Frenkel and Mussa departed in quick succession, Chicago lost
its two major international macroeconomists. Several attempts to attract
other leading people in the field failed, and international macroeconomics was left to the GSB economists.[285]

# CHAPTER SIX

# The Power of Markets

## *The Case for Limited Government*

THE BASIC MESSAGE OF PIONEERING ECONOMISTS ADAM SMITH and Alfred Marshall was simple: under certain conditions, an economic system based on free competition will create an optimal allocation of the scarce resources that society has at its disposal to satisfy citizens' wants. But what if those "certain conditions" do not hold?

Arthur Pigou, Marshall's successor to the chair of political economy at the University of Cambridge, initiated research on market failures (i.e., situations in which market forces, if left alone, lead to suboptimal allocations). Market failures tend to arise when private and social (marginal) costs and benefits are not equal. This divergence gives rise to what is described in the economist's jargon as externalities, which are costs and benefits that accrue to society but not to those who cause them. In his landmark book *The Economics of Welfare,* Pigou concluded that the free-market mechanism leads to suboptimal outcomes for such phenomena as pollution, information, invention, and congestion.

Particularly after World War II, the desire to cure externalities and the fear of monopoly (that other manifestation of market failure) became driving forces behind the expansion of the role of government in economic matters. The case for this more intense government intervention was mostly unchallenged until the 1960s. Just as Chicago economists like Milton Friedman and Robert Lucas had played a decisive role in the demise of Keynesian macroeconomics, another group of Chicago

economists fundamentally questioned the role of government intervention in the economy. The University of Chicago largely shaped the economics of regulation and deregulation. Frank Knight, who pointed out a
major shortcoming in Pigou's analysis of externalities in 1924, and Aaron
Director, who revolutionized thinking on monopoly, pioneered this
work; George Stigler and Ronald Coase were the two most prominent
thinkers who built on their efforts. Later, Lester Telser, Yale Brozen, Sam
Peltzman, Reuben Kessel, and Gary Becker continued the work.[286]

A belief in the power of markets and the related case for limited government are standard components of economics at the University of Chicago.
Although it may be hard to imagine at the start of the 21st century, this has
not always been true. During the 1930s and 1940s in particular, the idea
government had a decisive role to play in the fight against monopolistic
tendencies in the economy was a strongly held belief at the University of
Chicago. No one personifies this deep-seated fear of monopoly better than
Henry Simons, one of the leading Chicago scholars on monetary issues.

## RED HENRY

Simons's best-known publication is 1934's *A Positive Program for Laissez
Faire*. In the introduction, Simons (1934, 1) describes his essay as "frankly a
propagandist tract—a defense of traditional liberalism." Simons reached
his main conclusions just a few paragraphs into the first chapter: "The
great enemy of democracy is monopoly, in all its forms: gigantic corporations, trade associations and other agencies for price control, trade
unions or, in general, organization and concentration of power within
functional classes ... The petty warfare of competition within groups can
be kept on such a level that it protects and actually promotes the general
welfare. The warfare among organized economic groups, on the other
hand, is unlikely to be more controllable or less destructive than warfare
among nations" (4,5).

Simons would generally be classified ideologically as right wing and
conservative, but many of his proposals are left wing by the standards of
the early 21st century. Simons (1934) wrote that "public regulation of private monopoly would seem to be, at best, an anomalous arrangement,
tolerable only as a temporary expedient ... The state should face the ne-

cessity of actually taking over, owning and managing directly, both the railroads and utilities, and all other industries in which it is impossible to maintain effectively competitive conditions" (11–12).

Simons's opinion of what should be done with big companies was equally drastic: "Few of our gigantic corporations can be defended on the ground that their present size is necessary to reasonably full exploitation of production economies; their existence is to be explained in terms of opportunities for promoting profits, personal ambitions of industrial and financial 'Napoleons,' and advantages of monopoly power" (20,21). This analysis led Simons to recommend policies such as dismantling gigantic corporations, prohibiting horizontal combinations, limiting the amount of property a corporation can own, prohibiting people from serving as an officer in more than one corporation in the same line of business, prohibiting officers in an investment corporation from serving as an officer in an operating company, and making the Federal Trade Commission the most powerful government agency (19–20).

Simons was at least as critical of organized labor as he was of big companies. "The main device of trade-union strategy is the maintenance of the standard rate of pay through collective bargaining," Simons wrote in his *Pamphlet* (1934, 9); he continued his argument by saying: "… the raising of rates of wages in a particular field above the competitive level, by whatever methods of coercion, serves to diminish the volume of employment available within that field—including economy of such labor by substitution (of machinery and other labor) and relative contraction of the industries requiring such labor."

Over the next ten years, Simons developed his position on organized labor—as a matter of fact, his reflections on syndicalism had been on the shelf for three years. He begins his paper by explaining why it took so long to be published: "Questioning the virtues of the organized labor movement is like attacking religion, monogamy, motherhood or the home … Discussion of the sceptical views runs almost entirely in terms of how one came by such persuasions, as though they were symptoms of some disease" (Simons 1944, 1). Simons described unions as little more than specialized interest groups and concluded that "large and powerful unions are integral elements in a total institutional complex whose development is everywhere antithetical to economic freedom, to political liberty, and to world peace" (Simons 1944, 3). Simons's focus on liberty and freedom also made him an outspoken critic of both the welfare state discussed in the Beveridge Report and the Keynesian doctrine of macro-economic stabilization policy that came to the United States primarily through the work of Harvard's Alvin Hansen (1942, 1945).

Simons argued against any form of indirect taxation, such as sales tax. To reduce income inequality, which was something he regarded as "immensely important" (Simons 1934, 26), he argued strongly in favor of a broadly based, progressive income tax that could be installed "without much loss of efficiency in the system and without much impairing the attractiveness of the economic game" (26). A few years later, Simons repeated his call for the introduction of a progressive income tax regime (Simons 1938). He pleaded in favor of several remarkable tax measures: "Elimination of all special treatment for capital gains ... Levy upon estates under the income tax with respect to all unrealized appreciation of investment assets ... Treatment of all inheritances, bequests and (large) gifts inter vivos as personal income of the recipient for the year in which received" (Simons 1934, 27–28). At the end of his exposé on taxation, Simons remarks, almost as an aside, that "these proposals look toward arrangements whereby something like 10% of the whole national income would pass via personal income-taxation, into the hands of government" (29).

Simons also reached what today would be called a strongly un-Chicagoan conclusion about advertising: "The possibility of profitably utilizing resources to manipulate demand is, perhaps, the greatest source of diseconomy under the existing system. If present tendencies continue, we may soon reach a situation where most of our resources are utilized in persuading people to buy one thing rather than another and only a minor fraction actually employed in creating things to be bought" (Simons 1934, 32). Hence, Simons made a plea for heavy taxation on advertising: "There are interesting possibilities in progressive taxes on manufacturers and jobbers according to the percentage of selling expenses to total expenses" (34). Simons preached about the dangers of advertising at the University of Chicago, but a quarter of a century later, the exact opposite position—advocating the information advertising provides and the effects of this information on the organization and efficiency of markets—was initiated at Chicago.

To put Simons's views in perspective, consider Friedman's 1983 comments from *A Positive Program for Laissez Faire*:

> I've gone back and reread the *Positive Program* and been astounded at what I read. To think that I thought at the time that it was strongly pro free market in its orientation! Remember probably in 1934 when it appeared, I would say that close to a majority of the social scientists and the students in the social sciences at the University of Chicago were either members of the Communist party or very close to it. That was the environment in which Frank Knight gave a series of lectures under the title, 'The Case for Communism: From the Standpoint of an Ex-Liberal.' It was an environment in which the general intellectual atmosphere was strongly pro socialist. It was strongly in favor of government going all the way to take over the whole economy. Relative to that kind of atmosphere, the pamphlet created a stir because it was wildly interpreted as being, if you want, reactionary, strongly in favor of a lesser role for government than a greater role for government. (Kitch 1983a, 178,179)

## FROM HERESY TO PROPHECY

In 1960, after he succeeded Simons as the economist at Chicago's law school, Aaron Director organized a seminar at his home. In his memoir, Stigler characterized the magic of that meeting as follows: "Scientific discoveries are usually the product of dozens upon dozens of tentative explorations, with almost as many blind alleys followed too long. The rare idea that grows into a hypothesis, even more rarely overcomes the difficulties and contradictions it soon encounters. An Archimedes who suddenly has a marvelous idea and shouts 'Eureka!' is the hero of the rarest of events. I have spent all my professional life in the company of first-class scholars but only once have I encountered something like the sudden Archimedean revelation—as an observer" (Stigler 1988b, 73).

Englishman Ronald H. Coase was the man who created the "eureka" feeling Stigler enthusiastically described. Coase made his point about the Pigouvian analysis of externalities before 20 Chicago economists at

Director's home. Every Chicago economist present at the meeting initially rejected a specific part of Coase's analysis, as they were already familiar with it because it was part of research he had published on the allocation of radio and television frequencies by the Federal Communications Commission (Coase 1959). According to Stigler (1988a, 76), intellectual history was written that evening in Director's home: "Milton Friedman did most of the talking, as usual. He also did much of the thinking, as usual. In the course of two hours' argument, the vote went from twenty against and one for Coase to twenty-one for Coase. What an exhilarating event! I lamented afterward that we had not had the clairvoyance to tape it." It is interesting to note that Friedman disagreed with Stigler on this issue: "It was very important for Ronald Coase and the rest of his career as an economist. However, I would very much hesitate to state that the Coase Theorem really changed the basic approach toward economic analysis and research in Chicago. Of course, a lot of subsequent research was inspired by it but with respect to my own work I cannot think of one single piece of analysis that would have been substantially different if that evening in Aaron's home hadn't take place."[287]

Coase was 50 years old when he managed to convince the Chicago economists about his theory. He was born in 1910 in Willesden, near London, and suffered serious problems with his legs during his youth; this physical handicap intensified his interest in reading and intellectual exercise.

Coase entered the LSE in 1929. During his student days at the LSE, Coase was strongly influenced by Arnold Plant, who was appointed as LSE's professor of commerce in 1930. Most other economists at the LSE were preoccupied with the development of pure economic theory and had practically no interest in business. Plant's lectures opened up a new world to Coase, who in those days was a firm believer in socialist principles. Plant "explained how a competitive economic system co-ordinated by prices would lead to the production of goods and services which consumers valued most highly ... After Plant's seminar I had a coherent view of the economic system. He introduced me to Adam Smith's 'invisible hand'" (Coase 1991, 4). Despite the insights obtained from Plant's lectures at the LSE, Coase had the feeling that something essential was missing: "The view of the pricing system as the coordinating mechanism was clearly right but there were aspects of the argument that troubled me … Competition, according to Plant, acting through a system of prices, would do all the co-ordination necessary. And yet we had a factor of production, management, whose function was to co-ordinate. Why was it needed if the pricing system provided all the co-ordination necessary? (Coase 1991, 7)." These questions led Coase to write "The Nature of the Firm."

While at the LSE, Coase earned the Cassel Travelling Scholarship, which enabled him to visit the United States from 1931 to 1932. After returning from the United States, Coase taught for two years at the newly established Dundee School of Economics and Commerce in Scotland. In 1934, he attended the University of Liverpool for one year; there, he started work on his PhD, which he obtained in 1951 from the University of London. During his Dundee days, his economics were moving toward the Chicago Tradition. As Duncan Black, his good friend and colleague in Dundee, remarked: "He wanted an Economics that would both deal with the real world and do so in an exact manner" (Breit and Hirsch, 2004, 195). Coase was an early subscriber to a basic ingredient of the Chicago Tradition during the Friedman era—that theoretical developments have to be backed up by empirical evidence. By the 1930s, Coase had developed "a strong interest in measuring the concepts which were usually only treated theoretically by economists. In this, I was greatly influenced by the work of Henry Schultz of the University of Chicago in deriving statistical demand schedules" (Breit and Hirsch, 2004, 196).

From 1935 until 1951, Coase lectured at the LSE, where celebrated economists such as Lionel Robbins, Friedrich Hayek, Nicholas Kaldor, and John Hicks were among his colleagues. During World War II, Coase held various government positions, mainly in departments involved in statistical work. Coase criticized the viewpoints of postwar British economists, and he was inspired to start talking about "blackboard economics." By this he meant theoretical economics usually cast in sophisticated mathematical terms that have no (or very little) link with reality and hence only exist in the papers and "on the blackboards" of the economists involved. Coase's attack on the position that state enterprises should strictly adhere to a policy of marginal cost pricing, which was fervently defended by such well-known economists as James Meade and Abba Lerner, was typical of this attitude. Keynes, who was an adviser to the British Treasury in those days, seems to have been sympathetic to Coase's criticism of the argument made by Meade and his supporters (Breit and Hirsch 2004).

Coase emigrated to the United States in 1951. He took this step because of "a lack of faith in the future of socialist Britain, a liking for life in America ... and an admiration for American economics. Among the older economists it was Frank Knight that I most admired; among my contemporaries it was George Stigler" (Breit and Hirsch 2004, 199). After he arrived in the United States, he spent seven years at the University of Buffalo and followed that period with six years at the University of Virginia. In 1964—four years after that memorable evening in Director's house—he joined the University of Chicago, where he became one of the leading figures of the influential law and economics movement that Director started. In 1991, Coase received the Nobel Prize in economics for two of his articles.

In his Nobel lecture, Coase claimed that he had already found the answer to the questions raised in 1932, but it would take him five more years to get his argument formally down on paper—that paper was the article "The Nature of the Firm." Coase declared that the paper's purpose was "to bridge what appears to be the gap in economic theory between the assumption (made for some purposes) that resources are allocated by means of the price mechanism and the assumption (made for other purposes) that this allocation is dependent on the entrepreneur-coordinator" (Coase 1937, 39). In 1960, Coase published another article, "The Problem of Social Cost," that built on the earlier paper at the behest of many of the Chicago economists who were present that evening in Director's home. These two articles are among the most often cited pieces of analysis in the history of economics, which is a clear illustration of their importance. Some disagreed strongly with this qualification and went quite out of their way to predict that "Coase will never win the Nobel Prize in economics" (Schwab, 1989, 1190); two years later, the naysayers were proven wrong. Although the 1960 paper was an instant success, the 1937 paper went largely unnoticed for many years.

## THE FREE MARKET IS NOT FREE

In "The Nature of the Firm," Coase argued that using the price mechanism to coordinate market transactions is not cost-free. Coase referred to these costs as "marketing costs," but they came to be known in the literature as "transaction costs." The existence of firms is intimately related to the existence of such transaction costs as negotiations to be undertaken, contracts to be drawn up, inspections to be made, and arrangements to be made to settle disputes, but "the most obvious cost of 'organizing' production through the price mechanism is that of discovering what the relevant prices are" (Coase 1937, 40). As Karl Brunner (1992, 11) wrote about "The Nature of the Firm": "The peculiar characteristic of the firm can be recognized in the fact that it circumvents markets and market transactions. It replaces markets with an organizational structure represented by a set of contractual relationships. Economic agents thus confront a choice: they can organize their activities via market transactions or with the aid of a firm's coordinative structure."

In his Nobel lecture, Coase stated (1991, 8):

In "The Nature of the Firm" I argued that in a competitive system there would be an optimum of planning since a firm, that little planned society, could only continue to exist if it performed its co-ordination function at a lower cost than would be incurred if co-ordination were achieved by means of market transactions and also at a lower cost than this same function could be performed by another firm. To have an efficient economic system it is necessary not only to have markets but also areas of planning within organizations of the appropriate size. What this mix should be we find as a result of competition.

"The question always is," wrote Coase (1937, 50), "will it pay to bring an extra exchange transaction under the organizing authority? At the margin, the costs of organizing within the firm will be equal either to the costs of organizing in another firm or to the costs involved in leaving the transaction to be 'organized' by the price mechanism. Business men will be constantly experimenting, controlling more or less, and in this way equilibrium will be maintained."

Although Coase had a great deal of respect for Knight, his analysis in "The Nature of the Firm" brought him into conflict with some aspects of Knight's analysis in *Risk, Uncertainty and Profit*. Brunner characterized the intellectual conflict as follows:

> Knight anchors the existence of the firm in the fact of a pervasive uncertainty. The primary problem under the circumstances is to decide what to do and how to do it. The entrepreneur and his peculiar characterization thus emerge. Entrepreneurial ability is moreover not uniformly distributed and neither is the attitude towards risk taking. This comparative advantage explains according to Knight the occurrence of firms with their wage system. Coase objects that the existence of persons with better judgement hardly explains, in the absence of any transaction costs, the existence of firms. Such persons will simply sell their advice on the market. Knight offers according to Coase's judgement no reason why the market mechanism should be partly replaced by firms (Brunner 1992, 12).

The transaction-costs approach which he first covered in "The Nature of the Firm," also formed a fundamental building block of Coase's analysis in "The Problem of Social Cost."[288] The origin of this article lies in a 1959 paper Coase published in the *Journal of Law and Economics* that analyzed the way the Federal Communications Commission allocated available radio frequencies. This was the paper Coase came to defend on that historic evening in Director's house.

One of Coase's conclusions was that the price mechanism should be used in the process of allocating radio frequencies (Coase 1959). This was not something new for Chicago people: Leo Herzel (1951), then a student at Chicago's law school, had proposed exactly the same mechanism. In a second and much bolder assertion, Coase said that whatever the initial distribution of the legal right to use these frequencies, the competitive system would, in the absence of transaction costs, bring about an optimal distribution of these rights—provided the rights were well-defined and transferable. The first conclusion was easily accepted by the Chicago economists, but they assembled at Director's house to convince Coase that his second conclusion was wrong.

The discussion at Director's home convinced Coase of the hold Pigou's analysis of market failures and externalities had on his fellow economists.[289] According to Coase, a basic flaw in Pigou's analysis was that the reciprocal nature of so-called externalities was most often not recognized: "The problem we face in dealing with actions which have harmful effects is not simply one of restraining those responsible for them. What has to be decided is whether the gain from preventing the harm is greater than the loss which would be suffered elsewhere as a result of stopping the action which produces the harm" (Coase 1960, 27). As one of many examples, Coase (1960, 13) uses straying cattle that destroy crops on neighboring land: " ... it is true that there would be no crop damage without the cattle. It is equally true that that there would be no crop damage without the crop."

The analysis in "The Problem of Social Cost" first assumes that there are no transaction costs for the individuals and/or firms concerned. In this case, Coase proves that the assignment of legal rights does not make any difference at all regarding the allocation of resources. Stigler christened this proposition the "Coase Theorem."[290] This theorem states that "when transactions costs are zero and rights are fully specified, parties to a dispute will bargain to an efficient outcome, regardless of the initial assignment of rights" (Medema 1994, 10). However, Coase seemed to doubt whether or not the invention of the theorem was really a good thing. In his Nobel lecture, he said (1991, 11):

> I tend to regard the Coase Theorem as a stepping stone on
> the way to an analysis of an economy with positive transaction
> costs. The significance to me of the Coase Theorem is that it un-
> dermines the Pigouvian system. Since standard economic theory
> assumes transaction costs to be zero, the Coase Theorem dem-
> onstrates that the Pigouvian solutions are unnecessary in these

circumstances. Of course, it does not imply, when transaction costs are positive, that government actions (such as government operation, regulation or taxation, including subsidies) could not produce a better result than relying on negotiations between individuals in the market. Whether this would be so could be discovered not by studying imaginary governments but what real governments actually do.

In the case of positive transaction costs, Coase concluded that what should be done from the policy point of view could only be determined by working out empirical case studies. Coase tried to stimulate production of these case studies as much as possible while he was the editor of the *Journal of Law and Economics*. Most of this research showed that in a world of positive transaction costs, the characteristics of the legal system were vitally important for the functioning of the economic system. "It makes little sense for economists to discuss the process of exchange without specifying the institutional setting within which the trading takes place since this affects the incentives to produce and the costs of transacting," Coase concluded (1991, 12).

## KNIGHT'S HEIR

In "The Problem of Social Cost," Coase concluded:

It is clear that the government has powers which might enable it to get some things done at a lower cost than could a private organization ... But the government administrative machine is not itself costless. It can, in fact, on occasion be extremely costly. Furthermore, there's no reason to suppose that the restrictive and zoning regulations made by fallible administrations subject to political pressures and operating without any competitive check, will necessarily always be those which increase the efficiency with which the economic system operates. Furthermore, such general regulations which must apply to a wide variety of cases will be enforced in some cases in which they are clearly inappropriate. From those considerations it follows that direct government regulation will not necessarily give better results than leaving the problem to be solved by the market or the firm (Coase 1960, 17–18).

After Coase's pioneering work, scholars at the University of Chicago continued the economic analysis of government regulation along the same lines. A leader among these pioneers was Stigler, who "won the Nobel Prize in economics in 1982 for his work on the theory of economic regulation but if there were a Nobel prize for beautiful, polished papers on economic theory, industrial organization, and the history of economic thought, it should long ago have been given to him" (Blaug 1985, 239).

George J. Stigler, an only child, was born in 1911 in Renton, a small town near Seattle. The young Stigler was "an insatiable and utterly indiscriminate reader" (Stigler 1988b, 15) who focused on courses in business administration at the University of Washington. He planned to follow in his father's footsteps and pursue a life of trade. However, the Great Depression was already hitting hard upon Stigler's graduation in 1931; instead of joining the search for scarce jobs, he obtained a scholarship to Northwestern University in Chicago, where he earned an MBA. At Northwestern, he became interested in economics and in academic life in general.[291] Stigler went back to Seattle but then returned to Chicago in 1933—this time, to the University of Chicago. Later, he recalled: "There I met three economists I still consider to be outstanding: Frank Knight and Henry Simons, and ... Jacob Viner ... Knight ... communicated beyond any possible confusion the message that intellectual inquiry was a sacred calling ... One thing that Knight and Simons both succeeded in teaching me, in fact overtaught, was that great reputation and big office deserve little respect in scientific argument. We were told to listen to the argument and look at the evidence, but ignore the position, degrees, and age of the speaker ... Viner was the founder of the Chicago tradition of detailed training in neoclassical microeconomics" (Breit and Hirsch 2004, 81–82).

Among his fellow students at the University of Chicago were Allen Wallis and Milton Friedman, with whom Stigler developed an intense and lifelong friendship. Wallis got involved in the management of universities, first in Chicago as dean of the GSB and later as president of the University of Rochester, and he also held various government positions. Stigler and Friedman came to be known worldwide as, respectively, Mr. Micro and Mr. Macro (the physical height of the two men was inversely related to their economic nicknames, which gave rise to numerous jokes). Friedman, Stigler, Wallis, and Director formed the backbone of what Melvin Reder described as the "Knight affinity group" (Reder 1982, 7). As Wallis recalled: "Frequently George, Milton Friedman, and I ate dinner together. Those were long, drawn-out sessions, with our jaws doing more talking than chewing. The dominant subject was Frank Knight: What did he say and what did he mean? Did he make sense and was he right? ... Our attitude toward Knight was essentially hero worship" (Wallis 1993, 775,777). Friedman (1993, 771) writes of "[Stigler's] mentor Frank Knight." Coase confirms that Knight was the teacher who had the most decisive impact on the young Stigler: "it was Knight ... who most influenced him. Knight gave him his vision of economics and strongly reinforced what must have been innate in George Stigler, his love of scholarship" (Coase 1994, 200). Only Becker holds a somewhat different view: "Viner may have had the greater long-run impact through his emphasis on the empirical relevance of microeconomic theory, and on the necessity of testing a theory with historical and empirical evidence" (Becker 1993b, 761).

In 1936, Stigler left Chicago for Iowa State College, where T. W. Schultz was trying to build an economics department. Two years later, Stigler moved to the University of Minnesota, and in 1942 he took a sustained leave of absence—first to go to the National Bureau of Economic Research and then to the Statistical Research Group at Columbia University. Both jobs emphasized empirical work. Stigler again worked with his old pals Friedman and Wallis there, and he also worked with such distinguished economists and statisticians as Arthur Burns, Solomon Fabricant, Harold Hotelling, L.J. Savage, and Abraham Wald during this period. In 1946, Stigler went to Brown University, and a year later, he went to Columbia University, where he taught the graduate course on economic theory with Albert Hart and William Vickrey, the 1996 winner of the Nobel Prize in economics.

In 1946, an event took place that, in hindsight, can only be described as amazing. Wallis's recollection is as follows: "The Chicago economics department wanted to appoint George, but President Colwell pronounced him a raw empiricist with no appreciation of theory, and refused to allow the appointment. Then in 1950 George performed so spectacularly at a conference attended by several trustees, including the chairman of the board, that the trustees took the faculty to task for not having him at Chicago. So an offer was made (at double the salary that would have been offered 4 years earlier), but George turned it down" (Wallis 1993, 778). In his memoir, Stigler is extremely brief on this topic: "the professorship was offered to Milton Friedman, and President Colwell and I have launched the new Chicago School. We both deserve credit for that appointment, although for a long time I was not inclined to share it with Colwell" (Stigler 1988b, 40). Friedman is probably correct in his assessment that this episode left a deep wound in Stigler's soul: "Though he always treated his initial rejection as a joke, as in his *Memoirs,* he had clearly been deeply hurt. I have no doubt that that was the real reason that he turned down the offers from Chicago" (Friedman 1993, 770).

At the end of 1957, Stigler's good friend Wallis finally succeeded in getting Stigler back to the place where he stayed until his death in December 1991. Stigler became the Charles Walgreen Professor for the GSB and the economics department. His classroom at the University of Chicago was, according to his student Thomas Sowell, "... an intellectual Demolition Derby where fashionable cant and tempting fallacies were sent crashing to the junk heap" (Sowell 1991, 16). He edited the *Journal of Political Economy* for 19 years, and in 1947, he, Friedman, Director, and Hayek cofounded the famous Mont Pelerin Society in Switzerland.

## The Point of No More Search

Stigler was an extraordinary personality. Becker (1993b, 766) describes the 6 foot 3 inch tall Stigler as:

> ... An imposing figure, not only in his intellect and appearance but in his manner. On more than one occasion middle-aged men asked me to put some question or request to Stigler. They were too afraid to ask him directly ... Stigler could not tolerate half-baked arguments or those baked on little evidence, even

when they were advanced by close friends or were used to defend positions that he believed to be true ... This attitude and his intimidating personality frightened many students. They flocked to his classes but were reluctant to ask him to supervise their dissertations ... To Stigler's inner circle he was a warm and dear friend, generous with both his time and wallet.

The imposing nature of Stigler's personality probably explains why he, like Knight, supervised only a handful of doctoral dissertations.[292]

Friedman emphasizes Stigler's "quickness of mind, cleverness of repartee, and unmatched capacity for smart cracks" (Friedman 1993, 768). Some of these wisecracks or witty one-liners merit mention in this discussion. Once, Paul Samuelson preceded Stigler on a panel discussion and ended his remarks by saying, "I know what George Stigler's going to say and he's all wrong." At that, Stigler stood up, said "2 + 2 = 4," and sat down (Friedland 1993, 782). He introduced his talks with remarks such as, "I shall face the stupendous problem of speaking for 5 minutes in a way that will be remembered for 10 minutes" (Friedland 1993, 782).

While Stigler visited London in 1948 to deliver his Five Lectures on Economic Problems, he complained in a letter to Friedman about the inconvertibility of the pound and the inedible yet still rationed food there: "So here I am losing weight and gaining pounds" (Friedman 1993, 771). In another instance, a reporter who was interviewing Stigler commented on the fact that Stigler had written only 100 articles; the reporter had recently interviewed interviewed Harry Johnson, who had written 500. Stigler's response was succinct: "Mine are all different" (Friedland 1993, 781).

When speculating on the different reasons why economists gradually started to like antitrust policies, Stigler noticed (1982a, 12) that "the rate of compensation for economists in this activity is not in violation of the federal minimum wage law." Even when discussing royalty, Stigler could combine great wisdom and witty presentation: "Monarchies rely upon the dice of genetics to produce able leadership, and the phenomenon of regression to the mean is sufficient guarantee that on average the monarch will not be among the most able people of his time" (Stigler 1988a, x).

Among Stigler's most intriguing personality characteristics was directness in communicating his opinions. Claire Friedland, who worked as Stigler's assistant for 33 years at the University of Chicago, remarked: "He meant to lower the cost of information to anyone seeking his opinion by telling him or her the perfect truth, no matter how unpleasant" (Friedland 1993, 781). In this respect, Stigler seemingly applied the results of his research work on the economics of information to daily life. Stigler argued that his contributions to the economics of deregulation, his work on monopoly, or his efforts on the history of economic thought were not the high points of his legacy as an economist; instead, the "... much the most important contribution I have made to economics is information theory" (Stigler in Breit and Hirsch 2004, 89). The Nobel Prize Committee also stressed Stigler's work on information because, thanks to that work, "... phenomena such as price rigidity, variations in delivery periods, queuing and unutilized resources, which are essential features of market processes, can be afforded a strict explanation within the framework of basic economic assumptions" (Coase 1994, 204).

In the textbook model of a market characterized by perfect competition and a homogeneous product, there exists only one price: the price that equilibrates supply and demand. Underlying this model is the hypothesis that all market participants have perfect information on the prices being offered and demanded. One of the basic characteristics of theories of monopolistic competition is the focus on the lack of realism involved in accepting the hypothesis of perfect information. However, the analysis of information as an economic asset was left for Stigler to develop. Deploring the fact that information "occupies a slum dwelling in the house of economics," Stigler (1968, 171) argued that people look for information in a rational, reasoned way, and that they will pursue the search for additional information up to the point where the cost associated with acquiring one extra bit of information is equal to the benefit derived from that last piece of additional information. The main cost component in the search for information is the time one has to invest in gathering information. In his memoir, Stigler (1988b, 80) describes his work on the economics of information as "complementary to Coase's work because I had been examining a major component of transaction costs and, in fact, my article appeared at about the same time as his."

Stigler applied his general treatment of information to the labor market and proved that employers and employees look for better opportunities following the same rule—that is, up to the point where the marginal cost equals the marginal benefit of additional search efforts (Stigler 1968). This article lies at the origin of the search models of unemployment, in which unemployment is the result of a voluntary choice made by individuals to methodically search for the best job at the highest possible wage. Stigler's work on the economics of information shed new light on such phenomena as advertising, business location, and dealer specialization, and it led to important related research.[293]

One of the major applications of his economics of information was Stigler's theory of oligopoly. "The present paper accepts the hypothesis that oligopolists wish to collude to maximize profits. It seeks to reconcile this wish with facts, such as that collusion is impossible for many firms and collusion is much more effective in some circumstances than in others. The reconciliation is found in the problem of policing a collusive agreement, which proves to be a problem in the theory of information" (Stigler 1968, 39).

## LESTER'S CORE BUSINESS

Stigler's seminal paper on the economics of information consists of two parts. The first part develops his general analysis of the nature and characteristics of the search process, and the second part applies his insights on the phenomenon of advertising, which he describes as "clearly an immensely powerful instrument for the elimination of ignorance ... The effect of advertising prices ... is equivalent to that of the introduction of a very large amount of search by a large portion of the potential buyers" (Stigler 1968, 182, 187). Stigler's work on the economics of information and advertising was a major source of inspiration for Lester Telser, who in his earlier research was also "very much stimulated by Aaron Director."[294] Telser found, "despite plausible theorizing to the contrary," very little empirical evidence "for an inverse association between advertising and competition" (Telser 1964, 558). He detected a negative relationship between the advertising intensity of industries and changes in their concentration ratios (Telser 1962, 1969a). Telser also analyzed the workings of the advertising market (Telser 1966).

Telser was born in Chicago in 1931. He earned his bachelor's degree from

Roosevelt University in 1951. After one year as a Harvard graduate student, he received a master's degree from the University of Chicago in 1953 and a PhD, written under Friedman's supervision, three years later. Telser considers himself, intellectually, to be "the grandson of John Maynard Keynes and the son of Milton Friedman. My dose of Keynesianism I got from Abba Lerner who was teaching at Roosevelt University during my student days."[295] From 1952 to 1954, he worked as assistant to Hendrik Houthakker at the Cowles Commission, and the young scholar witnessed the frequent clashes between the Cowles crowd and the University of Chicago's department of economics.[296] After one year at Iowa State College (1955–56) and two years as a statistical consultant to the U.S. Army, he joined the faculty of Chicago's GSB in 1958. From 1965 forward, he was a professor in the department of economics.

Telser remembers his years at the Cowles Commission vividly.[297] There, he met John von Neumann, the father of game theory[298]:

> ... von Neumann is one of the most fascinating men that I ever came across. He used to come to visit the Cowles Commission for a few days every three months. Everybody would then line up to present to him the mathematical problems they weren't able to solve themselves. John von Neumann was the closest to a genius I've ever seen. Actually, Milton Friedman once told me that the theory of games was the one thing he really would like to have invented himself. I think Milton was serious on this remark since modern game theory comes quite close to what at one time he had been doing with Jimmy Savage.[299]

Whereas Director, Friedman, and Stigler instructed him in the richness of traditional price theory, Telser inherited a love of econometrics and mathematical economics from the people at the Cowles Commission. This didn't make life easy for him: "The original version of my first paper on resale price maintenance was highly mathematical. After long discussions, Aaron Director convinced me that it was better to leave much of the math aside because, as he put it, 'nobody would read the paper.'"[300] The article on resale price maintenance became Telser's (1960) first important contribution to economics.

Telser blended two elements—the competitive system, with its price mechanism, and a high level of abstraction through mathematical economics—in his theory of the core (Telser 1978, 1996). There can be no doubt that Telser's theory of the core is his most important contribution to economic theory.[301] The starting point of the theory of the core is the fundamental characteristic of a competitive equilibrium: no individual buyer (seller) or group of buyers (sellers) has an incentive to break away from the price-quantity pair typical of the equilibrium position. This situation is generally known as one of Pareto optimality. Following the pathbreaking analysis of the 19th-century British economist Francis Y. Edgeworth, Telser's theory of the core examines the way in which individuals can and will form coalitions and the incentives that determine their choices. Telser (1994, 152) summarized the theory as follows: "the theory of the core has three elements: individuals; the various groups they can form, called coalitions; and functions that measure the results of the actions taken by the individuals and coalitions ... Depending on the number of individuals and the process of recontracting, the core will sometimes consist of a range of outcomes, sometimes a single outcome and sometimes the core will not exist at all."

## Damsel In Distress

Although Stigler regards his work on the economics of information as his most important contribution to the field, there is also much to be said for the claim made by his Chicago colleague Coase when he declared that "the Swedish Academy made no mention of Stigler's studies of the history of economic thought, but in them he is, I believe, seen at his best" (Coase 1994, 201). In his dissertation—Stigler was one of the very few who succeeded in bringing a PhD under Knight's supervision to a favorable conclusion—he analyzed the intellectual history of the marginal productivity theory (Stigler 1940). Stigler published on the life and work of Adam Smith, David Ricardo, John Stuart Mill, Alfred Marshall, and others.[302] Becker described the mixed feelings Stigler must have experienced with respect to the subject of the history of economic thought: "Stigler became the world's greatest expert on the history of economic doctrine, but he recognized that this field attracted less and less interest from the vast majority of economists ... He continued to believe, however, that the great economists of the past were far more stimulating to read than all but a small fraction of contemporary writing on economics" (Becker 1993c, 762–63).

Most of Stigler's work—certainly on the history of economic thought— is characterized by a great affection for traditional economic analysis; it was a neoclassical synthesis of the classical theory developed by Smith and Ricardo and the marginal analysis personified by Alfred Marshall. As Claire Friedland wrote: "Much of his work centered around saving the damsel in distress, neoclassicism, from her attackers" (Friedland 1993, 780). Harold Demsetz remarked that Stigler "felt strongly that the neoclassical theoretical apparatus was, on the whole, quite powerful, and, after a half century's investment in its development, that it should not be abandoned lightly" (Demsetz 1993, 794). His dedication to neoclassical economics made Stigler into a lifelong opponent of one of the most influential books of the 20th century on the economics of the firm, *The Modern Corporation and Private Property* (1932), by Adolf Berle and Gardiner Means. In it, Berle and Means pleaded for a fundamental rethinking of economic organization.[303]

Stigler defended the market economy or the free-enterprise system on the grounds of efficiency and ethics. As is clear from the opening paragraphs of his 1981 Tanner Lectures, Stigler relied heavily on his historical knowledge to make this point: "Until the mid-nineteenth century, the virtues of the enterprise system were as widely accepted as the belief in its efficiency ... It is true that considerable lists have been compiled of the public tasks which the classical economists assigned to the state to correct or reinforce private actions, but they were not widespread or systematic *programs*, rather a spattering of Band-Aids to be put on the body economic."

Given his profound knowledge of the neoclassical heritage, it is surprising to note that he never lectured on price theory in the Economics 301 course at the University of Chicago. Some who knew Stigler well, including Claire Friedland and James Heckman, see this as a reflection of Stigler's admiration for Friedman and Becker.[304] Stigler's son Stephen, a professor of statistics at the University of Chicago, argues that, after lecturing for almost a decade on price theory at Columbia University, Stigler got tired of teaching it. Says Stephen Stigler: "By the time he returned to Chicago, his intellectual interests lay much more in the field of applied price theory."[305] During his stay at Columbia University, Stigler did indeed teach price theory, and in 1942, he published the handbook *The Theory of Competitive Price*. It was revised several times afterwards, the last being in 1987; along the way, the title changed to *The Theory of Price* (Stigler 1987).

A close challenger to George Stigler with respect to the defense of neoclassical economic analysis and the free market economy was Yale Brozen, who came to the University of Chicago's GSB in 1957, the same year as Stigler. Born in 1910 in Kansas City, Brozen earned two bachelor's degrees: one in chemical engineering at MIT and one in economics at the University of Chicago, where he also earned a PhD in 1942. After a short spell at the University of Florida, he joined the Army, and after World War II, Brozen successively taught at the Illinois Institute of Technology, the University of Minnesota, and Northwestern University. In 1957, he returned to the University of Chicago as a professor at the GSB. He retired from the business school in 1987 and died in 1998. "Yale was a real loner. Breaking new intellectual ground was not his primary objective. He wanted to bring the typical Chicago message to as broad a public as possible," Sam Peltzman commented on the day of Brozen's death.[306]

Brozen's major scientific contribution relates to the final report delivered in 1968 by the Task Force on Antitrust Policy headed by Phil Neal, who was at that time the dean of the law school at the University of Chicago.[307] The Task Force made the case for a much more interventionist government policy in concentrated industries. In the October 1971 issue of the *Journal of Law and Economics*, an intense discussion developed between Brozen and the defenders of the Task Force's conclusions on concentration and the policy to deal with it. Brozen offered substantial evidence against the case made by the Task Force that high and stable concentration levels in individual industries appear to be associated with persistently high levels of profitability for these industries as a whole and/or for their leading firms.

The concentration controversy stayed with Brozen for the rest of his life. He also regularly challenged the traditional paradigm of industrial economics that "structure determines conduct and performance," arguing instead that the "reality is that conduct and performance are more likely to determine structure and that, in the absence of governmental intervention, structure will be forced by the market in the direction dictated by efficiency" (Brozen 1982, 82–83). He always argued that there was an almost inherent contradiction between dominance and collusive behavior:

> If firms grow to where their market shares concentrate an industry or make one firm dominant, it must be because of superior management, economies of scale, or the production of better products that satisfy a major portion of buyers at a lower cost to them. The growth must be not only the result of lower costs but also of competitive behavior. The benefits of lower costs, to make low-cost firms 'dominant,' must be passed on to buyers in sufficient amount to attract them to low-cost firms. To maintain a large market share, the dominant firm or firms cannot restrict output to maintain price but must expand with the industry. Any attempt at monopolistic or collusive behavior requires restriction of output. Such attempts entail a consequent sacrifice of market share. (Brozen and Bittlingmayer 1982, 397).

## FLEXIBLE, MORE OR LESS

If a defense of neoclassical price theory was the primary characteristic of Stigler's approach to economics, then the need for economists to empirically verify their theories certainly came second. Demsetz (1993, 793) characterized Stigler as a "mid-century neoclassicist with a passion to quantify." One of his most powerful pleas in this respect was delivered in his 1964 presidential address to the AEA Annual Meeting. Referring to the limited role Adam Smith and his followers assigned to the state, Stigler asked: "By what methods did later economists who favored state control of railroads, stock exchanges, wage rates and prices, farm output, and a thousand other things, prove that these were better directed or operated by the state?" (Stigler 1975, 38). His answer:

> From 1776 to 1964 the chief instrument of empirical demonstration on the economic competence of the state has been the telling anecdote ... Even when economists took an active and direct interest in a policy issue, they did not make systematic empirical studies to establish the extent and nature of a problem or the probable efficiency of alternative methods of solving the problem ... No economist deemed it necessary to document his belief that the state could effectively discharge the new duties he proposed to give to it ... If [economists] have anything of their own to contribute to the popular discussion of economic policy, it is some special understanding of the relationship between policies and results of policies. (Stigler 1975, 39, 46, 49, 50)

His loyalty to this damsel in distress and his passion for empirical verification is clearly present in Stigler's work in the field of industrial organization. On the very first page of *The Organization of Industry*, a collection of Stigler's papers on this topic, he bluntly states: "... there is no such subject as industrial organization" (Stigler 1968, 1). Demsetz (1993) argued that most of Stigler's work in the field of industrial organization can be interpreted as a defense of neoclassical price theory, and Demsetz's thesis can be illustrated with Stigler's critique of Edward Chamberlin's theory of monopolistic competition (Stigler 1975)[308] and Harvey Leibenstein's "X-efficiency." Leibenstein challenged the neoclassical proposition that competition makes it impossible for inefficient companies to survive. Stigler (1976) criticized the Leibenstein theory because he believed measured profit is not an adequate index of efficiency and of the degree of utility maximization being achieved by companies.[309]

Stigler's critique of Leibenstein's theory was also related to one of his first contributions in the field of industrial organization: the survivor principle. Stigler conducted an empirical analysis of the theory of economies of scale that started with the observation that this theory "limped along for a century, collecting large pieces of good reasoning and small chunks of empirical evidence but never achieving scientific prosperity"

(Stigler 1968, 71). He concluded " ... there is a fairly wide range of optimum sizes" (Stigler 1968, 88).

There is little doubt that Stigler's research on such issues as the kinked demand schedule (Stigler 1968) and administered or rigid prices (Stigler and Kindahl 1970) was largely inspired by the fact that both issues undermined the notion of flexible prices, a critical hypothesis for a market economy to function well. On the empirical relevance of administered prices, Stigler strongly disagreed with Gardiner Means (1972), who thought the phenomenon was dominant in a modern market economy.[310] Like Stigler, Dennis Carlton became a major contributor to this field of research. In 1986, Carlton published a paper in which he reexamined the Stigler-Kindahl data and concluded that "the degree of price rigidity in many industries is significant" (Carlton 1986, 638).

At the end of the 20th century, another major Chicago economist in the field of industrial organization, Sam Peltzman, considered the issue of price flexibility. The title of Peltzman's paper says it all: "Prices rise faster than they fall."[311] The basic conclusion of Peltzman's empirical investigation was that "output prices tend to respond faster to input increases than to decreases ... It is found as frequently in producer goods markets as in consumer goods markets ... On average, the immediate response to a positive cost shock is at least twice the response to a negative shock" (Peltzman 2000, 466). These findings, Peltzman (2000, 493–94) readily admitted, posed "a challenge to theory ... The theoretical puzzle is unlikely to be solved by a roundup of the usual suspects. Price asymmetry is as characteristic of 'competitive' as 'oligopoly' market structures. It is found where the buyers are numerous and unsophisticated consumers as well as where they are large and presumably sophisticated industrial purchasers. Neither inventory holdings nor menu-costs seem a key ingredient in producing price asymmetries." Peltzman suggested that asymmetric adjustment costs and eventual vertical markets linkages were likely explanations for the observed price asymmetry.

## THE MONOPOLY SHIFT

Next to externalities, monopoly is the other major problem related the convergence of private and social costs and benefits. Over the years, Stigler fundamentally changed his mind about monopoly. Under the influence of Henry Simons, Stigler had considered monopoly to be a major problem in the 1940s and 1950s. In 1952, Stigler published an article in *Fortune Magazine* titled "The Case Against Big Business;" in the article, he wrote that "there are two fundamental criticisms to be made of big business: they act monopolistically, and they encourage and justify bigness in labor and government" (123). Stigler argued, "... the obvious and economical solution ... is to break up the giant companies" (164). By 1955, Stigler was already more restrained, arguing that "the history of the American economy in the twentieth century testifies that a modest program of combatting monopoly is enough to prevent any considerable decline in competition" (Stigler 1968, 297).

In his memoir, Stigler points to two scholars who helped change his mind about monopoly. Joseph Schumpeter emphasized that the competition from new commodities, new technologies, new sources of supply, new types of organization, and so on is what really matters. Through detailed study of different business practices, Aaron Director brought monopoly down from "its near-monopoly position in explaining business behavior. The research of Peltzman, Demsetz, Telser, and others reinforced the smaller role assigned to monopoly" (Stigler 1988b, 103). In his memoir, Stigler does not mention the role Arnold Harberger played in the changing thinking on monopoly. When Harberger was an associate professor at the University of Chicago, he published a paper that estimated the efficiency loss from monopoly to be only around 0.1 percent of national income (Harberger 1954).[312]

Becker must also have played an important role in changing Stigler's thinking about monopoly. In a 1958 paper, "Competition and Democracy," Becker concluded:

> I am inclined to believe that monopoly and other imperfections are at least as important, and perhaps substantially more so, in the political sector as in the market place. If this belief is even approximately correct, it has important implications ... Does the existence of market imperfections justify government intervention? The answer would be "no" if the imperfections in government behavior were greater than those in the market. It may be preferable not to regulate economic monopolies and to suffer

their bad effects, rather than to regulate them and suffer the effects of political imperfections. (Becker 1976, 37–38)

Stigler's final point of view on monopoly and antitrust laws was given in his Ely Lecture from 1981: "Economists have their glories, but I do not believe that the body of American antitrust law is one of them ... We have provided precious little tested economic knowledge to guide policy. No one can believe that we have established a precise relationship between concentration and market power ... The prosecution and defense both find economists to their liking, but that hardly establishes the direction of causation" (Stigler 1982a, 15). Stigler's changed attitude toward monopoly had at least as much to do with the basic economic analysis of monopoly as with the characteristics of government policies to fight monopoly. In Becker's words:

Early in his career he favored an activist antitrust policy, including extensive restrictions on mergers presumed to reduce competition, and the bust-up of companies convicted of having significant monopoly power. But he radically altered these positions in the 1960's as he became convinced ... that government officials and political appointees in charge of antitrust enforcement often have a different agenda ... Stigler began supporting a minimalist antitrust policy that would permit essentially all honest business practices except conspiracies to raise prices and divide up markets. The way to prevent monopolistic practices, he came to believe, is to encourage domestic and foreign competition, not through detailed regulation of business" (Becker 1993c, 764).

Stigler's work on regulation brought his name to the attention of the general public. Though Becker stated, "Stigler's changing views on antimonopoly policy colored his approach to other regulatory agencies" (Becker 1993c, 764), it should not be forgotten that Stigler had already analyzed a major regulation back in the mid-1940s—the minimum wage legislation that was introduced in 1938. On theoretical and empirical grounds, Stigler (1946, 7) argued that a minimum wage imposed by law has a negative impact on employment and on the level and degree of poverty in society.[313]

## REGULATION UNMASKED: PART 1

"The literature of public regulation is so vast that it must touch on everything, but it touches seldom and lightly on the most basic question one can ask about regulation: does it make a difference in the behavior of an industry?" stated the opening sentence of the seminal 1962 article by Stigler and his assistant Friedland (1962, 25). They investigated the regulation of electricity utilities in the United and found no significant impact of regulation on the behavior of these utilities. In the words of Paul Joskow and Nancy Rose (1989, 1495): "Systematic analysis of the effects of economic regulation originated with Stigler and Friedland's 1962 paper."

The early 1960s were very productive for the economics of regulation. In 1962, two researchers at the RAND Corporation, Harvey Averch and Leland Johnson, produced theoretical and empirical evidence that suggested that firms operating under regulatory constraints tend to work inefficiently, with a tendency to overinvest in capital. In another piece of research, Chicago economist Robert Gerwig pointed out considerable price-increasing consequences of government regulation in the gas sector. Two years later, Stigler published "Public Regulation of the Securities Market" (Stigler 1975), an analysis that indicated the inefficiencies of the Securities and Exchange Commission's regulation of the securities markets. Peltzman focused on the affects of regulatory agencies on entry into an industry, such as the banking sector. After Peltzman's pioneering work, much empirical work was done at the University of Chicago and elsewhere, as well. But more theoretically inspired work on regulation also surfaced, as in Demsetz's work.

"To what degree should legislation and regulation replace the market in the utilities or in other industries, and what forms should such legislation take?" Demsetz wrote (1968, 65). He carried the questioning of regulation one step further: "Although public utility regulation recently has been criticized because of its ineffectiveness or because of the undesirable indirect effects it produces, the basic intellectual arguments for believing that truly effective regulation is desirable have not been challenged" (Demsetz 1968, 55). Demsetz intended to meet that intellectual challenge by examining the issue of technical or natural monopoly (i.e., a situation where production takes place under conditions of decreasing average costs). Having two or more producers is clearly inefficient, but having only one raises the prospect of monopoly pricing.

Demsetz (1968, 57) argued, "... the determinants of competition in market negotiations differ from and should not be confused with the determinants of the number of firms from which production will issue after contractual negotiations have been completed." Stigler (1968, 19) used a similar argument to recommend "... customers can auction off the right to sell electricity, using the state as instrument to conduct the auction." Richard Posner (1972) saw a useful application of franchise bidding in the cable TV industry.

The Demsetz-inspired analysis can be considered a forerunner of the theory of contestable markets, and Demsetz's advocacy of franchise bidding led to an intense discussion with a colleague at the University of Chicago, Lester Telser (1969b), who argued that franchise bidding offers no assurance that pricing will be in accordance with marginal cost terms.[314] Kenneth Dam (1974) of Chicago's law school advocated franchise bidding for the development of North Sea oil and gas.

By the end of the 1960s, regulation had been unmasked: it was not "a *deus ex machina* which eliminated one or another unfortunate allocative consequence or market failure" (Peltzman 1998, 155). If regulations often proved to be inefficient, how it is possible that such regulation comes about in the first place?

By 1971, Stigler formulated his answer—the capture theory of regulation, which Roger Noll (1989, 1254) described as "the watershed event" in the analysis of the politics of regulation. The basic point of the capture theory is that "as a rule, regulation is acquired by the industry and is designed and operated primarily for its benefit." (Stigler 1975, 114). The view that the regulatory process is dominated by specific interest groups—"the industry," in Stigler's initial terminology—who try to use it to their own advantage, is diametrically opposed to the traditional view that regulation is primarily instituted by a benevolent political authority in order to protect the public. The roots of Stigler's approach to regulation go back to such early political scientists at the University of Chicago as Arthur F. Bentley (1908) and Harold Lasswell (1938). As early as 1906, an economist at the University of Chicago named Hugo Meyer (1906) had questioned the regulatory interventions of the Interstate Commerce Commission; however, the interest-group approach was largely absent from his analysis.

Elements of the public choice theory developed by James Buchanan and Gordon Tullock (1962) and William Niskanen (1971) also influenced Stigler's thinking on regulation. Public choice theory posits that politicians and bureaucrats are primarily interested in maximizing their own utility (e.g., power, votes, money, budget size, and so on). Mancur Olson's (1965) theory of the logic of collective action also influenced Stigler.

Another forerunner of Stigler's theory of regulation and University of Chicago scholar deserves mention: Ed Renshaw. In 1958, Renshaw, an instructor in the department of economics, investigated the effects of utility regulation. Renshaw (1958) concluded that government regulation of utilities often stimulates price fixing and other monopolistic practices instead of protecting the public against such practices.

## REGULATION UNMASKED: PART 2

In his theory of regulation, Stigler laid down the four ways an industry will try to use the coercive powers of the state to increase its profitability: subsidies, control over entry into the industry, policies affecting substitutes and complementary goods or services, and price fixing. "To explain," Stigler wrote in 1975, "why many industries are able to employ the political machinery to their own ends, we must examine the nature of the political process in a democracy" (123). Stigler points to two crucial characteristics of the democratic political process. First, democratic political decisions must be made "simultaneously by a large number of persons," and second, the democratic decision process must involve the entire community. Like Anthony Downs's (1957) rationally ignorant average voter, Stigler notes:

> The voter's expenditure to learn the merits of individual policy proposals and to express his preferences (by individual and

group representation as well as by voting) are determined by expected costs and returns, just as they are in the private marketplace. The costs of comprehensive information are higher in the political arena because information must be sought on many issues of little or no direct concern to the individual, and accordingly he will know little about most matters before the legislature. The expressions of preferences in voting will be less precise than the expressions of preferences in the marketplace because many uninformed people will be voting and affecting the decision. (Stigler 1975, 125–26)

Stigler (1975, 125–26) concluded that the chief method of coping with these characteristics of the democratic political process is "to employ more or less full-time representatives organized in (disciplined by) firms which are called political parties." The demand for regulation by industries is restrained by the fact that regulation is not a free good; its supply entails costs: "… the representative and his party must find a coalition of voter interests more durable than the anti-industry side of every industry policy proposal." Hence, "… the industry which seeks regulation must be prepared to pay with the two things a party needs: votes and resources."

In the same issue of the *Bell Journal of Economics and Management Science,* Stigler published his theory of regulation and Posner, who, like Simons, Director, and Coase, is a major figure in the law and economics movement at Chicago, made a major contribution to the understanding of regulation. Posner pointed out that regulated industries show a tendency toward "internal subsidies whereby unremunerative services are provided … out of the profits from other services" (Posner 1971, 22). According to Posner, none of the existing theories of regulation can explain the systematic occurrence of internal subsidies: "… the deliberate and continued provision of many services at lower rates and in larger quantities than would be offered in an unregulated competitive market, or, *a fortiori,* an unregulated monopolistic one" (Posner 1971, 22). The fact that cross-subsidization is clearly present in many regulated industries led Posner to conclude that "one of the functions of regulation is to perform distributive and allocative chores usually associated with the taxing or financial branch of government ... A firm provides a service below its real cost, and the deficit is made up by (usually) other customers of the firm who pay higher prices than they would otherwise. Were it not for the power of the state, acting through the regulatory agency, to control entry, the system would not be viable" (Posner 1971, 23,29). A decade later, Richard Epstein (1982, 434) also emphasized the equivalence of regulation and taxation "as instruments of confiscation."

By the time Stigler had published his theory of economic regulation, many academics at the University of Chicago were involved in research projects on regulation. One was Reuben Kessel, whom Stigler described as someone whose "skepticism was almost pathological" (Stigler 1988b, 158). According to Coase and Miller, Kessel showed "little tolerance for abstract theorizing about unobservables. His characteristic question to students (and colleagues) was always: 'What is your evidence for that proposition?'" (Kessel 1980, viii).[315]

Kessel was born and raised in Chicago, and he first came to the campus of the University of Chicago while in the army during World War II, when he attended a meteorological training course. Kessel returned in 1946 to earn an MBA. In 1949, he earned a PhD with a dissertation on the wealth redistribution effects of inflation. The interaction of price theory and monetary analysis clearly shows Friedman's impact on Kessel's work.[316]

Other important influences on Kessel's research include Aaron Director, H. Gregg Lewis, George Stigler, and Armen Alchian. In the 1950s, Kessel spent four years at the RAND Corporation in California, where Alchian was a colleague. Kessel wrote several papers jointly with Alchian; their 1967 paper "The Cyclical Behavior of the Term Structure of Interest Rates" (Kessel 1980) examined what is most likely to happen when regulation prevents monopolists from maximizing their profits. Alchian and Kessel argued that a monopolist's attention will turn in undesirable directions: more sumptuous offices, more pronounced outing of prejudices (even racist ones), and so on. In 1957, Kessel returned to the University of Chicago, first as a member of the department of economics and from 1962 forward as a faculty member in the GSB. Regulatory issues were the focal point of his research.[317]

His most lasting contribution on regulatory issues, however, deals with the medical sector; he argued that free-market principles lead to the best results where general welfare is concerned. His 1974 article "Transfused Blood, Serum Hepatitis, and the Coase Theorem" (Kessel 1980, 92) pointed out that the quality of the transfusion blood provided by the medical establishment is too low because of "too little commercialism." Although Friedman and Kuznets (1945) had pointed out that, in practice, doctors act as price-discriminating monopolists, Kessel was the first to point to the mechanisms that keep this price discrimination from being eroded by competition. These mechanisms include "withdrawal of staff privileges in hospitals ... *no criticism-rules*, professional courtesy or the free treatment by doctors of other doctors and their families, prohibition of advertising that might reallocate market shares among producers, preventing doctors from testifying against one another in malpractice suits, and the selection of candidates for medical schools and post graduate training in the surgical specialties that have a relatively low probability of being price cutters" (Kessel 1980, 35). In later papers on the same topic, including the 1970 article "The A.M.A. and the Supply of Physicians," the American Medical Association (AMA) became Kessel's *bête noir*: "Both the production (education) of physicians and the delivery of health care have suffered from common problems—[the] inability of institutions and individuals to innovate because of restraints imposed by organized medicine" (Keller 1980, 51).

## THE COALITION PERSPECTIVE

Stigler's theory indicated that regulatory benefits accrue to a single group such as, for example, the medical profession, and Stigler's student and colleague, Sam Peltzman, broadened his approach. Peltzman developed a model in which politicians and regulatory agencies actually play a much more active role than in Stigler's approach. In a 1976 article, "Towards a More General Theory of Regulation," Peltzman (1980) argued that they allocate benefits across different groups in society according to the principle of redistribution—up to the point where equality between marginal costs and marginal benefits of all regulatory actions is reached.

Peltzman deduced from his "more general theory of regulation" that a regulator who is behaving rationally will neither levy a uniform tax nor distribute benefits equally. Instead, the regulator will look for the combination of costs and benefits that maximizes his or her own political returns. Politicians and regulators take some of the wealth of organized interest groups away and distribute it to "buy off" the opposition. Peltzman's analysis induced him to characterize the process of regulation as "the search for coalitions that can sustain the regulatory enterprise" and the regulators themselves as "rational maximizers whose primary task [is] self-preservation' (Peltzman 1998, x–xi). In doing so, Peltzman explained a contradiction in Stigler's theory—if regulation is captured by interest groups, why is practically all regulation initially opposed by the organized groups it concerns? Peltzman showed that active, utility-maximizing politicians and regulators provide the explanation.

Peltzman's more general theory of regulation pointed to redistributional aspects that politicians and their regulatory agencies try to maximize to their own benefit. This line of reasoning had already been explored in a paper Peltzman had written five years earlier on the pricing policies of public and private enterprises. In it, he started with the assumption that "an important object of utility to the management of government enterprises, one for which they are willing to trade owner wealth, is the maintenance of political support for the enterprise and for the continued tenure of the managers" (Peltzman 1971, 112). The main conclusions, which he reached through empirical research, were: "In order to maintain its political support, the government firm must determine the appropriate amount of benefits to distribute to each benefited group. In making this determination, government firms will tend to treat different customer groups more uniformly than private firms: government firms will tend to spread the particular costs of serving one group of customers to all groups" (Peltzman 1971, 146).

Peltzman was born in 1940 in Brooklyn, New York. Dreaming of a career on Wall Street, he went to the City College of New York, where he was much influenced by Jacob Mincer, one of the fathers of the theory of human capital, and Robert Weintraub, who had a PhD from the University of Chicago. Weintraub's courses on price and value theory carried a substantial Chicago flavor that was not wasted on the young Peltzman, who promptly forgot about his Wall Street ambitions. He went to the University of Chicago to do his graduate work and, under Stigler's supervision, earned a PhD in 1965. Before joining the GSB in Chicago, Peltzman spent nine years (1964–73) in UCLA's economics department. In his memoir, Stigler (1988b, 160) described Peltzman as "once a gifted student and now a superb colleague, whose scholarship is creative and as colorful as his taste in clothing."

Peltzman set the tone for most of his academic work with his doctoral dissertation on the impact of regulation of the banking industry. He came to be identified with empirical research on regulation.[318] His best-known investigations into the consequences of regulation concern drugs and pharmaceuticals (Peltzman 1973), car safety (Peltzman 1975), advertising (Peltzman 1981), and health (Peltzman 1987).

The economics of regulation led Peltzman to analyze the democratic political system. Specifically, Peltzman searched for explanations for the growth of government in the 20th-century industrialized world. Sixteen years later, Peltzman described this study as "probably the most important paper I've ever written."[319] The main conclusion Peltzman reached on the determinants of government growth is expressed in the "ability-equality nexus":

> Our results imply that the *leveling* of income differences across a large part of the population—the growth of the 'middle class'—has in fact been a major source of the growth of government in the developed world over the last fifty years ... This leveling process, which has characterized almost every economically developed society in the latter stages of industrialization, created the necessary conditions for growth of government: a broadening of the political base that stood to gain from redistribution generally and thus provided a fertile source of political support for expansion of specific programs ... On our interpretation, this simultaneous growth of "ability" served to catalyze politically the spreading economic interest in redistribution. (Peltzman 1998, 268)

During the 1980s and early 1990s, Peltzman's inquiry into the determinants of the growth of government led him to analyze the voting market. Peltzman concluded that the average voter is fairly rational: "The electorate comes off surprisingly well informed. It appropriately rewards good performance by those in office and penalizes bad. It understands its interests and votes accordingly ... Somehow the decisions of millions of rationally ignorant individuals add up to a more or less sensible collective outcome. Moreover, the broad pattern of voting by legislators emerging from my work is one of faithful representation of the interests of their constituents" (Peltzman 1998, vii).

In the 1990s, Peltzman focused on another aspect of the role of government in a modern society: the provider of a public schooling system. This investigation, Peltzman claimed, was following "a strain in the economic analysis of politics whose lineage includes Anthony Downs, Mancur Olson, and George Stigler. This emphasizes the political effectiveness of compact, organized groups ... It is naive ... to treat school systems as if they seek only to maximize literacy or numeracy" (Peltzman 1993a, 332). He defined education's basic issue as follows: "The record of 1965-80 is truly astonishing. Real expenditures per student nearly doubled, and student/teacher ratios declined by about one-fourth ... Yet student achievement deteriorated badly by every measure we have ... What has happened since 1980? ... On the whole, schools today are performing at roughly the level at which they were in 1980" (Peltzman 1993b, 45). Peltzman's investigation showed that the decline in school performance had little to do with the rising crime rate, the increasing prevalence of single-parent families, or the movement to desegregate the schools. Peltzman found that the two most logical explanations for declining school performance were the increasing degree of teacher unionization and the increasing degree of centralization of school funding.

## DEADWEIGHT'S EFFICIENCY

After Stigler, Posner, and Peltzman, the fourth University of Chicago scholar to make a major contribution to the economic theory of regulation was Gary Becker. He focused on the way in which political influence leading to subsidies, regulation, and other interventions is actually generated. In Becker's analysis, pressure groups play the crucial role in this process. Politicians and bureaucrats are "assumed to be hired to further the collective interests of pressure groups who fire or repudiate them by elections and impeachment when they deviate excessively from these interests ... however ... bureaucrats and politicians may have significant political power when pressure groups cannot repudiate them easily" (Becker 1983, 396). The analyses developed by Stigler, Posner, and Peltzman tended to conclude that the way in which regulation comes about inevitably creates considerable inefficiencies, but Becker concluded that the fight for political influence keeps these inefficiencies in check.

The starting point of Becker's analysis is that the political process is characterized by competition:

> The total amount raised from taxes, including hidden taxes like inflation, equals the total amount available for subsidies, including hidden subsidies like restrictions on entry into an industry. This government budget equation implies that a change in the influence of any group that affects its taxes and subsidies must affect the subsidies and taxes, and hence the influence, of other groups. Therefore, groups do not entirely win or lose the competition for political influence because even heavily taxed groups can raise their influence and cut their taxes by additional expenditures on political activities. (Becker 1983, 372)

This competition for political influence is strongly influenced by deadweight costs, which are "the distortions in the use of resources induced by different taxes and subsidies" (Becker 1983, 373) or "the winner's gain less the loser's loss from the regulation-induced change in output. These gains and losses are [in Becker's analysis] what motivate the competing pressures on the political process. So rising marginal deadweight loss must progressively enfeeble the winners relative to the losers" (Peltzman 1998, 296).

Rising taxes and subsidies that drive output further and further away from its optimal level tend to increase deadweight costs. This leads to a competitive process that in the end promotes efficiency:

> An increase in the deadweight cost of a subsidy discourages pressure by the subsidized group because a given revenue from taxes then yields a smaller subsidy. An increase in the deadweight cost

of a tax, on the other hand, encourages pressure from the taxpayers because a given reduction in their taxes then has a smaller
effect on the amount available as a subsidy. Consequently, deadweight costs give taxpayers an intrinsic advantage in the competition for influence. Groups that receive large subsidies presumably have managed to offset their intrinsic disadvantage by
efficiency, an optimal size, or easy access to political influence ...
Policies that raise efficiency are likely to win out in the competition for influence because they produce gains rather than deadweight costs, so that groups benefited have the intrinsic advantage compared to groups harmed. (Becker 1983, 395–96)

Becker did not unconditionally follow the major conclusions that
Stigler and others had drawn: that smaller groups tend to be more efficient in acquiring regulatory protection. Instead, Becker saw forces at
work in different directions:

Efficiency in producing pressure is partly determined by the cost
of controlling free riding among members. Greater control over
free riding raises the optimal pressure by a group and does increase its subsidy or reduces its taxes. Efficiency is also determined by the size of a group, not only because size affects free
riding, but also because small groups may not be able to take
advantage of scale economies in the production of pressure ...
Since deadweight costs to taxpayers fall as the tax per person
falls, the opposition of taxpayers to subsidies decreases as the
number of taxpayers increases. Therefore, groups can more readily obtain subsidies when they are small relative to the number
of taxpayers. This may well explain why farmers in rich countries and urban dwellers in poor countries are politically successful. (Becker 1983, 395)

Fundamentally, Becker's contribution to the theory of regulation, and
more specifically to the role therein of the competitive process among
pressure groups, led to conclusions that run parallel to those reached in
welfare economics, especially regarding the so-called compensation principle. Becker argued:

If the gain to groups that benefit exceeds the loss to groups that suffer, and if access to political influence were otherwise the same for all groups, gainers would exert more political pressure than losers, and a policy would tend to be implemented. Note that the criterion is whether gainers *could* compensate losers; actual compensation need not be paid to losers. If gainers could not compensate losers, a policy would not be implemented unless gainers had much better access to political influence. Therefore, the Compensation Principle combined with an analysis of the production of political influence provides a unified approach to the political feasibility both of public goods and other policies that raise social output (where gainers could compensate losers), and of policies that redistribute to favored groups (where gainers could not compensate). (Becker 1988, 101)

Among the younger generation of economists at the University of Chicago, Randall Kroszner certainly deserves mention as one who looked into the economics of regulation and the political process. Kroszner was born in 1963, earned a bachelor's degree in history from Brown University, and earned a PhD in economics from Harvard in 1990, the same year he joined Chicago's GSB. After consulting for several of the Federal Reserve Banks during the 1990s, Kroszner became a member of President George W. Bush's Council of Economic Advisers from 2001 to 2003. Kroszner's research focused on the interaction between interest groups and politicians (Kroszner and Stratman 1998), competition policy and deregulation (Kroszner and Strahan), and the regulation of international financial markets (Kroszner and Cowen). In March 2006, Kroszner became a member of the Federal Reserve Board in Washington.

## CHICAGO ON GOVERNMENT

Despite research on specific forms of regulation in specific industries, there were hardly any new developments about the general theory of regulation coming out of the University of Chicago other than the two Becker articles. However, general theory eventually played a role in more than just regulatory issues.

In 1988, Stigler edited a volume that contained most of the papers discussed in this chapter: *Chicago Studies in Political Economy.* Stigler's book did not attempt to bring forward a kind of synthetic general framework of the Chicago view on political economy. Rather, he stressed the need for further research, the ambition of which should be that "it should eventually be possible to offer general advice on the best ways to achieve the goals of policy" (Stigler 1988a, xvii).

Although the book shows Stigler to be a bit hesitant (for once), it can be argued that from the research described in this chapter, a Chicago theory of government, and hence a theory on how to achieve policy goals, can be described. According to Roger Noll of Stanford University, this Chicago theory of government has three essential characteristics:

> One is that changes in the opportunities for using the coercive power of the state to capture rents lead to institutional change ... A second component is that the costs of effective political organization differ among economic interests and so affect who is likely to be the winning bidder in the competition for the use of the coercive power of the state to generate rents ... The third component of the Chicago theory, emphasized more by Gary Becker and Richard Posner than by Peltzman and Stigler, is the convergence of policy towards efficiency ... The reason, of course, is that inefficient institutions leave potential rents uncollected, so that in principle all parties to a policy can find a Pareto improving change to which they can agree. The limitation to the convergence to efficiency is simply the transaction cost of identifying the change and organizing to acquire it from government. (Peltzman 1989, 48–49)

In his synthesis of what he calls "the economic theory of regulation," Peltzman stressed the importance of the coalitional aspects of politics and awarded a central role to the need for regulators to balance pressures emanating from competing interest groups. Looked at in this way, the economic theory of regulation offers an explanation of deregulation. Peltzman believed the economic theory of regulation-related explanation of deregulation was confirmed in the timing of deregulation and the way in which it came about in U.S. industries such as railroads, airlines, stock brokerages, and banking:

> When the deregulation benefits become large relative to the associated losses, the probability that the option will be exercised rises. This situation is more likely to occur if the regulation itself has generated inefficiencies, so that shedding the inefficiency through deregulation provides a potential source of benefits ... Regulation occurs when there is a wide discrepancy between the political balance of pressures and the unregulated distribution of wealth. The regulation (of, say, price) then creates incentives for wealth dissipation (through, say, cost increases), which ultimately make restoration of the preregulation status quo more attractive than continuing regulation. In such a model deregulation is not the correction of some belatedly recognized policy error. It is the last stage in a process about which, in principle, all the actors could have had perfect foresight at the beginning. (Peltzman 1998, 320–21)

It is only appropriate to end this chapter with the thoughts on regulation, deregulation, and a Chicago theory of government that Stigler expressed toward the end of his life. Clearly, they deviate from Peltzman's conclusions.

Stigler was rather pessimistic in his 1987 Adam Smith Lecture, which he delivered before the National Association of Business Economics. After reviewing the available evidence, he had come to the conclusion that "we shall experience episodes of deregulation as well as episodes of increased regulation, but the relative preponderance of the latter episodes is so great that it is more appropriate to speak of eras of increased regulation and flurries of deregulation. A substantial period within which deregulation is widespread is most uncommon in modern western history" (Stigler 1988c, 12). Surprisingly, he gave the definite impression of being ready for something close to intellectual capitulation on the basis of the principle—or even the paradox—of legitimacy.

What he had in mind about this principle of legitimacy is the following:

No matter what law is passed, we can and must find a set of
Congressional values that justifies that action: we are simply
applying the doctrine of revealed preferences to the legislature
... *Ex ante*, every public action is expected to be non-mistaken;
*ex ante*, the state is infallible ... So every tariff, every rent control statute, every usury law, every tax loophole, every industry
handout yields a benefit at least equal to its cost in the eyes of
the political authorities ... The Principle of Legitimacy tells us
that these are desirable transfers, i.e., that one dollar taken from
the general consumer and given to a well-paid employee of the
merchant marine constitutes a net increase in the utility of the
nation. If I challenge this interpretation, all that I will be doing is asserting that George Stigler's tastes are not those of the
Congress, and who, besides myself, cares about that? Indeed,
even I have become reconciled to the fact that American society
does not fully share my preferences. (Stigler 1988c, 8–9)

The theory of government that Stigler put forward in the last years of
his life led him to become less worried about the growth of government
and stood in sharp contrast with the way in which his lifelong friend
Friedman saw government policy and the affect economists and activists
can have on that policy. Stigler's conclusion was that he assigned "little
influence of economists' preachings on actual public policy" (Stigler
1988c, 12). On the other hand, "Milton Friedman's lifetime mission," as
Robert Nelson noted (2001, 151), "has been to persuade the American
public of the correct ideas, and thus the correct form of government, a
task to which he devoted great energy, in writing *Newsweek* columns, ap-
pearing on television shows, writing popular books and other efforts to
publicize his views."

# CHAPTER SEVEN

# The Business School

## *A Great Economics Department*

IN 1996, DOUGLAS IRWIN PUBLISHED *AGAINST THE TIDE*, A BOOK
that traced the intellectual history of the doctrine of free trade. At the
time, Irwin was not a scholar teaching the history of economic thought
at some remote university that had not yet abolished its course in this
discipline; instead, he was a professor at the GSB.[320]

Irwin's example illustrates the two basic characteristics of business
education at the University of Chicago. The first is that the broadness of
the program was strongly emphasized. As early as 1925, Ernest DeWitt
Burton, the University's third president, argued that the business school
"will not undertake to be a trade school, fitting men for business by
teaching them a standardized technique. It will continue to emphasize
broad *education* for business administration rather than narrow *training*"
(Murphy and Bruckner 1976, 361). Hence, at Chicago's GSB, the education of future managers and entrepreneurs goes hand-in-hand with the
presence of scholars such as Irwin who write books on the intellectual
history of the doctrine of free trade.

The second basic characteristic of business education at the University
of Chicago is the emphasis on the general use of a rigorous analytical
framework. During the last half century, neoclassical price theory—in
the words of George Stigler, "the mature, stable corpus of economic theory" (Stigler 1946, v) —formed the backbone of that rigorous analytical
framework. The importance attached to theoretical rigor explains why

Chicago's GSB has attracted such scholars as Stigler, Sam Peltzman, and Kevin Murphy, who would be in the economics department of most other universities. Stigler and Murphy are economists whose approach can be considered typical of the basic philosophy followed at Chicago's GSB. In fact, Stigler was the first Nobel laureate in economics to be affiliated with a business school. The GSB's Peter Pashigian was the author of *Price Theory and Applications* (1995), one of the most widely used textbooks in undergraduate microeconomics.

Although their spells at the business school were separated by almost half a century, two scholars are close to perfect embodiments of these two characteristics that have, for decades now, earned Chicago's GSB a permanent place among the world's leading business schools: Robert W. Fogel, the 1993 colaureate of the Nobel Prize in economics, and Theodore O. Yntema.

## FROM VINER TO FORD

Few other people have been as successful as Yntema in both the university community and the world of business. Yntema was born in 1900 in Holland, Michigan and graduated from Hope College. Afterward, he earned two master's degrees in just two years: one in chemistry from the University of Illinois and one in business from the University of Chicago. In 1929, Yntema was awarded a PhD for a dissertation entitled "A Mathematical Reformulation of the General Theory of International Trade," which was a treatment of the subject that was particularly theoretically rigorous for its time.

Yntema remained on the University of Chicago's faculty from 1923 to 1949, first as a professor of statistics and later as a professor of business and economic policy. He was appointed director of research of the Cowles Commission for Research in Economics when it relocated to Chicago in 1939.[321]

After doing extensive consulting work for the Ford Motor Company over the previous years, Yntema became Ford's vice president of finance in 1949. He retired from Ford in 1966 after serving numerous roles, including chairman of the board, and returned to the GSB as a professorial lecturer. Yntema died in 1985. The Theodore O. Yntema Professorship in Finance was established at the GSB in 1973, and Eugene Fama was its first recipient.

In the introduction to his doctoral dissertation, Yntema stated that the work "was conceived under the stimulus of lectures on 'International Economic Policies' delivered by Professor Jacob Viner ... From Professor Henry Schultz, I have received constant encouragement and, out of his wide knowledge of mathematical economics, technical aid which has been invaluable" (Yntema 1932, ix). This PhD dissertation, which was one of the very first to rely heavily on mathematics, wasn't Yntema's first important publication. Three years earlier, he published an article on dumping that was chosen as one of the *Journal of Political Economy's* landmark articles when the journal celebrated its 50th anniversary (Yntema 1938).

However, Yntema was always more interested in the broader policy picture; this led him to accept the directorship of research at the Committee for Economic Development, which was set up in 1942. This committee was the brainchild of three men who were linked to the University of Chicago: President Robert Hutchins, vice president William Benton, and trustee Paul Hoffman, who was also president of the Studebaker Company. Its immediate goal was to focus on the postwar economic conditions of the country in order to avert a repetition of the Great Depression of the 1930s. The Committee for Economic Development eventually evolved into a business-oriented think tank on economic policy.

In his publications from the 1940s, Yntema frequently defended large enterprises and rejected quick fixes in terms of macroeconomic policies. Yntema argued, "... the benefits to be derived from reducing the role of large-scale enterprise tend to be overestimated ... It is true that the history of pools, trusts, and combinations provides a strong basis in experience for associating bigness with the exercise of monopoly power, but the essential fact is that the aggregate of monopoly profits and avoidable costs of excess capacity attributable to size is now a very small portion of the national income" (Yntema 1941, 846).[322]

A 1944 essay reflects Yntema's thoughts on macroeconomic policy. Under the heading "how not to do it," he wrote: "Deficit financing is a dangerous drug ... After the war, there will be a clamor for solving the unemployment problem by shortening hours, spreading the work and thus reducing the supply of labor. As a stopgap remedy, this will spread the burden of existing unemployment and lessen the intensity of its incidence. But we shall never raise our standards of living by producing less. This is the council of despair" (Yntema 1944, 110).

Toward the end of his career, Yntema increasingly stressed the importance of education to further economic development.[323] At a time when socialist thinking was rather fashionable, Yntema was a strong defender of capitalism. "The relative merits of capitalism and communism," he claimed, "depend on three factors: first, the advantage of private ownership versus state ownership of capital; second, the advantages of economic organization through prices established in free, competitive markets versus centralized planning and control by edict; and third, the implications of each system for political organization—control by minority Communist party (dictatorship of the proletariat) versus democracy" (Yntema 1964, 16). Yntema concluded that for each of these three points, "we can expect private enterprise to serve us better" (Yntema 1964, 17).

## WRITING HISTORY

Robert Fogel is a more recent personification of the twin characteristics of the GSB's basic program—a broadly oriented approach and a rigorous theoretical grounding. Fogel became one of the leading scholars in the field Blaug described as "new economic history" and characterized as "the appeal to standard price theory, the imaginative use of available statistical data, the constant attention to the specification of property rights, and the emphasis on information and transaction costs" (Blaug 1985, 160).

His parents emigrated to the United States from Odessa, Russia in 1922, and Fogel was born four years later in New York City. His early education was in New York's public schools, and in 1948, he earned a bachelor's degree from Cornell University. The communist sympathies he cherished during the 1940s disappeared after he left Cornell: "Two things made me change my mind. First, the constant predictions of the Marxian economists that the United States and the world economy would collapse were clearly wrong. There was growth and full employment all around. Second, gradually more became known about the terrible things going on in the Soviet Union of Josef Stalin."[324]

Out went Marx, and in came Stigler. In those days, Stigler taught price theory at Columbia University, where Fogel earned a master's degree in economics in 1960. According to Fogel, "Stigler made price theory really come alive."[325] From Columbia, Fogel moved to Johns Hopkins University where, under the supervision of Simon Kuznets, he earned a PhD in 1963. In his dissertation, Fogel (1964) concluded that the railroads were less important as an engine of economic progress in 19th-century America than was generally believed.[326]

Fogel was an assistant professor at the University of Rochester from 1960 to 1964, the year he moved to the Chicago's department of economics. In 1975, he transferred to Harvard University, and six years later, he returned to the University of Chicago—this time to teach at the GSB.

In 1974, Fogel and Stanley Engerman published *Time on the Cross: The Economics of American Slavery*, a book that is among the most controversial ever written on U.S. socioeconomic history. The controversy was not surprising, given the book's central conclusions: slave agriculture was not inefficient compared with free agriculture; the belief that slave breeding, sexual exploitation, and promiscuity destroyed the black family is a myth; and the rate of expropriation of the slaves was much lower than generally thought, as slaves were allowed to keep about 90 percent of the income they produced over their life cycles. Fogel wrote *Without Consent or Contract: The Rise and Fall of American Slavery* 15 years later; this book ended with a six-page "moral indictment of slavery," but his economic analysis was essentially untouched (Fogel 1989, 393). This book tried to counter the view that was widespread among those who passionately criticized his first book on slavery that Fogel implicitly considered slavery to be a morally defensible phenomenon.

By the time his second book on slavery was published, Fogel had already been focusing for some time on another issue: the secular decline in mortality, which was the theme of his Nobel lecture. In his Nobel lecture, he argued on the basis of a broad range of empirical evidence that it was not so much diseases or famines but instead chronic malnutrition that was the cause of the high mortality rates of days past. Improvements in nutrition also played a major role in the acceleration of economic growth that took place from the early 18th century forward (Fogel 1997).

By the start of the 21st century, this research had led Fogel to an optimistic view of the future of humanity:

> Despite the increasing complexities of social life, the profound new ethical challenges and the potential for disaster, my predictions for the next six decades include longer and healthier lives, more abundant food supplies, improved housing and environments, higher levels of education for larger numbers of people, the narrowing of both material and spiritual inequality (not only within the country but internationally), better paying and flexible jobs, more time for parenting, stronger families that spend more leisure time together, lower rates of crime or corruption, and greater ethnic and racial harmony (Fogel 2000, 13).

Although Fogel was beyond any doubt the most important scholar at the University of Chicago in the field of economic history, he was certainly not the only one. When Fogel arrived in Chicago in 1964, he joined another colorful economic historian, the Mississippi-born Earl J. Hamilton.[327] Hamilton had earned a PhD at Harvard in 1929 and had taught at Duke University (1927–44) and Northwestern (1944–47) before T.W. Schultz brought him to the University of Chicago, where he stayed until his retirement in 1968. Hamilton edited the *Journal of Political Economy* from 1948 to 1954 and served as president of the Economic History Association in 1951–52 and president of the AEA in 1955. With the quantity theory of money as a basic building block of his work and armed with fluency in seven languages, Hamilton focused his research on international financial relations.[328]

Other major contributors to the research program in economic history at the University of Chicago were Arcadius Kahan, Deirdre McCloskey, and David Galenson.

On the run from the aftermath of the Holocaust and a communist dictatorship, Kahan, a Lithuanian, arrived in the United States in 1950. Four years later, he earned a PhD in economics at Rutgers University. In 1955, he joined the University of Chicago as D. Gale Johnson's assistant. Kahan's areas of specialization were the economic history of Russian and European Jewry.[329]

Deirdre McCloskey was, educationally speaking, an all-Harvard product: bachelor's degree in 1964, master's degree in 1967, and PhD in 1970. McCloskey began teaching at the University of Chicago in 1968 and left for the University of Iowa in 1980. Her focus was the economic history of Britain (McCloskey 1981). She also became increasingly critical of the ways in which modern economics had developed (McCloskey 1994).

Like McCloskey, Galenson received his entire education at Harvard, where in 1979, with Fogel as supervisor, he earned a PhD. Galenson began teaching at the University of Chicago in 1978, and his research focused on such topics as the development of markets in history (Galenson 1989) and career evolution over longer periods (Galenson 1993).

## DIFFICULT START

The combination of a rigorous theoretical approach and a broadly oriented program was a key feature of education at the University of Chicago's business school right from the start. In 1894, when James Laughlin first began to talk to William Harper about establishing a school of commerce and industry,[330] there was only one business school in the United States—the Wharton School, which had been established at the University of Pennsylvania in 1881. Laughlin strongly believed that "business, like divinity, medicine or law, was a profession that required specialized preparation" (Streeten 1991, 49). Despite considerable resistance from within the university,[331] Laughlin was finally given the green light to found the College of Commerce and Politics in 1898. However, he was disappointed, because the idea of a professional school in management had not really won.[332]

The College had a difficult start, and three different deans, Henry Hatfield, Francis Shepardson, and Charles Merriam, served from 1902 to 1909. It was Leon C. Marshall, who became dean in 1909, who really got the institute off the ground.[333]

Marshall wanted a business education that "falls little short of being as broad, as inclusive, as life itself in its motives, aspirations, and social obligations" (Graduate School of Business 1998, 12). The 1920 launch of the first scholarly business journal in the United States, *The Journal of*

*Business,* underlined the importance attached to the broad perspective and related research efforts.

Marshall's deanship was important for Chicago's business school in several other ways. First, the business college awarded its first master's degrees in 1915 and its first two business PhDs in 1922 (to Albert C. Hodge and Waldo F. Mitchell);[334] second, Marshall cofounded the American Association of Collegiate Schools of Business in 1915; and third, Chicago-born philanthropist Hobart W. Williams donated prime downtown Chicago property valued at $2 million to the university in 1916. This new situation made it possible for the school to run its affairs on a more independent basis. Last, Marshall launched a series of textbooks under the title *Materials for the Study of Business* in 1916. This publication grew into a set of 40 volumes and played a prominent role in business education all over the United States.

In 1924, Marshall handed over the deanship to William Homer Spencer, who had been teaching at the College since 1913. Spencer was forced to deal with the impact of the Great Depression and with University President Robert Hutchins's manifold intrusions into the affairs of the business school.[335] Hutchins regarded the business school as a vehicle for career preparation, and he believed an academic community should not concern itself with such things. As Jim Lorie commented: "Hutchins didn't exactly abolish the business school, but he really came very close."[336] In 1932, the College became the School of Business and three years later, it awarded its first MBA degree. Spencer succeeded in attracting several young and promising scholars to Chicago, some of whom became rather famous later, including George H. Brown (who became president of the American Marketing Association and director of the U.S. Census Bureau), Paul Douglas, and Michael Davis, who in 1934 organized the Graduate Program in Hospital Administration, a milestone in the field of health care economics. Another Spencer appointment was Garfield Cox, who took over Spencer's position as dean in 1942.

Cox was born in 1893 in Fairmont, Indiana, and he earned a PhD at the University of Chicago in 1929. Cox was a pioneer in the field of forecasting for business purposes, although over the years he became more involved in finance research. Under Cox's leadership, the school went through a difficult period; a lack of financial resources and a decrease in staff and faculty morale mutually reinforced each other in a downward spiral. Many scholars left because of what was known as the "4E contract," which obliged faculty members to turn any consulting fees they earned over to the university. Nevertheless, Cox succeeded in developing the Executive Program, which launched in 1943. This Executive Program was the first of its kind in the United States and was designed to create a close interaction between teachers and businessmen.

The next dean of Chicago's business school, John Jeuck, inherited a challenge when he took over from Cox in 1952. The Chicago-born Jeuck had received his entire education at the University of Chicago (bachelor's and master's degrees and a PhD); however, even with that level of knowledge of the university, he could not really turn the tide, but he did succeed in ending the practice of the 4E contract. After three years as its dean, Jeuck left the GSB to join the Harvard Business School.

During the late 1940s, the University of Chicago's business school was rapidly losing ground in the field of business education. In the realm of research, for example, the Graduate School of Industrial Administration of the Carnegie Institute of Technology and not Chicago was clearly in the lead.

By the beginning of the 1950s, George Leland Bach had shaped a scientific curriculum for an MBA program at the Graduate School of Industrial Administration. Bach was born in 1915 in Victoria, Iowa,[337] and graduated from Iowa's Grinnell College. He joined Chicago's doctoral program in economics and was one of the very few to complete a PhD under the supervision of Frank Knight. A year before obtaining his PhD, Bach was hired by T.W. Schultz to teach at Iowa State College. Schultz "became a lifelong mentor of Bach's" (Gleeson and Schlossman 1995, 3). Schultz helped Bach get the job of special assistant to the Board of Governors of the Federal Reserve System in 1941 and later persuaded Robert Doherty of the Carnegie Institute of Technology—which was primarily known as an engineering school—that Bach was the man he needed for the postwar revival of Carnegie's economics department. In 1946, Bach accepted this challenge, on two conditions, "… both of which revealed his Chicago roots: first, he wanted leeway in choosing his own faculty; second, he wanted the university to commit to starting up a graduate program as soon as the budget allowed" (Gleeson and Schlossman 1995, 5).

By the late 1940s, Schultz brought Bach into the inner circle of the Ford Foundation. During the early 1950s, Robert Hutchins was another major player in the Ford Foundation. Hutchins was highly critical of university-based management education and related research, and Bach played a major role in convincing the Ford Foundation to support the expansion of business schools.

In the late 1950s, two widely debated reports on the future of business education were published, and it was generally recognized that "Bach's unique stamp on both reports was self-evident. The reports confirmed Bach's position as the leading intellectual in the field" (Gleeson and Schlossman 1995, 22). Bach urged business schools to organize their MBA curricula on three foundations: economic analysis, statistics, and the administrative process and organizational behavior (Pierson 1959). Bach believed that traditional areas of business education, such as finance, marketing, and organization, were nothing more than applied problem areas to which managers should apply the tools provided by the three foundations.

The Bach-inspired program at Carnegie included such great economists as Herbert Simon, a 1943 PhD graduate from the University of Chicago and 1978 Nobel laureate for his work on areas such as bounded rationality; Charles Holt; John Muth, another recipient of a PhD from the University of Chicago who was the intellectual father of the rational expectations revolution; Franco Modigliani, the 1985 Nobel Prize laureate; Richard Cyert and James March, whose efforts revolutionized thinking on corporate behavior (Cyert and March, 1953); and, last but not least, Merton Miller, 1990 Nobel laureate and one of the pillars of the later successes of Chicago's GSB. Miller and Modigliani developed their famous theorem on corporate finance at Carnegie. During the 1960s, Robert Lucas spent several years at Carnegie's business school before returning to the University of Chicago; at Carnegie, Lucas picked up Muth's grand vision of rational expectations.

## THE WALLIS-LORIE DOCTRINE

W. Allen Wallis replaced Jeuck as dean in 1956. Wallis was born to an academic Philadelphia family in 1912. His father was a respected anthropologist and philosopher who taught at various universities. Wallis majored in psychology at the University of Minnesota and graduated in 1932, but by that time, economics and statistics had become his major areas of interest. Starting in 1933, he spent two years at the University of Chicago where, with Milton Friedman and George Stigler, he received his economics education from Jacob Viner, Henry Simons, and Frank Knight. After short spells at Columbia University, the Natural Resources Committee in Washington, DC, and Yale University, Wallis joined the Stanford University's department of economics in 1938. In June 1942, he was appointed director of research of the Statistical Research Group at Columbia University. This group included eminent statisticians, such as Harold Hotelling, Abraham Wald, and Leonard J. Savage, and prominent economists, including Friedman and Stigler.[338] In the fall of 1946, Wallis returned to the University of Chicago, where he became a professor of statistics and economics at the GSB. Throughout his life, Wallis remained a passionate defender of the free market economy.[339]

In 1952, Wallis turned down an offer to become dean of the GSB. Four years later, he was again asked to lead the troubled business school. Wallis accepted the GSB's offer on the condition that Jim Lorie would be his assistant dean. "The challenge was enormous," Lorie remembered 40 years later, "The business school was in a very bad situation. There was no money, no zeal, no imagination, not even telephones anymore. Allen Wallis persuaded me to join the effort. Apart from his many talents, he had an immensely important asset: Wallis knew his way around the University."[340]

However, Wallis was also absent a lot: he spent most of 1957 at Stanford, and in subsequent years, Vice President Richard Nixon frequently called him to Washington, DC. Wallis was the driving force behind President Eisenhower's Cabinet Committee on Price Stability for Economic Growth. While he and Lorie carried out a successful reengineering of the business school, Wallis eventually began to show interest in the presidency of the University of Chicago. When it became clear that Ed Levi would be the next president, Wallis accepted an offer to become president of the University of Rochester in 1962.

Lorie, whom Stigler called "the owner of the most sardonic wit I have met" (Stigler 1988b, 159), had a very different background. Lorie was born in 1922 in Kansas City, Missouri, and he earned a master's degree in agricultural economics from Cornell University in 1945. Lorie moved to the University of Chicago, where by 1947 he had finished his PhD on the livestock industry: "I hurried because I wanted to go West to raise cattle with my stepbrother. However, being a cowboy wasn't my cup of tea."[341] In 1947, he returned to the University of Chicago, which he would never leave again except for the two years (1950–52) that he served as adviser to the Board of Governors of the Federal Reserve System. His first academic interests were in marketing and consumer spending, which led to the creation of a handbook on marketing research in 1951 (Lorie and Roberts 1951). Under the influence of Garfield Cox, Lorie's attention gradually shifted to finance and investment.[342] In 1974, he prepared a public policy report on the capital markets for the Treasury Department (Lorie 1974), and from 1964 to 1984, he directed the biannual Seminar on the Analysis of Security Prices. In 1973, he cowrote a book with Mary Hamilton that provided a nontechnical description of the whole body of modern finance as it had developed up to that time (Lorie and Hamilton 1973).

Wallis and Lorie created the modern Chicago approach to business education: "Harper's concept of a College of Practical Arts, Laughlin's vision of a School that would combine the practical with the theoretical, the cosmic view of Marshall who saw business education in the forefront of social change, now came full circle with Wallis and Lorie" (Dreiser 1971, 17–18). At the GSB Centennial Gala, Merton Miller (1997, 1) summarized what Wallis and Lorie had done for Chicago's business school: "The Wallis-Lorie team gave us our Constitution and also our Declaration of Independence." Wallis spelled that constitution out in 1958:

> Instead of asking 'What are the things that businessmen must know?,' we should ask, 'Of all the things that businessmen should learn during their lives, which are best taught during the few years around the age of twenty that are devoted to academic professional training?' ... [therefore] universities should teach the broad underlying fields of knowledge that are basic to the practice of business and they should teach the fields of business practice in a broad analytical framework ... The basic disciplines may be classified under four headings: (1) economics, (2) quantitative meth-

ods, (3) behavioral science, and (4) law ... The teaching of business subjects should be organized ... around the functions that are common to all businesses ... These functional fields may be grouped also into four categories: (1) production, (2) marketing, (3) finance, and (4) personnel." (Wallis, 1958, 3–5)

That this constitution of the GSB drew heavily on Bach's approach at Carnegie's Graduate School of Industrial Administration can hardly be questioned. However, Lorie points to a crucial difference: "Bach's approach was entirely based on the scientific analysis of business decisions. Our concept went one important step further. We at the GSB consider not only the scientific analysis of business decisions in finance, marketing, industrial relations, and production, but also analyze the structure and functions of business organizations, and examine the total environment of business."[343]

Next to the constitution there was, to use Miller's words, the declaration of independence. Lorie said: "When we took over, the annual budget of the business school was $375,000. We said to university president Kimpton: 'Double this budget for the next year and afterwards we'll never again ask for one dime.' Kimpton agreed. With the assistance of our two resident advisors, Al Harberger and Edward Shils, we drew up a 10-year plan."[344] This plan impressed the people at the Ford Foundation (where Bach had played a pivotal role during the 1950s and 1960s), and a grant of $1.4 million was made available to Chicago's business school. With this money, Wallis and Lorie went on a recruiting tour through the United States, bringing George Shultz (labor economics), Sydney Davidson (accounting), Wallis's student friend Stigler, and others to Chicago.

Another Wallis-Lorie appointment was Victor Zarnowitz, who arrived in 1959 and spent 31 years at Chicago's GSB. Zarnowitz, who was born in Lancut, Poland in 1919, managed to survive Nazism and Stalinist communism. In 1951, he earned a PhD in economics at the University of Heidelberg, and he came to the United States in 1952. Zarnowitz got a job as a research assistant at the National Bureau of Economic Research in New York that was soon followed by an appointment as a lecturer at Columbia University, where Stigler a leading economist.

Stigler joined the GSB in 1957, and Zarnowitz followed him there in 1959. Zamowitz unquestionably shared Stigler's passion for empirical verification. "I don't see," argued Zarnowitz 40 years later, "economics as a deductive science. It is all too easy to spin theories starting from certain axioms."[345]

Zarnowitz is best known for his work on the business cycle.[346] His work followed the tradition of Wesley C. Mitchell, the cofounder of the National Bureau and a pioneer in empirical business cycle analysis. Zarnowitz was suspicious of monocausal explanations of the business cycle, including those of Chicago colleagues like Friedman and Lucas: "Business cycles are not all alike and cannot be ascribed to any single factor or mechanism. Real, financial, and expectational variables all participate and interact" (Zarnowitz 1992, xvi).

## RATIONALITY QUESTIONED

According to Wallis, economics, quantitative methods, behavioral sciences, and law are the four basic disciplines of business education at Chicago's GSB. Yet although several appointments were made in the behavioral sciences, the field never really developed into an attractive area for students or a creative field of research. "I think there was a general disillusionment with behavioral sciences in business schools after the promise of the 1950s. It never had the intellectual rigor to match its promise," according to Hillel Einhorn (Arbeiter 1985, 4). Robin Hogarth highlights another factor: "Some of the early behaviorists at the GSB were stressing sociology, others psychology, anthropology, or organizational theory. There was a lack of unifying, overall vision."[347] Most of the behavioral science developments at the GSB were attributable to the efforts of Einhorn and Hogarth.

Hillel Einhorn was born in 1941 in Brooklyn, New York.[348] He attended Brooklyn College and earned a bachelor's degree in philosophy and a master's degree in experimental psychology. For his doctoral studies, Einhorn attended Wayne State University, where he earned a PhD in industrial psychology in 1969. That same year, he joined the GSB as an assistant professor in behavioral science. By the mid-1970s, dissatisfaction with the behavioral sciences was so intense that some called for a complete elimination of them from the curriculum. In 1976, Einhorn proposed a complete reorganization that would place more emphasis on behavioral decision making, a more quantitative field that is close to economics and statistics. Dean Richard Rosett gave the green light, and in 1977 the Center for Decision Research was established. Within a decade, this Center served as an example for comparable initiatives at the business schools at MIT, Carnegie-Mellon, and Wharton, among other institutions.

Under Einhorn's leadership, the Center for Decision Research increasingly criticized the traditional economic model of rationality as the dominant force in human behavior.[349] The two basic building blocks of behavioral decision theory were Herbert Simon's concept of bounded rationality and the statistical decision theory, which Chicago's L.J. Savage played an important role in developing. Hogarth describes how the research agenda of the Center grew out of a dissatisfaction with conventional economic accounts of how people make decisions: "People cannot optimize all the time. They often rely on intuition to make decisions. Among the major problems with the assumption of rationality are limits to perception and information processing, inability to test hypotheses accurately, dependence on the order in which information is acquired, and denial of uncertainty."[350]

The researchers at the Center faced considerable opposition from economists at the GSB and elsewhere in the University of Chicago, and this situation forced them to constantly raise their intellectual standards so that they—and their ideas—could survive. A parallel can be drawn here with the department of economics and the Cowles Commission, whose researchers produced scientific research of the highest quality amidst a rather hostile environment at the University of Chicago. As Hogarth says: "You need fire and water to make the pot boil."[351] Crucial to the survival of the Center for Decision Research was the combination of a scientifically and analytically rigorous approach with an emphasis on empirical research.

Einhorn always emphasized that the decision to bring Hogarth back to the University of Chicago was crucial to the successful development of the Center for Decision Research.[352] Hogarth was born in India in 1942, which at that time was still a British colony (Hogarth maintains

his British citizenship to this day). He received his high school education in Scotland. After studying at France's INSEAD (European Institute
of Business Administration) in 1967–68, Hogarth enrolled at the GSB,
where he earned a PhD in 1972 (in fact, he was Einhorn's first PhD student). Hogarth returned to INSEAD, but Einhorn brought him back
to the University of Chicago in 1979. In 1982, Einhorn became a professor of behavioral science at the GSB, and one year later, he became the
director of the Center of Decision Research. Hogarth, who had always
taken a keen interest in business education,[353] served as deputy dean of
Chicago's GSB from 1993 to 1998.

Under Hogarth's leadership, the behavioral approach at the GSB
started to develop a new perspective. Says Hogarth: "We realized that
our students needed a broader perspective. That's why we added the
study of social networks in all their variety;"[354] hence the appointment
of the sociologically oriented Ron Burt. Hogarth also played an important role in bringing the economist Richard Thaler to the GSB. A major
researcher in the area of behavioral finance, Thaler is very critical of the
efficient-market hypothesis that became the trademark of GSB scholars in finance.

## High Noon

In the early 1960s, there was a change in the leadership of the GSB.
Associate Dean Lorie had almost worked himself to death in his campaign to rebuild Chicago's GSB over the second half of the 1950s, and in
1961, he had to step aside because of health problems. A year later, Dean
Wallis left to assume the presidency of the University of Rochester, and
George Shultz took over as dean at the GSB. Shultz and the deans who
followed him further refined and expanded the Wallis-Lorie concept.
This is the context in which several centers for research were established
at the GSB in the early 1960s: the Center for Research in Security Prices,
the Center for Health Administration, the Institute of Professional
Accounting, and the Center for Mathematical Studies in Business and
Economics. Econometrician Henri Theil became the director of the latter in the fall of 1965.

The roots of econometrics lie in Europe. Norwegian Ragnar Frisch and Dutchman Jan Tinbergen, the two economists who shared the first Nobel Prize in economics in 1969, deserve most of the credit for initiating the discipline. As a matter of fact, Frisch coined the term "econometrics" and founded the Econometric Society. After having been the director of the Netherlands Central Planning Bureau since it was established in 1945, Tinbergen became a full-time professor of development planning at the Netherlands School of Economics. Tinbergen had an enormous influence on the development of econometric techniques and on economic policymaking thought.[355]

Henri Theil was one of Tinbergen's most prominent students. Theil was born in Amsterdam in 1924 and attended the University of Amsterdam, where he was awarded a PhD in 1951. Theil then joined Tinbergen's staff at the Central Planning Bureau in 1952. From 1955 to 1956 he was a visiting professor at the department of economics of the University of Chicago. After visiting professorships at Stanford University and Harvard University, he came to Chicago on a permanent basis in the fall of 1965. Theil was thoroughly trained in the Tinbergen style of econometrics, which focused on "getting the job done" by looking at the practical problems at hand rather than engaging in sophisticated theoretical digressions.[356]

Two considerations led to Theil's arrival in Chicago. First of all, there was his no-nonsense approach to the quantification of economics; this particularly pleased Friedman, who was suspicious of the increasingly sophisticated quantitative techniques economists were using. To Theil and Friedman, the techniques were simply a means to achieve empirical verification of economic phenomena. The second consideration had to do with the departure of the Cowles Commission in 1955. Despite all the fights between the Chicago economists and the Cowles researchers, most economists realized that, if nothing was done, the University of Chicago risked falling behind in the quantitative arena. Theil's presence helped fill that gap. He became a close friend of Friedman and many others, including Merton Miller.

Theil's most important contribution to econometrics is the development of the method of two-stage least squares (2SLS),[357] which offered a solution to the problems of bias and inconsistency that often plague estimates made with the ordinary least-squares method. When Theil first came to the University of Chicago, the model builders at the Cowles

Commission (especially Lawrence Klein), were putting in endless hours of work to get their simultaneous-equations models estimated properly. Theil's 2SLS method was like a gift from heaven to the Cowles researchers, because it could be applied to just one equation in a system without immediately involving all other equations.

Scientifically, the 2SLS method was not waterproof, but it "got the job done." Theil's main problem with Bayesian econometrics was its lack of practical utility. Bayesian econometrics had origins in Bayesian statistics, which were chiefly developed by L.J. Savage (1954).[358] Savage also spent some time at the University of Chicago and wrote an influential paper with Friedman. The basic difference between traditional econometrics and the Bayesian version has to do with the use of *a priori* information. In traditional econometrics, the value of the parameters of an equation will be estimated from the available data, but Bayesian econometrists will use the data to check the knowledge that exists at that moment with respect to the value of a parameter.

Arnold Zellner (1997) was highly influential in the development of Bayesian econometrics. Theil brought Zellner to Chicago's GSB from the University of Wisconsin in 1966. A few years earlier, Theil and Zellner had produced the method of three-stage least squares, a further refinement of the 2SLS procedure (Theil and Zellner 1962). Although this looked like the start of a fruitful cooperation between these two talented men, it soon turned into one of the most bitter personal battles ever fought in the history of economics at the University of Chicago.

Zellner was born in 1927 in Brooklyn, New York. He earned a bachelor's degree in physics at Harvard in 1947, but for his graduate work in physics, he switched to the University of California at Berkeley. At Berkeley, he became acquainted with the study of economics through his brother Nathan and eventually earned a PhD in economics in 1957. After spells at the University of Washington (1955–60) and the University of Wisconsin (1960–66), Zellner joined Chicago's GSB. For more than 30 years, Zellner was one of the pillars of the faculty, and his office became a refuge for doctoral students who were desperate for advice or inspiration.

Zellner cofounded the *Journal of Econometrics* in 1972 and was a founding editor of the *Journal of Business and Economic Statistics* in 1981. His own first major contribution to the field of econometrics was on seemingly unrelated regressions. During the 1960s, Zellner gradually moved in the direction of Bayesian econometrics. Critics of Bayesian methods argue that they rely too much on prior information. Zellner rejects this argument: "Non-Bayesians sit around thinking about restrictions on simultaneous equation models. That's prior information. Others think about what to assume about the error terms properties. That's many times prior information. Others sit around thinking about how to formulate a model for the observations. That involves a tremendous amount of prior information. Others worry about how to choose a significance level and the power of their tests which involves a lot of prior information" (Rossi 1989, 301).

The split between Theil and Zellner—in the end, they literally stopped talking to each other and stood in opposition to each other[359]— was about more than the usefulness of Bayesian econometrics or other scientific arguments. First of all, they had extremely different personalities. Theil was more open and flexible, and Zellner was a real scientist, obsessed with his work and inflexible where scientific arguments were concerned. He could not accept Theil's total refutation of Bayesian statistics and econometrics.

Another important element of Zellner's animosity was the fact that Theil was not an especially good teacher and, moreover, did not care much for his students. Zellner was an able teacher who consistently showed great concern for his students. To put it bluntly: In Zellner's eyes, Theil was not doing his job properly. Last but not least, there was the fact that Theil never became an economist in the Chicago sense— basic price theory didn't interest him.

Disappointed, Theil left Chicago in 1981 to a become a professor of econometrics and decision sciences at the University of Florida in Gainesville. He died in Florida in 2000.

## Pioneers in Finance

The two fields in which the GSB gained the strongest reputation in the second half of the 20th century were not behavioral science or econometrics—instead, they were industrial organization and, especially, finance. Although Merton Miller and Eugene Fama are usually recognized as the originators of the GSB's success story in the area of finance, Charles O. Hardy deserves mention as well.

Hardy went through the economics curriculum as a graduate student at Chicago and earned a PhD in history in 1916 there as well. Hardy lectured at Chicago's business school from 1918 to 1922. In that period, he wrote his classic book *Risk and Risk Bearing* (1923).[360] In 1922 Hardy moved to the economics department at Iowa State University; there, he became a colleague of Frank Knight's. In the preface to his book *Risk, Profit and Uncertainty* Knight acknowledges his debt to Hardy, who was also one of the first to present a fully worked-out theory of hedging (Hardy and Lyon 1923). One of the issues Hardy analyzed in *Risk and Risk Bearing* would in today's jargon be called the futures market. On the basis of his empirical work, Hardy argued that, on average, speculators lose money and by doing so they render society a service because, through the individual losses of these speculators, other people can rid themselves of risks associated with their productive businesses.

Another pioneer in the field of finance is Chicago native Harry Markowitz, who shared the 1990 Nobel Prize with Merton Miller and William Sharpe. Markowitz, who was a member of the Cowles Commission as a PhD student, laid down the foundations of modern portfolio management in his 1952 dissertation at the University of Chicago. He earned his doctoral degree despite Milton Friedman's opposition to his thesis. Friedman contended that "this isn't a dissertation in economics … It's not math, it's not economics, it's not even business administration" (Bernstein 1992, 60). Starting with the familiar idea that risk and return are the two properties of any asset with which investors are concerned, Markowitz developed insights including the idea that the total risk of a portfolio is not only determined by the risk of the individual investments but also by the correlations between these risks. On the basis of Markowitz's analysis, it became accepted jargon to speak of an "efficient portfolio," i.e., "a portfolio that offers the highest expected return for any given degree of risk, or that has the lowest degree of risk for any given expected return" (Bernstein 1992, 53). Markowitz's work also provided his graduate student William Sharpe with the building blocks for the development of the illustrious capital-asset pricing model (CAPM). This model was basically a vehicle that made it possible to sidestep the enormous problem inherent in Markowitz's setup—the calculation of all the covariances among the individual stocks under consideration.

Sharpe's solution to this problem was to relate the variability of each stock to that of the market as a whole (Sharpe 1963).

Ezra Solomon was another pioneering scholar working in the field of modern finance at the University of Chicago. Solomon was born in 1920 in Rangoon, Burma. He graduated with a degree in economics from the University of Rangoon in 1940, but the Solomon family fled to India when the Japanese invaded Burma in 1941. Solomon served with the Burma Division of the Royal Navy Volunteer Reserve for five years. In 1947, he came to the University of Chicago as a Burma state scholar and earned a PhD in economics in 1950. A regime change in Rangoon made him decide to stay in the United States. In 1961, Solomon moved to Stanford University, partly because he "didn't feel comfortable with the Friedmanite label in monetary affairs, although there can be no doubt that Milton Friedman is one the greatest economists of the 20th century."[361] In his scholarly work, Solomon focused on such topics as investment portfolio theory and corporate finance (Solomon 1948, 1955).

Jim Lorie was another early pioneer in modern finance. As Wallis's right hand in the reshaping of Chicago's GSB, Lorie was much more of a clever number cruncher than a man of theory. Lorie got the Center for Research in Security Prices established with $150,000 in funding from Merrill Lynch, Pierce, Fenner & Smith. This was achieved in 1960, and the Center became the first institute to have a complete database of historical information on every stock listed on the New York Stock Exchange (NYSE). Lorie says: "We wanted to answer one basic question: 'What has been, over the long haul, the experience of the average investor in common stocks?'"[362] The Center's unique database allowed Lorie and statistician Lawrence Fisher to publish a groundbreaking piece of empirical analysis on the returns of all NYSE stocks between 1926 and 1960 (Fisher and Lorie 1964).[363] This analysis was truly innovative because unlike earlier work on the subject, it analyzed total returns—not only changes in stock prices but also dividends paid.

In an article he contributed to the *Wall Street Journal* on the occasion of the Dow Jones Industrial's centennial in 1996, Lorie summarized the general conclusions to be drawn from more than 30 years of empirical research on the stock market:

One dollar invested in 1926 in large companies such as those represented on the Dow Jones Industrial Average, would, with dividends reinvested, have grown to over $1,100 by the end of 1995. The average annual percentage return is 10.5 percent. The picture is less cheery if one takes into account inflation, taxes and transaction costs ... [then] the average annual rate of return would have been 4.8 percent ... The data do indicate that common stocks have been the best investments for all long periods of time. Stocks in small companies have been best of all ... The two prolonged periods of poor performance for the stock market (the 1930s and 1970s) seem to have been caused by what we see—in hindsight only—were major mistakes in monetary policy.[364]

## AGENT FAMA

Eugene Fama is one of the most important researchers in modern finance at the GSB. Born in Boston in 1939, Fama did his undergraduate studies in 1960 at Tufts University while dreaming of a career in football or baseball.[365] He graduated with a degree in romance languages, but knowledge of the French language and civilization did not offer impressive career opportunities. Harry Ernst, a Tufts professor who published a stock market newsletter, aroused Fama's interest in the stock market. In 1960, Fama transferred to Chicago's GSB, where he earned an MBA in 1963 and a PhD in 1964. His dissertation on the behavior of stock market prices was the first at Chicago to be completed under the supervision of Merton Miller. Fama's lifelong stay at the GSB was interrupted only by a few visiting professorships, including spells at Belgium's Catholic University of Leuven and UCLA's Anderson Graduate School of Management.

In addition to an impressive number of articles in journals, Fama produced two textbooks in the field of finance (Fama and Miller 1972; Fama 1976) and also made interesting contributions to the theory of the firm. The classical model viewed the firm as an entity owned and managed by a single person. By the 1950s, this model came under increasing criticism, and attention shifted to the managers who did not own their company and the areas of potential conflict between these managers and the owners. Although basic characteristics were already present in the work of Ronald Coase, and even, some would argue, in that of Adam Smith. Armen Alchian, Harold Demsetz, Michael Jensen, and William Meckling are generally considered to be the founding fathers of the theory of the firm in which agency problems are the central concept.[366] The basic idea behind this approach is that a firm can best be viewed as a set of contracts among the factors of production, with each of these factors acting in its own best interest.

Fama carried this contractual approach one step further, arguing that the modern separation of management and risk-bearing is an efficient form of economic organization. Fama saw the basic problem of the owner-risk bearers as follows: "When management and risk bearing are viewed as naturally separate factors of production, looking at the market for risk bearing from the viewpoint of portfolio theory tells us that risk bearers are likely to spread their wealth across many firms and so not to be interested in directly controlling the management of any individual firm" (Fama 1980, 295). In this setup, managerial labor markets ensure that managers are disciplined, and outside takeovers are the ultimate police force.[367] In several papers written with his former student Jensen (who was by then at the University of Rochester), Fama elaborated further on his contractual theory of the firm. Starting from the observation that most goods and services can be produced by any form of organization, and that there is competition among organizational forms for survival in any activity, they concluded that "absent fiat, the form of organization that survives in an activity is the one that delivers the product demanded by customers at the lowest price while covering costs" (Fama and Jensen 1983, 301).

Despite these different contributions to the theory of the firm, it is no exaggeration to state that one question has dominated Fama's career: Are capital markets efficient or not? Fama's answer has always been yes; in this context, efficiency means that the prices of stocks, bonds, and other securities reflect all the information that is available at any point in time. Fama began researching the stock market and eventually produced the random walk hypothesis, which posits that successive price changes of individual stocks are unpredictable because stock market prices rapidly adjust to every bit of new information that becomes available on the company involved.[368] Fama's paper "Tomorrow on the New York Stock Exchange" (1965c) appeared in the same issue of the *Journal of Business* as a similar exercise on the Amsterdam Stock Exchange that was supervised by Theil (Theil and Leenders 1965). The random walk hypothesis led to the conclusion that no investor can hope to beat the market systematically. The chance of this happening is comparable to the so-called millionth monkey effect—the likelihood that one in a million monkeys with a PC will write out Shakespeare's Macbeth.

However, the concept of the random walk hypothesis was not new when Fama came up with it. As a matter of fact, just one year before Fama's articles were published, MIT professor Paul Cootner had edited a book entitled *The Random Walk of Stock Prices* (1964). Among the more striking pre-Fama works on random walks is a seminal 1959 paper by the GSB's Harry Roberts (1959). Paul Samuelson also subscribed to the random walk hypothesis (1965), and Alfred Cowles had reached similar conclusions in 1944.

In 1970, Fama produced evidence that the market efficiency hypothesis held for the stock market and also for all capital markets in general. This finding brought him extensive coverage in the popular media and caused a huge controversy among economists. Sanford Grossman and Joseph Stiglitz (1980) developed a theoretical model that showed that perfectly efficient markets are only possible on the improbable condition that information and trading costs are always zero. Robert Schiller (1984) and Lawrence Summers (1986) produced evidence that stock prices might be predictable over the longer term. Although they challenged these findings on the basis of data distortions caused by the Great Depression, Fama and Kenneth French (1988), one of Fama's students who later taught at the Yale School of Management, produced evidence that some part of the longer-term returns on stocks and bonds may indeed be predictable.

Over time, Fama watered down his version of the efficiency market hypothesis. In 1970, he contended that "the evidence in support of the efficient markets model is extensive and (somewhat uniquely in economics) contradictory evidence is sparse" (Fama 1970, 416). Contrast this with the proposition he wrote 21 years later: "Since there are surely positive information and trading costs, the extreme version of the market efficiency hypothesis is surely false ... A weaker and economically more sensible version of the efficiency hypothesis says that prices reflect information to the point where the marginal benefits of acting on information (the profits to be made) do not exceed the marginal costs" (Fama 1991, 1575).[369] Does Fama's view on efficient capital markets mean security analysis and active trading don't make any sense? Not at all. By 1965, Fama (1965c) had noted that analysts and traders play a crucial role in narrowing the discrepancies between actual prices and intrinsic values and cause actual prices—on average—to adjust to changes in intrinsic values.

Through their empirical research, Fama and French produced evidence that went against another finance paradigm: the famous beta of CAPM, which was first developed by William Sharpe (1970). This beta reduced risk related to securities to a single dimension: the sensitivity of stocks or other securities to changes in returns on the market. In other words, an asset's volatility relative to the market determines its riskiness. In several papers, Fama and French (1992, 1996) came up with two other important risk factors or, to put it another way, two factors that capture much of the cross-section of average stock returns. These factors are size as captured by market equity (stock price times shares outstanding) and the ratio of book value to market value. These results further fueled the discussion, and the behavioral finance researchers fundamentally challenged the concept of market efficiency.

## THE WORLD OF M AND M

Like Lorie and Fama, Merton Miller played a prominent role in the story of Chicago and modern finance. Miller won a Nobel prize in economics for having "established the foundation for the field 'Financial Economics and Corporate Finance'" (Lindbeck 1992, 272). According to Gregg Jarrell, former chief economist at the Securities and Exchange Commission and a professor at the business school of the University of Rochester, "Mr. Miller, armed with enormous intelligence, humor, energy, and a genius of a co-author, won over the finance profession and started the field on its way to becoming rich with scientifically rigorous theories and statistically sophisticated empirical knowledge."[370] In his search for "the improbable origins of modern Wall Street," Peter Bernstein assigned a similar pivotal role to Miller: "As financial markets multiplied and as institutions and professional managers became the principal players, innovation was inevitable. But innovation must be preceded by theory ... Throughout this story, Merton Miller has played the role of power broker. He had encouraged Eugene Fama, still a novice, to teach entirely new material. He had guided Scholes into finance. He had introduced Treynor to Modigliani. He had immediately recognized Sharpe's talent. And finally he was instrumental in providing Black and Scholes with the notice that their work surely deserved" (Bernstein 1992, 221). In all of this, Miller succeeded in combining thorough analysis with a great sense of humor.[371]

Merton Miller was born in 1923 in Boston and was educated at Harvard (a bachelor's degree in 1944) and Johns Hopkins University (a PhD in 1952). "I chose Johns Hopkins," Miller recalled almost a half century later, "because I was intrigued by the work of Fritz Machlup who taught there. Together with George Stigler, Machlup was the economist that influenced me most."[372] From 1943 to 1947, Miller worked in the research department of the U.S. Treasury, followed by two years at the Federal Reserve System in Washington, DC. After one year at the LSE, Miller joined the Graduate School of Industrial Administration of the Carnegie Institute of Technology in 1953. Eight years later, he joined Chicago's GSB, where he stayed for the rest of his life.

At Carnegie, Miller teamed up with another future Nobel Prize winner, Franco Modigliani, the "genius of a co-author" Gregg Jarrell referred to. They produced the Modigliani-Miller (MM) theorem in 1958. In 1988, when Miller looked back on their 1958 paper, he wrote that he was reflecting on "three decades of intense scrutiny and often bitter controversy ... The view that ... 'nothing matters' in corporate finance, though still sometimes attributed to us ... is far from what we ever actually said about the real-world applications of our theoretical propositions" (Miller 1993, 129–130). Some parallels can also be drawn between the MM theorem and the Coase Theorem. Both are built on strong assumptions that made it possible to derive even stronger conclusions. Too often, however, these assumptions have been forgotten.

In the paper that resulted in the MM theorem, Miller and Modigliani set out to develop "an adequate theory of the effect of financial structure on market evaluation" and then "a theory of investment of the firm under uncertainty" (Modigliani and Miller 1958, 264). They found the traditional approach to be unsatisfactory because it simply equalized the cost of capital to the market rate of interest—thereby implying that investment will tend to be pushed to the point where the marginal yield on physical assets is equal to that market interest rate. A cornerstone of their analysis was the concept first introduced by Irving Fisher that a corporation should be regarded as a vehicle that produces a stream of cash flows.

The MM theorem basically consisted of two propositions. First, "the market value of any firm is independent of its capital structure and is given by capitalizing its expected returns at the rate $p_k$ appropriate to its class" (Modigliani and Miller, 1958, 268). In this case, "class" refers to risk-equivalent assets that generate comparable income streams. The second proposition stated—as Miller rephrased it in 1988—that "the cost of equity capital was a linear function of the debt/equity ratio. Any gains from using more of what might seem to be cheaper debt capital would thus be offset by the correspondingly higher cost of the now riskier equity capital" (Miller 1993, 130). Hence, nothing could be gained by changing the leverage of a company. These propositions were derived from a model with strong assumptions, of which two are crucial. The first assumption is that markets are perfect in the sense of exhibiting zero transaction costs and perfect information, and the second assumption is that investors continuously optimize their positions by taking advantage of every arbitrage opportunity that appears between leveraged and unleveraged companies.

MIT's David Durand led the critique of the MM theorem. Durand (1959) seriously questioned the arbitrage assumption and also argued that the existence of dividends undermined the MM propositions. With respect to Durand and the first MM proposition, history took a rather ironic turn. In 1952, Durand presented a paper during a conference that was sponsored by the National Bureau of Economic Research. The paper contemplated the idea that the value of a company might be independent of its capital structure. However, he rejected this idea because it did not conform to the real business world. This paper was published one year before Modigliani and Miller's article (Durand 1957).

Modigliani and Miller rejected the dividend-related criticism in two follow-up papers (Modigliani and Miller 1959, 1961). That issues concerning dividend policy are much less important than is often assumed remained a constant line of thought in Miller's work (Miller and Scholes 1978).

A third critique of the original MM propositions related to the importance of taxes for the capital structure of firms. In 1963, Modigliani and Miller admitted that—contrary to their original position—the tax rate and the degree of leverage did indeed play a role in the decisions of rational investors. In his 1977 paper "Debt and Taxes," Miller further analyzed the issue of taxes, capital structure, and finance. A frequent question would arise—why didn't companies resort more heavily to debt financing, as the tax rate on profit had gone up substantially in the United States since the 1920s? Miller offered that tax advantages can be viewed as a government subsidy in favor of debt financing as an explanation for this phenomenon. This subsidization increases the demand for debt financing, but more companies issuing more bonds will tend to lower the price of bonds, thus triggering an increase in the interest rate. At that point, debt financing becomes less attractive once again.

In the late 1990s, Fama and French (1997) examined data on more than 2,000 companies for the period 1965 to 1992 and found that a clear separation line could be drawn between real investment decisions and decisions related to financing.[373] In conformity with the MM logic, nothing in the Fama and French data indicated that high debt ratios tend to deter investment.

In another piece of largely empirical research, Fama and French (1998) found no link between tax effects of financing decisions and firm value. As Miller himself explained, the MM theorem and the efficient market hypothesis are clearly linked: "The M&M Propositions, like the Efficient Markets Hypothesis, are about equilibrium in the capital markets—what equilibrium looks like and what forces are set in motion once it is disturbed" (Miller 1998, 13).

## No Chernobyl

Over time, the concept of leverage, which is closely related to the MM theorem, became ever more important in corporate finance. In fact,

Miller chose "Leverage" as the title for his 1990 Nobel lecture. Remaining faithful to the message of the 1963 article—tax issues do make a difference, but not a very important one—Miller argued that the main reasons for leveraged buyouts (LBOs) should not be sought in the tax advantages of debt financing, and he believed "that the LBO entrepreneurs have achieved substantial real efficiency gains by reconcentrating corporate control and redeploying assets" (Miller 1992, 292). Furthermore, Miller argued that most of the fallout fears with respect to overleveraging are groundless. He made four points on this issue: "first, that losses and defaults on junk bonds need not mean that overleveraging did in fact occur; second, paradoxical as it may sound, that increased leveraging by corporations does not imply increased risk for the economy as a whole; third, that the financial distress being suffered by some highly leveraged firms involves mainly private, not social costs; and finally, that the capital markets have built-in controls against overleveraging" (Miller 1992, 292).

Miller developed a similar defense of the derivative markets (e.g., options, futures), whose role was hotly debated when the likes of Orange County, Metallgesellschaft, Barings Bank, and LTCM left huge losses in their wakes. These markets grew enormously "because they have ... allowed firms and banks, at long last, to manage effectively and at low cost business and financial risks that have plagued them for decades" (Miller 1994, 1–2). On the social costs associated with big losses in the derivatives markets, Miller argued, "... derivatives *always* have two sides, a long and a short. And, at all times, the positions cancel. The gains and losses thus represent what economists call pure *transfers* of wealth between the parties, not changes in *aggregate* social wealth" (Miller 1996, 3). But what about the so-called systemic risk—"the fear that a failure by one big bank will bring down another big bank which will bring down another until the world's whole financial system melts down in some cataclysmic Chernobyl. That *can* happen of course, but it's most unlikely. The big banks of this world are ... all very heavily capitalized, highly diversified in their portfolios, thanks in part to derivatives, incidentally, and constantly monitoring their aggregate risk exposure" (Miller 1996, 13). Big financial crashes, Miller argued (1994, 2), "are *policy* disasters, tracing not to transactions between *private-sector* parties but to deliberately deflationary actions of a central bank somewhere." The central banks of the world, moreover, "have the power, though not always the will or the wisdom, to stop in its tracks any downward cascading financial spiral. Our own Federal Reserve System failed miserably on that count in the early 1930s, but at least learned some important lessons in the process that have made the prospect of a recurrence of the 1930s for the U.S. virtually unthinkable" (Miller 1996, 13).

Influenced by the work of GSB colleagues Stigler and Peltzman on regulation, Miller examined government regulation in the financial arena.[374] He came to argue that practically all financial innovation is borne out of a desire to mitigate the effects of regulation.[375] As to the recurring demand for more regulation of the derivatives markets, he argued that what this was all about was clearly shown in the aftermath of the crash of October 1987 with:

> ... The campaign waged by the New York Stock Exchange,
> the SEC [Securities and Exchange Commission], and parts of
> the New York brokerage industry for tighter regulation of the
> Chicago futures exchanges. The New York attackers were claim-
> ing that index arbitrage was causing market crashes and rais-
> ing market volatility, which was false. What they *really* meant,
> of course, was that the new Chicago index futures products were
> taking commission and fee income away from the New York
> firms, which was certainly true. Such are the conventions of
> American politics, however, that the brokerage industry and the
> SEC couldn't come right out and say that. They had to frame
> their case in higher, public-interest terms by demanding tighter
> regulation of the interlopers. (Miller 1994, 10)

Through his work on corporate finance and regulation, Miller became involved with the Chicago Board of Trade (CBOT) and the Chicago Mercantile Exchange (CME). Miller held the University of Chicago's seat on the board of the CBOT during the period 1983–1985 and joined the CME's board in 1990. Both organizations played a crucial role in developing the market for financial derivatives. The intellectual roots of the derivatives market can be found at the University of Chicago. As the story goes, Friedman played the role of catalyst.

By the end of the 1960s, Friedman was firmly convinced that the

British welfare system had become untenable and would inevitably lead to a devaluation of the pound. Friedman wanted to put his money where his mouth was and asked his banker whether he could short-sell the pound. He found out traditional banking did not offer him this opportunity.[376] Friedman's complaint reached the ears of the CME's Leo Melamed, who had been thinking along Friedman's lines and decided that the time had come to create the market for this type of transactions. In April 1973, the CME opened the first modern options exchange in Chicago. One month later, one of the most influential articles in the history of economics appeared in the University of Chicago's *Journal of Political Economy*: "The Pricing of Options and Corporate Liabilities."

Fischer Black and Myron Scholes, the authors of that famous article, were the first to solve the options pricing puzzle. A race in the academic circles had developed to get to that solution first. Samuelson recalled more than 20 years later: "It was like the race to the North Pole, and they were the first to get there. I had worked on the problem, too, and I was close, but no cigar."[377]

Black was born in 1938 and died on August 30, 1995 of throat cancer. As the British weekly *The Economist* commented in its obituary, he was "one of the most productive economic minds of his century and, had he lived, would surely have won a Nobel Prize."[378] In 1959, Black graduated from Harvard with a bachelor's degree in physics, and five years later he obtained a PhD in applied mathematics from Harvard. In 1965, he joined Arthur D. Little, where Jack Treynor sparked his interest in finance. According to Black (1989), Treynor had already developed the CAPM a few years before Sharpe had.

Black left Arthur D. Little in 1969 to start his own consulting firm, Associates in Finance. Miller succeeded in attracting Black to Chicago's GSB in 1972: "With his strong belief in markets and rational behavior he out-Chicagoed Chicago" (Merton and Scholes 1995, 1360). Black returned to Boston in 1975 to become a professor of finance at MIT's Sloan School of Management, and he left MIT in 1984 to join Goldman Sachs.

## The Magic of a Formula

While working for Arthur D. Little in Boston, Black met Scholes. This was the start of a fruitful cooperation.[379] The birth of the article and its famous option formula has already been documented in detail (Black 1989; Bernstein, 1992). Black and Scholes initially ran into strong opposition to their article, and it took the sustained support of Merton Miller, Eugene Fama, and Harry Johnson to finally get it published in Chicago's *Journal of Political Economy* (like everyone else, the *Journal* had turned it down at first) in 1973, even though a first draft had been complete as early as 1970. It took Chicago's readiness to support new ideas, no matter how controversial, and make the Black-Scholes formula a success story.

By the end of the 1960s, Black, inspired by Treynor and soon joined by Scholes, started working on the question of the pricing of options. Black and Scholes finally came up with a formula that was innovative: it made it possible to determine the value of an option not only at the expiry date but at any point in time. MIT's Robert Merton played a crucial role in the development of the formula; in fact, Black pointed out 15 years later that because Merton gave them the arbitrage argument for deriving the formula, the article should be called the Black-Merton-Scholes paper.

The Black-Scholes formula for pricing options indicated that the value of, for example, a call option on stock X increases with increases in the price of stock X, the time remaining until the option expires, the interest rate, and the volatility of stock X. This volatility is particularly important for options pricing. To be able to derive a specific option price on the basis of the formula, Black and Scholes had to make some rather heroic assumptions, such as the known volatility of the stock, a constant short-term interest rate, and no trading costs. Although researchers have tried to refine and extend the Black-Scholes formula, the basic Black-Scholes formula is still widely used. Scholars gradually came to realize that the methodology Black and Scholes developed could also be used to value any contract whose worth depends on the uncertain value of an asset. Princeton's Avinash Dixit argued: "... if you ask what idea in the last 50 or 60 years coming from economic research has had the biggest impact on the world, this is it."[380]

It would be a mistake to reduce the significance of Fischer Black as an economist to the Black-Scholes formula and his subsequent contributions to the area of options and derivatives.[381] He also contributed to research on such topics as asset pricing, portfolio management, the design of financial institutions, and the effects of taxation. In his 15-minute-long 1985 presidential address to the American Finance Association, Black introduced the concept of "noise" as "what makes our observations imperfect" (Black 1986, 259). Black (1986) showed how noise made economic analysis, and drawing firm conclusions, very difficult in the fields of finance, econometrics, and macroeconomics.[382] With his distinction between information traders—those acting on hard evidence and solid news—and noise traders —those acting on anything else—Black made an important contribution to what would become known as behavioral finance.

Black also became interested in macroeconomics, particularly monetary theory. In fact, the only two books he ever published were in this field (Black 1987, 1995a). He was among the first to warn that control of the money supply would become more and more complicated as financial innovation progressed. His business cycle analysis was very close to what would become known as the real business cycle theory.

*The Economist* argued in Black's 1995 obituary that "… had he lived, [he] would surely have won a Nobel Prize." This was explicitly confirmed by the Royal Swedish Academy of Sciences two years later when it awarded the 1997 Nobel Prize in economics to Robert C. Merton and Scholes. For the first time, the importance of an economist no longer living was emphasized by the Academy. "Robert C. Merton and Myron S. Scholes have, in collaboration with the late Fischer Black, developed a pioneering formula for the valuation of stock options. Their methodology has paved the way for economic valuations in many areas. It has also generated new types of financial instruments and facilitated more efficient risk management in society," were the opening words of the Royal Swedish Academy of Sciences press release.

The Nobel Prize for Scholes was also a win for the GSB. Scholes was born in 1941 in Timmins, Canada, but he would later became a U.S. citizen. He earned a bachelor's degree in 1962 at Toronto's McMaster University; afterward, he attended Chicago's GSB and received an MBA in 1964 and a PhD five years later under Miller's supervision. After only one year as an instructor at Chicago, Scholes joined MIT's Sloan School of Management, where he stayed until 1973. Scholes spent 1973–82 back at the GSB where, among other responsibilities, he was director of the Center for Research in Security Prices for six years. After Chicago came Stanford, where he taught finance and tax law, and there he argued that further refinements in financial products and markets played an important role in the process of economic growth (Scholes 1996). It is undeniable, however, that Scholes's output as a scholar declined significantly after he left the University of Chicago.

Scholes joined Salomon Brothers as managing director in the autumn of 1991. Salomon's vice chairman John Meriwether, a legendary trader and fellow University of Chicago graduate, welcomed him to his brain trust on bond trading. After a scandal concerning Treasury bond deals, Meriwether left Salomon and set up his own trading house, Long-Term Capital Management (LTCM). Most who enjoyed great success at Salomon, including Scholes and Merton, joined Meriwether there as partners.[383] On the day Merton and Scholes got their Nobel Prize, the *Wall Street Journal* commented: "The success of Long-Term Capital, where the partners have shared more than $1 billion in profits, makes the two men among the richest Nobel Laureates ever."[384]

But even brilliant Nobel Prize winners can be wrong. When LTCM went belly-up in September 1998, it wiped out a big chunk of the personal fortunes of both Scholes and Merton.[385] Ironically, in his Nobel lecture, which was delivered nine months before the LTCM disaster, Scholes said that it could hardly be argued "that we have seen the end of derivative failures. There will be losses sustained as in many other business activities" (Scholes 1998, 363).

## Nothing But Disconnected Paradoxes?

A firm belief in the rationality of markets is central to the work of prominent GSB finance scholars, including Miller, Fama, and Scholes. The quasi-consensus among Chicago's finance people on this issue was shaken in 1995 when Richard Thaler, one of the founding fathers of behavioral finance, joined the GSB.

Four years earlier, Fama had written: "De Bondt and Thaler mount an aggressive empirical attack on market efficiency, directed at unmasking irrational bubbles" (Fama, 1991, 1581). Fama was referring to two papers Richard Thaler and his student Werner De Bondt[386] had published in the second half of the 1980s in which they offered evidence in support of the "overreaction hypothesis" (De Bondt and Thaler 1987, 557). "The financial world as described in Eugene Fama's 1970 efficient market survey," Thaler argued, "was one that had no urgent need for people. Markets were efficient, prices were unpredictable, and financial economists did not know how to spell the word *anomaly*" (Thaler, 1993, xvi). Thaler and De Bondt argued that investors not only tend to overreact to news but also to overweigh recent information; they found that extreme performers on the NYSE tended to show a strong reversal of that performance in later periods.[387]

Richard Thaler was born in 1945 in East Orange, New Jersey. He attended the University of Rochester and earned a master's degree in 1970 and a PhD in economics in 1974, and he later taught at Rochester's Graduate School of Management. In the summer of 1978 he moved from Rochester to Cornell's Graduate School of Business and Public Administration. Thaler stayed at Cornell until 1995, when he came to Chicago's GSB. "I consider myself to be a typical modern Chicago economist, since empirical work dominates my research," Thaler said.[388] "Thaler's hiring is a characteristic Chicago move. His work is of high quality, although still quite controversial. It might in the end lead to nothing but it might also give us another Nobel win," explained a GSB man involved in hiring Thaler.[389]

The subject of Thaler's doctoral dissertation, which was written under the supervision of Sherwin Rosen, was the value of a human life (Rosen and Thaler 1976). "While working on this dissertation," Thaler recalls, "I began to realize that, even for economists, it might be more interesting to ask people questions directly instead of just running regressions."[390] Thaler's discovery of the work done by Daniel Kahneman and Amos Tversky, two leading scholars in the field of behavioral decision theory, were crucial to the development of his dissertation.[391] In 1977 and 1978, Thaler spent 15 months at Stanford University and collaborated with Kahneman and Tversky. Almost 20 years later, Thaler was still unequivocal: "This period left a major impact on my thinking for the rest of my life."[392] Thaler based much of his work on direct experiments with people through questioning them. This approach led to remarkable insights on such topics as consumer choice, saving decisions, self-control, and the Coase Theorem.[393]

In 1992, Thaler published a book on anomalies in traditional economic analysis. The book's title, *The Winner's Curse*, refers to Thaler's proposition that "in an auction with many bidders, the winning bidder is often a loser" for the simple reason that the nature of the bidding process often leads the winner to bid too high (Thaler 1992, 1). It goes without saying that such a statement sounds suspicious to a neoclassical economist. "But," Thaler argues, "take a close look at three or four decades of economic research and you'll see that the focus has been overwhelmingly on research on prices and not on people, and there's absolutely nothing that can make one believe that markets are really different from anything else. We know people matter everywhere else ... why not in the analysis of the behavior of markets?"[394]

Recognizing that "we are still much closer to the beginning of the research agenda than we are to the end," Thaler and Nicholas Barberis[395] concluded in 2003 that "behavioral finance argues that some financial phenomena can plausibly be understood using models in which some agents are not fully rational. The field has two building blocks: *limits to arbitrage*, which argues that it can be difficult for rational traders to undo the dislocations caused by less rational traders; and *psychology*, which catalogues the kinds of deviations from full rationality we might expect to see" (Barberis and Thaler 2003, 1114).

Miller saw little future for the research program on behavioral finance, referring to it as:

> ... little more than some disconnected paradoxes, optical illusions and the usual mantras I've been hearing for 40 years ... on the supposed importance of more realistic psychological assumptions in modeling individual choice behavior. But why should we, as economists, care about that kind of realism? We're perfectly willing to leave the detailed description of *individual* choices to our colleagues in psychology. Our concern in finance and economics has always been the essentially *impersonal* behavior of *markets* and *market prices*. Rationality, as *we* use it, means simply that people are assumed to prefer more wealth to less. Or, in the words of comedian Joe E. Lewis: "I've been rich and I've been poor. And rich is better" (Miller 1998, 8–9).

On the basis of his own empirical research, Fama saw two essential reasons why market efficiency should not be abandoned. First, "consistent with the market efficiency hypothesis that the anomalies are chance results, apparent over-reaction of stock prices is about as common as under-reaction" and, second, "post-event continuation of pre-event abnormal returns is about as frequent as post-event reversal." The second argument for market efficiency is that "the long-term anomalies are fragile. They tend to disappear with reasonable changes in the way they are measured" (Fama 1998b, 304).[396]

Another point of disagreement between Fama and Thaler was the equity premium puzzle.[397] This equity premium puzzle refers to the fact that over longer periods, returns on equity are higher than on risk-free Treasury bills. The explanation seems to be that investors have levels of risk aversion well in excess of the level generally assumed for the average investor. Thaler argued that the solution to this equity premium puzzle lies in "characteristics of the psychology of human decision making that are fundamentally at odds with the theory of market efficiency."[398] French and Fama, who examined the period 1872–1999, found that investors just got lucky: they earned more than they expected to earn when they made their investments "due to unexpected capital gains, the result of a decline in discount rates" (Fama and French 2000, i).

## THE GLAMOR OF VALUE

When Thaler arrived at the GSB in 1995, he found that Robert Vishny was a strong ally for his research program on behavioral finance. Born in 1959 and raised in Chicago, Vishny earned a bachelor's degree from the University of Michigan in 1981. Afterward, he moved on to MIT, where he teamed up with Andrei Shleifer. After graduation, both men moved to the University of Chicago. As he considered his move from MIT to Chicago, Vishny commented: "I got the better part of my education as an economist when I was an assistant professor at the University of Chicago, with people like Gary Becker and Bob Lucas playing a decisive role."[399] In 1989, just before his 30th birthday, Robert Vishny became a full professor at Chicago's GSB.

One of Vishny's early lines of research grew out of the PhD work he did at MIT. Instead of writing one dissertation, Vishny worked with Shleifer to produce three papers, which earned them both PhDs. Two of the papers found their way into the literature and dealt with corporate governance and ownership structure (Shleifer and Vishny 1986a, 1986b).[400] Vishny and Shleifer's first papers on the financial and investment markets dealt with the performance of money managers. In a paper coauthored with Richard Thaler and Josef Lakonishok, Shleifer and Vishny had already shown that money managers sometimes windowdress their portfolios to impress investors (Lakonishok et al. 1991); in the new paper, they calculated that from 1982 to 1989, fund managers underperformed the market considerably (Lakonishok, Shleifer, and Vishny 1992).[401]

In 1994, Shleifer, Vishny, and Lakonishok published the first of two major contributions to the critique of the efficient market hypothesis (Lakonishok, Shleifer, and Vishny 1994). They found that, for the period 1968 to 1990, "value strategies" outperform "glamor strategies" (1542). Whereas "value strategies call for buying stocks that have low prices relative to earnings, dividends, historical prices, book assets, or other measures of value" (1541), "glamor" or "naïve" strategies, on the other hand, "might range from extrapolating past earnings growth too far into the future, to assuming a trend in stock prices, to overreacting to good or bad news, or to simply equating a good investment with a well-run company irrespective of price" (1542). Although amateur investors may make these mistakes because of judgment errors, the three authors refer to the agency problem as the cause for professional investors: "Institutions might prefer glamor stocks because they appear to be 'prudent' investments, and hence are easy to justify to sponsors" (1576).

Shleifer and Vishny's second contribution deals with a crucial hypothesis underlying the efficient market model: the existence of numerous small arbitrageurs that drive prices toward their equilibrium values. In the real world, however, "arbitrage is conducted by relatively few professional, highly specialized investors who combine their knowledge with resources of outside investors to take large positions. The fundamental feature of such arbitrage is that brains and resources are separated by an agency relationship. The money comes from wealthy individuals, banks, endowments, and other investors with only a limited knowledge of individual markets, and is invested by arbitrageurs with highly specialized knowledge of these markets" (Shleifer and Vishny 1997, 36–37). They conclude: "… professional arbitrageurs may avoid extremely volatile 'arbitrage' positions. Although such positions offer attractive average returns, the volatility also exposes arbitrageurs to risk of losses and the need to liquidate the portfolio under pressure from investors in the fund" (Shleifer and Vishny 1997, 54). This agency problem may explain the persistence of some anomalies in the financial markets.

Almost a decade later, Shleifer and Vishny resumed their PhD work on corporate governance—this time in an international context. They found that differences in the nature of financial systems in different countries have a lot to do with differences in investor protection against expropriation by insiders (La Porta et al. 1996). Common-law countries such as the United Kingdom and the United States offer better legal protection to investors than countries with a legal system based more on the French civil-law tradition. Countries with the weakest legal protection framework for investors also tend to have the least developed capital markets (La Porta et al. 1997). Corporate governance and the characteristics of the legal system were also important issues for the privatizations in former communist countries.

Vishny and Shleifer became deeply involved in the huge privatization effort in Russia. In November 1991, they joined the team of Russia's reform tsar, Anatoly Chubais. In the book *Privatizing Russia*, Shleifer, Vishny, and their Russian coauthor Maxim Boycko describe this episode in detail (Boycko, Shleifer, and Vishny 1995). On the basis of this Russian experience, Shleifer and Vishny (1998) elaborated on the different models of government in a second book.

## The International Factor

The success of Chicago's GSB in the broad field of finance also had an international component. In the 1970s and 1980s, the GSB hosted Michael Mussa, a leading international macroeconomist.

Robert Aliber also belongs in the international niche. Although he has been working at the University of Chicago for more than 30 years, Aliber, who specializes in international finance and international business, is an atypical Chicago economist. Unlike most of the other finance people, he is not obsessed with empirical research; instead, he focuses more on institutional and conceptual issues. He is suspicious of what he labeled "house dogmas:" "I subscribe to the belief that price theory is the basic building block of serious economic analysis. But I reject the idea that markets always do a better job. With respect to international macroeconomics, I strongly reject the case for floating exchange rates that was, especially during Milton Friedman's days, a house dogma here in Chicago."[402]

Aliber, who was born in 1930 in Keene, New Hampshire, earned a master's degree in economics in 1958 from the University of Cambridge. Aliber moved from Cambridge to Yale University, where James Tobin and Robert Triffin were major influences. Triffin convinced Aliber that the U.S. balance of payments deficit of the 1950s was mainly the result of excess foreign demand for dollars, a situation that in turn had come about because the United States was viewed as the ultimate provider of international liquidity. Aliber argued (1990) that the United States moved from being the world's largest creditor country to becoming the world's largest debtor country as a consequence of the increased foreign demand for dollar securities and real assets due to the relatively higher returns these assets earned.

In 1961, Aliber began working for the Committee for Economic Development in Washington, DC. In those days, Herbert Stein, another PhD from the University of Chicago and a protégé of Friedman's, was director of research in the agency. Stein had an enduring impact on Aliber: "Although undoubtedly a staunch defender of the free market economy, Stein was less dogmatic than his two great Chicago teachers, Milton Friedman and George Stigler."[403] Attracted by Dean George Shultz, Aliber joined Chicago's GSB in 1965 as professor of international economics and finance. He became a prolific writer in the specialized academic journals and also in books aimed at the general public. His books *The International Money Game* (1973) and *Your Money and Your Life* (1982) became national bestsellers. With Thomas Mayer and James Duesenberry,

Robert Aliber coauthored *Money, Banking and the Economy*, a widely used textbook (Aliber, Duesenberry, and Mayer 1981).

Aliber regarded his analysis of foreign direct investment as "most probably his major contribution."[404] In *The Multinational Paradigm*, Aliber presented his "revised exchange risk theory of foreign direct investment" (Aliber 1993, 195). According to this theory, monetary factors like the real exchange rate and interest rate differentials go hand in hand with real factors such as ownership advantages as determinants of foreign direct investment.

Anil Kashyap, Raghuram Rajan, Luigi Zingales, and Alwyn Young are standouts among the younger generation of economists at the GSB today who focus on the international aspects of finance and international economics in general. Of Indian origin, Anil Kashyap first studied at the University of California, Davis and earned a PhD in economics at MIT in 1989. After working as a research assistant at the Federal Reserve in Washington, DC, he joined Chicago's GSB in 1991 because of "the stimulating environment for applied economic research."[405] Kashyap's research has focused on such areas as the business cycle, the monetary transmission mechanism, banking and capital markets, and the Japanese financial system (Cechetti, Kashyap, and Wilcox 1997; Angeloni, Kashyap, and Mojon 2003; Kashyap and Takeo).

The careers of Rajan and Zingales, both born in 1963, have many parallels. Rajan, who was born in India, graduated in 1985 with an electrical engineering degree from the Indian Institute of Technology in Delhi. Zingalis, who was born in Italy, graduated with an economics degree from Bocconi University in Milan in 1987. They started their collaboration while at MIT, where they both earned PhDs in economics in the early 1990s. Afterward, they both joined Chicago's GSB. In 2003, Rajan was awarded the first Fischer Black Prize by the American Finance Association for contributions to finance by an economist under 40. That same year, he left Chicago's GSB to become economic counselor and director of research at the IMF in Washington.

In their mostly joint research efforts, Rajan and Zingales have focused on the theory of organizations and, more specifically, on financial institutions and their role in economic development. The results of much of this research were brought together in the book *Saving Capitalism from the Capitalists,* which hit the bestseller lists (Rajan and Zingales 2003). Pointing out the forces continuously undermining the beneficial functioning of free markets ("those in power ... feel threatened by free markets"), Rajan and Zingales documented the crucial role played by financial markets and institutions in keeping the wealth-creating free market economy vibrant and innovative: "The greater availability of capital is slowly redressing many of the evils of capitalism—the tyranny of capital over labor, the excessive concentration of industry, the unequal distribution of income in favor of the owners of capital, the lack of opportunity for the poor" (Rajan and Zingales 2003, 10,312).

Although he has concentrated less frequently on purely financial issues, Alwyn Young has made important contributions to the field of international economics. With PhDs in law and diplomacy (Tufts University, 1989) and economics (Columbia University, 1990), Young taught first at MIT's Sloan School of Management (1990–95) and Boston University (1995–97) before joining Chicago's GSB. Specializing in international trade and economic growth, Young contributed to an understanding of the East Asian growth miracle. Young proved that dramatic growth miracles had much less to do with extraordinary productivity gains than with the dramatic rise of factor inputs—especially labor (Young 1992, 1995).[406]

## STIGLER'S TORCH

It was not only finance that earned the GSB a reputation for excellence during the second half of the 20th century. The GSB also became renowned for its research in the field of industrial organization. Stigler laid the foundations for the successes in industrial organization with the assistance of Ronald Coase, Aaron Director, and others, and Dennis Carlton became the main torchbearer of this tradition.

Born in Boston in 1951, Carlton was educated entirely on the East Coast. After earning a bachelor's degree in applied mathematics and economics at Harvard in 1972, Carlton moved to MIT, where he earned a PhD in economics in 1975. His doctoral dissertation formed the backbone of his first book (Carlton 1984b). At Chicago, Carlton worked in the department of economics (1976–80), the law school (1980–84), and, from 1984 forward, the GSB. Regarding the economists who influenced him most, Carlton commented: "At MIT, Frank Fisher, my PhD supervisor, and Robert Hall were the major influences. Robert Hall taught me that micro- and macroeconomics need to be more interlinked than was fashionable in the 1970s. In Chicago, I was very much influenced by Gary Becker, George Stigler, and Ronald Coase."[407]

Carlton published a leading textbook on industrial organization with Jeffrey Perloff.[408] As one of his first research topics, Carlton followed in the footsteps of his Chicago colleague Lester Telser by looking into the role of futures markets. Like Telser, Carlton described this role as largely beneficial for the workings of the economic system (Carlton 1984; Telser 1981).

Allocative theory was another major area of research for Carlton. Carlton (1989, 1991) analyzed delivery lags and rationing as market-clearing alternatives to the price mechanism. In a related field, he also investigated the macroeconomic consequences of imperfections in market clearing. In the Beckerian tradition of the economic analysis of discrimination, Carlton also analyzed how economic transactions can generate hostility that leads to the destruction of property and even life. A substantial part of Carlton's research efforts has concentrated on theoretical and applied aspects of antitrust such as vertical integration, merger policy, antitrust and higher education, antitrust and credit card networks, communication among competitors, the Microsoft case, antitrust and the Internet, barriers to entry, and intellectual property.[409] Over the years, Carlton has earned a good reputation as a consultant to private companies in legal battles concerning antitrust and related issues.

Just like Carlton, Robert Gertner, who was born in 1959, was educated entirely on the East Coast—a bachelor's degree in economics from Princeton in 1981 and a PhD from MIT five years later. "At Princeton, Bob Willig had a major influence on me as well as MIT's Bob Solow, Frank Fisher, and Peter Diamond. It was, however, Oliver Hart and Jean Tirole who attracted me to industrial organization," Gertner comments.[410] Tirole's influence is clear from Gertner's choice of PhD topic: "Essays in Theoretical Industrial Organization," in which game theory played an important role. "Game theory is a way of thinking about the competitive process that allows us to model analytically complicated issues. Game theory has shown us that the world is a lot more ambiguous than we thought. We now believe less and less stuff that wasn't true in the first place," argued Gertner.[411]

Gertner came to the GSB in 1986 and became a full professor in 1995. Despite the fact that game theory was rejected by the bulk of economists working at Chicago, it occupies a central place in most of Gertner's research.[412]

Austan Goolsbee[413] and Lars Stole are also MIT graduates who focused on industrial organization at the GSB. Goolsbee's dissertation work was the basis for a paper in which he showed that an investment tax credit primarily leads to price and wage increases in the capital goods sector (Goolsbee 1997). Similarly, Goolsbee showed that increased government funding of research and development does not increase the amount of inventive activity that takes place. This government money mostly finds its way into higher salaries for the researchers. Goolsbee estimated that this phenomenon led to an overestimation of the social return of research and development by 30 to 50 percent (Goolsbee 1998a). Goolsbee also examined a variety of tax issues (Goolsbee 1998, 2004).[414]

Stole, born in 1964, came to Chicago's GSB in 1991. "What attracted me most was the reputation of the University of Chicago as a place where scientific boundaries are continually pushed further," Stole recalls.[415] Stole earned a bachelor's degree at the University of Illinois in June 1985 and a PhD in economics at MIT in 1991 with a dissertation on the economics of contracts and organizations. Most of Stole's further work concentrated on these and other closely related issues. As opposed to the mostly applied and empirical work of Goolsbee, Stole's publications have a strong theoretical flavor.[416]

## More Than Just Rocket Scientists

Robert Hamada, the 14th dean of the GSB, emerged directly from the circle of the successful finance group. In 1993, Hamada inherited a business school that was finalizing a process of repositioning itself within the business education community. To put this into perspective, one has to go back to the glorious days of Allen Wallis and Jim Lorie who, to repeat the words of Merton Miller, gave the GSB its constitution as well as its declaration of independence. The essence of that constitution was that the GSB focused on the scientific content of business education. It kept its broad perspective, but nevertheless the GSB increasingly emphasized the purely scientific aspects of the different branches and deemphasized the business applications. As a senior faculty member put it: "During the sixties and the seventies, we got more and more into the business of training rocket scientists than that of training future entrepreneurs and business executives."[417] As a result of this evolution, the GSB lost some of its attractiveness for students and for the business community.

The problem was not so much the scientific content of the courses offered, but the fact that the other skills MBAs need in their professional life—especially those related to leadership, social contact, and group work—were relatively neglected. This tendency grew more apparent under the deanships of George Shultz and Sydney Davidson and reached its zenith under Richard Rosett. Among the most important appointments Shultz made were those of Henri Theil, John Gould, and Hamada. Shultz helped create the Center for Mathematical Studies in Business and Economics, the Center for Health Administration Studies, the Center for Research in Security Prices, and the Institute for Professional Accounting. Shultz also launched Careers for Negroes in Management, a program designed to improve the integration of minorities; he particularly cherished this creation.

Shultz had a very close relationship with his associate dean, Walter "Bud" Fackler, a man who became something of a legend at the GSB through his extraordinary care for fellow faculty members and students. After eight years as associate dean, Fackler was acting dean for one year in 1968–69 and subsequently served from 1970 to 1987 as director of the GSB's Executive MBA Program.

In 1969, Sydney Davidson succeeded Shultz as dean of the GSB, a position he held for five years. As the Ford Foundation began to reduce its grants to the GSB, Davidson negotiated a new financial arrangement with the university's central administration.

Davidson was born in Chicago in 1919 but grew up in Flint, Michigan. Davidson received his entire education at the University of Michigan, and he earned a PhD in economics and accounting there in 1950. He taught at Johns Hopkins University until 1958, the year he moved to the GSB; he stayed there for the rest of his academic career. Apart from his reputation as an outstanding teacher, Davidson is regarded as one of the leading authorities on accounting in postwar America. Several of his books became standard works (Davidson 1983, 1991). Davidson turned the deanship over to Rosett in 1974.

Born in Baltimore in 1928, Rosett earned a bachelor's degree from Columbia University and a PhD in economics from Yale University in 1957, and he spent two years at the Cowles Foundation at Yale before moving to the University of Rochester. He left Rochester to become dean of the GSB.

Rosett consolidated the financial independence of the GSB through a successful fundraising campaign. Under his deanship, the Center for the Study of the Economy and the State, the New Product Laboratory, the Center for Research in Future Markets, and the Center for Population Economics were created. A major innovation introduced under Rosett was the course and interview bidding system, by which students can compose their programs through an auction-like mechanism.

Rosett's publications as a professional academic are testimony to his preference for theoretical economics and econometrics. Therefore, it is no coincidence that the emphasis on economic theory and quantitative methods that resulted in more "rocket scientists" than business-oriented graduates reached a high point during Rosett's ten years at the helm of Chicago's GSB. However, the business education market clearly signaled to Chicago's GSB that it was losing ground.

The GSB had to adjust, and it did so under the deanship of John Gould, who set as a major goal "to respond to critiques from alumni and other business people that the school ranked high academically but low in leadership training and to empower students to solve real problems" (Graduate School of Business, 1998, 82).

Unlike Rosett, Gould came from within the GSB. Born in Chicago in 1939, Gould studied first at Northwestern University and subsequently at the University of Chicago, where he earned a PhD in economics in 1966. In 1965 he joined the faculty of the GSB and became a full professor in 1974. In 1969–70, he served as a special assistant to his former dean, George Shultz, who was then Secretary of Labor.

Gould's research was focused on different aspects of the investment process (Gould 1967; Gould and Waud 1973). Like other Chicago scholars such as Coase and Stigler, Gould (Gould 1980a, 1980b) also investigated the characteristics of the market process and the role of information. Against considerable opposition from several faculty members, Gould forwarded the idea that is was no longer sufficient to only graduate "rocket scientists." The faculty's opposition to this idea is evidenced by the fact that it took Gould five years to push through his LEAD (Leadership Exploration and Development) project, which was intended to correct the lack of emphasis in the GSB courses on the social skills needed by business executives. The whole idea was to bring the students together to discuss any problems with their education as they experienced them and to press the students to come up with their own solutions to these problems.

Also, under Gould's guidance, the Argonne National Laboratory/ University of Chicago Development Corporation (ARCH) was established in 1986 to capitalize on the commercial potential of research done at the University of Chicago.

As participation in the part-time programs grew rapidly, the GSB's downtown facilities became increasingly inadequate. Gould oversaw the construction of the new Gleacher Center, named after its main benefactor Eric Gleacher, a GSB graduate turned successful New York investment banker, in the heart of downtown Chicago.

In 1993, Hamada succeeded Gould as the GSB's dean. Born in San Francisco in 1938, Hamada was educated on the East Coast—he earned a bachelor's degree in chemical engineering from Yale and a master's degree and PhD in finance from MIT. In 1966, Hamada joined the GSB, and from 1985 to 1990, he served as its deputy dean. He also served four years as director of the CBOT. In 1999, Hamada accepted a second term as dean of Chicago's GSB.

Hamada's academic research focused on the impact of taxes and risk on financial decisions in corporations and on the interrelations between corporate strategy and corporate finance (Hamada 1979). A third element of his research effort concerned the increasing internationalization of business activity. Hamada's interest in the international aspects of business became evident as the GSB opened two new International Executive MBA Programs—one in Barcelona in 1994 and one in Singapore in 2000. Also under Hamada, the Center for International Business Education and Research was established.

Hamada continued along the path that Gould had laid, giving top priority to close contact with students. "Under Gould and Hamada," a senior faculty member concludes, "the GSB has become more 'humane' in the sense that it is no longer required that you have the intellectual resources of a sophisticated rocket scientist to feel at home here."

In 2001, Edward Snyder, the former dean of the Darden Business School at the University of Virginia and a Chicago PhD himself, took over from Bob Hamada. With this new dean, the GSB continued down the same road.

# CHAPTER EIGHT

# Law and Economics
## *Justice through Efficiency*

OVER THE DECADES, ANALYSIS OF GOVERNMENT INTERVENTIONS in economic processes has become a pioneering research area for University of Chicago scholars. However, students of the regulatory process inevitably have to deal with legal issues. Examining the law in all of its dimensions through the lens of neoclassical price theory became known as the modern study of law and economics, a subfield with close ties to the University of Chicago. Like Aaron Director, Ronald Coase, and George Stigler, many other Chicago scholars became major contributors to the research program on law and economics, including Richard Posner, Robert Bork, Walter Blum, Edmund Kitch, William Landes, Frank Easterbrook, Dennis Carlton, Richard Epstein, Daniel Fischel, Douglas Baird, and Alan Sykes.

However, the process of studying the interaction between legal and economic processes did not begin at the University of Chicago. In 1897, when the University of Chicago was still in its infancy, legal scholar Oliver Wendell Holmes, a U.S. Supreme Court justice from 1902 to 1932, wrote: "For the rational study of the law, the black-letter man may be the man of the present, but the man of the future is the man of statistics and the master of economics." (Holmes, 1897) Such scholars as Warren Samuels, Heath Pearson, and Steve Medema have traced the origins of what is now called law and economics as far back as the ancient Greek and Roman civilizations.

The more modern intellectual roots of this field of inquiry go back to such 18th and 19th century European *grands savants* as Adam Smith, Jeremy Bentham, Thomas Hobbes, and Karl Knies. Prominent American economists such as John Bates Clark, the institutionalist John Commons, and Irving Fisher showed great interest in the interactions between the legal domain and the economic domain (Samuels 1993; Pearson 1997; Medema 1998).

## Early Freunds

Although the creation of the subfield of law and economics at the University of Chicago is usually considered to have begun in 1950s, the tradition of analyzing legal and economic issues simultaneously goes back much further. As a matter of fact, the foundations of Chicago's law school were laid at Chicago's department of political economy:

> Movement towards creating a professional school of law [at the University of Chicago] began in 1894 when the Department of Political Economy introduced a course in 'Roman Law and Jurisprudence,' taught by a young New York attorney, Ernest Freund ... When Rockefeller provided funds for the establishment of the Law School in 1902, Freund drafted a proposed curriculum outline for president Harper. In addition to the standard legal courses, the second and third years of the program included ... courses [covering] a range of topics, from psychology and urban sociology to economics and diplomatic history. (Streeten 1991, 47)[418]

James Laughlin and Leon C. Marshall, a later chairman of the department of political economy and dean of the business school, also taught and published on legal matters.

Law and economics have traveled a long way since those early beginnings. Posner, who is one of the most important Chicago scholars in this field, wrote, "... [today] economic analysis of law— has both positive (that is, descriptive) and normative aspects. It tries to explain and predict the behavior of participants in and persons regulated by law. It also tries to improve law by pointing out respects in which existing or proposed laws have unintended or undesirable consequences, whether on economic efficiency, or the distribution of income and wealth, or other values" (Posner 1998, 3).

"The principal intellectual foundation of 'law and economics,'" wrote Edmund Kitch (Kitch 1983b, 184,192), "has been its relative success in illuminating two fundamental questions. First, what effects do legal rules have upon society? And second, how do social forces shape and determine the law? ... Law and economics is not a set of analytic propositions that follow inexorably from first principles. It is a tradition of inquiry, analysis, and exploration of law."

David Friedman (1991, 371), a former fellow at the University of Chicago's law school and the son of Milton and Rose Friedman, divided the subject into "three distinct but related enterprises. The first is the use of economics to predict the effects of legal rules. The second is the use of economics to determine what legal rules are economically efficient, in order to recommend what the legal rules ought to be. The third is the use of economics to predict what the legal rules will be."

The evolution of law and economics can be divided into two periods. In the first, which lasted up to the early 1960s, attention was concentrated on traditional economic issues, such as monopoly, antitrust, public utilities, regulation, and corporate law. By 1937, Harvard's Edward Mason had argued in favor of more consultation between lawyers and economists to make antitrust policy more effective. It was characteristic of the contributions coming out of the University of Chicago during this period that, mainly under Director's influence, price theory formed the analytical framework in which the analyses took place.

The second era in the history of law and economics started with two articles published at the beginning of the 1960s—an article on social cost by Coase (1960) and an article on tort law by Yale's Guido Calabresi (1961). Stigler noted that "in the field of law and/or economics, B.C. means Before Coase" (Stigler 1992). As to the importance of Calabresi's contribution, Chicago's Richard Epstein remarked (1995, 317): "Guido Calabresi introduced the fertile idea that the function of tort law was to minimize the sum of administrative costs, accident costs, and the costs of accident prevention, *subject* to the constraint of justice." In the second era of law and economics, the economic approach was applied to common law (contracts, property, torts); to constitutional law; to civil, criminal, and administrative procedure; and to the determination of litigations and damages.

From the beginning, most traditional law scholars strongly opposed this broad law and economics movement. First of all, there is the claim that the hypotheses on which the economic models are based are too simplistic for the complex world in which we live, which is an argument that is often made against neoclassical price theory in general.[419] The second major argument against the economic analysis of law is the alleged ignorance of justice, to which Posner replies:

> One must distinguish between the different meanings of [justice]. Sometimes it means distributive justice, the proper degree of economic equality. Although economists cannot tell society what that degree is, they have much to say that is relevant— about the actual amounts of inequality in different societies and in different periods, about the difference between real economic inequality and inequalities in pecuniary incomes that merely offset cost differences or reflect different positions in the life cycle, and about the cost of achieving greater equality ... A second meaning of justice, perhaps the most common, is efficiency ... when people describe as unjust convicting a person without a trial, taking property without just compensation, or failing to make a negligent automobile driver answer in damages to the victim of his negligence, this means nothing more pretentious than that the conduct wastes resources" (Posner 1992, 27).

Yet Posner qualifies his own argument: "There is more to notions of justice than a concern with efficiency. It is not obviously inefficient to allow suicide pacts, to flog prisoners, to allow babies to be sold for adoption ... there is more to justice than economics" (Posner 1992, 27).[420]

Some of the early critics of the economic approach to law, like the University of Texas's H.H. Liebhafsky, were quite sharp:

> This literature has been produced largely by economists who know no law and a handful of lawyers who have learned their

economics from these same economists, all of whom are bound together by their acceptance of eighteenth-century hedonism ... Some of this literature has attained the status of "classic" because it confirms to the Gordon-Liebhafsky Theorem, which states: "Provided that it achieves a certain threshold level of intelligibility, the greater the obscurity of a piece written by an economist, the greater is the likelihood that it will be recognized as a classic or seminal work." (Samuels 1992, 254)

The opponents of the economic analysis of law, however, too often took their own wishes for reality. A typical example is law professor Morton Horowitz, who in 1980 declared: "I have a strong feeling that the economic analysis of law has 'peaked out' as the latest fad in legal scholarship" (Landes and Posner 1993, 388). In 1989, law professor Owen Fiss concluded: "... law and economics ... seemed to have peaked" (Landes and Posner 1993, 388). Landes and Posner (1993) assembled citation evidence to the contrary.

In 1995, Anthony Kronman, dean of the Yale Law School and himself a known critic of the law and economics approach, wrote: "The law and economics movement was and continues to be an enormous enlivening force in American legal thought and, I would say, today continues and remains the single most influential jurisprudential school in this country (Posner 1998, 2)."

## STARTING WITH THE BRAKES ON

Director deserves most of the credit for establishing the foundations of modern law and economics at the University of Chicago. Other than the largely unnoticed stay of economic institutionalist Walton Hamilton at the Yale Law School, Henry Simons must be regarded as the first economist to ever teach at a law school. Thus, Simons's appointment in 1934 is often seen as the start of the economic approach to law. Symbolically, this claim may have some validity, but this is too simplistic a presentation because plain coincidence played a major role in Simons's arrival at the law school, and developments totally unrelated to Simons's appointment created an environment that was favorable to the development of law and economics. With respect to the coincidence factor, Simons's appointment to the law school was essentially a compromise intended to end a disagreement between Frank Knight, who supported Simons, and Paul Douglas, who strongly disliked Simons. As Milton Friedman said: "Douglas came close to driving Henry Simons out. In the end, Robert Hutchins, the president of the University of Chicago who had become a personal friend of Simons, refused to dismiss Henry Simons."[421]

Hutchins also played an important role in the creation of a favorable intellectual environment for the development of law and economics. While a law student at Yale University, Hutchins came under the influence of legal realism, a movement focused on bringing the law into closer relation with social reality and hence with the social sciences such as economics, anthropology, sociology, and political science. Wilber Katz, who served for several years as dean of Chicago's law school, played an important role in linking law to the social sciences.[422] According to Walter Blum, Katz argued that "precedent no longer worked in the court system as well as it had in the past ... So it was necessary to have some kind of additional technique, and that meant that lawyers had to be more broadly trained, at least so that they would know how to deal with experts from other disciplines. He did not expect that lawyers would become accountants, or economists, or psychologists, or psychiatrists, but that they would know enough to deal with them in a courtroom or adversary situation" (Kitch 1983a, 168). In the second part of the 1930s, Katz formally introduced economics and accounting to the legal studies curriculum (Katz 1937).

Katz did all he could to attract students to Simons's lectures. But, as already noted, Simons's main field of interest was monetary analysis. Although he was well trained in price theory, Simons had little more to say on industrial organization than what he wrote in his book *Positive Program for Laissez-Faire* (1934) about the omnipresence of monopoly and the need to nationalize large parts of the economy. As far as Simons's role in law and economics is concerned, Coase concluded: "... in dealing with industrial organization, Simons provides no empirical backing for his contentions, makes no serious investigation of what the effects of his proposals would be on the efficiency with which the economic system would operate ... Simons' approach is the very antithesis of that which was to become dominant as a result of the emergence of that new subject, law and economics" (Coase 1993b, 242).

By the end of World War II, Simons was desperate about the state of the world, and in 1945 he wrote a memorandum that urged Chicago to create a center "… to which economic liberals everywhere may look for intellectual leadership or support … Chicago economics still has some distinctively traditional-liberal connotations and some prestige … The outlook at Chicago, if better than elsewhere, is not very promising" (Coase 1993b, 244-245). Simons sent a copy of his memorandum to Friedrich Hayek, who was at the LSE at the time. Hayek, who largely shared Simons's fears, had come to know Director at the LSE, as Director spent 1937 and 1938 at the LSE before joining several government agencies in Washington.

At this point, Harold Luhnow of the Kansas City–based William Volker Fund stepped into the picture. Luhnow was an admirer of the writings of Ludwig von Mises and Hayek. Hayek and Simons worked out the details of what came to be known as the "Hayek Research Project," which Director would direct and the William Volker Fund would sponsor.[423] It was agreed that the project should focus on "a study of a suitable legal and institutional framework of an effective competitive system" (Coase 1993b, 246). It came to be located in the Chicago's law school, something Dean Wilber Katz only agreed to on the condition that Director would also do some teaching at the law school. In 1946, Director took over Simons's classes on basic price theory.

Soon, Director began teaching the antitrust course with Edward Levi. Robert Bork described Levi as "without question the most brilliant classroom teacher I have ever seen" (Bork 1978, xv). Levi's grandfather, Rabbi Emil Hirsch, had been the first Jewish member of the faculty of the University of Chicago.

As a child, Levi attended kindergarten, elementary, and high school near the University, and at Chicago's law school he earned PhB and JD degrees and started as an assistant professor in 1936. He served as dean of the law school (1950–62), provost of the University (1962–68), and president of the University (1968–75). In 1975, President Gerald Ford appointed Levi to head the U.S. Department of Justice, which was, in the wake of the traumatic Watergate affair, going through one of the worst crises in its existence. As a legal scholar and a specialist in higher education, Levi produced several seminal contributions (Levi 1949).

At the time Director joined him, Levi's major area of legal expertise was American antitrust laws, which are designed to safeguard a fair, competitive environment. The Federal Trade Commission and the Department of Justice are responsible for supervising antitrust laws. Chicago students of the 1940s and 1950s have vivid memories of the antitrust course taught by Levi and Director. Wesley Liebeler recalls: "For four days each week Ed Levi would develop the law and would use the traditional techniques of legal reasoning to relate the cases to each other and create a synthesis ... For four days Ed would do this, and for one day each week Aaron Director would tell us that everything that Levi had told us the preceding four days was nonsense. He used economic analysis to show us that the legal analysis would not stand up" (Kitch 1983a, 183). It would take Levi several years to convert to the Director doctrine.[424]

## The Inspirator

Director's impact did not limit itself to the antitrust course, as Henry Manne, a Chicago student in the early 1950s and a major law and economics scholar himself, testified: "It was clear to me very early that economics was important in most of the courses I was taking in law school" (Kitch 1983a, 184). One of the courses Manne singled out was the course on bankruptcy given by Walter Blum.

Blum was born in Chicago in 1918 and attended the University of Chicago Laboratory Schools. In 1939, he received a bachelor's degree from the University of Chicago, and in 1941, he received a JD from the Law School. From 1941 to 1943, Blum served as an attorney in the Office of Price Administration in Washington, DC. In 1943 he joined the armed forces and returned to Chicago's law school in 1946.

Blum spent the rest of his life at the University of Chicago law school and died in Chicago in 1994. At Chicago, he was regularly consulted by presidents, provosts, deans, and students.[425] Blum also played an active role in the Atomic Scientists of Chicago, a group formed around the scientists of the University of Chicago's Metallurgic Laboratory, where the plutonium used in the Nagasaki atomic bomb was developed. The Atomic Scientists of Chicago sought to prevent the further development and use of nuclear weapons.

Blum taught courses in taxation, insurance, bankruptcy, and corporate reorganization. In 1953, he and Harry Kalven Jr. published *The Uneasy Case for Progressive Taxation* (Blum and Kalven 1953). The basic point of Blum and Kalven's analysis was that progressive taxation distorts economic incentives for the rich and the poor and it strongly encourages tax avoidance. Instead of a progressive income tax, they argued in favor of introducing a tax on consumer spending. In 1975, when Arthur Okun advocated a government-supported program that would guarantee every citizen an income equal to at least half the median income in society financed exclusively through higher taxation of higher incomes, Blum reacted promptly and rejected Okun's proposal on economic, social, and democratic grounds.[426]

However, even Blum is no match for Director in importance and relevance to the development of law and economics. Medema (1998, 209) describes Director as " ... the individual most responsible for firmly establishing the Chicago law and economics tradition ... [and who had] ... a formidable influence on Chicago law students." In the preface to his book *The Antitrust Paradox,* Bork refers to Director as "the seminal thinker on antitrust economics and industrial organization. His reputation is immense among those who know him; that it is not more widespread is entirely due to his choice to publish little and rest content with the establishment of a strong oral tradition at the law school of the University of Chicago ... It is impossible to capture the impressiveness of the man for the reader who does not know him ... He is my idea of what a real intellectual is like" (Bork 1978, xv).

The way in which Director created an oral tradition and influenced so many students was totally different from the style of his contemporaries Friedman and Stigler. The latter two loved to fight it out in public, even in the workshops they attended. Director hardly ever spoke when attending the presentation of a paper. "Only when Aaron started chewing his moustache you got a clear sign that he had problems with the argument being developed or the evidence being presented," Lester Telser remembers.[427] Director preferred to persuade others privately.

Director brought about a sea change at the University of Chicago with respect to monopoly and antitrust. Up until at least the late 1940s, the dominant opinion in Chicago was that monopoly was a very serious problem, and that vigorous application of very broad antitrust legislation should be high on society's agenda.[428] This point of view was not universal at the University of Chicago, however. Chester Wright, who taught at the University of Chicago from 1907 to 1944, offered a typical example of a more nuanced approach to the monopoly (or trust) problem. At the end of his 1912 analysis of "the trust problem," Wright concluded that his study

> ... shows that (a) since the trusts may have an element of good in them which would be destroyed under the present policy of annihilating unreasonable trusts, and (b) since the trusts show many characteristics which closely correspond to those prevailing in industries controlled by public-service operations where (c) a policy of regulation has accomplished so much more; therefore we should inquire whether a policy of regulation discriminating between trusts and trust evils, and based on preventive methods, should not be substituted for our present indiscriminate, purely alleviative, and generally ineffective policy of destruction and enforced competition. (Wright 1912, 587)

One of the most discussed pieces of research inspired by Director was John McGee's study of the allegation that John D. Rockefeller's Standard Oil was guilty of predatory pricing, a policy of price cutting aimed at driving competitors out of business in order to reap monopoly-sized profits later. McGee concluded from his empirical investigation that "... Standard Oil did not systematically, if ever, use local price cutting in retailing, or anywhere else, to reduce competition" (McGee 1958, 168). Twenty-two years after his initial research, McGee saw no new evidence that would lead him to change his prior conclusion on the issue: "Predatory pricing has proved to be a durable subject if not a durable practice ... Most kinds of predation that economists and historians have worried about are *more* costly to predator than to prey" (McGee 1980, 290–95).

Another program inspired by Director concerned vertical integration[429] and vertical restraints.[430] Typical examples of vertical restraints are resale price maintenance, exclusive territories, and exclusive outlets.

The crucial element in cases of vertical restraints is the free-rider problem. In the case of resale price maintenance, a manufacturer may find it necessary to differentiate his product through expensive advertising, thus requiring his retailers to offer some special service to their customers. If he allows other retailers than the ones who keep to the required price to sell the product, they will benefit from the advertising without having to offer the service. Hence, they will be able to sell the product at a discount.

Director also played an important role in a research project on industry concentration and merger policy. General opinion during the 1950s and 1960s held that the link observed between industry concentration and profitability was proof of market power and hence the setting of prices above the competitive level. Not so, the Chicago answer went, because companies grow big and profitable because they are efficient.[431] If those companies tried to exert market power and raise their prices substantially, others would enter the market. The issue of concentrated industries led to an intense discussion among scholars at the University of Chicago. In 1969, the White House Task Force on Antitrust Policy published the Neal Report (named after its chairman, Phil Neal, who was at the time dean of the Chicago law school). The Neal Report proposed a Concentrated Industries Act that would lead to vigorous action in concentrated industries. In fact, the Act never became law.

## Lonely On The Midway

Almost 30 years after he came to the University of Chicago, Coase remarked, "… it is probable that without the *Journal*, I would not have come to Chicago" (Coase 1993b, 252). Coase remained editor of the *Journal of Law and Economics* until 1982. Soon after Coase's arrival in Chicago, Director retired and Coase took over his courses in antitrust and price theory.[432] Although Coase and Director had different styles and addressed different topics, there was a common theme defined by Harold Demsetz as the assumption that "people try to maximize and that really there is competition in the attempt to maximize" (Kitch 1983a, 204).

Despite that common trait Demsetz observed, over time a certain unease developed in the relationship between Coase and other economists at the University of Chicago. During the 1970s, a gap became visible between the methodology favored by Coase and the methodology defended by others, notably Stigler.[433] Stigler saw the study of industrial organization and the related legal issues as merely an application of basic price theory (Stigler 1968). Coase wanted a broader framework that paid more attention to the institutions of capitalism—two of the most important ones being the market and the firm.[434]

Several sources on the University of Chicago campus confirmed that this methodological disagreement strained the relationship between Stigler and Coase, but their mutual respect remained strong. From Stigler's side, this is obvious, considering the enthusiastic way in which Stigler wrote about Coase and his contribution to economics in his memoir. William Landes recalled Coase's devastation when he heard about Stigler's unexpected death.[435]

In the early 1990s, the discussion on methodology continued—this time between Coase and Posner. In the March 1993 issue of the *Journal of Institutional and Theoretical Economics,* this discussion turned rather nasty, as is evident from the opening sections of Coase's reply to Posner's paper that compared new institutional economics and law and economics; Posner's paper had criticized Coase's attitude to economic methodology.

> My first reaction on reading Posner's paper was one of amusement. It recalled to my mind Miss Elliott's description of Alfred Marshall's lectures on Henry George. She said that Marshall reminded her of a boa constrictor that slobbered over its victim before swallowing it. In saying this, I had no intention of equating Posner with Marshall, still less with any kind of snake, although I must confess that the wicked thought did flicker through my mind as I studied his paper with more care and ceased to be amused ... [I have] expressed my astonishment that Posner, writing about my views, had not bothered to ask me what they were." (Coase 1993a, 96, 98).

Coase further specified: "Posner states that I 'want to go back to the earlier, simpler, looser, nonmathematical theory of Adam Smith.' This is the opposite of the truth ... Posner also refers to my 'dislike of abstraction.' This is wrong" (Coase 1993a, 96, 97).

Despite Coase's objections, Posner persisted. In 1993, he argued that what is most striking about Coase's economics is "the *narrowness* of his conception of the domain and methodology—and hence of the past, present and future—of economics … [Coase] thinks that the two centuries since the publication of [Adam Smith's] *Wealth of Nations* have been largely wasted in economics and we must turn now to the study of large-scale collection of business records" (Posner 1993b, 203). In his recollection of the material Coase covered in his antitrust course, Benjamin Klein confirms this last point of Posner's: "What he did was copy large sections of the case record in major trust cases, and we would go through the record and try to figure out what was going on" (Kitch 1983a, 192). Posner commented further on Coase: "He writes in an English economics tradition shaped by Smith and Marshall and by Coase's teacher Arnold Plant … The mathematical and statistical movement in economics … has passed Coase by and indeed has become an object of his scorn" (Posner 1993b, 204–205). Landes states a more subtle conclusion: "It is one of the ironies of law and economics that the person whose pioneering work provided the foundation for the subject has been less than enthusiastic about its development" (Landes 1997, 36).

## Property Rights Get the Job Done

Of the many things Coase contributed to law and economics, his 1960 article on social cost—from which Stigler deduced the famous Coase Theorem—is by far the most important. More than 30 years later, Coase commented:

> What I wanted to do was to improve our analysis of the working of the economic system. Law came into the article because, in a regime of positive transaction costs, the character of the law becomes one of the main factors determining the performance of the economy. If transactions costs were zero (as is assumed in standard economic theory) we can imagine people contracting around the law whenever the value of production would be increased by a change in the legal position. But in a regime of positive transaction costs, such contracting would not occur whenever transaction costs were greater than the gain that

such a redistribution of rights would bring. As a consequence
the rights which individuals possess will commonly be those established by the law, which in these circumstances can be said to
control the economy. (Coase 1993b, 250–51)

Property rights are the rights of individuals to the use of scarce resources and transaction costs are the costs associated with the definition,
the enforcement, and the transfer of property rights.

More than three decades later, Richard Epstein, a professor at the
Chicago's law school who had been highly critical of the Coasian analysis
in the earlier stages of his own research (Epstein 1973), still reduced most
of law and economics to what Coase had written in 1960:

> With positive transactions costs, a summary of the entire pro-
> gram of analysis within the law and economics movement be-
> comes as easy as one, two, three. One is the situation where the
> single owner knows his own preferences, and his sole task is to
> array the resources to maximize their satisfaction. Two is the
> case where two persons must interact only with each other and
> must therefore adopt bargaining strategies that will allow them
> to maximize through exchange of their original endowments the
> desired resources at their command. The world is now compli-
> cated by strategic behavior, monitoring, and asymmetric infor-
> mation … Three is a world with three players, in which coali-
> tions are possible that can alter the balance of power among the
> players at hand … Beyond three, the numbers of permutations
> and combinations of ordinary exchanges and complex coalitions
> are powerful indeed … The object of the law is to develop a set
> of rules that promotes the closest possible approximation to the
> world of zero transaction costs. (Epstein 1993, 556)

Coase's 1960 article originated a huge body of literature on property
rights, and Armen Alchian and Demsetz were among the pioneering researchers in the field.[436] Alchian lived in California for his entire life—he
was born in Fresno in 1914, earned a PhD from Stanford in 1944, was an
economist with the RAND Corporation in Santa Monica from 1947 to

1964, and was a professor at UCLA from 1964 forward—but as an economist, he was as close to Chicago as one can get without actually working and living there.[437]

Demsetz, on the other hand, was born (in 1930) and raised in Chicago. He received an MBA and a PhD (in 1959) from Northwestern University. After two years at the University of Michigan and three at UCLA, he came to the University of Chicago in 1963 to teach at the law school and the GSB. After eight years there, Demsetz left Chicago for California, where he was the first Senior Research Fellow at the Hoover Institution at Stanford. In 1978, he joined Alchian at UCLA.

Almost simultaneously, Alchian (1965) and Demsetz (1964) wrote two seminal papers on property rights. Demsetz formulated the more generalized theory of property rights. "When a transaction is concluded in the marketplace, two bundles of property rights are exchanged," reads the first sentence of this paper; afterward, Demsetz develops the link between property rights and externalities:

> Property rights specify how persons may be benefited and harmed, and, therefore, who must pay whom to modify the actions taken by persons. The recognition of this leads easily to the close relationship between property rights and externalities ... What converts a harmful or beneficial effect into an externality is that the cost of bringing the effect to bear on the decisions of one or more of the interacting persons is too high to make it worthwhile ... "Internalizing" such effects refers to a process, usually a change in property rights, that enables these effects to bear (in greater degree) on all interacting persons. A primary function of property rights is that of guiding incentives to achieve a greater internalization of externalities. (Demsetz 1967, 347–48)

The next step in Demsetz's analysis was to relate property rights and externalities to transaction costs: "The cost of a transaction in the rights between parties (internalization) must exceed the gains from internalization. In general, transacting costs can be large relative to gains because of 'natural' difficulties in trading or they can be large because of legal reasons ... Property rights develop to internalize externalities when the gains of internalization become larger than the cost of internalization" (Demsetz 1967, 348,350).

Demsetz's Chicago work did not concentrate solely on property rights; he also worked in the field of regulation. In another paper, Demsetz took issue with Kenneth Arrow's (1962) claim that a free-market economy tends to underinvest in research to such a degree that the government is required to step in. Demsetz argued that "[Arrow's] *nirvana approach*" leads to "three logical fallacies—*the grass is always greener fallacy, the fallacy of the free lunch,* and *the people could be different fallacy*" (Demsetz 1969, 1–2). It is far from evident, Demsetz concluded, that the competitive system will underperform with respect to invention and research.

Demsetz also extensively analyzed the political market: "Voter sovereignty, expressed through ballots, replaces consumer sovereignty, expressed through dollar votes" (Demsetz 1982, 69). However, voting costs—that is, the costs to individual voters of informing themselves—distort political competition even more than transaction costs do with perfect competition. It is to these voting costs that political parties ultimately owe their *raison d'être,* just as firms owe theirs to the existence of transaction costs.

## Patents and Stuff

In the wake of Coase, Alchian, and Demsetz, the economics of property rights became a major area of research for economists and law scholars at the University of Chicago, and Director was a major source of inspiration.[438] Posner and Charles Meyers developed a system for transferring water rights between states. Landes and Posner (1989) analyzed trademark law and copyright law as it applied to intellectual property rights. Friedman, Landes, and Posner (1991) criticized traditional patenting.

However, at Chicago, the study of the patent system from the economic point of view is largely identified with Edmund Kitch, who considers himself to be "more on the lawyer's side of the law and economics research project."[439] Kitch was born in 1939 in Wichita, Kansas. He earned a bachelor's degree from Yale University in 1961 and a JD from the University of Chicago in 1964. More than three decades later, Kitch pointed to Director and Stigler as the Chicago teachers who had a major influence on him.[440] Kitch was a member of the faculty of Chicago's law school from 1965 until 1982, when he became a law professor at the University of Virginia.

Kitch analyzed, and strongly criticized, the regulation of the natural gas market (Kitch 1972) and that of the taxicab market in Chicago (Kitch, Isaacson, and Kasper 1971). Although he also did some research on antitrust (Kitch 1985) and wrote on the general development of law and economics (Kitch 1983a, 1983b), most of his reputation came from his work on intellectual property rights—mainly patents, copyrights, and trademarks. In 1990, Kitch summarized his basic position on these rights: "They are a subtle and complex system of private empowerment. These systems of rights exist to enable private parties to engage in the activity of investment in innovation, authorship, and development of positive relationships with customers" (Kitch 1990, 3).

In his seminal contribution on the patent system, Kitch proposed his prospect theory as an alternative to the then-generally accepted reward theory (Kitch 1977, 1983b, and 1990). The traditional reward theory goes back to the work of Coase's teacher Arnold Plant; it views the patent system as permitting inventors to capture the returns from their investments. By the late 1950s, Harvard's Fritz Machlup (1958) expressed fears about the strong monopoly effects of this patent system. Kitch challenged Machlup's thesis, arguing that the feared output-reducing monopoly effects were often exaggerated. The basic characteristic of his prospect theory is that the patent system actually increases the output from resources used for technological innovation. Instead, Kitch advocated the allowance of broadly defined patents. This would, first of all, give the inventor an incentive to release more information than if his patent had only been narrowly defined. Second, with a broader patent, the inventor could do a more efficient job of coordinating the activities of those who follow up on his ideas.

The study of the patent system was then taken up by Kenneth Dam (1994, 266), who claimed: "A patent system should not only avoid wasteful competitive R&D, but it should also avoid encroaching on future R&D that is socially desirable." Since the 1982 creation of a federal appellate court specializing in the administration of patent laws, the U.S. authorities, Dam argued, had been rather successful at limiting the three secondary economic problems that arise when property rights in inventions are created (which is what patents do). This trio consists of "monopoly, rent-seeking, and inhibition-of-future-innovation problems" (Dam 1994, 249). In related research, Dam investigated the issues involved with intellectual property protection in such new sectors as software, biotechnology, and the Internet.

Dennis Carlton and Daniel Fischel developed another intriguing application of the theory of property rights with respect to the regulation of insider trading. In short, they argued that it is hard to find good reasons why the proper legal response to insider trading should be different from that to other forms of management compensation such as salaries, bonuses, and vacation leave.

The Carlton and Fischel analysis was strongly in the spirit of the pioneering work on insider trading of Henry Manne. Born in 1928 in New Orleans, Manne earned a JD in 1952 at Chicago's law school. He left Chicago to undertake a pilgrimage as an apostle of the Chicago version of law and economics.

Manne taught at St. Louis University (1956–62), George Washington University (1962–68), University of Rochester (1968–74), University of Miami (1974–80), Emory University (1980–86), and finally George Mason University (1986–96), where he served as dean of its School of Law. In 1996, the *National Law Journal* reported, "... although the University of Chicago is the birthplace of law and economics, only at George Mason does it permeate the entire curriculum" (Klein 1996).

Manne stepped down as dean of George Mason's law school in 1996, 30 years after he had obtained his JSD from Yale Law School with a dissertation on insider trading. One of the basic messages of Manne's dissertation was that the negative analysis so prevalent with respect to insider trading was often wrong (Manne 1966). Manne was also responsible for the idea of the existence of a market for corporate control (Manne 1965).

## A Sea Change in Antitrust

"The difference between Aaron's period and the period I was there was the interest of the law professors in economics," Coase commented a year after he gave up the editorship of the *Journal of Law and Economics* (Kitch 1983a, 222). Coase names three people explicitly: Dam, Kitch, and Posner, "… who had been set on the right road through his contact with Aaron Director at Stanford and who then moved to Chicago" (Coase 1993b, 251). Stigler wrote in his memoir about "… the brilliant lawyer (and excellent economist) Richard Posner who almost single-handedly created the field of economic analysis of law" (Stigler 1988b, 160).

President Reagan appointed Posner as a judge in the U.S. Courts of Appeal (7th Circuit) in 1981. This appointment meant Posner had to leave Lexecon Inc., a highly successful consulting firm that specializes in the economic analysis of legal cases. Posner had set up Lexecon in 1977 with Landes and their former student Andrew Rosenfield. During the 1980s, Fischel and Carlton also joined Lexecon.

Posner was born in 1939 in New York. He was the son of a lawyer and a schoolteacher, and he drifted into law because he "… didn't have any strong pull in some other direction" (Ciccone 1999, 265). He got his education in law at Yale (bachelor's degree) and Harvard (LLB in 1962). From 1963 to 1968 Posner was on the staff of the Federal Trade Commission and the U.S. Solicitor General and served as general counsel to the President's Task Force on Communications Policy. He was teaching at Stanford's law school when he first met Director, who visited the school. It took Director only a few lunchtime sessions to convert Posner—who was highly skeptical at first—to his ideas about the economic approach to law.[441] Posner entered Chicago's law school in 1969.

Posner's first important contributions were to regulation (Posner 1971, 1974) and legal precedent, which Posner and his coauthor, Landes, viewed as a capital stock depreciating over time due to obsolescence (Landes and Posner 1976). In 1973, Posner published the first edition of what would become one of the leading textbooks on the economic analysis of law (Posner 1992). In 2002, the sixth edition of *Economic Analysis of Law* was published. By that time, Posner had already become something of a legend. In the mid-1980s, law professor John Donohue declared: "He's one of the great geniuses of the 20th century" (Ciccone 1999, 266). U.S. Supreme Court Justice William Brennan "reportedly once said that Posner and Supreme Court Justice William O. Douglas were the only true geniuses he ever encountered" (Ciccone 1999, 265).

Adds Landes: "It is just incredible what Posner is capable of doing in 24 hours. He does not seem to be time-constrained."[442]

Inevitably, the U.S. antitrust laws were extensively covered by Posner's research. He was highly suspicious of too broad an interpretation of the Sherman Act and the antitrust laws in general. In a *Wall Street Journal* contribution written for the occasion of the centennial of the Sherman Act, Posner saw a more or less "normal" application of the antitrust law through time up until the term of Attorney General Thurman Arnold, who

> ... reinvigorated antitrust enforcement in the 1940s, which was fine, but he and his successors also began attempting to use antitrust for improper purposes—to promote quixotic political goals such as restoring a nation of small businessmen, to redistribute wealth ... Too often the antitrust suits ... were brought by or on behalf of inefficient competitors against their deservedly more successful rivals ... With the appointment of William Baxter as head of the antitrust division in 1981 ... antitrust enforcement was gradually pruned back.[443]

Twenty-five years after its first publication, a second edition of Posner's book *Antitrust Law* was published.[444] In it, Posner emphasized that "my ideas on antitrust continue to bear the stamp of Aaron Director and the late George Stigler" (Posner 2001a, xi). "Today, antitrust law is a body of economically rational principles ... The basic phenomenon [that antitrust has to deal with]," Posner argued at the start of the 21st century, "is that of monopoly ... The economic theory of monopoly provides the only sound basis for antitrust policy" (Posner 2001a, viii,1,9,26).

As Posner pointed out, a sea change in the interpretation of antitrust took place in the 1980s. This change was a victory for the Chicago analysis of antitrust, and Robert Bork was crucial in bringing about this change. To Bork, who was born in Pittsburgh in 1927, Director's course at the University of Chicago was a real eye-opener. In his youth, Bork had declared himself to be a socialist, and although he remained rebellious for the rest of his life, he lost the socialism. After one year as a research assistant in Chicago (1953–54), he went into corporate law practice as an antitrust specialist. There, he felt intellectually frustrated, so he took a huge pay cut and left for Yale Law School. At Yale, Bork was influenced by Alexander Bickell, an expert on constitutional law. From Bickell, Bork inherited the principles of judicial restraint and literal interpretation of the Constitution's wording as the cornerstone of his legal thinking. This led him to controversial points of view on such issues as freedom of speech, school prayer, abortion, privacy, and civil rights.

His conservative views brought him to the attention of President Richard Nixon, who appointed him as Solicitor General, one of the top positions at the Department of Justice, in 1973. A few months later he occupied center stage in the firing—on President Nixon's orders—of Archibald Cox, the special prosecutor in the Watergate affair.[445] In 1977, Bork returned to Yale, but in 1981, President Ronald Reagan appointed him to the federal court of appeals for the District of Columbia. Six years later, Reagan made him a candidate for the Supreme Court, which led to a fierce controversy. The liberal anti-Borkians were victorious, and the Senate voted 58 to 42 against him. In two subsequent books, Bork argued that he had become the victim of a liberal witch-hunt (Bork 1989) and that modern liberalism was more or less the cause of everything that was wrong with the United States.

As an academic scholar, Bork is best known for his book *The Antitrust Paradox*, in which he concluded, "… modern antitrust has so decayed that the policy is no longer intellectually respectable. Some of it is no longer respectable as law; more of it is not respectable as economics; and … a great deal of antitrust is not even respectable as politics" (Bork 1978/1993, x). According to Bork, much of the intellectual decay antitrust laws had suffered was due to the liberal and egalitarian way Chief Justice Earl Warren's Supreme Court had been interpreting the antitrust laws. As Posner already indicated, a change in court personnel that was essentially engineered by President Reagan greatly changed that picture.

A second factor in bringing about the sea change in antitrust thinking was the rise to prominence of a largely University of Chicago–inspired view of antitrust. In the new introduction to the 1993 edition of his book on antitrust, Bork set out two major characteristics of this "new body of antitrust scholarship": "The first is the insistence that the exclusive goal of antitrust adjudication, the sole consideration the judge must bear in mind, is the maximization of consumer welfare ... Second, the Chicagoans applied economic analysis more rigorously than was common at the time to test the propositions of the law and to understand the impact of business behavior on consumer welfare" (Bork 1978/1993, xi). As a result, Bork concluded, "courts now customarily speak the language of economics rather than pop sociology and political philosophy" (Bork 1978/1993, 427).

Dwelling on what, specifically, had changed in the way judges and courts applied antitrust legislation, Bork remarked: "One of the most satisfactory developments in the law has been the way in which corporate size and methods of attaining size are now dealt with. Size is achieved, of course, by internal growth, predation, or merger. This book argued that no firm size created by internal growth should be attacked by antitrust. The reason, of course, is that the achievement of large size by internal growth, whether the result is monopoly or membership in an oligopoly, demonstrates superior efficiency over the range of the market held" (Bork 1978/1993, 430). Although he still saw significant "demagoguery" surrounding the subject of predation, Bork seemed very satisfied as far as mergers were concerned: "Antitrust concern with conglomerate mergers seems to have disappeared without a trace. Although the government has a few guidelines about the circumstances in which it will move against vertical mergers, the guidelines are quite mild ... Horizontal mergers remain a subject of the law, as they should" (Bork 1978/1993, 434).

## JUDGE REMAINS CONTROVERSIAL SCHOLAR

Over the years, Bork became increasingly critical of the expansion of the economic approach to law:

> The application of economics to law soon transcended antitrust so that a broader law and economics movement was born. That movement has contributed greatly to the understanding of the utility of legal rules in various fields, though it has also been carried to excess by those who think that economics can explain all human behavior. Economics, as Coase has said, is most power-

ful when it deals with markets and values that can be measured in dollars. As economic explanations move further and further away from real markets, they gradually lose rigor and explanatory power, and finally lapse into self-parody" (Bork 1978/1993. xii).

Bork gave his critique a personal touch: "Judge Posner attempts to apply economics to wider areas than some of us do. I don't think that works" (Gibbons 1985). Indeed, Posner constantly pushed the frontiers of law and economics. In 1994, he published *Overcoming Law*. Recognizing that the rule of law is "a public good of immense value," Posner concluded that major parts of the law should be overcome, because they are "pretentious, uninformed, prejudiced and spurious" and need to be improved by more "pragmatism" (Posner 1994, 20–21). According to Posner, the "three keys to legal theory" are "economics, classical liberalism [and] pragmatism" (Posner 1994, viii).

Shortly after *Overcoming Law*, Posner published a book on a totally different subject. In *Aging and Old Age*, he presented an economic analysis of the aging process that was not limited to retirement issues such as the determinants of the age of retirement and the financing of consumption during retirement. Leaning heavily on human capital theory, Posner developed a positive economic theory of aging; the multiple-selves perspective plays a crucial role in it: "the difference between one's young and one's old self may be so profound that the two selves are more fruitfully viewed as two persons rather than one" (Posner 1995, 8–9). The last part of the book is more normative as Posner delves into subjects like euthanasia, compulsory and subsidized pensions, the allocation of medical research, and the political power of the elderly.

Posner pays particular attention in *Aging and Old Age* to the "rip-off" question—are the old ripping off the young?—and the relationship between the older and younger generations. Posner argues that

> ... it is probably true that the old people in the United States of the present day do not command the respect and affection they once did ... loss of popularity is the price that elderly Americans pay, probably willingly in most cases, for the dramatic increase in their prosperity and political influence ... Demographic

changes ... have greatly increased both the relative size and the absolute size of the elderly population. They are less scarce, so less valued. Most important perhaps are social changes, including mass education and the increasing rapidity of social, economic, and technological change—the increasing dynamism of American society—that have reduced the social value of the memories, wisdom, and experience of the elderly ... When [the elderly] were less wealthy, they had more respect; as they became wealthier, respect for them declined. The keel remains even. (Posner 1995, 360)

Posner concludes that financing rising costs caused by the elderly "presents a policy dilemma, since the young will resist being forced to pay either in taxes or in compelled savings for the level of care that their old selves will demand or that the current old are demanding. Multiple-selves analysis does not point the way to a solution to this dilemma; on the contrary, it shows why a solution will be difficult to devise" (Posner 1995, 362).

Another interesting piece of research by Posner deals with community, wealth, and equality —specifically, the possible political consequences of increasing income inequality. On the basis of theoretical, historical, and empirical evidence, Posner concludes: "... it is the *level* of income, rather than income *equality*, that is important to the maintenance of political community" (Posner 1997a, 1). Despite these more traditional economist-like excursions, Posner remains first a man of law and economics. When delivering the Clarendon Law Lectures in England in 1995, Posner openly called on the English to apply the economic approach more intensely to common law; he said that they were working in a much more Continental European than an American way.

Like Gary Becker, Posner also investigated social norms from an economic perspective—specifically their relationship with the law (Posner 1997b). At the end of the 20th century, Posner became deeply involved in the Microsoft antitrust case and commented on the impeachment procedure of President Bill Clinton. Appalled by the poor quality of commentary on these issues by academics writing outside their field, Posner tried to develop an economic theory to explain this decline.

## Bomb Throwers

Although Posner was certainly pivotal in extending the range of law and economics, the approach was most successful in the field of antitrust. Director, Coase, Telser, McGee, Posner, and Bork produced seminal contributions to antitrust analysis, but several others at the University of Chicago also excelled in this sphere, including, of course, Stigler.

Other important players on the Chicago antitrust field are Frank Easterbrook, Daniel Fischel, William Landes, and Dennis Carlton. When President Reagan appointed Easterbrook to the U.S. Court of Appeals for the 7th Circuit in 1984, the Chicago scholar became the youngest federal judge since William Howard Taft almost a century earlier. Described as "a brilliant lawyer" with "a fierce intellectual aggressiveness" (Marcus 1988), Easterbrook acknowledges that he's "generally viewed as a bomb thrower of one sort or another."[446]

Born in 1948 in Buffalo, New York, Easterbrook earned a bachelor's degree from Swarthmore College in 1970 and a JD from the University of Chicago in 1973. From 1974 to 1977 he served as an assistant to the U.S. Solicitor General and later became Deputy Solicitor General of the United States. In 1979, he began teaching at Chicago's law school. Since 1985, Easterbrook has divided his time between the U.S. Court of Appeals, lecturing at the University of Chicago's law school, and consulting at Lexecon.

At Chicago's law school, Easterbrook was close to Posner; in 1980, he published the first edition of *Antitrust: Cases, Notes and Other Materials* with Posner. In 1995, the book went into a third edition. A few years after the publication of *Antitrust*, Easterbrook referred to Chicago thinking on antitrust as the Workable Antitrust Policy School, and he described its most basic characteristic as the need for antitrust authorities to distinguish efficient from inefficient practices (Easterbrook 1984, 1986b). Writing on the limits of antitrust, Easterbrook concluded: "… antitrust is costly. The judges act with imperfect information about the effects of the practices at stake. The costs of action and information are the limits of antitrust ... Antitrust is an imperfect tool for the preservation of competition. Imperfect because we rarely know the right amount of competition to preserve, because neither judges nor juries are particularly good at handling complex economic arguments, and because plaintiffs are interested in restraining rather than promoting competition" (Easterbrook 1984, 4,43).

With his Chicago law school colleague Daniel Fischel, Easterbrook analyzed antitrust cases initiated by the management of a company that had become the object of a tender offer. They concluded that usually, such tenders are unsettling for current management but not harmful to consumers or the competitive environment. This analysis followed a hotly debated paper that Easterbrook and Fischel had published a year earlier. In that 1981 paper, they argued that management resistance to tender offers is almost always disadvantageous to shareholders (Easterbrook and Fischel 1981). These papers were the start of intensified cooperation between Easterbrook and Fischel on corporate law. This work culminated in the 1991 publication of *The Economic Structure of Corporate Law,* which analyzed such topics as limited liability, shareholder voting, corporate control, insider trading, and securities laws.

Fischel joined the University of Chicago's Law School in 1981 and became head of its program in law and economics in 1984. In 1999, he succeeded Douglas Baird as dean of the law school. Fischel was among those who brought new blood into the law school in the mid 1980s. Born in 1950, Fischel earned a bachelor's degree in 1972 from Cornell University and, two years later, a master's degree in American history from Brown University. After he earned a JD at the University of Chicago in 1977, Fischel worked for a few years as a law clerk in several courts and in private law practice. After a year at Northwestern University's law school, he returned to the University of Chicago in 1981.

Fischel's work was often prime example of the penchant for controversy typical of Chicago-style law and economics. In addition to the hotly debated research he published with Easterbrook, there was also his work with Carlton on the beneficial impact of insider trading (Carlton and Fischel 1983).

Corporate criminal liability was the subject of a paper by Fischel and his Chicago colleague Alan Sykes. They argued that corporations should not be prosecuted for criminal acts of their employees because "... the civil liability system is better suited to calculate appropriate fines and penalties for organizational defendants ... Corporate criminal liability is often heaped on top of substantial civil liability in circumstances where there is no reason to believe that civil liability alone would not produce appropriate deterrence. The result is overdeterrence ex ante, and an excessive investment of resources in litigation ex post" (Fischel and Sykes 1996, 321).

Fischel reached unprecedented heights of controversy with the 1995 publication of *Payback*, a book that defended Michael Milken, the "junk-bond king" of the 1980s. At Lexecon, Fischel worked as a consultant for Milken and his company Drexel Burnham Lambert. "Some people believe in UFO's. Some people believe in the tooth fairy. The author of this book believes in the innocence of Drexel's junk-bond king, Michael Milken," were the opening words of the *Washington Post*'s review of *Payback*.[447] Fischel argued that a coalition of four interest groups—prosecutors with political ambitions, the old financial establishment, the popular media, and congressional regulators—played a dirty game to bring about Milken's downfall.[448] Fischel rejected the claim that Milken and other junk-bond kings caused the disaster that hit the savings and loan industry in the United States. The key lesson Fischel draws from the Milken case is that we need to "guard against the arbitrary exercise of power by the government against those who are unpopular because they threaten the economic establishment. We need to be particularly suspicious about the rhetoric of greed. Powerful interest groups and their allies in the government use the rhetoric of greed to discredit and delegitimize the success of others" (Fischel 1995, 303–4).

In addition to Easterbrook and Fischel, Landes and Carlton also made important contributions to antitrust research. Landes made two important contributions to the economic analysis of antitrust. Landes published a 1981 paper with Posner that dealt with the issue of market power and antitrust cases (Landes and Posner 1981). Two years later, Landes tried to develop rules for determining the optimal sanctions for antitrust violations (Landes 1983).

Landes was born in 1939 in New York City. He started out as an arts major at the High School of Music and Art and from there moved to

Columbia University, where he was quickly "Beckerized": in the second year Landes spent at Columbia, Becker's "... course on human capital marked the beginning of my training as an economist" (Landes 1997, 32). Many years later, Landes is still convinced that "Gary Becker and the way he teaches economics really transforms you."[449] Under Becker's supervision, Landes completed a PhD dissertation that analyzed whether fair employment laws improved the economic situation of nonwhites in the United States—and his answer tended to be "no" (Landes 1968). After a short spell at Stanford University, Landes was an assistant professor at the University of Chicago's department of economics for three years, after which he returned to Columbia and the National Bureau of Economic Research in New York. In 1973, he rejoined Chicago, but this time at the law school.

One of Landes's important contributions was his investigation of court settlements, an analysis that clearly bore the imprint of Becker's work on crime. An interesting conclusion of his analysis was that although 90 percent of criminal cases end with plea bargains and hence do not go to trial, plea bargains made criminals worse off as a group, because the practice freed resources and time to pursue more criminals than would be the case if effective trials had been dominant. In 1975, Landes published his first two joint papers with Posner, the first of which dealt with how interest groups and their activities affect the independence of the judiciary (Landes and Posner 1975a) and the second of which elaborated further on Becker and Stigler's analysis of private law enforcement (Landes and Posner 1975b).

Carlton, who also recognizes Becker's influence on his own work, is coauthor of *Modern Industrial Organisation*, a widely used textbook on industrial organization (Carlton and Perloff 1989). In his more specific research on antitrust issues, Carlton focused on such topics as market power in durable goods markets, price fixing in college fees, and the antitrust economics of credit card networks.[450]

## THE OTHER GUYS

Not all scholars working in the field of law and economics at the University of Chicago have focused on antitrust, however. Some typical examples would be Richard Epstein, Douglas Baird, Randall Picker, and Alan Sykes.

Epstein, who was born in Brooklyn, New York in 1943, graduated from Columbia University in 1964. After graduation he spent two years at Oxford University and then went on to earn an LLB from Yale Law School in 1968. After a few years at the University of Southern California, he joined Chicago's law school in 1972. Epstein's first major publication, *Takings* (1985), immediately put him on a controversial footing with the American intellectual community.[451] He solidly remained there after publishing *Forbidden Grounds: The Case Against Employment Discrimination Laws.*

In *Forbidden Grounds,* Epstein (1992 2) concentrates on "the economic and social consequences that are generated by antidiscrimination laws." Although he also touches on sex, age, and disability discrimination, Epstein focuses primarily on racial discrimination—specifically, on the Civil Rights Act of 1964.[452] Recognizing that federal government action brought "enormous successes in changing a misguided, and often hateful, pattern of race relations" (1), Epstein concluded that the whole battery of ensuing anti-discrimination laws left everybody worse off in the end—including those whose destiny they were supposed to improve. Moreover, "the antidiscrimination law does not satisfy any condition of formal equality because some forms of discrimination are allowed while others are forbidden" (496). "The modern civil rights laws," Epstein concluded, "are a new form of imperialism that threatens the political liberty and intellectual freedom of us all" (505). These conclusions created a nationwide outcry of indignation.[453] Epstein's position on antidiscrimination laws was entirely in line with the position of Antonin Scalia, the controversial law scholar who became a member of the Supreme Court in 1986 and who spent 1977 to 1982 at the University of Chicago.

In 1997, Epstein again provoked controversy when he published an analysis of the health care system in the United States. Epstein believed that health policy discussion should center on what can be provided for the largest number of people, given the nation's limited resources. "Scarcity," Epstein argued, "is not an artificial assumption … it is the inevitable constraint that any and all systems of social order must confront—before it confronts them" (Epstein 1997, xi).

Epstein rejected Kenneth Arrow's argument (1963) on market failures in health care provision. Instead, Epstein (1997, 2) stressed government failure, which "exacerbates problems of information, uncertainty and monopoly." He saw government intervention mechanisms as "an endless tangle of hidden subsidies, perverse incentives, and administrative nightmares" (Epstein 1997, 2). Epstein advocated the unregulated provision of health care, which, in the long run, would guarantee greater access to quality medical care for more people. Other research areas in which Epstein has made significant contributions are product liability and the underground economy (Epstein 1988, 1994).

Two of the "other guys" are Baird and Picker, who coauthored the book *Game Theory and the Law* (1994) with Robert Gertner. In *Game Theory*, the authors apply the analytical apparatus of game theory to legal issues.

Baird was born in 1953 in Philadelphia. He received a bachelor's degree in English from Yale in 1975 and graduated four years later from Stanford's law school. He joined the law school at the University of Chicago in 1980. From 1984 to 1987, he served as associate dean, and in 1994, he succeeded Geoffrey Stone as the tenth dean of the law school. Baird also served as director of the law and economics program, but nevertheless, he cautions against viewing the economic approach as the only form of legal scholarship: "If you put law and economics first and foremost, you're not going to get a complete view of family law, for example. You can use it to an extent, but it is not the driving force behind the discipline."[454] Baird's main area of expertise is bankruptcy law (Baird 1992).

Picker, who was born in 1959, can be considered an authentic exponent of the Chicago brand of law and economics.[455] At Chicago's department of economics, he earned bachelor's and master's degrees in economics; afterward, he turned to the law school, where he earned a JD in 1985. After a year working as a clerk for Posner, Picker joined the Chicago law firm of Sidley and Austin. In 1989, he returned to the Chicago's law school.

Sykes, the fourth "other guy," was among the first to apply economic analysis to international law. Born in 1954, Sykes holds two academic degrees. In 1982, he graduated from Yale Law School, and five years later he also earned a PhD in economics from Yale University. Before joining the faculty of the University of Chicago law school, Sykes lectured at the University of Pennsylvania's law school. In 2006, Sykes left Chicago to join the Stanford Law School. "The general approach in Chicago," Sykes argued, "offers a broad framework for thinking about legal issues. The basic element is that people again and again respond to incentives and that economics has a lot to tell about incentives and how to analyze them."[456]

Sykes's analysis of the welfare economics of immigration law, which he sees as a form of protectionism that diminishes the degree of competition domestic workers have to face in the labor market (Sykes 1992), is typical of his research. Sykes's most important contributions are to be found in the field of international trade law. He has studied countervailing duties, unilateral threats, and the escape clause in the General Agreement on Tariffs and Trade (GATT) agreement (Sykes 1989, 1991).

Inspired by the debate between the United States and the European Union on beef from animals treated with growth hormones, Sykes investigated regulatory protectionism: "... any cost disadvantage imposed on foreign firms by a regulatory policy that discriminates against them or that otherwise disadvantages them in a manner that is unnecessary to the attainment of some genuine, nonprotectionist regulatory objective" (Sykes 1999, 3).

How can it be explained that the World Trade Organization condemns regulatory protectionism while at the same time allowing certain overt types of protectionism such as tariffs, subsidies, and quotas? Sykes showed that "... in most cases regulatory protectionism causes additional deadweight losses that make it considerably more inefficient than other instruments of protectionism such as tariffs, quotas, and subsidies" (5). Hence, regulatory protectionism "... holds little temptation for savvy political officials who are free to select among the alternative instruments of protection ... Where the self-interest of political actors requires an inefficient transfer of rents to well-organized interest groups ... it is often best to make that inefficient transfer as efficient as possible" (45,46). Hence, it should be no surprise that multilateral trading agreements strongly prohibit regulatory protectionism.

## THE IN-HOUSE FIGHT

Law and economics did not escape from one of the basic characteristics of the Chicago Tradition—the constant push to discuss and question accepted dogma. The way in which Director dismissed Levi's antitrust analysis was an early example. Another typical example was the early 1990s discussion between Posner and Coase on the domain and the methodology of economics as a science.

Toward the end of his life, Stigler also voiced disagreement with Posner's view that the common law always seeks economic efficiency. Stigler argued that "… ruling political groups produce and retain the doctrines of common law that serve them best" (Stigler 1992, 460). Stigler concluded: "The difference between a discipline that seeks to explain economic life (and, indeed, all rational behavior) and a discipline that seeks to achieve justice in regulating all aspects of human behavior is profound. This difference means that, basically, the economist and the lawyer live in different worlds and speak different languages" (463).

Fundamental discussions on the substance and future of law and economics are not the only points of dispute among legal scholars and economists at the University of Chicago. Cass Sunstein is a Chicago law school legal scholar who also has strong reservations about the economic approach to law as such.

Sunstein, who was born in 1954 in Salem, Massachusetts, is entirely Harvard-educated, and he earned a JD there in 1978. Three years later, he arrived at Chicago's law school as a specialist in constitutional law and regulation. In *Free Markets and Social Justice,* he acknowledged free markets as "the engine of economic productivity," but questions free markets as a requirement for social justice (Sunstein 1997, 3). He claimed free markets not only "can produce a great deal of injustice" but can also "sharply limit freedom" (4).

Sunstein developed his case around five key points. First, there's the "myth of laissez-faire"—that free markets "should be understood as a legal construct … rather than as a part of nature" (Sunstein 1997, 5). Second, preferences should not be considered to be a given: "Social norms are an important determinant of behavior, and they have received far too little attention from those interested in free markets" (4). Certainly, Sunstein argued, legal scholars should not agree to the notion that existing preferences should be accepted without any questions asked: "Unjust institutions can breed preferences that produce individual and collective harm" (5). Hence, laws can (and should) shape preferences. Third, "economists and economically oriented analysts of law sometimes think they can derive, from particular choices, large-scale or acontextual accounts of how much people value various goods" (6). Sunstein considered this to be a fundamental mistake as "choices are a function of context" (6). Fourth, Sunstein questioned the axiom of human rationality, referring to recent research that suggests "... people's choices and judgments are quite different from what traditional economists predict" (7).[457] Fifth, laws should be about a fair distribution of income and resources.

Two years after *Free Markets and Social Justice,* Sunstein published *The Cost of Rights,* in which he stressed the vital link between the protection of liberty and strong democratic government, which must collect taxes in order to be able to codify, protect, and enforce the rights to property, speech, and religion (Holmes and Sunstein 1999).

Although Sunstein did not present his arguments in this way, large parts of his analysis can be considered as a reply to Epstein's book *Simple Rules for a Complex World,* which was written two years before Sunstein's *Free Markets and Social Justice.* The basic message of Epstein's book was that "... every new legal wrinkle [should] pay its way by some improvement in the allocation of social resources. All too often, today's law does just the opposite: it makes more complex rules that hamper the productive efficiency of the society they regulate." The "simple rules" Epstein identified are "individual autonomy, first possession, voluntary exchange, control of aggression, limited privileges for cases of necessity, and just compensation for takings of private property, with a reluctant nod toward redistribution within the framework of flat taxes" (Epstein 1995, 307). In the last chapter of *Simple Rules,* Epstein takes issue with what would become the basic points of Sunstein's argumentation.

## New Recruits

At the start of the 21st century, the field of law and economics is very much alive at the University of Chicago's Law School, and several young scholars are coming to the forefront.[458] The most eye-catching name among these new faculty members is that of Eric A. Posner, son of Richard Posner. Born in 1965 in Chicago, Eric Posner earned a master's degree in philosophy from Yale in 1988 and a JD from Harvard three years later. After one year as law clerk for Judge Stephen F. Williams and another as attorney adviser at the U.S. Department of Justice, Eric Posner joined the University of Pennsylvania's law school in 1993. Since 1998, he has been a professor of law at the University of Chicago's law school: "What attracted me most was the prominence of the law and economics program here."[459] Eric Posner focuses on contract law, bankruptcy law, and the interaction between law and social standards. On this last issue, he has written a book that attempts to answer why people conform to social standards and what the role of the law is in a society where these social standards play such an important role (Posner 2000).

The other major new recruits are Lisa Bernstein, Saul Levmore, Douglas Lichtman, George Triantis, and David Weisbach.

Bernstein holds an economics degree from the University of Chicago and earned a JD at Harvard in 1991. Before joining Chicago's law school in 1998, she taught at Boston University and Georgetown University. Bernstein specializes in private commercial law.

Levmore studied law and economics at Yale and holds a PhD in economics from Columbia. He also joined Chicago's law school in 1998. Since 1980, he has taught at the University of Virginia School of Law, but he has frequently left for visiting professorships at Yale, Harvard, and Chicago, among others. Levmore's research focused on corporate tax, commercial law, and public choice.

In 1994, Lichtman earned a degree in electrical engineering and computer science from Duke University. In 1997, he completed a JD at Yale Law School, and one year later, he moved to Chicago, where he focused on the impact of technology on the legal system.

Triantis earned a JD at Stanford and taught at the University of Toronto (1989–94) and the University of Virginia (1994–99). His main fields of interest are contracts, commercial law, and debtor-creditor relations.

Weisbach earned a bachelor's degree in mathematics from the University of Michigan in 1985 and a JD from Harvard in 1989. In 1996, he joined the Georgetown Law Center; two years later, he transferred to Chicago. His work is focused on federal taxation.

One final remark on the field of law and economics at the University of Chicago: interaction between the law school, the department of economics, and the GSB has certainly diminished in recent years. Landes can be considered a privileged observer of this evolution. His explanation points to three factors: "First, the disappearance of people like Ronald Coase and George Stigler, who were very important for the link between the law people and the economists. Secondly, there are now many legal scholars well trained in economics. A lot of them have joined degrees. Thirdly, there's the seemingly ever-increasing degree of technicality of economics. Sometimes one gets the impression that it has become applied mathematics."[460] Dam adds: "I increasingly have the feeling that the legal people are closer to daily reality than the economists. The mathematization of economics is too often an excuse to write papers and dissertations just to repeat the obvious."[461]

Nevertheless, Fischel, speaking shortly after his appointment as dean of the Chicago law school, remained more confident than ever that this law school retained its leading position in the development of law and economics. "Despite sometimes fierce opposition, this law school has succeeded in bringing every aspect of the law under the scrutiny of economic analysis. It is indeed true that the cooperation with the economists across the Midway is less intense as it used to be. But I see signs that this is changing again."[462] Fischel and all the others were convinced that, while they certainly agreed with Charles Rowley's claim for the past, they would prove him wrong about the future of Chicago's role in law and economics: "The future of law and economics is extremely bright and although Chicago cannot expect to dominate the future of the discipline as effectively has it has dominated the past thirty years, it has surely earned an eternal reputation as the founding father of what is perhaps with public choice, one of the two most successful research programs in the social sciences of the second half of the twentieth century" (Newman 1998, 485).

# CHAPTER NINE

# Chicago and Politics

## *A Rare Breed*

GEORGE STIGLER RECEIVED THE NOBEL PRIZE IN ECONOMICS IN 1982. At that time, President Ronald Reagan's administration was fighting a deep recession in the United States and trying to strengthen public support for its program of supply-side economics. As they were convinced that an economist from the University of Chicago would not hesitate to help out a staunchly pro-free market administration, Nobel laureate Stigler was invited to the White House. However, this public relations exercise backfired badly for the Reagan administration. In front of the Washington press corps, Stigler talked about the economy being in "a depression" and described the supply-side program as something between "a gimmick and a slogan."[463] This episode is characteristic of the uneasy relationship between economists at the University of Chicago and the world of politics and public policy. However, many Chicago economists have spent some time in one or more governmental organizations; in addition to Stigler, the list includes Theodore Yntema, Ronald Coase, Aaron Director, Milton Friedman, Merton Miller, Sam Peltzman, Robert Aliber, Robert Vishny, Anil Kashyap, Randall Kroszner, Tomas Philipson, and Raghuram Rajan. Even James Laughlin was closely involved in shaping what would become the Federal Reserve System, and Jacob Viner and Charles Hardy worked for the U.S. Treasury during the Great Depression.

Most Chicago economists' involvement with government has had two basic characteristics. First, these entanglements usually transpired when the economists were young or, as in the case of Coase, Director, Friedman, and Stigler, in special circumstances such as World War II. Second, and more importantly, none of these men seemed to have had the ambition to leave university life and focus their energies on a political career. Only two Chicago economists are clear-cut examples of people who left the university for a full-blown political career: George Shultz and Paul Douglas.

There is a somewhat inverted relationship between the careers of these two extraordinary men. Although both men had careers in politics and in economics, Shultz's lasting contributions were more in the political arena and Douglas's were more in economics.

In addition to Shultz and Douglas, several other Chicago economists played influential roles in government, including Kenneth Dam, Arthur Laffer, Friedrich Hayek, Bert Hoselitz, Arnold Harberger, and Larry Sjaastad.

## "Senior But Not Old"

George Pratt Shultz was born in midtown Manhattan in 1920. "As a child of the 1930s and of the Depression, I was attracted to economics and to what I thought of as the real side of the economy," he remembered more than half a century later (Shultz 1993, 25). In 1942, he graduated from Princeton with a bachelor's degree in economics. Shortly after the Japanese attack on Pearl Harbor, he joined the U.S. Marines, and he stayed there until 1945.

After the war, Shultz pursued graduate studies at MIT. Among the teachers who most influenced him there were Paul Samuelson and Harold Freeman, "a wonderful teacher of statistics" (Shultz 1993, 27). In 1949, he earned a PhD in industrial economics at MIT with a specialty in labor economics. He taught at MIT until Allen Wallis brought him to Chicago's GSB in 1957. As Jim Lorie recalled: "I asked Al Rees to name the outstanding man in America in labor economics, someone who was senior but not old, and he said that man was George Shultz" (Dreiser 1971, 18). Shultz's labor economics diverged considerably from the then dominant Keynesian macroeconomics, which related employment to the evolution of aggregate demand in the economy, by emphasizing supply, demand, prices, and the market process.[464]

Shultz defended what he termed the "labor market approach" to unemployment:

> From the standpoint of meeting long-term manpower developments as well as immediate unemployment problems, [it is important] to make the labor market process as efficient as possible. We are talking here, of course, about human beings and their movement to the places and jobs in which they can be most productive. But, while human beings are involved, what they are involved in is a market process—a fact hard for many to accept, since so much has been made of the idea that "labor is not a commodity." Nevertheless, we ignore at our peril the fact that this market like others relies on good information about supply and demand, the possibility of movement away from one industry, occupation, or area and of entry into others, and that the price of labor in a given market will have impact on the quantity demanded ... To neglect the operation of labor markets and the institutional arrangements which shape their character is to invite an approach confined to the aggregate level, likely to be inflationary, and therefore employed with a timidity inappropriate to the seriousness of the problem. (Shultz 1963, 3,4)

At the GSB, Shultz ran a seminar and taught a course on industrial relations, and in 1962, he succeeded Wallis as dean. During the six years he served as dean, George Shultz consolidated the change and expansion Chicago's GSB had begun under Wallis and Lorie. With Walter "Bud" Fackler as associate dean, however, Shultz did more than just consolidate the Wallis-Lorie heritage. As dean at the GSB and during his later political career, Shultz became the living example of his own definition of an economist: "An economist is by training a strategist who will try to understand the constellation of forces present in a situation and try to arrange them to point toward a desirable result" (Shultz 1993, 31).

Shultz first became involved in government in 1955 and 1956, when he served as a senior staff economist on President Dwight Eisenhower's

Council of Economic Advisers. In 1959 and 1960, Shultz was a consultant to James Mitchell, the Secretary of Labor. One year later, President John F. Kennedy appointed him to a seat on the Advisory Committee on Labor Management Policy. In January 1969, Shultz took a leave of absence from the GSB and entered President Richard Nixon's Cabinet as Secretary of Labor. His knowledge of labor economics and his proven ability to act as a successful negotiator in labor conflicts got him the job. From the previous administration, Shultz inherited a major strike of longshoremen along the East and Gulf Coasts, which then-President Lyndon Johnson had declared a "national emergency." Shultz's strategy was to state publicly that the strike was not a concern of the federal government and then acted accordingly. When government intervention ceased, the strike was settled within weeks.

In the summer of 1970, the old Budget Bureau was transformed into the Office of Management and the Budget, and Nixon made Shultz its first director. Less than two years later, Shultz replaced John Connally as Secretary of the Treasury. At that moment, the always cool and calm Shultz was already indisputably "President Nixon's number one guy on virtually all domestic issues." "Check it with George" was a favorite sentence of Nixon's, despite the fact that Shultz had to be considered "the most apolitical member of the president's inner circle."[465]

As Secretary of the Treasury, Shultz had to deal with the breakdown of the Bretton Woods system of fixed exchange rates. In the meantime, the Nixon administration was getting into more and more difficulties because of the Watergate affair, but it was a matter of economic policy that spurred Shultz to leave the administration in the spring of 1974.

In the early 1970s, the United States paid the price of the expansionary monetary policy fueled by Johnson's Great Society expenditures and the cost of the Vietnam War. That price, of course, was inflation. Although Friedman's monetarist message was gradually gaining credibility and support, most economists and policymakers were still convinced that the inflationary bandwagon could not be stopped by monetary restraint. Nixon came under increasing pressure to accept wage and price controls to bring inflation under control, and he first introduced such controls in August 1971. In September of that year, Friedman visited Nixon, who said, "Don't blame George [Shultz] for this monstrosity [wage and price controls]." Friedman replied: "I don't blame George. I blame you, Mr. President" (Friedman and Friedman 1998, 387). Shultz disagreed with the policy of controls but, as he faced difficulties on many fronts, Nixon asked Shultz to withhold his resignation. However, in the summer of 1974, Shultz finally left the administration to become executive vice president of the Bechtel Corporation, a leading California engineering and construction company. During his eight years at Bechtel, Shultz taught part-time at Stanford University.

In July 1982, President Ronald Reagan called on Shultz to replace Alexander Haig as Secretary of State. As Shultz himself has documented in *Triumph and Turmoil*, his seven years at the State Department were full of big crises and major events, such as the end of the Marcos regime, the invasion of Grenada, the historic meeting between Reagan and Gorbachev in Reykjavik, the struggle to oust Noriega, the Iran-Contra affair, and the beginning of the downfall of the Soviet empire. Shultz was something of a shadow president in the Nixon administration, and this was probably even more evident during the Reagan administration. Shultz left his post as Secretary of State in January 1989 to become the Jack Steele Parker Professor of International Economics at Stanford's Graduate School of Business.

## CHICAGO GOES WASHINGTON

At the State Department, Shultz assembled a group of people whose common denominator was the University of Chicago. The three most important people were Kenneth Dam, Allen Wallis, and Arthur Laffer.

Shultz chose Wallis, his predecessor as dean of Chicago's GSB, for the post of Undersecretary for Economic Affairs. "Decisions might not go his way for political reasons, but as a forceful advocate of the free market, he never failed to leave his mark," said Shultz (1993, 34) of Wallis.

Dam, of Chicago's law school, had already collaborated with Shultz in previous government jobs. "Ken had a brilliant mind," Shultz (1993, 33) commented later, "honed to a keen edge in the seminar rooms of Chicago; he had as well the common sense associated with Kansas, his home state." Dam brought not only legal expertise but also a thorough knowledge of the international monetary system and of the energy markets. Shultz, Dam, and Wallis played a pivotal role in keeping the Reagan administration on the free-trade track at a time when the protectionist pressures emanating from Congress were strong.

Kenneth W. Dam was born to a Marysville, Kansas, farming family in 1932. He graduated from the University of Kansas in 1954 and earned a law degree from the University of Chicago three years later. After serving as a law clerk to U.S. Supreme Court Justice Charles E. Whitaker, he went into private law practice. In 1960, Dam joined the faculty of the Chicago's law school, where he was attracted to the rapidly expanding field of law and economics. Nevertheless, almost 40 years later, Dam still stressed: "I always was and still am first and foremost a lawyer. Over the years the legal profession has, I think, kept closer to the daily reality of business and politics than the economics profession."[466]

When Dam joined the law school's faculty, Aaron Director was still teaching his almost legendary course in antitrust. Soon, Director invited Dam to join him in this effort. As with so many others at the University of Chicago, Director left a lifelong impression on Dam: "He was an intellectual and a real gentleman. The basics of the economics I mastered over the years I got from Aaron Director."[467] Given Director's influence, it can be no surprise that antitrust-related issues such as price discrimination, trademarks, and mergers took a central place in his first publications.[468]

In his first eleven years at Chicago's law school, however, Dam's name was most closely linked to the issue of North Sea oil and gas licensing. He strongly favored the "price system" with its "great advantages of objectivity," as opposed to the discretionary licensing system then used to solve the allocative problems that surfaced in the development of the fields (Dam 1965, 74). His later articles further explored the auction system, arguing that "the auction system holds out the best possibility of capturing all the economic rents for the state" (Dam 1970b, 43). In 1974, Dam published an article on licensing policy that summarized the basic conclusions he had drawn by that time. Any licensing policy, Dam argued, "must satisfy two basic requirements. On the one hand, the system must attract private capital and technical capability ... On the other hand, in seeking to attract the private sector, the system cannot be seen by the voters to be a giveaway to the private companies of the nation's resources ... The auction system is ... excellent from the standpoint of allocative efficiency ... Whether the auction system meets the second requirement is a more complicated question" (Dam 1974, 261–62).[469]

In 1971, Shultz called on Dam to become assistant director of the Office of Management and the Budget. "George asked me to analyze the newly created Office of Management and the Budget. I accepted the offer because I wanted to see the government from the inside. I was surprised when the request came because I barely knew George Shultz at that time. My only direct contact with him was in discussions on an eventual joint degree between the law school and the GSB," Dam recalls.[470]

In 1973, Shultz appointed Dam as the executive director of the Council on Economic Policy, a platform for coordinating U.S. domestic and international economic policy. In 1974, Dam returned to Chicago's law school, and in 1980, he was chosen to be provost of the University, a job he left two years later when Shultz called on him again. Until 1985, Dam held the position of deputy secretary of state in the Reagan administration, and from 1985 to 1992, Dam served as vice president for law and external relations at IBM. In 1992, he agreed to become interim president of the United Way of America and clean up a scandal at that organization.

The close cooperation between Shultz and Dam led to the 1977 publication of *Economic Policy Beyond the Headlines,* the second edition of which was published in 1998. This book contains their reflections on and conclusions from their years of direct involvement in government policymaking. Their policy experience confirmed their Chicago beliefs: "Contrary to the view of those who believe that legislators and officials are responsible for rising standards of living, the market system itself has been our most resilient and versatile economic tool—a superior problem-solver, both in satisfying private wants and in achieving public goals. Yet too often governmental economic policy tools have been misused, even abused, in attempting to achieve goals for which they are inappropriate, and market solutions have too often been set aside at precisely the time when most needed" (Shultz and Dam 1977, 200). Thus, it is hardly surprising that Shultz concluded: "… perhaps my two most important words during six years of government service were 'Do Nothing'" (Shultz and Dam 1977, 2).

In January 2001, Dam joined President George W. Bush's administration as Deputy Secretary of the Treasury. Shortly beforehand, he finished writing *The Rules of the Global Game: A New Look at U.S. International Economic Policymaking*, an attempt to provide "a conceptual framework for assessing … international economic policy" as "conventional wisdom" on these issues "has shallow roots" (Dam 2001, x). He distinguishes between the normative approach—asking what should be done—and the positive approach—focusing on what is actually done. In the positive approach, he emphasizes "three basic concepts: (1) rent seeking; (2) interest group politics; and (3) statecraft" (Dam 2001, 5) to explain why there is so often a difference between what is and what should be in international economic policy making. Armed with this framework and many years of experience, Dam analyzed U.S. policy on such issues as international trade, private foreign investment, the international monetary system, labor standards and the environment, and immigration. "I do not believe in an all-wise bureaucratic state where civil servants … would formulate and carry out the best policies … free from the demands of politics … Some of our most important and far-reaching policies would never have been adopted without the pressure of interest groups," he concluded (Dam 2001, 291–92).

In addition to Dam and Wallis, Shultz brought Arthur Laffer from the University of Chicago to Washington. In 1980, Robert Mundell, from whom Laffer "borrowed" one of the basic ideas of the supply-side revolution, described Laffer as "the most controversial economist in the United States today—as well as one of the most influential;" John K. Galbraith described Laffer's theories and policy prescriptions as "witchcraft."[471] Laffer will forever be identified with the Laffer Curve, which was drawn, as history has it, on a restaurant napkin during a dinner meeting in a restaurant in Washington with Jude Wanniski in December 1974. In those days, Wanniski was an editorial writer for the *Wall Street Journal*, and he became a major protagonist of the tax cuts pushed through by President Reagan.

The Laffer Curve showed that tax receipts would first increase as the rate of taxation is pushed up. At a certain point, however, the disincentive effects of taxation become dominant, so as the rate of taxation continues to rise, tax receipts actually start to fall (Laffer 1980; Laffer and Seymour 1979). The idea of something like the Laffer Curve was nothing new—after all, Adam Smith wrote in *Wealth of Nations*: "High taxes, sometimes by diminishing the consumption of the taxed commodities and sometimes by encouraging smuggling, afford a smaller revenue to government than might be drawn from more moderate taxes" (Smith 1776, book V, 414).

Arthur Laffer was born in 1940 in Youngstown, Ohio. He obtained a bachelor's degree in economics from Yale University and then moved on to Stanford, where he earned an MBA in 1965 and a PhD in 1971 with a dissertation on short-term capital movements and the voluntary credit restraint program. In 1967, the University of Chicago offered him an assistant professorship, and he eventually won tenure at the unusually young age of 28. Laffer's main area of research at Chicago was monetary matters; he stressed such topics as the importance of the world supply of money for the evolution of inflation—even in countries as big as the United States (Laffer and Meiselman 1975). When Shultz became the first director of the Office of Management and the Budget in 1970, he made Laffer the Office's economist.

In 1974, Laffer returned to Chicago, but by that time he had become more of a political activist than an academic researcher. After two more years in Chicago, he moved to the University of Southern California, where his tax crusade gained full momentum. He was one of the major defenders of California's Proposition 13, which resulted in a huge cut in real estate taxes.

## MARINE AT 50

Laffer's name will be forever identified with the Laffer Curve, and Paul Douglas will be forever associated with the Cobb-Douglas production function. "If Nobel Prizes," Paul Samuelson, a student of Douglas's at the University of Chicago, wrote, "had been awarded in economics after 1901, as they were in physics, chemistry, medicine, peace, and literature, Paul H. Douglas would probably have received one before World War II for his pioneering econometric attempts to measure marginal productivities and quantify the demands for factor inputs" (Samuelson 1979, 923). Albert Rees, another student of Douglas's, testifies to Douglas's great skill as an empirical economist when he argues that "the similarity between many of the Douglas results and those of later investigators is a tribute to his ingenuity" (Rees 1979, 920).

Paul H. Douglas was born in Salem, Massachusetts in 1892. His mother died when Douglas was only four, and because of his father's nomadic lifestyle, he was raised by an uncle near Moorhead Lake, Maine. He paid for his own schooling by working as a lumberjack, farmer, fisherman, and clerk. In 1909, he entered Bowdoin College in Brunswick, Maine, where he became interested in economics. "John Stuart Mill became an inspiration," Douglas recalled, "and has remained so throughout my life" (Douglas 1972, 24). After graduating from Bowdoin in 1913, Douglas moved to Columbia University, where he obtained a master's degree in political science in 1915. At Columbia, Douglas was greatly influenced by John Bates Clark and by the econometrician Henry Moore.

In 1915, Douglas went to Harvard to study economics, and there he experienced the bullying of F. W. Taussig. After endless humiliations at Taussig's hands, Douglas ended up openly challenging him on Clark's marginal productivity theory: "No student except Jacob Viner had dared do this" (Douglas 1972, 34). After short teaching assignments at the University of Illinois and at Reed College, Oregon, he worked for the Emergency Fleet Corporation at the end of World War I. In 1919, he started teaching at the University of Washington, and in 1921, he earned a PhD in economics from Columbia University.

In 1920, Douglas was called to the University of Chicago by Leon C. Marshall, at a time when Chicago "was entering the most disgraceful decades that any American city has ever experienced" (Douglas 1972, 44), mainly because of organized crime and political corruption. In Chicago, he became a colleague of John Maurice Clark, the son of his teacher John Bates Clark. Douglas stayed at the University of Chicago for the rest of his academic life, which ended in 1948 when he became a U.S. senator.

For Douglas, it did not suffice to understand the nature of social and economic problems—he also wanted to change things. Involvement in politics was the next logical step. In 1930 and 1931, he acted as adviser to the Committee on Stabilization of Employment established by New York Governor Franklin D. Roosevelt. Also during the 1930s, he served on the Pennsylvania Committee on Unemployment, on the Illinois Housing Commission, and on the National Recovery Administration.

As chairman of the Illinois Utility and Consumer's League, Douglas fought a fierce battle against the monopolistic utility empire of Samuel Insull, "the uncrowned king of both Chicago and Illinois ... [who was] ... reaching out for the utilities of a large portion of the nation" (Douglas 1972, 44,55). Four decades later he wrote in his memoir: "The Insull forces put heavy pressure on the university either to fire or to muzzle me ... to the credit of the university authorities, no one interfered with me, and the new president, Robert M. Hutchins, was particularly firm in his stand for academic freedom" (Douglas 1972, 57). In 1939, Douglas won a seat on the Chicago City Council, and in 1942 he ran unsuccessfully for the U.S. Senate as a Democrat.

The day after this defeat, he enlisted as a private in the U.S. Marines at the age of 50. Although he was a lifelong pacifist, he was disgusted by the atrocities committed by the German, Japanese, and Italian fascists, as well as by the terror-ridden police state in Russia. He was severely wounded at Okinawa and returned from World War II without the use of his left arm.

Douglas ran for the Senate again in 1948, and this time he was elected. He served three terms in the U.S. Senate, finally losing his seat in 1966. Although he was already 74 years old, Douglas resumed his academic career at the New School for Social Research in New York. He retired in 1969 and died in 1976.

At the University of Chicago, Douglas was in constant dispute with Frank Knight, who dominated the economics scene at the University of Chicago during the 1930s and 1940s.[472] Other than their more personal animosities, Knight had two problems with Douglas. First, he had very strong reservations about Douglas's empirical approach, which he tried to use to go beyond Knight's more theoretical argumentation. Second, Knight reproached Douglas for being out of line as an academic because of his political activities. George Stigler (1988b, 186–187) wrote that Knight "believed that for a scholar to give explicit solutions to hard social problems on the basis of inadequate knowledge was almost immoral," and he described Douglas as "a buoyant, hyperactive liberal reformer" (182). It is not hard to imagine who Douglas had in mind when, in the preface to *The Theory of Wages*, he stated that as to "the inductive, statistical and quasi-mathematical method" in economics, "an excellent beginning has been made ... during the last twenty years by such scholars as Henry L. Moore, Schultz ... and Marschak ... The victory of these men is not yet won for there are still those who sneer at all attempts to introduce greater precision and who at times seem to take a perverse pleasure in muddying the waters" (Douglas 1934, xii).

In his memoir, Douglas (1972, 44) left no doubt about his feelings toward the University of Chicago: "I still have a deep affection for it and the values it has fostered." However, he had different feelings when he returned to the University in 1946: "The university I had loved so much seemed to be a different place. Schultz was dead, Viner was gone, Knight was openly hostile, and his disciples seemed to be everywhere. If I stayed, it would be in an unfriendly environment. I felt stifled and did not think I could live in that atmosphere" ((Douglas 1972, 128). He found that "the economic and political conservatives had acquired an almost complete dominance over my department and taught that market decisions were always right and profit values the supreme ones. The doctrine of noninterference with the market meant, in practice, clear the track for big business. Inequalities of bargaining power, knowledge, and income were brushed aside, and the realities of monopoly, quasi monopoly and imperfect competition were treated as either immaterial or nonexistent" (Douglas 1972, 127).

In his political career, Douglas became "a champion of liberal causes."[473] Douglas fought tough but rather lonely battles for such issues as unemployment insurance, old-age pensions, union protection legislation, and disclosure of financial positions by politicians. He also had outspoken liberal views on civil rights—Douglas was close to Martin Luther King—and ecological issues. Because of his controversial positions, the FBI began to investigate Douglas in 1941 and placed his name on a list of people "whose arrest might be considered necessary in wartime." The Bureau described Douglas as "outstanding in communist activities."[474]

In response to these accusations, Douglas wrote in his memoir that he and his wife "had 'adopted' a Spanish orphan and were paying for her through the Foster Parents organization. This was broadcast as proof that I was a communist. So were the facts that I had favored the recognition of the Soviet Union, had tried to help the unemployed, and had opposed Franco" (Douglas 1972, 90). Douglas's strong belief in the domino theory in international politics and his support for the U.S.'s role in the Vietnam War were quite at odds with these alleged "communist sympathies." Despite his liberal positions on many issues, Douglas consistently argued against unbalanced budgets and for more frugality, efficiency, and higher standards of ethics on the part of politicians (Douglas 1952a, 1952b).

Douglas divided his life more or less half and half between academia and politics. It is not clear which of the two careers he cherished most. Friedman remembers that shortly after his 1966 electoral defeat, Douglas was invited to the University of Chicago to give a lecture: "When a number of us had lunch with him, I commented that he looked far more relaxed and in much better shape than he had while in office or during the campaign, and said 'So, Paul, maybe your defeat was a blessing in disguise.' He reacted violently, saying, 'Oh no! It's the worst thing that ever happened to me. There is no better job in the world than being a U.S. Senator'" (Friedman and Friedman 1998, 196). In the late 1960s, a reporter asked what he loved most—teaching or politics—and Douglas replied: "I think teaching. In teaching, one is aloof from the power struggle."[475]

## STILL AN EXCELLENT APPROXIMATION

One of Douglas's major academic achievements was the Cobb-Douglas (CD) production function; through it, he gained "a certain immortality" (Stigler 1946, 153). In his presidential address to the AEA in December 1947, Douglas described its birth:

> It was twenty years ago last spring that, having computed indexes for American manufacturing of the numbers of workers employed per year from 1899 to 1922, as well as indexes of the amounts of fixed capital in manufacturing deflated to dollars of approximately constant purchasing power, and then plotting these on a log scale together with the Day index of physical

production for manufacturing, I observed that the product curve lay consistently between the two curves for the factors of production and tended to be approximately a quarter of the relative distance between the curve of the index for labor ... and that of the index of capital ... Since I was lecturing at Amherst College at the time, I suggested to my friend, Charles W. Cobb, that we seek to develop a formula which would measure the relative effect of labor and capital upon product during this period. (Douglas 1948, 6)

Douglas and mathematician Cobb arrived at the formula $P = bL^kC^{1-k}$, in which P stands for production, L for labor input, and C for capital input. For the period 1899 to 1922, they estimated the parameters to be b=1.01 and k=0.75. The CD production function showed constant returns to scale, and the function inherently implied diminishing returns to each factor of production. Moreover, technological progress played only a very marginal role in the CD function.

These and other criticisms were voiced by Douglas and Cobb's contemporaries, including Joseph Schumpeter, John Maurice Clark, Ragnar Frisch, and David Durand.[476] Despite these critiques, for Paul Douglas the CD production function remained a reasonable description of reality.[477] As Stigler (1946, 153) argued in the 1980s: "It is now customary practice in economics to deny the CD production function's validity and then to use it as an excellent approximation."[478]

For Douglas, the production function and the eventual laws of production were not the primary purpose of his research. Like Henry Moore, he wanted to get to a verification of the marginal productivity theory of his other teacher, John Bates Clark. Douglas realized that he needed a theory of production or, preferably, laws of production, to be able to verify the general marginal productivity theory; this in turn formed the basis for his theory of wages developed in *The Theory of Wages* (1934), which is generally recognized as his real magnum opus.

"Does the process of distribution approximate the apparent laws of production?" or, alternatively, "To what degree do the shares labor and capital receive of the product approximate the proportions we would expect from the values of the production function?"—these were the real questions Douglas wanted to answer (Cobb and Douglas 1928, 161;

Douglas, 1948, 36). His research led Douglas to a rather unconditional "yes" as the answer to both questions. Given the assumptions of constant returns and perfect competition, the mathematics of the CD production function do indeed lead to the conclusion that each factor of production—labor and capital—would receive the fraction of total output that is indicated by the exponents k and 1 − k. Hence, 75 percent of total output (national income) is expected to go to labor and 25 percent to capital, which is very close to what the national accounts actually show. Douglas concluded that the laws of production and the laws of distribution, in conformity with the marginal productivity theory, reinforce each other as theoretically and empirically valuable vehicles.

But, if the data indicated that the marginal productivity theory held up as a law of distribution, why, then, did the same man who empirically verified this theory take so many initiatives as a politician that would bring about a change in the distribution of income (e.g., legally enforced minimum wages, unemployment insurance, greater union power)? According to Blaug (1985, 55), Douglas "never adequately discussed the tensions between his academic views and his political life." On several occasions, however, Douglas did shed light on this issue. In 1928, Cobb and Douglas pointed out that the "decided tendency for distribution to follow the laws of imputed productivity" should not lead to the conclusion that

> ... this lends an ethical justification to the existing social and economic order ... it should be pointed out that even if there were a precise correspondence, it would not furnish any light upon the question as to whether capital for example should be privately owned to the degree to which it is in our society. For while capital may be "productive," it does not follow that the capitalist always is. Capital would still be "productive" even though its ownership were changed. Nor does it follow that the uses to which the capitalists put the income which they receive are on the whole socially the best. (Cobb and Douglas 1928, 163–64)

Twenty years later, Douglas (1948, 38) conceded that the apparent conformity between the laws of production and the marginal productivity theory raises the "problem of reconciling these results with the known facts of imperfect competition, oligopoly and monopoly. Such conditions ... do exist, and, in fact, characterize a large sector of our economy. It is, therefore, puzzling to find labor's share approximately equal to that which we would expect under conditions of perfect competition ... I would ... suggest that one answer to the paradox may be that the quasi-monopolies and oligopolies may have shared with their workers the excess gains which they have made at the expense of the consumers." Given this analysis, the logical next step is to try to reinforce the rights and bargaining position of the weaker segments of the work force and of the population in general. As a senator, Douglas worked energetically to that end.

An integral part of Douglas's research on the marginal productivity theory was his analysis of wages and of the labor market in general. In this field, Douglas did pioneering empirical work. Because the federal government at that time had poor to nonexistent statistics on these issues, Douglas personally constructed indices of the cost of living and of wages in several industries, which enabled him to calculate the evolution of real wages. He even calculated a time series on the estimated average weekly salaries of domestic servants based on help-wanted advertisements in the Chicago newspapers (Douglas and Hanson 1930). The data on wages provided Douglas and his assistants with the raw material that allowed them to dig into questions of labor demand and labor supply in a very innovative way.[479]

Given the Depression of the 1930s, it was hardly surprising that a labor economist such as Douglas also focused on the unemployment problem. In 1934, Douglas and Director (who was Douglas's research assistant at the time) published *The Problem of Unemployment.* After describing the extent and costs of unemployment, Director and Douglas analyzed seasonal, cyclical, and technological unemployment and the impact of technological advances on employment. Douglas and Director pleaded for the introduction of an unemployment insurance system by the government and the installation of public employment offices throughout the country and also for the active use of public works planning to reduce fluctuations in employment and the average level of unemployment. Even the planning system of the Soviet Union is regarded favorably by the authors: "A planned economy managed for the social good may well have a greater capacity to prevent depressions and to keep the laboring force more steadily employed than an uncoordinated system of private establishments necessarily motivated by profit where the ultimate governor in the distribution of productive resources is the tendency of profits and wages to flow towards an equality" (Director and Douglas 1934, 62).

## "Two Stubborn Men of Principle"

Douglas's most important book on the Great Depression of the 1930s is *Controlling Depressions*, which was published one year before Keynes's *General Theory*. "The two great rocks upon which the capitalistic system may founder," Douglas (1935, 277,280-281) wrote, "are wars and business depressions ... It is more than doubtful whether the capitalistic system can survive more than two or three more such depressions." Douglas's tract must be seen in the context of the thinking on the Depression that prevailed at the University of Chicago in those days. The Public Policy Pamphlet No. 1, *Balancing the Budget*, offers a good summary of this Chicago thinking. Nevertheless, Douglas introduced his own emphases into the analysis and the policy recommendations. Though Viner and most other Chicagoans argued for government action in the face of a severe depression, they fundamentally believed in the long-run equilibrating forces of a market economy. Douglas's beliefs were closer to those of John Maynard Keynes—that a market economy was fundamentally unstable and that continuous government monitoring was necessary. Building on the acceleration principle of his former Chicago colleague John Maurice Clark, Douglas (1935, 13) argued that investment was much more volatile than consumption: "... the demand for capital goods is a function not only of the total demand for consumer goods but rather of the *rate of change* in the demand for these latter products."

Douglas argued that a recovery could only come from an increase in consumer demand, but that there was no guarantee that this would happen automatically, because a depression usually severely reduces the purchasing power of the average consumer. "Without vigorous constructive action, even ultimate recovery is by no means certain, while it is, in any event, likely to be long-delayed," Douglas concluded (1935, 95). The obvious next question was, "What kind of vigorous constructive action should be pursued by the authorities?" Douglas did not believe the classical instruments of monetary policy— changes in the interest rates and open-market operations—could do the trick. The "vigorous constructive action" Douglas pleaded for was increased government spending, especially through a program of public works. As Douglas was conscious of the need to expand the monetary supply, he believed that these public works should not be financed by higher taxation. Instead, a combination of borrowing through the bond market and money creation should be pursued, with Douglas having a clear preference for the latter. Although Douglas defended an intentional policy of compensatory public finance over the business cycle, he thought it necessary that the government budget should be "approximatively balanced over a ten-year period" (Douglas 1935, 278).

"Paul Douglas," concluded J. Ronnie Davis (1971, 59), "built an explanation of and a remedy for depression along Keynesian lines ... Like Keynes, he did disavow an older tradition of aggregate economics, principally identified with J.B. Say, whose followers treated total effective demand as transferable, but incapable of creation or destruction." Furthermore, Douglas (1935) thought it necessary to deprive "private banking of the power of creating commercial credit [and to lodge] this function in a socialized agency" (278) and to carry out a "thoroughgoing reorganization of our economic system, and a distinct curbing of the hitherto enormous powers of private monopolists and big bankers" (280).

Someone who was fundamentally at odds with Douglas's analysis of the Great Depression was Friedrich Hayek, who came to the University of Chicago a few years after Douglas had left. Hayek rejected those theories that explained the Great Depression as a fundamental consequence of underconsumption, and Douglas clearly belonged to the underconsumptionist camp. On the occasion of Hayek's death on March 23, 1992, David Broder of the *Washington Post* pointed out the remarkable coincidence that just one day later, Washington would commemorate the 100th birthday of the late Paul Douglas; Broder described Hayek and Douglas as "two stubborn men of principle,"[480] but in their views on economics and the world in general, Douglas and Hayek were light years apart. Unlike Douglas, Hayek never went into active politics. So why include Hayek in this chapter? First, as a political philosopher, he has always been a major source of inspiration for politicians and, second, his major work, *The Constitution of Liberty*, is primarily a tract in political philosophy.

Friedrich A. von Hayek was born in 1899 to a Viennese family with a long academic tradition; the famous philosopher Ludwig Wittgenstein was one of his cousins.[481] Hayek studied law at the University of Vienna, but he also followed the lectures of the physicist Ernst Mach and the economists Friedrich von Wieser and Othmar Spann. Hayek (1994, 48) later recalled, "I really got hooked [on economics] when I found [Carl] Menger's *Grundsätze* such a fascinating book." The young Hayek became part of the famous Austrian or Viennese School of Economics; Ludwig von Mises was another important member.[482] Hayek was part of a generation of Austrian-school economists that included such future luminaries as Gottfried Haberler, Fritz Machlup, and Oscar Morgenstern.

After receiving his doctoral degree in political science in 1923, Hayek took a trip to the United States, during which his attention was drawn to Wesley Mitchell's empirical work on the business cycle at Columbia University. A few years after his return to Vienna, Hayek and Mises started the Austrian Institute for Business Cycle Research. Though he was intrigued by the progress made in the United States on data collection and analysis, Hayek thought it necessary to first develop a theory explaining the statistical regularities observed.

Using Eugen von Böhm-Bawerk's framework of average periods of production, Hayek developed his own theory of the business cycle.[483] Hayek's distinctly monetary business cycle theory leads to the conclusion that excessive credit creation inevitably leads to rising inflation and depressed economic activity—something that was impossible in the basic Keynesian analysis, but which plagued every Western economy in the 1970s.[484]

Hayek's work attracted the attention of the British economist Lionel Robbins, who invited the young Austrian economist to give four lectures at the LSE in 1930 and 1931. In 1931, Hayek was the first foreigner to obtain a full-time professorship at the prestigious LSE, and in 1938, he exchanged Austrian for British citizenship.

Hayek remained in England for the next 18 years, where he quickly became "the only intellectual opponent of John Maynard Keynes" (Leube and Nishiyama 1984, xix).[485] In 1930, Keynes had published *Treatise on Money*, which Hayek attacked. Hayek never reviewed Keynes's *General Theory*, which appeared in 1936.[486] Half a century later, and with Keynes long dead, Hayek (1983) summed up his view of Keynes as follows: "I am claiming that perhaps the most impressive intellectual figure I have ever encountered and whose general intellectual superiority I have readily acknowledged, was wholly wrong in the scientific work for which he was chiefly known."[487]

## No Chicago Economist

The publication of *The Pure Theory of Capital* in 1941 rounded out Hayek's research on monetary theory. By that time, he was much more concerned with two interrelated popular ideas of the early 1940s, the first that the Nazi regime in Germany had to be seen as a capitalist reaction against socialism, and the other that some form of government planning had not only become necessary but even desirable.

Hayek's rejection of these ideas was made most forcefully in *The Road to Serfdom*, which was written during the period 1940 to 1943 and was dedicated to "the socialists of all parties" (Hayek 1944, iv). "Few are ready," according to Hayek (1944, 3), "to recognize that the rise of Fascism and Nazism was not a reaction against the socialist trends of the preceding period, but a necessary outcome of these tendencies. This is a truth which most people are unwilling to see even when the similarities of many of the repellent features of the internal regimes in communist Russia and national-socialist Germany were widely recognized." In the United States, the book appeared in *Reader's Digest* in condensed form and provoked highly negative comments.[488] "The American intelligentsia," according to Hayek (1994, 102), "felt that this [book] was a betrayal of the highest ideals which intellectuals ought to defend." David Warsh (1993, 120) said: "It's hard now to recall the fury that greeted *The Road to Serfdom* when it was published in 1944, a time when John Maynard Keynes, Joseph Schumpeter, Karl Polanyi, Karl Mannheim and Harold Laski were trumpeting the death of capitalism and the inevitability of planning."

From March to May 1945, when *The Road to Serfdom* was a best seller in the United States, Hayek was on a lecture tour in the country. During this tour, he used the University of Chicago as his headquarters, as he was close to Henry Simons and Aaron Director. Harold Luhnow of the William Volker Fund became enthusiastic about Hayek's message and started a campaign to persuade Hayek to come to the United States. Hayek met Luhnow only once, in the Quadrangle Club on the campus of the University of Chicago, but "I have every reason to suspect that when a little later John Nef began to make attempts to persuade Hutchins to call me to Chicago, he was instrumental. I was proposed first to the faculty of economics but they turned me down" (Hayek 1994, 128). Nef (1973, 237–38) confirms Hayek's account: "The Economics Department welcomed his connection with Social Thought, although the economists had opposed his appointment in economics four years before largely because they regarded his *Road to Serfdom* as too popular a work for a respectable scholar to perpetrate. It was all right to have him at the University of Chicago so long as he wasn't identified with the economists." In 1950, Nef finally succeeded in luring Hayek to the University of Chicago with Luhnow's money,[489] giving him a chair as professor of social and moral science on the Committee on Social Thought—which Nef had personally set up not long before.

What led economists at the University of Chicago to refuse Hayek? According to Friedman, the economists at the Department in Chicago "didn't agree with [Hayek's] economics" (Ebenstein 2001, 174). Hayek indicated that the opposition was strongest among the econometricians (Ebenstein 2001, 175). Two sources confirmed that the close link between Hayek and Simons made several leading economists in the department very suspicious of Hayek,[490] and the same sources point out that Douglas took a negative attitude towards Hayek.

What exact role did Friedman play? Friedman leaves no doubt that the discussion on Hayek was already over and done with by the time he arrived in Chicago.[491] However, the same two sources referred to above claim that Friedman was at least consulted about the issue and spoke out against Hayek joining the department of economics. I was not able to settle this issue, but there are reasons to believe Friedman was not terribly enthusiastic about Hayek in 1946. In the early 1940s, Hayek was increasingly hostile to what he described as "scientism or scientistic prejudice" (Hayek 1942, 269) in economics.[492] Imitation of the methods used in the physical sciences is sure, Hayek argued, to lead to grave errors in economic analysis.

By contrast, Friedman believed that of the human sciences, economics was by far closest to those physical sciences. In his essay on "The Methodology of Positive Economics," Friedman (1953, 4) claims that "positive economics is, or can be, an 'objective' science, in precisely the same sense as the physical sciences." Hayek (1994, 145) later described "Milton's [*Essays in*] *Positive Economics*" as a book "which in a way is quite as dangerous a book ... as Keynes's treatise." In his memoir, Friedman touches briefly on Hayek's joining the Committee on Social Thought, but without further comment. On other occasions, however, Friedman admired Hayek's work.[493]

In 1947, Hayek was joined by Knight, Friedman, Director, and Stigler in creating the Mont Pèlerin Society.[494] With the financial and organizational help of Swiss businessman Albert Hunold, Hayek succeeded at bringing together a group of people who were prepared for "efforts to revive the liberal tradition" in the postwar area (Hayek 1994, 132–33)[495] In the spring of 1947, thirty-six scholars and publicists attended a ten-day conference in Mont Pèlerin, Switzerland. After 1947, the Society met annually at different locations. In his memoir, Friedman writes enthusiastically about his membership in "a society that has played a major role in preserving and strengthening liberal ideas" (Friedman and Friedman 1998, 159).

Hayek's major publication during his twelve years at the University of Chicago was undoubtedly *The Constitution of Liberty*. According to Hayek's biographer, the book "was intended as his magnum opus ... [Hayek] hoped *The Constitution of Liberty* would be the *Wealth of Nations* of the twentieth century" (Ebenstein 2001, 196). Hayek got the idea for the book when he obtained a grant from the Guggenheim Foundation in 1954 that allowed him to retrace the journey John Stuart Mill had made through France and Italy. Just as Mill had conceived the idea of writing his famous tract *On Liberty* during this long trip, Hayek came back to Chicago with the plan of *The Constitution of Liberty* in his head. In it, Hayek (1960, 6, 11) defined liberty as "that condition of men in which coercion of some by others is reduced as much as possible in society."

Hayek regarded the state as the major source of possible coercion; hence, strict limitations on the powers of all government were absolutely necessary to preserve freedom. Hayek remained in line with the Chicago tradition on monetary policy when he argued that "... some mechanical rule which aims at what is desirable in the long run and ties the hands of authority in its short-term decisions is likely to produce a better monetary policy than principles which give to the authorities more power and discretion" (Hayek 1960, 261). He saw "... the whole basis of our free society [as] gravely threatened by the powers arrogated by the unions ... The unions cannot achieve their principal aims unless they obtain complete control of the supply of the type of labor with which they are concerned" (Hayek 1960, 269, 273). He also opposed the modern welfare state as "... an instrument for the compulsory redistribution of income" involving "not a majority of givers who determine what should be given to the unfortunate few, but a majority of takers who decide what they will take from a wealthier minority" (Hayek 1960, 289).

It is fair to say that most of the economists at the University of Chicago's department of economics agreed with what Hayek wrote in *The Constitution of Liberty*. However, as an academic economist, Hayek always remained on a different wavelength than the majority of Chicago economists. On the question of whether his time at the University of Chicago had any influence on the economists there, he answered: "[Henry] Simons I should have had a great hope for, and his death was a catastrophe. The others ... are in effect macroeconomists and not microeconomists. Stigler least of all; Friedman very much ... Milton and I agree on almost everything except monetary policy ... They believe economic phenomena can be explained as macrophenomena, that you can ascertain causes and effects from aggregates and averages" (Hayek 1994, 144). Combine this with a statement like "I don't think statistical information has anything to contribute to ... general theory" (Hayek 1994, 148), and it becomes obvious that Hayek felt rather uneasy among the economists at the University of Chicago. Hence, "much as I enjoyed the intellectual environment that the University of Chicago offered, I never came to feel as much at home in the United States as I had done in England" (Hayek 1994, 131). In 1962, Hayek, who had fallen into a severe depression in 1960, left Chicago for the University of Freiburg in Germany.

In the late 1970s, Hayek regained respectability as an economist at Chicago's department of economics. His book *Monetary Theory and the Trade Cycle* argued that "... the incorporation of cyclical phenomena into the system of economic equilibrium theory, with which they are in apparent contradiction, remains the crucial problem of Trade Cycle Theory" (Hayek 1929, 33). For Robert Lucas (1977, 8), who also emphasized the general equilibrium approach to business cycle analysis, this was enough to characterize Hayek's method as "roughly equivalent to ours." David Laidler (1981, 12) also concluded that Hayek and Mises should be considered the true "predecessors of Lucas, Sargent and their associates."[496]

## FIGHTING THE PREBISCH DOCTRINE

In 1974, Hayek shared the Nobel Prize in economics with Gunnar Myrdal "... for their pioneering work in the theory of money and economic fluctuations and for their penetrating analysis of the interdependence of economic, social, and institutional phenomena."[497] Those who were on the left side of the political spectrum did not welcome Hayek's selection. However, the commotion following Hayek's Nobel Prize was minor compared with what erupted when it became public knowledge that the Chilean dictator Augusto Pinochet was receiving assistance from a team of economists, many of which were trained at the University of Chicago. The image of the "Chicago Boys" was born: a group of amoral, ruthless, and antidemocratic hyper-technicians, who believed the free-market economy was the only thing worth worrying about. The story of the Chicago Boys in Chile has already been told in great detail elsewhere,[498] but it must also be covered here.

The fundamental issue regarding Chile and the Chicago Boys is the debate on development economics.[499] Friedman (1958, 85) argued that a sensible development policy would consist of "strengthening of free-market economies in the less-developed nations, the removal of obstacles to private international trade, and the fostering of a climate favorable to private international investment," so as to bring out the best in the "millions of able, active, and vigorous people ... [that] ... exist in every underdeveloped country." In the early 1970s, Arnold Harberger (1972, 353) claimed, "… the amount of progress that can be generated by a dollar of foreign aid has been greatly exaggerated by the proponents of aid."

The Chicago approach to development economics stood in sharp contrast to that developed by the Economic Commission for Latin America of the United Nations (ECLA) under the auspices of its first executive secretary, the Argentinean economist Raul Prebisch. The Prebisch doctrine, which was inspired by the Harrod-Domar model, became very popular during the 1950s and 1960s. It rejected the free market as a way of escaping underdevelopment and poverty and preached trade protectionism, capital controls, infant industry protection, and central economic planning. Viner wrote:

> All that I find in Prebisch's study and in the other literature
> along similar lines emanating from the United Nations and else-
> where is the dogmatic identification of agriculture with poverty,
> and the explanation of agricultural poverty by inherent natural
> historical laws by virtue of which agricultural products tend to
> exchange on ever-deteriorating terms for manufactures, techno-
> logical progress tends to confine its blessings to manufacturing
> industry, and agricultural populations do not get the benefit of
> technological progress in manufactures even as purchasers, be-
> cause the prices of manufactured products do not fall with the
> decline in real costs. These natural laws seem to me for the most
> part mischievous fantasies, or conjectural or distorted history.
> (Viner 1952, 44)

Harry Johnson's book *Economic Policies Toward Less Developed Countries* (1967b) echoed Viner's harsh verdict.

T.W. Schultz also dismissed the view associated with Prebisch and ECLA as "having little to recommend it either as a good economic policy or as a useful theory" (Schultz 1956b, 16). What was most missing in those theories, Schultz argued, was the human capital factor. By the early 1950s, Schultz and Jacob Mincer had developed the concept of human capital. Schultz concluded that investment in people was crucial to the process of economic development. As a matter of fact, Schultz discovered the relevance of human capital when studying the Latin American experience in the late 1940s and early 1950s.

One scholar who was on the same wavelength as Schultz on development issues was Bert Hoselitz. Hoselitz was born in Vienna in 1913, and he earned a doctoral degree in law at the University of Vienna in 1936. A Jew, he fled the Nazis and came to the University of Chicago, where he earned a master's degree in economics in 1945. That same year he joined the department of economics at the University of Chicago, and he stayed there until he retired in 1978. Hoselitz focused his research mainly on economic growth in underdeveloped countries, paying special attention to associated social, political, and cultural aspects. Working as a governmental adviser in such countries as El Salvador and India, Hoselitz combined academic research with practical experience. Hoselitz constantly emphasized the importance of "institutional arrangements in the legal, educational, familial, or motivational orders" for economic growth in every stage of development (Hoselitz 1957, 29).[500]

## RIGHTING THE BALANCE

"One day in late 1953, T.W. Schultz walked into my office," Albion W. Patterson recalled almost 40 years later (Valdes 1995, 114). Patterson was one of the most remarkable pioneers in the postwar U.S. international aid programs for Latin America (Thorp 1971). Schultz convinced Patterson that what was really needed was a plan to develop Latin American higher education in "the strategic fields of economics, agricultural technology, engineering, business administration, industrial engineering, and public administration" (Valdes 1995, 114). Cold War considerations certainly played a role in the plans Patterson and Schultz devised. Given the prominence of Marxist, Prebisch, and ECLA economics in the university curriculums in Latin America, Patterson thought it imperative "to right the balance of university economics" (Valdes 1995, 116).

As the leading university in opposition to statist and interventionist development economics, the choice of the University of Chicago as the major institute for changing Latin American university economics was almost inevitable. The University of Chicago welcomed this because, among other benefits, it allowed Chicago to diversify its foreign student body and attracted government funds for financing its graduate program (Valdes 1995). The choice of Chile followed from the fact that Patterson knew Chile best of all Latin American countries, from the location of the ECLA's headquarters in the Chilean capital of Santiago, and, last but not least, from Chile's long tradition of protectionist and interventionist policies. Patterson initially contacted the Universidad de Chile, but cooperation was eventually established between the University of Chicago and the Universidad Catolica de Chile (UCC).

In June 1955, Schultz and three other members of Chicago's department of economics—Earl Hamilton, Simon Rottenberg,[501] and Arnold Harberger—went to Chile for discussions with the UCC. On March 29 and 30 of 1956, the final contracts were signed, and by September 1956, the first three young Chileans arrived in Chicago: Sergio de Castro, Carlos Massad, and Ernesto Fontaine. A hundred Chileans attended the University of Chicago from 1957 to 1970. Upon their return to Chile, they gradually adjusted the economics program at the UCC to what they had learned at the University of Chicago.[502]

In 1965, de Castro became chairman of the faculty of economics at the UCC. It was around this time that Chilean entrepreneurs began to take an interest in what was going on at the UCC. In September 1970, Salvador Allende and his Unidad Popular won the presidential election and intensified the policies of trade protectionism, socialization, and nationalization. The results were disastrous: inflation and unemployment shot up, and the deficits on the budget and the current account of the balance of payments soared (Larrain and Meller 1991). Allende's militia conducted a vicious war against its adversaries, including the economists at the UCC. "The situation was totally insane," Larry Sjaastad, the Chicago economist who was in Santiago in those days, remembers, "with, for example, the salaries being blocked for all economists thought of as anti-socialist."[503]

In secret, the Chicago-trained UCC economists wrote out a diagnosis of the social and economic disaster their country was experiencing and a plan for recovery. They summarized their detailed plan in a brief document that became known as "El Ladrillo," or "the brick." This document strongly advocated the introduction of a free-market economy, but also devoted considerable attention to educational reform, infant nutrition, hygiene programs, better provision of social services for the poor, and housing programs.

In September 1973, the military coup led by General Augusto Pinochet ended the Allende presidency. The military first tried to solve the economic crisis, but failed. In the spring of 1975 they brought in "Los Chee-Ca-Go Boys," as they were nicknamed in Chile. De Castro, a man "known for the almost magical quality of his leadership ... [and] ... without the slightest political ambition of his own" (Harberger 1993, 345), is generally recognized as the leader of the first generation of Chicago Boys. According to Sjaastad, de Castro was "the only one of the economics faculty at the Universidad Catolica who stayed there, despite all the intimidation, during the years of the Allende insanity."[504] The team de Castro finally assembled, a group that "included among many others, Juan Carlos Mendez, who implemented Chile's tax reforms of the mid-1970s; Sergio de la Cuadra, who designed the calendar of trade liberalization; Miguel Kast, who coordinated the social policies aimed at alleviating extreme poverty and who played a major role in Chile's deregulation effort; and José Pinera, who drafted the law implementing El Ladrillo's social-security program, and major labor and mining legislation as well" (Harberger 1993, 346).

Harberger also identifies Hernan Buchi (who was educated at Columbia University, not at Chicago) as the major figure among the second group of economic technicians who took center stage after the deep recession of the early 1980s. Buchi's major accomplishments were the implementation of "a clear-cut strategy of export-led growth" and the privatization of the major public utilities, in which a key element was "a sort of voucher system for public employees" (Harberger 1993, 346–47). In Harberger's words: "What [the Chicago Boys] have been doing are things wise old men at the World Bank and the International Monetary Fund have been saying for 25 years."[505] Although the worldwide economic recession of the early 1980s and the Third World debt crisis of the same period hit the Chilean economy hard, Chile gradually became a model economy, with policies that lesser-developed countries should follow to better their situations.[506]

With Sjaastad and Harberger as the driving forces from the University of Chicago, the Chile project was brought to other Latin American countries during the 1960s, financed primarily by the Ford and Rockefeller Foundations. The first to follow in the footsteps of the UCC were the National University of Cuyo in Mendoza, Argentina, and the University of del Valle in Cali, Colombia. By the late 1960s, Harberger and Sjaastad had set up a network of economists and institutions all over Latin America that was closely linked to the University of Chicago. In 1984, James Trowbridge of the Ford Foundation noted, "... through careful negotiation at the outset and diligent administration and maintenance of quality thereafter, Professor Harberger made the Foundation's investment in the University of Chicago's department of economics a highly fruitful one for the economics profession in Latin America" (Valdes 1995, 194).

## THE TRIANGLE MAN

Although T. W. Schultz pioneered the Chile project and H. Gregg Lewis was the project's coordinator, it was Friedman who was pushed into the role of *bête noir* by the international press.[507] But Harberger was the real intellectual father of the Chicago Boys. At one point, Harberger declared, "... a great piece of my life is involved with these *Latinamericanos* ... [and] ... I feel prouder about my students than of anything I have written" (Valdes 1995, 156).[508] However, his contributions to the academic literature should not be underestimated. In 1997, Warsh described Harberger as "one of the most interesting members of his generation if one of the least known, arguably on a par in terms of influence with Paul Samuelson and Milton Friedman."[509]

Arnold C. Harberger was born in 1924 in Newark, New Jersey. He went to Johns Hopkins University and then to the University of Chicago, where he received a master's degree in international relations in 1947 and a PhD in economics in 1950. During this first Chicago period, he was in close contact with the people at the Cowles Commission. In 1949, Harberger joined the faculty of Johns Hopkins University, but he returned to Chicago's department of economics in 1953 and became a full professor in 1959. Harberger twice served as chairman of the department of economics: from 1964 to 1971, and from 1975 to 1980.

In 1980, Harvard University invited Harberger to become head of its Institute for International Development, but after a month-long controversy over Harberger's Chilean connection, he turned the offer down. From 1984 forward, he combined his professorship at the University of Chicago with one at UCLA. After 1991, he was at UCLA exclusively.[510]

Harberger (1984, 1), who described himself as a "representative of the neoclassical tradition of economic science," covered a wide variety of subjects in his academic work. The common denominator in his research was what became known—even outside the University of Chicago— as the "Harberger triangles:" economic losses caused by a departure from the competitive equilibrium. In the standard graphic representation of supply and demand curves, these losses usually take the form of triangles. When Deirdre McCloskey referred to Harberger as "the inventor of modern cost benefit analysis" (McCloskey 1994, 356), it was mainly Harberger's triangles that she had in mind. An important part of Harberger's scholarly output does deal with issues related to both the theoretical aspects and the practical applications of cost-benefit analysis and welfare economics in general.[511] Also closely linked to the "triangles" is Harberger's work on taxation, as he produced seminal contributions to the economic analysis of corporate tax (1962, 1974).

In 1995, when Saul Estrin and Alan Marin (1995, 1) brought together "some of the seminal papers in microeconomics and macroeconomics," their volume contained Harberger's "Monopoly and Resource Allocation." Harberger's paper attempted to "get some quantitative notion of the allocative and welfare effects of monopoly" in order to be able to check the then-prevailing "impression that some 20 or 30 or 40 per cent of our economy is effectively monopolized" (Harberger 1954, 77). On the basis of some strong assumptions, Harberger (1954, 82) estimated that eliminating all monopolistic elements in U.S. industry would increase consumer welfare by "59 million dollars—less than one-tenth of 1 percent of the national income."

Stigler, who was still teaching at Columbia University, was a major critic of Harberger's seminal paper on the welfare cost of monopoly. Stigler criticized Harberger's analysis on two points. First, he considered the hypothesis of a price elasticity of demand of –1 as unrealistic, given the fact that monopolists will always try to operate in the zone where this elasticity is greater than one. Second, Stigler (1956) argued that in monopolistic industries, profits tend to be underreported and assets tend to be blown up, resulting in a downward-biased return on assets. However, later empirical work that took Stigler's remarks into account resulted in a maximum estimate of the welfare loss from monopoly of something like 0.5 percent of national income—substantially higher than Harberger's estimate, but still rather low (Worcester 1973). It is not clear whether this discussion between Harberger and Stigler played a major role in the cool relationship between the two during the many years they were together at the University of Chicago.[512] It is striking that in his memoir, Stigler refers to Harberger only once, as "a colleague of distinction who worked in fields in which I was not active" (Stigler 1988b, 160).

However, Harberger did cover many other subjects than just the monopoly problem and triangle-related issues. His analysis of the demand for durable goods is still a classic (Harberger 1960). He also regularly turned his attention to macroeconomic issues such as economic growth, inflation, trade policy, and the real exchange rate (Harberger 1978, 1985, and 1988). But at the end of the day, Harberger will be first remembered as the American economist who played a pivotal role in bringing Chicago economics to Latin America.

## ARGENTINA

When it came to introducing Chicago-style economics to Latin American universities, Harberger's brother-in-arms was Larry Sjaastad. Although he was also engaged in the Chilean project, from 1962 forward Sjaastad focused on Argentina.[513] Almost 40 years later, Sjaastad recalled:

> We set up a cooperation between the University of Chicago and the University of Cuyo in Mendoza. Although the whole concept was pretty much the same, Cuyo was never as successful as UCC in Chile. The main reason for this was that Cuyo was a state-run university so that we had to deal constantly with political interference. In 1972 all the professors had to sign a document in which they swore loyalty to the Peronist movement. A climax in absurdity was reached when four years later

the military seized power and immediately fired those who had signed that 1972 document. Soon all the better economists were gone."[514]

The son of Scandinavian immigrants, Sjaastad was born in North Dakota in 1934. By the mid-1950s, the McCarthy witch-hunt for communists also hit North Dakota University, where Sjaastad was studying economics. He was among those students who came to the defense of three professors who were fired: "The fight for these three men proved to be unwinnable. When one of them, Cecil Haver, left for the University of Chicago, I went along with him."[515] He earned a master's degree from Chicago in 1958 and a PhD in 1962. After two years as an assistant professor at the University of Minnesota, Sjaastad returned to the University of Chicago in 1962. Only visiting professorships—mainly at Latin American and Australian universities—interrupted his time at Chicago, and he stayed there for the rest of his career.

Although international macroeconomics was his major area of professional interest, Sjaastad also produced several papers outside this field. His doctoral dissertation was the first to apply the concept of human capital to the phenomenon of migration. Sjaastad (1962) tried to measure costs and benefits related to migration to arrive at a rate of return on the investment people make when they decide to migrate.

Sjaastad also examined the cost of protectionism. His basic conclusion was that protectionist measures translate inevitably into a creeping tax on export industries, because protection against imports results in increases in "the market price of both actual imports and domestically-produced import substitutes," with wage rates acting as "the shifting agent" (Sjaastad and Clements 1984, 49).

Over the years, Sjaastad's attention turned increasingly in the direction of monetary macroeconomics; this tendency was reinforced by his involvement with Latin American projects, as most of these countries suffered from chronic inflation in those days. In the late 1970s, he was one of the very first to point out that serious trouble was in the air for the developing countries with respect to their capacity to honor their foreign debt (Sjaastad 1979). Although he was also one of the first to ask whether it was time for the World Bank to be fundamentally reformed (Sjaastad

1991), his research during the 1990s focused on the topic of purchasing power parity and the real exchange rate, with much emphasis in each case on the empirical verification of the theories offered.[516] In the end, however, Sjaastad closely echoed his good friend and long-time colleague Harberger: "If I somehow have made an important contribution to economics, it is most probably through the many South American students I worked with so closely."[517]

# Epilogue

KENNETH ELZINGA WROTE, "THE TRULY INFLUENTIAL ECONO-
mist is one who affects how economists view fundamental problems
in their own discipline and affects how non-specialists come to view
the world of economic reality" (Elzinga, 1984, 572). Judged by Elzinga's
standard, a defensible case can be made that Chicago economists have
been among the most influential ones in their profession over the last
century. Evidence can be found in the disproportionately large share of
Nobel Prize winners but also in the seminal contributions of such towering Chicago economists as Thorstein Veblen, John Maurice Clark,
Frank Knight, Jacob Viner, Theodore Schultz, Milton Friedman, George
Stigler, Ronald Coase, Merton Miller, Robert Fogel, Richard Posner,
Gary Becker, Robert Lucas, Kevin Murphy, and Steven Levitt. The degree to which some of these names have become well-known far outside
the field of professional economics is evidence of how Chicago economists have been able to influence the views of non-economists.

The same conclusion holds if we use the Elzinga standard to judge
the impact of economists on social and economic policies pursued by
national governments and international institutions. Over the decades,
Chicago economists have shown great consistency in defending the free-
market approach. Certainly during the 1950s and 1960s, the interventionist Keynesian vision strongly dominated social and economic policymaking. Chicago economists played a dominant role in the research
work that led to the demise of the Keynesian dogma.

The intellectual roots of the Reagan and Thatcher revolutions of the 1980s can be found at the University of Chicago. Over the past quarter-century, one by one many developing countries have adopted free-market oriented economic policies, and the same holds true for them. China, India and the countries of the former Soviet Union are the highest-profile examples, but many other smaller countries followed the same route. Although some contest it, globalization, which is nothing more than the application of free-market policies across borders, cultures, and continents, has triumphed worldwide on a heretofore unseen scale. Hence, it can be argued that globalization's success is a triumph of the work done over more than a century by Chicago economists.

In the first chapter of this book, the Chicago Tradition was defined; it goes a long way in explaining the remarkable successes of Chicago economics. This Chicago Tradition consists of six elements: a fanatical work ethic, a strong emphasis on academic excellence, unlimited freedom to criticize on a scientific basis, the recognition of neoclassical price theory as a true science, the need to constantly back up theoretical work with empirical evidence, and the two-dimensional geographical isolation of the University of Chicago. Apart from the last one, several of these characteristics of the Chicago Tradition could be found at other universities. What makes economic scholarship at the University of Chicago unique is that all these characteristics have been consistently respected for decades by a majority of economists working in Chicago's department of economics, the GSB, and the law school.

Adherence to the Chicago Tradition is no coincidence. First, the rule that most Chicago economists want to see applied for economic life in general—competition leads to the best results—is constantly applied at the university. Survival of the fittest is a core truth at Chicago. Inevitably, the highly competitive process of selecting and tenuring leads to the selection of strong personalities. A tradition defended by strong personalities has a higher survival probability—not least because the quality of those personalities also tends to lead to the selection of promising research programs.

Second, Chicago's famous system of workshops led to a "distinctive style of inquiry ... [that] ... came to dominate Chicago graduate training and research in all fields of economics" (Nerlove, 1999, 732). In the University of Chicago's economics workshop system, there is no place for prestige, rank, past honor, or personal sensitivities. Intellectual discipline and rigor are always required at workshop sessions, and this rigor strongly underpins the Chicago Tradition.

Did adherence to the Chicago Tradition make economics at University of Chicago more monolithic, or even narrow-minded? There is no simple "yes" or "no" answer for this question. It cannot be denied that during the second part of the 20th century, the economic research coming out of the University of Chicago was somewhat more monolithic. The strong influence of powerful intellectuals such as Milton Friedman and George Stigler probably played a significant role in this. However, dissenters have always a part of the University of Chicago.

Among the first appointments at the department of economics was Thorstein Veblen, a man who categorically rejected neoclassical economics and capitalism. Frank Knight was a pathological dissenter from any accepted truth. Oskar Lange and many economists at the Cowles Commission were ideologically opposed to the department of economics' mainstream views during the 1940s and 1950s. While Milton Friedman led an attack on Keynesian economics, the department recruited Lloyd Metzler, a leading Keynesian. Researchers at the GSB's Center for Decision Research (including Hillel Einhorn, Robin Hogarth, and Richard Thaler) seriously question the concept of the homo economics that is so central to almost everything economics at the University of Chicago stands for. Chicago's law school, the birthplace of law and economics, is the home of Cass Sunstein, one of the most articulate critics of this research program.

The role of the dissenters has been crucial. Leading economists working at the University of Chicago have always shown an almost unshakable belief in the correctness of their approach. However, they have realized that in order to keep the Chicago Tradition alive and strong, it must be challenged—not only by economists in faraway institutions, but also by scholars in the same building and by economists visiting the same workshops. Moreover, the possibility was always present that one day, a new paradigm might surface. If the objective is to be the birthplace of brilliant new ideas, then good dissenters are necessary.

Will the successful 20th century be followed by an equally successful 21st century at Chicago's department of economics? The answer to this question depends on whether or not the Chicago Tradition will survive. Obviously, the Tradition's element of isolation no longer holds. Internet, e-mail, and the relative convenience of international travel have connected scholars worldwide.

But other characteristics remain in question. First, price theory and partial equilibrium analysis are strongly challenged by general equilibrium analysis at Chicago's department of economics, and the pressure to back up theory with empirical evidence has diminished. It is not an exaggeration to say that today, the old Chicago Tradition is more alive at the GSB than at the department of economics.

Chicago's scholars have always been engaged in developments that were described elsewhere as "crazy," "on the lunatic fringe," "a dead-end street," and/or "useless." Eventually, some of these "stupidities" became mainstream economics, and some were even considered worthy of the Nobel Prize.

Adherence to the Chicago Tradition has played a crucial role in managing this process and making sure that at the end of the day, intellectual rigor and discipline always triumph. Many people, including some at the University of Chicago, are inclined to argue that history won't repeat itself, and that the University is losing its unique and leading position in the field of economics because the Tradition is weakening.

Consider this book as a warning against this kind of pessimism. The successful story of economics at the University of Chicago is that of a cat with far more than nine lives.

# Bibliography

Abu-Lughod, J.L. 1999. *New York, Chicago, Los Angeles: America's global cities.* Minneapolis: University of Minnesota Press.

Alchian, A. 1965. Some economics of property rights. In *Economic forces at work.* New York: Liberty Press, 1977.

Alchian, A., and H. Demsetz. 1972. Production, information costs, and economic organization. *American Economic Review.* December.

Alchian, A., and R. Kessel. 1960. The meaning and validity of the inflation-induced lag of wages. *American Economic Review.* March.

Alexander, S. 1959. The effects of devaluation: A simplified synthesis of elasticities and absorption approaches. *American Economic Review.* March.

Aliber, R.Z. 1973. *The International Money Game.* 4th ed. New York: Basic Books.

———. 1982. *Your money and your life.* New York: Basic Books.

———. 1990. The US trade deficit and US fiscal deficit: Cause and effect. In *International finance and financial policy,* ed. H. Stoll, 83-99. New York: Quorum Books.

———. 1993. *The Multinational Paradigm.* Cambridge, MA: MIT Press.

Aliber, R.Z., J. Duesenberry, and T. Mayer. 1981. *Money, banking, and the economy.* New York: W.W. Norton.

Allen, J. 1995. At the University of Chicago, risk taking is part of the program. *American Banker.* September 19.

Ando, A., and F. Modigliani. 1965. The relative stability of the monetary velocity and the investment multiplier. *American Economic Review.* September.

Angell, J. 1933. Monetary control and general business stabilization. In *Economic Essays in Honour of Gustav Cassel.* London: Allen and Unwin.

Angeloni, I., A. Kashyap, and B. Mojon, eds. 2003. *Monetary policy transmission in the Euro-area.* Cambridge: Cambridge University Press.

Antle, J.M., and D.A. Sumner. eds. 1996. *Papers in honor of D. Gale Johnson.* Vol. 2 of The Economics of Agriculture. Chicago: University of Chicago Press.

Arbeiter, L. 1985. Rationality under fire. GSB Chicago, mimeo, Autumn.

Arrow, K. 1962. The economic implications of learning by doing. *Review of Economic Studies.* June.

———. 1963. Uncertainty and the welfare economics of medical care. *American Economic Review.* December.

———. 1973. Higher education as filter. *Journal of Public Economics.* Vol. 2: July. 193-216.

————. 1979. Marshak, Jacob. In *International Encyclopedia of the Social Sciences*, ed. D.K. Sills. Vol. 18. New York: The Free Press.

Ashenfelter, O. 1994. H. Gregg Lewis memorial comments. *Journal of Labor Economics.* 12 (1): 138.

Aslanbeigui, N., and S. Medema. 1998. Beyond dark clouds: Pigou and Coase on social cost. *History of Political Economy.* Winter.

Aspromourgos, T. 1986. On the origins of the term "neoclassical." *Cambridge Journal of Economics.* 12(1):265-70.

Ault, R., and R. Ekelund. 1988. Habits in economic analysis: Veblen and the neoclassics. *History of Political Economy.* Fall.

Averch, H., and L. Johnson. 1962. The behavior of the firm under regulatory constraint. *American Economic Review.* December.

Bailey, M. 1957. Saving and the rate of interest. *Journal of Political Economy.* August.

Baird, D. 1992. *Elements of Bankruptcy.* New York: Foundation Press.

Baird, D.G., R.H. Gertner, and R.C. Picker. 1998. *Game theory and the law.* Cambridge, MA: Harvard University Press.

Barber, W.J. 1988. Political economy in an atmosphere of academic entrepreneurship: The University of Chicago. In *Breaking the academic mould: Economics and American learning in the nineteenth century,* ed. W. Barber. Middletown, CT: Wesleyan University Press.

Barberis, N., and M. Huang. 2001. Mental accounting, loss aversion, and individual stock returns. *Journal of Finance.* Vol. LVI, No. 4, August 2001: 1247.

Barberis, N., and R. Thaler. 2003. A survey of behavioral finance. In *Handbook of the Economics of Finance,* eds. G. Constantinidis, M. Harris, and R. Stulz, 1051-1121. Amsterdam: North-Holland.

Barro, R., 1996. *Getting it right: markets and choices in a free society.* Cambridge, MA: MIT Press.

Barro, R., and X. Sala-I-Martin. 1995. *Economic growth,* New York: McGraw Hill.

Bateman, W. Clearing the ground: The demise of the social gospel movement and the rise of neo-classicism in American Economics. In Morgan and Rutherford 1998, 29-52.

Baumol, W.J. 1972. Jacob Viner at Princeton. *Journal of Political Economy.* January.

————. 2000. What Marshall *didn't* know: On the twentieth century's contributions to economics. *Quarterly Journal of Economics.* February.

Baumol, W., and G.S. Becker. 1952, The classical monetary theory: The outcome of A discussion, *Economica,* November.

Baumol, W., J. Panzar, and R. Willig. 1982. *Contestable markets and the theory of industry structure.* New York: Harcourt Brace Jovanovich.

Beaud, M., and G. Dostaler. 1995. *Economic thought since Keynes: A history and dictionary of major economists.* Cheltenham, UK, Edward Elgar Publishing.

Becker, G.S. 1957. *The economics of discrimination.* Chicago: Chicago University Press.

————. 1965. A theory of the allocation of time. *Economic Journal,* September.

————. 1968. Crime and punishment: An economic approach. *Journal of Political Economy.* March/April.

————. 1971. *Economic Theory.* New York: Alfred A. Knopf.

————. 1976. *The economic approach to human behavior.* Chicago: The University of Chicago Press.

————. 1981. *A treatise on the family.* Cambridge, MA: Harvard University Press.

————. 1983. A theory of competition among pressure groups for political influence. *Quarterly Journal of Economics.* August.

————. 1988. Public policies, pressure groups, and dead weight costs. In Stigler 1988a.

————. 1991. Milton Friedman. In Shils 1991, 138–146.

————. 1993a. *Human capital: A theoretical and empirical analysis with special reference to education.* 3rd ed. Chicago: The University of Chicago Press.

————. 1993b. Nobel Lecture: The economic way of looking at behavior. *Journal of Political Economy.* June.

————. 1993c, George Joseph Stigler: January, 17, 1911 - December, 1, 1991 *Journal of Political Economy.* October.

————. 1995. Foreword to *The new economics of human behavior,* ed. by M. Tommasi and K. Ierulli. Cambridge: Cambridge University Press.

————. 1996. *Accounting for tastes.* Cambridge, MA: Harvard University Press.

Becker G., and G.N. Becker. 1997. *The economics of life: From baseball to affirmative action to immigration, how real-world issues affect our everyday life.* New York: McGraw-Hill.

Becker, G.S., E.L. Glaeser, and K.M. Murphy. 1999. Population and economic growth. *AEA Papers and Proceedings.* May.

Becker, G., and W. Landes, eds. 1974, *Essays in the economics of crime and punishment.* New York: Columbia University Press.

Becker, G.S., and H.G. Lewis. 1976. On the interaction between the quantity and quality of children. In Becker 1976, S279-88.

Becker, G.S., and C.B. Mulligan. 1997. The endogenous determination of time preference. *Quarterly Journal of Economics.* August.

————. 1998. Deadweight costs and the size of government. Working Paper No. 144. Chicago, IL: George J. Stigler Center for the Study of the Economy and the State.

Becker, G.S., and K.M. Murphy 1999. *Social economics: market behavior in a social environment.* Cambridge, MA: Harvard University Press.

Becker, G.S., K.M. Murphy, and R. Tamura. 1990. Human capital, fertility and economic growth. *Journal of Political Economy.* v. 98, no. 5, Part 2 (October 1990): S12-S37.

Becker, G.S, T. Philipson, and R. Soares. 2005. The quantity and quality of life and the evolution of world inequality. *American Economic Review.* March.

Becker, G.S., and G. Stigler. 1977. De gustibus non est disputandum. *American Economic Review.* December.

Beckman, M.J. 1991. Tjalling C. Koopmans. In Shils 1991.

Benartzi, S., and R. Thaler, R. 1995. Myopic risk aversion and the equity premium puzzle. *Quarterly Journal of Economics.* February.

Ben-Porath, Y. 1982. Economics and the family—match or mismatch? A review of Becker's *Treatise on the Family. Journal of Economic Literature.* 20(1), pp. 52-64.

Bernanke, B. 2000. *Essays on the Great Depression,* Princeton, NJ: Princeton University Press.

Bentley, A. 1908. *The process of government.* Chicago: University of Chicago Press.

Bernstein, L. 1992. *Capital ideas.* New York: The Free Press.

————. 1996. *Against the gods: The remarkable story of risk.* New York: John Wiley & Sons.

Bhagwati, J. 1982. Remembering Harry G. Johnson. *Journal of International Economics.* supplement. January.

Biddle, J.E. 1996. H. Gregg Lewis. In Samuels, W., ed. *American Economists of the Late Twentieth Century.* Cheltenham, UK, Edward Elgar Publishing.

Bickerdike, C.F. 1920. The instability of foreign exchange. *Economic Journal.* March.

Black, F. 1982. The trouble with econometric models. *Financial Analysts Journal.* March/April.

————. 1986. Noise. *Journal of Finance.* July.

————. 1987. *Business cycles and equilibrium.* New York: Blackwell.

————. 1988. On Robert C. Merton. *MIT Management.* Fall.

————. 1989. How we came up with the option formula. *Journal of Portfolio Management.* Winter.

————. 1995a. *Exploring general equilibrium.* Cambridge, MA: MIT Press.

————. 1995b. Interest rates as options. *Journal of Finance.* December.

Black, F., M. Jensen, and M. Scholes. 1972. The capital asset pricing model: Some empirical tests. In *Studies in the theory of capital markets,* ed. M. Jensen, New York: Praeger.

Black, F., M.H. Miller, and R.A. Posner. 1978. An approach to the regulation of bank holding companies. *Journal of Business*. July.

Black, F., and M.S. Scholes. 1973. The pricing of options and corporate liabilities. *Journal of Political Economy*. May.

Blaug, M. 1985. *Great economists since Keynes*. London: Wheatsheaf Books Ltd.

———. W. Eltis, D. O'Brien, R. Skidelsky, and D. Patinkin. 1995. *The quantity theory of money. From Locke to Keynes and Friedman*. Cheltenham, U.K.: Edward Elgar Publishing.

———. 1997. *Economic theory in retrospect*. 5th ed. Cambridge: Cambridge University Press.

——— 2001. No history of ideas, please, we're economists. *Journal of Economic Perspectives*. Winter.

Blinder, A. 1997. The rise and fall of Keynesian Economics. In Snowdon and Vane.

Bloomfield, A.I. 1992. On the centenary of Jacob Viner's birth: A retrospective view of the man and his work. *Journal of Economic Literature*. December.

Blum, W. 1976. The uneasy case for progressive taxation in 1976. Occasional papers, no. 11, University of Chicago, Law School.

Blum, W., and H. Kalven. 1953. *The uneasy case for progressive taxation*. Chicago: University of Chicago Press.

Blundell, R. 2001. James Heckman's contributions to economics and econometrics. *Scandinavian Journal of Economics*. 103 (2).

Bordo, M. 1989. The contribution of "A Monetary History of the United States, 1867-1960" to monetary history. In *Money, history and international finance: Essays in honor of Anna J. Schwartz*, ed. M. Bordo. Chicago: University of Chicago Press.

Bork, R. 1954. Vertical integration and the Sherman Act: The legal history of an economic misconception. *University of Chicago Law Review*. Autumn.

———. 1978. *The antitrust paradox*. New York: Basic Books, 1993.

———. 1979. The legacy of Alexander M. Bickel. *Yale Law Report*. Fall.

———. 1989. *The tempting of America: The political seduction of the law*. New York: Free Press.

———. 1996. *Slouching towards Gomorrah: Modern liberalism and American decline*. New York: Regan Books.

Bornemann, A. 1940. *J. Laurence Laughlin*. Washington, DC: American Council on Foreign Affairs.

Bosworth, B., R. Dornbush, and R. Laban, eds. 1994. *The Chilean economy: policy lessons and challenges*. Washington, DC: Brookings Institution.

Boulding, K.E. 1958. *The skills of an economist*. Cleveland, OH: Howard Allen.

———. 1992. From chemistry to economics and beyond. In Szenberg 1992.

Bourneuf, A., E. Domar, and P. Samuelson, eds., 1973. *Collected papers: Lloyd A. Metzler*. Cambridge, MA: Harvard University Press.

Bowman, M.J. 1980. On Theodore W. Schultz's contributions to economics. *Scandinavian Journal of Economics*, 82.

Bowman, W. 1952. Resale price maintenance—A monopoly problem. *The Journal of Business*. July.

Boycko, M., A. Schleifer, and R. Vishny. 1995. *Privatizing Russia*. Cambridge, MA: MIT Press.

Brady, D., and R. Director-Friedman. 1947. *Savings and the income distribution*. Studies in Income and Wealth, No. 10. New York: National Bureau of Economic Research.

Breit, W., and B. Hirsch. 2004. *Lives of the laureates*. Cambridge, Mass., MIT Press.

Breit, W., and R.L. Ransom. 1998. *The academic scribblers*. Princeton, NJ: Princeton University Press.

Bronfenbrenner, M. 1962. Observations on the "Chicago Schools." *Journal of Political Economy*. February.

Brooks, K., and D.G. Johnson. 1983. *Prospects for Soviet agriculture in the 1980s*. Bloomington: Indiana University Press.

Brown, E., Douglas, P., Harbison, F., et al. 1949. Harry Alvin Millis, 1873-1948. *American Economic Review*. Vol. 39, No. 3 (Jun., 1949), pp. 742-750.

Brozen, Y. 1957. The economics of automation. *American Economic Review*. May.

———. 1962. Minimum wage rates and household workers. *Journal of Law and Economics* October.

———. 1982. *Mergers in perspective*. Washington, DC: American Enterprise Institute.

Brozen, Y., and G. Bittlinger. 1982. *Concentration, mergers, and public policy*. New York: Macmillan.

Brunner, K. 1968. The role of money and monetary policy. *Federal Reserve Bank of St. Louis Review*. 50 (7): 9-24.

———. ed. 1981. *The Great Depression revisited*. Boston: Martinus Nijhoff Publishing.

———. 1992. My quest for economic knowledge. In Szenberg 1992.

———. 1992. Ronald Coase—old-fashioned scholar. *Scandinavian Journal of Economics*. No. 1.

Buchanan, J.M. 1991. Frank H. Knight. In Shils 1991.

Buchanan, J., and G. Tullock. 1962. *The calculus of consent*. Ann Arbor: University of Michigan Press.

Bulmer, M. 1984. *The Chicago School of Sociology*. Chicago: University of Chicago Press.

Cagan, P. 1965. *Determinants of effects of changes in the money stock 1875-1960*, New York: National Bureau of Economic Research.

Cairncross, A. 1953. Home and foreign investment 1870-1913. Cambridge: Cambridge University Press.

Calabresi, G. 1961. Some thoughts on risk distribution and the law of torts. *Yale Law Review*. No. 70.

Caldwell, B. 1998. Why didn't Hayek review Keynes' General Theory? *History of Political Economy*. Winter.

Carlton, D.W. 1984a, Futures markets: Their purpose, their history, their growth, their successes and failures. *Journal of Futures Markets*. Fall.

———. 1984b. *Market behavior under uncertainty*. New York: Garland.

———. 1986. The rigidity of prices. *American Economic Review*. September.

———. 1989. The theory and facts of how markets clear: Is industrial organization valuable for understanding macroeconomics? In *Handbook of Industrial Organization*, eds. R. Schmalensee and R. Willig, Amsterdam: North-Holland.

———. 1991. The theory of allocation and its implications for marketing and industrial structure: Why rationing is efficient. *Journal of Law and Economics*. October.

———. 1995. Economic organization and conflict. *Journal of Institutional and Theoretical Economics*. March.

———. 1997. A critical assessment of the role of imperfect competition in macroeconomics. In *Market behaviour and macroeconomic modelling*, eds. S. Brakman, H. Van Ees, S. Kuipers, New York: Macmillan.

Carlton, D.W., and D.R. Fishel. 1983. The regulation of insider trading. *Stanford Law Review*. May.

Carlton, D.W. and J.M. Perloff. 2004. *Modern industrial organization*, 4th ed. Glenview, IL: Addison Wesley.

Cechetti, S., A. Kashyap, and D. Wilcox. 1997. Interactions between the seasonal and the business cycles in production and inventories. *American Economic Review*. December.

Chamberlin, E.H. 1957. *Towards a more general theory of value*. New York: Oxford University Press.

Chao, H.-K. 2003. Milton Friedman and the emergence of the permanent income hypothesis. *History of Political Economy.* Spring.

Chari, V.V. 1998. Nobel Laureate Robert E. Lucas Jr.: Architect of modern macroeconomics. *Journal of Economic Perspectives.* Winter.

Chernow, R. 1998. *Titan: The Life of John D. Rockefeller, Sr.* New York: Random House.

Christ, C. 1994. The Cowles Commission's contributions to econometrics at Chicago. *Journal of Economic Literature.* March.

Ciccone, F.R. 1999. *Chicago and the American century.* Chicago: Contemporary Books.

Clark, J. ed. 1996. *James S. Coleman.* London, Falmer Press.

Clark, J.M. 1917. Business acceleration and the law of demand: A technical factor in economic cycles. *Journal of Political Economy.* March.

———. 1918. Economics and modern psychology. *Journal of Political Economy.* January/February.

———. 1919. Economic theory in an era of social readjustment. *AEA Papers and Proceedings.* March.

———. 1923. *Studies in the economics of overhead costs.* Chicago, University of Chicago Press.

———. 1926. *Social control of business.* Chicago: University of Chicago Press.

———. 1929. Thorstein Bundy Veblen. *American Economic Review.* December.

Coase, R.H. 1937. The nature of the firm. In *Essential readings in economics,* ed. S. Estrin and A. Marin. London: Macmillan, 1995.

———. 1959. The Federal Communications Commission. *Journal of Law and Economics.* October.

———. 1960. The problem of social cost. *Journal of Law and Economics.* October.

———. 1984. The new institutional economics. *Journal of Institutional and Theoretical Economics.* March.

———. 1991. The institutional structure of production. In *Essays on economics and economists.* Chicago: University of Chicago.

———. 1993a. Coase on Posner on Coase. *Journal of Institutional and Theoretical Economics.* March.

———. 1993b. Law and economics at Chicago. *Journal of Law & Economics.* April.

———. 1994. *Essays on economics and economists.* Chicago: University of Chicago Press.

———. 1997. The institutional structure of production. In Persson 1997.

Coats, A.W. 1963. The origins of the Chicago School. *Journal of Political Economy.* October.

———. 1985. The American Economic Association and the economics profession. *Journal of Economic Literature.* December.

Cobb, C.W., and P.H. Douglas. 1928. A theory of production. *American Economic Review.* March.

Cohen, A. 1998. Frank Knight's position on capital and interest. In Rutherford 1998.

Colander, D. 1991. *Why aren't economists as important as garbagemen? Essays on the state of economics.* Armonk, NY: M.E. Sharpe.

Coleman, J.S. 1961. *The adolescent society: The social life of the teenager and its impact on education.* Glencoe, IL: The Free Press.

———. 1985. *Schools, Families and Children. The 1985 Ryerson Lecture.* Chicago: The University of Chicago Press.

———. 1990. *Foundations of social theory.* Cambridge, MA: Harvard University Press.

Coleman, J. S. e.a. 1966. *Equality of educational opportunity.* Washington DC: U.S. Government Printing Office.

Coleman, J.S., T. Hoffer, and S. Kilgore. 1982. *High school achievement: Public, catholic, and private schools compared.* New York: Basic Books.

Coleman, J.S., S. Kelly, and J. Moore. 1975. *Trends in school segregation, 1968-73.* Washington DC: The Urban Institute.

Cootner, P.H., ed. 1964. *The random character of stock prices.* Cambridge, MA: MIT Press.

Corden, W.M. 1965. *Recent developments in the theory of international trade.* Special papers in the theory of international trade, No. 7. Princeton, NJ: Princeton University.

Corden, W.M. 1984. Harry Johnson's contributions to international trade theory. *Journal of Political Economy.* August.

Cowles, A. 1944. Stock market forecasting. *Econometrica.* July.

Cyert, R., and J. March, 1963. *A behavioral theory of the firm.* Englewood Cliffs, NJ: Prentice-Hall.

Dam, K.W. 1964. Trademarks, price discrimination and the Bureau of Customs. *Journal of Law and Economics.* October.

———. 1965. Oil and gas licensing and the North Sea. *Journal of Law and Economics.* October.

———. 1970b. The pricing of North Sea Gas in Britain. *Journal of Law and Economics.* April.

———. 1974. The evolution of North Sea licensing policy in Britain and Norway. *Journal of Law and Economics.* October.

———. 1976. *Oil resources: Who gets what how?* Chicago: University of Chicago Press.

———. 1994. The economic underpinnings of patent law. *The Journal of Legal Studies.* January.

———. 1995. Some economic considerations in the intellectual property protection of software. *The Journal of Legal Studies.* June.

———. 2001. *The rules of the game: A new look at US international policy making.* Chicago: University of Chicago Press.

Davenport, H. 1897. The real cost of tariff. *Journal of Political Economy.* September.

———. 1914. *Economics of enterprise.* New York: Macmillan, 1932.

Davidson, S., and R. Weil. 1983. *Handbook of modern accounting.* New York: McGraw-Hill.

Davidson, S., M. Maher, C. Stickney, and R. Weil. 1991. *Managerial accounting.* Chicago: Harcourt Brace Jovanovich.

Davis, H. ,and Hogarth, R. 1992. *Rethinking management education: A view from Chicago.* GSB, selected paper no. 72.

Davis, J.R. 1971. *The new economics and the old economists.* Ames: Iowa State University Press.

De Bondt, W., and R. Thaler. 1985. Does the stock market overreact? *Journal of Finance.* No. 40.

———. 1987. Further evidence on investor overreaction and stock market seasonality. *Journal of Finance.* No. 42.

De Long, J.B. 2000. The triumph of monetarism? *Journal of Economic Perspectives.* Winter.

Del Solar, B. 1992. The cradle of the Chicago Boys. *Que Pasa* (translation as available in the files of the Communications Department of the University of Chicago).

Demsetz, H. 1964. The exchange and enforcement of property rights. *Journal of Law and Economics.* October.

———. 1967. Towards a theory of property rights. *American Economic Review.* May.

———. 1968. Why regulate utilities? *Journal of Law and Economics.* April.

———. 1969, Information and Efficiency: Another Viewpoint. *Journal of Law and Economics.* April.

———. 1982. *Economic, legal and political dimensions of competition.* Amsterdam: North Holland.

———. 1993. George J. Stigler: Mid-century neoclassicalist with a passion to quantify. *Journal of Political Economy.* October.

Dimand, M.A., R.W. Dimand, and E.L. Forget, eds. 1996. Women of value: Feminist Essays on the History of Women in Economics. Aldershot, UK: Edward Elgar Publishing.

Director, A. 1930. Making use of public works. *Survey.* August 15.

———. 1932. *Unemployment.* Chicago: American Library Association.

———. 1933. The economics of technocracy. *Public Policy Pamphlets.* No. 2. Chicago: University of Chicago Press.

———. 1948. Preface to *Economic policy for a free society,* by Henry Simons. Chicago: University of Chicago Press.

———. 1964. The parity of the economic market place. *Journal of Law and Economics.* October.

Director, A., and Levi, E. 1956. Law and the future: Trade legislation. *Northwestern Law Review.* No.10.

Director, A., and P.H. Douglas. 1934. *The problem of unemployment.* New York: Macmillan.

Domar, E.D. 1992. How I tried to become an economist. In Szenberg 1992.

Donohue, J.J., and S.D. Levitt. 2001a. The impact of legalized abortion on crime. *Quarterly Journal of Economics.* May.

———. 2001b. The impact of race on policing and arrests. *Journal of Law and Economics.* October.

Dorfman, J. 1934. *Thorstein Veblen and his America.* New York: Viking Press.

———. 1959. *The Economic Mind in American Civilization.* New York: Viking Press.

Dornbush, R., 1976. Expectations and exchange rate dynamics. *Journal of Political Economy.* December.

Dornbush, R. 1996. Nobel savages. *The Economist.* March 30.

Dornbush, R, and S. Fisher. 1994. *Macroeconomics.* New York: McGraw Hill,

Dornbush, R., and J. Frenkel, J. 1973. Inflation and growth: Alternative approaches. *Journal of Money, Banking and Credit.* February.

Douglas, P.H. 1927. The modern technique of mass production and its relation to wages. *Proceedings of the Academy of Political Science.* July.

———. 1930. *Real wages in the United States, 1890-1926.* Boston: Houghton Mifflin.

———. 1934. *The theory of wages.* New York: Macmillan Company.

———. 1935. *Controlling depressions.* New York: Norton.

———. 1939. Henry Schultz as a colleague. *Econometrics.* April.

———. 1947. Antidote for communism. *University of Chicago Magazine.* December.

———. 1948. Are there laws of production? *American Economic Review.* March.

———. 1952a. *Economy in the national government.* Chicago: University of Chicago Press.

———. 1952b. *Ethics in government.* Chicago: University of Chicago Press.

———. 1972. *In the fullness of time.* New York: Harcourt, Brace, Jovanovich.

———. 1976. The Cobb-Douglas production function once again: Its history, its testing, and some empirical values. *Journal of Political Economy.* October.

Douglas, P., and A. Hanson. 1930. The wages of domestic labor in Chicago, 1890-1926. *Journal of American Statistical Association.* March.

Douglas, P., and E. Schoenberg. 1937. Studies in the supply of labor: The relation in 1929 between average earnings in American cities and the proportions seeking employment. *Journal of Political Economy.* February.

Downs, A. 1957. *An economic theory of democracy.* New York: Harper.

Dreiser, H. 1971. *The University of Chicago/Graduate School of Business: A Brief History.* Chicago: Graduate School of Business.

Duggan, M. 2001. More guns, more crime. *Journal of Political Economy.* October.

Dunsing, M., and M. Reid. 1958. Effect of varying degrees of transitory income on income elasticity of expenditures. *Journal of American Statistical Association.* June.

Durand, D. 1957. Growth stocks and the Petersburg paradox. *Journal of Finance.* September.

———. 1959. The cost of capital, corporation finance, and the theory of investment. *American Economic Review.* September.

Dybek, S. 1993. Introduction. In *Chicago stories: Tales of the city,* ed. J. Miller. San Francisco: Chronicle Books.

Dzuback, M.A. 1991. *Robert M. Hutchins: Portrait of an Educator.* Chicago: University of Chicago Press.

Easterbrook, F. 1984. *The Limits of Antitrust.* Working paper 20. University of Chicago Law School, Program in Law & Economics.

———. 1986. Workable antitrust policy. *Michigan Law Review.* August.

Easterbrook, F., and D. Fischel. 1981. The proper role of target's management in responding to a tender offer. *Harvard Law Review.* April.

———. 1982. Antitrust suits by targets of tender offers. *Michigan Law Review.* 80.

———. 1991. *The economic structure of corporate law.* Cambridge, MA: Harvard University Press.

Ebenstein, A. 2001. *Friedrich Hayek: A biography.* New York: Palgrave.

Edgell, S., and R. Tilman. 1991. John Rae and Thorstein Veblen on conspicuous consumption: A Neglected intellectual relationship. *History of Political Economy.* Winter.

Ehrlich, I. 1973. Participation in illegitimate activities: A theoretical and empirical investigation. *Journal of Political Economy.* May.

Einhorn, H.J., and R.M. Hogarth. 1987. Decision making: Going forward in reverse. *Harvard Business Review.* Jan./Feb.

Elzinga, K. 1984. Elzinga on Coase. In *Contemporary economists in perspective: Part B,* eds. H.W. Spiegel and W.J. Samuels. Greenwich, CT: JAI Press.

Emmett, R. 1998. Entrenching disciplinary competence: The role of general education and graduate study in Chicago economics. In Morgan and Rutherford 1998.

———. ed. 2002. *The Chicago tradition in economics 1892-1945.* 8 vols. New York: Routledge.

Epstein, R.A. 1973. A theory of strict liability. *Journal of Legal Studies.* 2, 151.

———. 1982. Taxation, regulation, and confiscation. *Osgoode Hall Law Journal.* September.

———. 1985. *Takings: Private property and the power of eminent domain.* Cambridge, MA: Harvard University Press.

———. 1988. The political economy of product liability reform. *AEA Papers and Proceedings* May.

———. 1990. The paradox of civil rights. *Yale Law & Policy Review.* 8 (2): 299.

———. 1992. *Forbidden grounds: The case against employment discrimination laws.* Cambridge, MA: Harvard University Press.

———. 1993. Holdouts, externalities, and the single owner: One more salute to Ronald Coase. *Journal of Law and Economics.* April.

———. 1994. The moral and practical dilemmas of an underground economy. *Yale Law & Policy Review.* June.

———. 1995. *Simple rules for a complex world.* Cambridge, MA: Harvard University Press.

———. 1997. *Mortal peril: Our inalienable right to health care?* New York: Addison-Wesley.

Estrin, S., and A. Marin, eds. 1995. *Essential readings in economics.* London: Macmillan.

Fama, E.F. 1963. Mandelbrot and the stable Paretian hypothesis. *Journal of Business.* October.

———. 1965a. The behavior of stock market prices. *Journal of Business.* January.

———. 1965b. Tomorrow on the New York Stock Exchange. *Journal of Business.* July.

———. 1965c. Random walks in stock market prices. *Financial Analysts Journal.* Sept.-Oct.

———. 1970. Efficient capital markets: A review of theory and empirical work. *Journal of Finance.* May.

———. 1976. *Foundations of finance.* New York: Basic Books.

———. 1980. Agency problems and the theory of the firm. *Journal of Political Economy.* April.

———. 1991. Efficient capital markets: II. *Journal of Finance.* December.

Fama, E.F., and French, K.R. 1992. The cross section of expected stock returns. *Journal of Finance.* June.

———. 1996. Multifactor explanations of asset pricing anomalies. *Journal of Finance.* March.

———. 1988. Dividend yields and expected stock returns. *Journal of Financial Economics.* October.

————. 1993. Common risk factors in the returns on bonds and stocks. *Journal of Financial Economics.* February.

————. 1998a, Taxes, financing decisions, and firm value. *Journal of Finance.* June.

————. 1998b. Value versus growth: the international evidence. *Journal of Finance.* December.

————. 2000. The equity premium. Working paper 522, The Center for Research in Security Prices, University of Chicago.

Fama, E.F., and M. Jensen. 1983. Separation of ownership and control. *Journal of Law and Economics.* June.

Fama, E.F., and M.H. Miller. 1972. *The theory of finance.* New York: Holt, Rinehart and Winston.

Favell, A. 1993. James Coleman: Social theorist and moral philosopher. *American Journal of Sociology.* November.

Fershtman, C., K. Murphy, and Y. Weiss. 1996, Social status, education, and growth. *Journal of Political Economy.* February.

Finer, H. 1946. *The road to reaction.* Boston: Little, Brown & Co.

Fischel, D. 1995. *Payback: The conspiracy to destroy Michael Milken and his financial revolution.* New York: Harper Business.

Fischel, D., and A. Sykes. 1996. Corporate crime. *The Journal of Legal Studies.* June.

Fisher, I. 1911, *The purchasing power of money: Its determination and relation to credit, interest and crises.* New York: Macmillan.

————. 1926. A statistical relation between unemployment and price changes. *International Labor Review.* June.

Fisher, S., Z. Griliches, and C. Kaysen. 1962, The costs of automobile changes since 1949. *Journal of Political Economy.* October.

Fisher, L., and J. Lorie. 1964. Rates of return on investments in common stocks. *Journal of Business.* January.

————. 1968. Rates of return on investments in common stocks: The year-by-year record, 1926-1965. *Journal of Business.* July.

Fleming, J.M., 1962, "Domestic Financial Policies under Fixed and under Floating Exchange Rates", IMF Staff Papers, March.

Fleming, M. 1971. On exchange rate unification. *Economic Journal.* September.

Fogel, R.W. 1964. *Railroads and American economic growth: Essays in econometric history.* Washington. DC: Johns Hopkins University Press.

————. 1989. *Without consent or contract: The rise and fall of American slavery.* New York: W.W. Norton & Co.

————. 1997. Economic growth, population theory, and physiology: The bearing of long-term processes on the making of economic policy. In Persson 1997.

————. 2000. *The fourth great awakening and the future of egalitarianism.* Chicago: University of Chicago Press.

Fogel, R.W., and S.L. Engerman. 1974. *Time on the cross: The economics of American negro slavery.* New York: Little, Brown.

Foss, N. 1994. *The Austrian School and modern economics: Essays in reassessment.* Copenhagen: Munksgaard International Publishers.

Frenkel, J. 1974. The demand for international reserves by developed and less-developed countries. *Economica.* February.

————. 1978. Purchasing power parity: Doctrinal perspective and empirical evidence from the 1920's. *Journal of International Economics.* May.

————. 1981. The collapse of purchasing power parities in the 1970s. *European Economic Review.* May.

Frenkel, J.A., and H.G. Johnson, eds. 1976. *The monetary approach to the balance of payments.* Toronto: University of Toronto Press.

Frenkel, J.A., and M.L. Mussa. 1980. The efficiency of the foreign exchange market and measures of turbulence. *AEA Papers and Proceedings.* May.

———. 1985. Asset markets, exchange rates and the balance of payments. In *Handbook of international economics,* ed. R. Jones and P. Kenen, Amsterdam: North-Holland.

Frenkel, J.A., and A. Razin. 1987. *The Mundell-Fleming model: A quarter century later.* IMF Staff Papers No. 34. Washington, DC: International Monetary Fund.

Freund, E. 1912. The enforcement provisions of the Sherman Law. *Journal of Political Economy.* May.

Friedland, C. 1993. "On Stigler and Stiglerisms." *Journal of Political Economy.* October.

Friedman, D. 1991. Law and Economics. In *The New Palgrave: The World of Economics,* eds. J. Eatwell, M. Milgate, and P. Newman, New York: W.W. Norton.

Friedman, D., W. Landes, and R. Posner. 1991, Some economics of trade secret law. *Journal of Economic Perspectives.* Winter.

Friedman, M. 1937. The use of ranks to avoid the assumption of normality implicit in the analysis of variance. *Journal of the American Statistical Association.* Vol. 32, No. 200 (Dec., 1937), pp. 675-701.

———. 1940. Review of *Business Cycles in the United States of America, 1919-32* by J. Tinbergen. *American Economic Review.* September.

———. 1941. Review of *Monopolistic Competition and General Equilibrium Theory* by R. Triffin. *Journal of Farm Economics.* February.

———. 1948. A monetary and fiscal framework for economic stability. *American Economic Review.* June.

———. 1953. *Essays in positive economics.* Chicago: University of Chicago Press.

———. 1955. The role of government in education. In *Economics and the Public Interest,* ed. R.A. Solo, New Brunswick: Rutgers University Press.

———, ed. 1956. *Studies in the quantity theory of money.* Chicago: University of Chicago Press.

———. 1957. *A theory of the consumption function.* Princeton, NJ: Princeton University Press.

———. 1958. Foreign economic aid: Means and objectives. In *The Essence of Friedman,* ed. K.R. Leube, 80. Stanford, CA: Hoover Institution Press, 1987.

———. 1960. *A program for monetary stability.* New York: Fordham University Press.

———. 1962. *Capitalism & freedom.* Chicago: University of Chicago Press.

———. 1966. What price guideposts? In *Guidelines: Informal contracts and the market place,* eds. G. Schultz and R. Aliber, Chicago: University of Chicago Press.

———. 1967a, The monetary theory and policy of Henry Simons. *Journal of Law and Economics.* October.

———. 1967b. Why not a voluntary army? In *The draft: A handbook of facts and alternatives,* ed. S. Tax. Chicago: University of Chicago Press.

———. 1968. The role of monetary policy. *American Economic Review.* March.

———. 1970. Social responsibility of business. *New York Times Magazine,* September 13.

———. 1974. *Schools at Chicago.* Archives of the Communications Department of the University of Chicago.

———. 1976a. *Price theory.* New York: Aldine de Gruyter.

———. 1976b. Inflation and unemployment. In *The Essence of Friedman,* ed. K. Leube, Stanford, CA: Hoover Institution Press, 1987.

———. 1978. Tax limitation, inflation, and the role of government. Dallas: The Fisher Institute.

———. 1992. *Money mischief: Episodes in monetary history.* New York: Harcourt Brace & Company.

———. 1993. George Stigler: A personal reminiscence. *Journal of Political Economy.* October.

———. 1997. John Maynard Keynes. Federal Reserve Bank of Richmond *Economic Quarterly* 83 (2).

Friedman, M., and R. Friedman R. 1979. *Free to Choose.* New York: Penguin Books.

————. 1998. *Memoirs: Two lucky people.* Chicago: University of Chicago Press.

Friedman, M., and S. Kuznets. 1945. *Income from independent professional practice.* Boston: National Bureau of Economic Research.

Friedman, M., and D. Meiselman.1963. The relative stability of monetary velocity and the investment multiplier in the United States. In *Commission on Money and Credit.* Stabilization Policies. Englewood Cliffs, NJ: Prentice-Hall.

Friedman, M. and L. Savage. 1948. The utility analysis of choices involving risks. *Journal of Political Economy.* August.

Friedman, M., and A. Schwartz. 1963. *A monetary history of the United States, 1867-1960.* Princeton, NJ: Princeton University Press.

————. 1982. *Monetary trends in the United States and the United Kingdom: Their relation to income, prices and interest rates, 1867-1975.* Chicago: The University of Chicago Press.

————. 1991. Alternative approaches to analyzing economic data. *American Economic Review.* March.

Furner, M. 1975. *Advocacy and objectivity: A crisis in the professionalization of American social science, 1865-1905.* Lexington: University of Kentucky Press.

Gaffney, M., and F. Harrison. 1994. *The corruption of economics.* London: Shepheard-Walwyn Publishers.

Galenson, D., ed. 1989. *Markets in history: Economic studies of the past.* Cambridge: Cambridge University Press.

————. 1993. The impact of economic and technological change on the careers of American men tennis players, 1960-1991. *Journal of Sport History.* Summer.

Gans, J., and G. Shepherd. 1994. Rejected classic articles by leading economists. *Journal of Economic Perspectives.* Winter.

Gerwig, R., 1962. Natural gas production: A study of costs of regulation. *Journal of Law and Economics.* October.

Gibbons, T. 1985. Bringing economics into law: The Chicago movement. *Illinois Issues.* June.

Gideonse H., 1935. National collectivism and Charles A. Beard. *Journal of Political Economy.* December.

Glaeser, E., H. Kallal, J. Scheinkman, and A. Schleifer. 1992. The growth of cities. *Journal of Political Economy.* February.

Glaeser, E., B. Sacerdote, and J. Scheinkman. 1996. Crime and social interactions. *Quarterly Journal of Economics.* May.

Glaeser, E., and J. Scheinkman. 1996. The transition to free markets: Where to begin privatization. *Journal of Comparative Economics.* February.

Gleeson, R., and S. Schlossman. 1995. George Leland Bach and the rebirth of graduate management education in the United States, 1945-75. *Selections* Spring.

Goodspeed, T.W. 1916. *A History of the University of Chicago: The first quarter-century.* Chicago: University of Chicago Press.

Goodwin, C. 1998. The patrons of economics in a time of transformation. In Morgan and Rutherford 1998.

Goodwin, D. 1998. Martin Bronfenbrenner, 1914-1997. *Economic Journal.* November.

Goolsbee, A. 1997. Investment tax incentives, prices, and the supply of capital goods. *Quarterly Journal of Economics.* August.

————. 1998a. Does R and D policy primarily benefit scientists and engineers? *AEA Papers and Proceedings.* May.

————. 1998b. In *A world without borders: The impact of taxes on Internet commerce.* Working paper 6863. National Bureau of Economic Research, Cambridge, MA.

————. 2004. The impact and inefficiency of the corporate income tax: Evidence from state organizational form data. *Journal of Public Economics.* September.

Gordon, R.A., ed. 1974. *Milton Friedman's monetary framework: A debate with his critics.* Chicago: University of Chicago Press.

Gordon, R., and J. Wilcox. 1981. Monetary interpretations of the Great Depression: An evaluation and critique. In Brunner 1981.

Gould, J. 1967. Market value and the theory of investment of the firm. *American Economic Review.* September.

Gould, J. 1980. The economics of markets: A simple model of market-making process. *Journal of Business.* July.

————. 1980. Privacy and the economics of information. *Journal of Legal Studies.* December.

Gould, J. and E. Lazear. 1986. *Microeconomic Theory.* Homewood, Ill.: Richard D. Irwin

Gould, J., and R. Waud. 1973. The neoclassical model of investment behavior: another view. *International Economic Review.* February.

Graduate School of Business. 1998. *Taking stock: A century of business education.* Chicago: The University of Chicago Graduate School of Business.

Greenaway, D., M. Bleaney, and I. Stewart. 1996. *A guide to modern economics.* London: Routledge.

Griliches, Z. 1957. Hybrid corn: An exploration in the economics of "technical change." *Econometrica.* October.

Griliches, Z. 1958. Research costs and social returns: Hybrid corn and related innovations. *Journal of Political Economy.* October.

————. 1959. The demand for inputs in agriculture and a derived supply elasticity. *Journal of Farm Economics.* 41.

————. 1961a. *Hedonic price indexes for automobiles: An econometric analysis of quality change.* The Price Statistics of the Federal Government, National Bureau of Economic Research, General Series. No. 73. Cambridge, MA: National Bureau of Economic Research.

————. 1961b. A note on serial correlation bias estimates in distributed lags. *Econometrica.* January.

————. 1963. The source of measured productivity growth: United States Agriculture: 1940-1960. *Journal of Political Economy.* August.

————. 1964. Research expenditures, education, and the aggregate agricultural production function. *American Economic Review.* December.

————. 1998. *Practicing econometrics: Essays in method and application.* Economists of the Twentieth Century, eds. M. Blaug and D. Colander. Cheltenham, UK, Edward Elgar Publishing.

Groenewegen, P. 2003. Classics and moderns in economics. Vol. II of *Nineteenth- and twentieth-century economic thought.* London: Routledge.

Hamilton, E. 1934. *American treasure and the price revolution in Spain, 1501-1650.* Cambridge, MA: Harvard University Press.

Hamilton, W. 1919. The institutionalist approach to economic theory. *American Economic Review.* March.

Hammond, D. 1996. *Theory and measurement: causality issues in Milton Friedman's monetary economics.* Cambridge: Cambridge University Press.

Harberger, A.C. 1954. Monopoly and resource allocation. *American Economic Review.* May.

————. 1960. *The demand for durable goods.* Chicago: The University of Chicago Press.

————. 1962. The incidence of the corporation income tax. *Journal of Political Economy.* June.

————. 1972a. Issues concerning capital assistance to less-developed countries. In Wall 1972.

————. 1972b. *Project evaluation.* Chicago: The University of Chicago Press.

————. 1974. *Taxation and welfare.* Boston: Little, Brown & Co.

———. 1978. A primer on inflation. *Journal of Money, Credit and Banking*. November.

———. 1984. *Economic science and economic policy*. University of Chicago, mimeo (files Communications Department).

———. ed. 1985. *World economic growth*. San Francisco, CA: Institute for Contemporary Studies.

———. 1988. *Trade policy and the real exchange rate*. Washington, DC: The World Bank Development Institute.

———. 1993. Secrets of success: A handful of heroes. *AEA Papers and Proceedings*. May.

Harding, C.M. 1955. *Freedom in agricultural education*. New York: Arno.

Hardy, C.O. 1923. *Risk and risk bearing*. Chicago: University of Chicago Press.

———. 1932. *Credit policies of the Federal Reserve System*. Washington, DC: Brookings Institution.

———. 1948. Liberalism in the modern state: The philosophy of Henry Simons. *Journal of Political Economy*. August.

Hardy, C.O., and L. Lyon. 1923. The theory of hedging. *Journal of Political Economy*. April.

Hart, A., 1940. *Anticipations, uncertainty, and dynamic planning*. Chicago: University of Chicago Press.

Hartwell, R.M.. 1995. *A history of the Mont Pèlerin Society*. Indianapolis: Liberty Press.

Hayek, F.A. 1929. *Monetary theory and the trade cycle*. London: Jonathan Cape.

———. 1931. *Prices and production*. New York: August M. Kelley.

———. 1942. Scientism and the study of society. *Economica*. August.

———. 1944. *The road to serfdom*. Chicago: University of Chicago Press, 1976.

———. 1960. *The constitution of liberty*. Chicago: University of Chicago Press.

———. 1974. The pretence of knowledge. In Leube and Nishiyama 1984.

———. 1975. Inflation, the misdirection of labor and unemployment. Occasional paper 45. Institute of Economic Affairs, London.

———. 1983. The Keynes century: The Austrian critique. *The Economist*. June 11.

———. 1994. *Hayek on Hayek: An autobiographical dialogue*, eds. S. Kresge, and L. Weinar. Chicago: University of Chicago Press.

Heckman, J. 1974a. The effect of child care programs on women's work effort. *Journal of Political Economy*. March/April (part II).

———. 1974b. Life cycle consumption and labor supply: An explanation of the relationship between income and consumption over the life cycle. *American Economic Review*. March.

———. 1974c. Shadow prices, market wages, and labor supply. *Econometrica*. 42 (4)

———. 1976. A life-cycle model of earnings, learning, and consumption. *Journal of Political Economy*. August (part II).

———. 1990. The central role of the South in accounting for the economic progress of black Americans. *American Economic Review*. May.

———. 1993. What has been learned about labor supply in the past twenty years. *American Economic Review*. May.

———. 1997. Henry Schultz. Mimeo, University of Chicago (received in March 1997).

———. 1998. Detecting discrimination. *Journal of Economic Perspectives*. Spring.

———. 2001. Micro data, heterogeneity, and the evaluation of public policy: Nobel Lecture. *Journal of Political Economy*. August.

Heckman, J., and M. Killingsworth. 1987. Female labor supply: A survey. In *Handbook of Labor Economics*, edited by O. Ashenfelter and R. Layard, Amsterdam: North-Holland.

Heckman, J., R. Roselius, and J. Smith. 1994. US education and training policy: A re-evaluation of the underlying assumptions behind the "new consensus." In *Labor Markets, Employment Policy, and Job Creation*, eds. L. Solmon and A. Levenson, Boulder, CO: Westview Press.

Heckman, J., and J. Verkerke, J. 1990. Racial disparity and employment discrimination laws: An economic perspective. *Yale Law and Policy Review*. 8 (2).

Hegeland, H. 1951. *The quantity theory of money.* Göteborg, Sweden: Elanders Boktryckeri.

Hendry, D., and N. Ericsson, N. 1991. An econometric Analysis of UK money demand in *Monetary Trends in the United States and the United Kingdom. American Economic Review.* March.

Herman, E.S. 1995. *The triumph of the market.* Boston: South End Press.

Herzel, L. 1951. Public interest and the market in color television regulation. *University of Chicago Law Review.* No. 18.

Hickman, C.A. 1975. *J.M. Clark.* New York: Columbia University Press.

Hicks, J. 1937. Mr. Keynes and the classics: A suggested interpretation. *Econometrica.* April.

Hicks, J., and W. Weber, eds. 1973. *Carl Menger and the Austrian School of Economics.* London, Oxford University Press.

Hildreth, C. 1986. *The Cowles Commission in Chicago, 1939-1955.* Berlin: Springer.

Hirsch, Abraham & de Marchi, Neil. 1990. *Milton Friedman. Economics in Theory and Practice,* Ann Arbor: The University of Michigan Press.

Hogarth, R.M., ed. 1990. *Insights in decision making: A tribute to Hillel J. Einhorn.* Chicago: University of Chicago Press.

Holmes, O.W. 1897. The path to laws. *Harvard Law Review.* Vol. 10.

Holmes, S., and C. Sunstein. 1999. *The cost of rights: Why liberty depends on taxes.* New York: Norton.

Homan, P.T. 1928. *Contemporary economic thought.* New York: Harper and Brothers.

———. 1931. Herbert Joseph Davenport. *Journal of Political Economy.* December.

Hotelling, H. 1939. The work of Henry Schultz. *Econometrica.* April.

Hoselitz, B.F. 1957. Economic growth and development – non-economic factors in economic development. *AEA Papers and Proceedings.* May.

———. 1960. Sociological aspects of economic growth. New York: Free Press.

Hovenkamp, H. 1986. Chicago and its alternatives. *Duke Law Journal.* December.

Hoxie, R. 1906. The demand and supply concepts: An introduction to the study of market prize. *Journal of Political Economy.* June/July.

Irwin, D.A. 1996. *Against the tide: An intellectual history of free trade.* Princeton, NJ: Princeton University Press.

Jacoby, N. 1950. Antitrust re-examined. *Journal of Political Economy.* February.

Jensen, M. 1968. The performance of mutual funds in the period 1945-64. *Journal of Finance.* May.

Jensen, M., and W. Meckling. 1976. Theory of the firm: Managerial behavior, agency costs, and ownership structure. *Journal of Financial Economics.* October.

Johnson, A.S. 1952. *Pilgrim's Progress.* New York: Viking Press.

Johnson, D.G. 1944. Contributions of price policy to income and resource problems in agriculture. *Journal of Farm Economics.* November.

Johnson, D.G. 1947. *Forward prices for agriculture.* Chicago: The University of Chicago Press.

———. 1948a. Allocation of agricultural income, *Journal of Farm Economics.* November.

———. 1948b. Mobility as a field of economic Research. *Southern Economic Journal.* October.

———. 1950. The nature of the supply function for agricultural products. *American Economic Review.* September.

———. 1958. Labor mobility and agricultural adjustment. In *Agricultural adjustment problems in a growing economy,* ed. E.H. Diesslin, et al. Ames: Iowa State University Press.

———. 1979. Schultz, Theodore W. *International encyclopaedia of the social sciences,* ed. D.L. Sills. New York: The Free Press.

———. 1991. *World agriculture in disarray,* Rev. ed. London: Macmillan.

———. 1997. Agriculture and the wealth of nations. *AEA Papers and Proceedings.* May.

Johnson, H.G. 1958. *International trade and economic growth.* London: Unwin.

———. 1960. The political economy of opulence. *Canadian Journal of Economic and Political Science.* November.

————. 1961. The *General Theory* after twenty-five years. *AEA Papers and Proceedings.* May.

————. 1962. Monetary theory and policy. *American Economic Review.* June.

————. 1965. A quantity theorist's monetary history of the United States. *Economic Journal.* June.

————. 1967a. The possibility of income losses from increased efficiency or factor accumulation in the presence of tariffs. *Economic Journal.* March.

————. 1967b. *Economic policies toward less developed countries.*Washington. The Brookings Institution.

————. 1971. *Aspects of the theory of tariffs.* London: Allen & Unwin.

————. 1972a. The Keynesian revolution and the monetarist counter-revolution. *AEA Papers and Proceedings.* May.

————. 1972b. *Macroeconomics and monetary theory.* London Gray-Mills.

————. 1975. Trade, development and dependence. Paper presented at the Conference on The New Nations Revisited, The University of Chicago, October 16-19.

————. 1976a. Monetary theory and Keynesian economics. In *Monetary Theory: Selected Readings,* ed. R. Clower. Baltimore, MD: Penguin.

————. 1976b. The Nobel Milton. *The Economist.*

————. 1976c. Towards a general theory of the balance of payments. In Frenkel and Johnson 1976.

Johnson, H.G., and E.S. Johnson, E.S. 1978. *The shadow of Keynes.* Oxford: Basil Blackwell.

Johnson, H.G., and H.K. Swoboda, eds. 1973. *The economics of common currencies.* London: Allen and Unwin.

Jolls, C., C. Sunstein, and R. Thaler. 1998. Behavioral approach to law and economics. Working paper 55. Law & Economics, University of Chicago Law Faculty.

Jones, M. 1944. Secular and cyclical saving propensities. *Journal of Business.* January.

Jorgenson, D., and Z. Griliches. 1967. The explanation of productivity change. *Review of Economics Statistics.* July.

Joskow, P., and N. Rose. 1989. The effects of regulation. In *The Handbook of Industrial Organization,* ed. R. Schmalensee and R. Willig, Amsterdam: North Holland.

Juhn, C., K. Murphy, and B. Pierce. 1993. Wage Inequality and the Rise in Returns to Skill, *Journal of Political Economy.* June.

Kahan, A. 1985. *The plow, the hammer, and the knout: An economic history of eighteenth-century Russia.* Chicago: University of Chicago Press.

————. 1986. *Essays in Jewish social and economic history,* ed. R. Weiss. Chicago, University of Chicago Press.

Kahneman, D., P. Slovic, and A. Tversky, eds. 1982. *Judgement under uncertainty: Heuristics and biases.* London: Cambridge University Press.

Kashyap, A., and H. Takeo. 2004. Japan's economic and financial crisis: An overview. *Journal of Economic Perspectives.* Winter.

Katz, W. 1937. A four-year program for legal education. *University of Chicago Law Review.* June.

Kaysen, C., and D. Turner. 1959. *Antitrust policy: An economic and legal analysis.* Cambridge, MA: Harvard University Press.

Kessel, R. 1980. *Essays in applied price theory,* eds. R.H. Coase and M.H. Miller. Chicago: University of Chicago Press.

Keuzenkamp, H. 1991. A precursor to Muth: Tinbergen's 1932 model of rational expectations. *Economic Journal.* September.

Keynes, J.M. 1936. *The general theory of employment, interest, and money.* London: MacMillan and Co.

————. 1937. The general theory of employment. *Quarterly Journal of Economics.* February.

Kiker, B.F. 1966. The historical roots of the concept of human capital. *Journal of Political Economy.* October.

———. ed. 1972. *Investment in human capital.* Columbia: University of South Carolina Press.

Kindleberger, C. 1973. *The world in depression 1929-39.* Berkeley: University of California Press.

———. 1999. *Essays in history.* Ann Arbor: The University of Michigan Press.

King, R., and C. Plosser. 1984. Money, credit and prices in a real business cycle model. *American Economic Review.* June.

Kitch, E.W. 1972. The shortage of natural gas. Occasional papers No. 2, Chicago Law School.

———. 1977. The nature and function of the patent system. *Journal of Law and Economics.* October.

———. 1983a. The fire of truth: A remembrance of law and economics at Chicago, 1932-1970. *Journal of Law and Economics.* April.

———. 1983b. The intellectual foundations of "Law and Economics." *Journal of Legal Education.* 33, 183.

———. 1985. The antitrust economics of joint ventures. *Antitrust Law Journal.* 54.

———. 1990. Property rights in inventions, writings and marks. *Harvard Journal of Law & Public Policy.* 13, 119.

Kitch, E., M. Isaacson, and D. Kasper. 1971. The regulation of taxicabs in Chicago. *Journal of Law and Economics* 14 (2).

Klamer, A. 1983. *Conversations with economists.* Totowa, NJ: Rowman & Allanheld.

Klein, C. 1996. Law and economics finds its niche. *The National Law Journal.* October 14.

Knight, F. 1921. *Risk, uncertainty and profit.* Boston: Houghton Mifflin.

———. 1932a. *The case for communism: From the standpoint of an ex-liberal.* Mimeo. Chicago: University of Chicago files.

———. 1932b. The newer economics and the control of economic activity. *Journal of Political Economy.* August.

———. 1933. *The economic organization.* Mimeo. Chicago: The University of Chicago.

———. 1936a. The quantity of capital and the rate of interest, part 1. *Journal of Political Economy.* August.

———. 1936b. The quantity of capital and the rate of interest, part 2. *Journal of Political Economy.* October.

———. 1937. Unemployment and Mr. Keynes's revolution in economic theory. *Canadian Journal of Economic and Political Science.* February.

———. 1938. Imperfect competition. *Journal of Marketing.* April.

———. 1944. Diminishing returns from investment. *Journal of Political Economy.* March.

———. 1951. *The ethics of competition and other essays.* New York: August M. Kelley.

———. 1956. *On the history and method of economics.* Chicago: University of Chicago Press.

———. 1997. *The ethics of competition.* New Brunswick, NJ: Transaction Publishers.

———. 1957. *Three essays on the state of economic sciences.* New York: McGraw-Hill.

Kroszner, R., and T. Cowen. 1989. Scottish banking before 1845: A model for laissez-faire? *Journal of Money, Credit and Banking.* May.

Kroszner, R., and P. Strahan. 1999. What drives deregulation? Economics and politics of the relaxation of bank branching restrictions. *Quarterly Journal of Economics.* November.

Kroszner, R., and T. Stratman. 1998. Interest group competition and the organization of Congress: Theory and evidence from financial services' political action committees. *American Economic Review.* December.

Krueger, A., and T. Taylor. 2000. Interview with Zvi Griliches, *Journal of Economic Perspectives.* Spring.

Kuznets, S. 1952. Proportion of capital formation to national product. *AEA Papers and Proceedings.* May.

Kydland, F.E., and E. Prescott. 1977. Rules rather than discretion: The inconsistency of optimal plans. *Journal of Political Economy.* June.

―――. 1982. Time to build and aggregate fluctuations. *Econometrica*. November.

Kyrk, H. 1953. *The family in the American economy.* Chicago: University of Chicago Press.

Laffer, A. 1980. *The ellipse: An explanation of the Laffer Curve in a two factor model.* Rolling Hill Estates, CA: A.B. Laffer Associates.

Laffer, A., and D. Meiselman, eds. 1975. *The phenomenon of worldwide inflation.* Washington, DC: American Enterprise Institute.

Laffer, A., and J. Seymour. 1979. *The economics of the tax revolt: A reader.* San Diego, CA: Harcourt Brace Jovanovich.

Laidler, D. 1981. Monetarism: An interpretation and an assessment. *Economic Journal.* March.

Lakonishok, J., A. Shleifer, R. Thaler, and R. Vishny. 1991. Window dressing by pension fund managers. *AEA Papers and Proceedings.* May.

Lakonishok J., A. Shleifer, and R. Vishny. 1992. *The structure and performance of the money management industry.* Brookings Papers on Economic Activity: Microeconomics. Washington, DC: The Brookings Institution.

―――. 1994. Contrarian investment, extrapolation and risk. *Journal of Finance.* December.

Landes, W. 1968. The economics of fair employment laws. *Journal of Political Economy.* July.

―――. 1971. An economic analysis of the courts. *Journal of Law and Economics.* July.

―――. 1983. Optimal sanctions for antitrust violations. *University of Chicago Law Review.* 50.

―――. 1997. The art of law and economics: An autobiographical essay. *The American Economist.* Spring.

Landes, W., L. Lessig, and M. Solimine. 1998. Judicial influence: A citation analysis of federal courts of appeals judges. *Journal of Legal Studies.* June.

Landes, W., and R. Posner. 1976. Legal precedent: A theoretical and empirical analysis. *Journal of Law and Economics.* April.

―――. 1981. Market Power and Antitrust Cases. *Harvard Law Review.* 94.

―――. 1989. An economic analysis of copyright law. *Journal of Legal Studies.* No. 18.

―――. 1975. The independent judiciary in an interest-group perspective. *Journal of Law and Economics.* April.

―――. 1975. The private enforcement of law. *Journal of Legal Studies.* 4.

―――. 1993. The influence of economics on law: A quantitative study. *Journal of Law & Economics.* April.

Landreth, H., and D. Colander. 1989. *History of Economic Theory.* Boston: Houghton Mifflin Company.

Lange, O. 1944. *Price flexibility and employment.* Bloomington, IN: Principia Press.

Lange, O., e.a. 1942, *Studies in Mathematical Economics and Econometrics.* Chicago: The University of Chicago Press.

La Porta, R., F. Lopez-de-Salinas, A. Shleifer, and R. Vishny. 1996. Law and finance. Working paper 5561, National Bureau of Economic Research, Cambridge, MA.

―――. 1997. Legal determinants of external finance. Working paper 5879, National Bureau of Economic Research, Cambridge, MA.

Larrain, F., and P. Meller. 1991. The socialist-populist Chilean experience: 1970-1973. In *The Macroeconomics of Populism in Latin America*, eds. R. Dornbush and S. Edwards. Chicago: University of Chicago Press.

Laswell, H. 1938. *Politics: Who gets what, when, how.* New York: Whittlesey House.

Laughlin, J.L. 1902. Prices and the international movement of specie. *Journal of Political Economy.* September.

―――. 1903. *Principles of money.* New York: Charles Scriber's Sons.

―――. 1906a. Academic liberty. *Journal of Political Economy.* January.

―――. 1906b. The union versus higher wages. *Journal of Political Economy.* March.

―――. 1909. *Latter-day problems.* New York: Charles Scribner's Sons.

————. 1912. The economic seminars. *Journal of Political Economy.* February.

————. 1914. The Banking and Currency Act of 1913, Parts I & II. *Journal of Political Economy.* April.

————. 1924. The quantity theory of money. *Journal of Political Economy.* June.

Lazear, E. 1977. Education: consumption or production? *Journal of Political Economy.* June.

————. 1980. Family background and optimal schooling decisions. *Review of Economics and Statistics.* February.

————. 1983. A competitive theory of monopoly unionism. *American Economic Review.* September.

————. 2000. Economic imperialism. *Quarterly Journal of Economics.* February.

Leeson, R. 2000. Patinkin, Johnson, and the shadow of Friedman. *History of Political Economy.* Winter.

Leibenstein, H. 1966. Allocative efficiency vs. x-efficiency. *American Economic Review.* June.

Leontief, W. 1953, The domestic production and foreign trade: The American capital position re-examined. *Proceedings of the American Philosophical Society.* September.

Levi, E. 1949. *An introduction to legal reasoning.* Chicago: University of Chicago Press.

Leube, K., and C. Nishiyama, eds. 1984. *The Essence of Hayek.* Stanford, CA: Hoover Institution Press.

Levi, E. 1977. Reminiscences. *University of Chicago Law Alumni Journal.*

Levitt, S.D. 1997. Using electoral cycles in police hiring to estimate the effect of police on crime. *American Economic Review.* June.

Levitt, S. 1998. Juvenile crime and punishment. *Journal of Political Economy.* October.

Lewis, H.G, 1951. The labor monopoly problem: A positive program, *Journal of Political Economy.* August.

————. 1963. *Unions and relative wages in the United States: An empirical enquiry.* Chicago: University of Chicago Press.

————. 1986. *Union relative wage effects: A survey.* Chicago: University of Chicago Press.

Lindbeck, A. 1985. The Prize in Economic Science in Memory of Alfred Nobel. *Journal of Economic Literature.* March.

————. 1992. Presentation. In Maler 1992.

Long, J., and C. Plosser. 1983. Real business cycles. *Journal of Political Economy.* February.

Lorie, J. 1974. *Public policy for American capital market.* Washington, DC: U.S. Government Printing Office.

Lorie, J., and M. Hamilton. 1973. *The stock market: Theories and evidence*, Homewood, Ill: Richard Irwin.

Lorie, J., and V. Niederhoffer. 1968. Predictive and statistical properties of insider trading. *Journal of Law and Economics.* April.

Lorie, J., and H. Roberts. 1951. *Basic methods of marketing research.* New York: McGraw-Hill.

Lott, J.R. 1998. *More guns, less crime.* Chicago: The University of Chicago Press.

Lowenstein, R. 2000. *When genius failed: The rise and fall of Long-Term Capital Management.* New York: Random House.

Lucas, R.E. 1972. Expectations and the neutrality of money. *Journal of Economic Theory.* April.

————. 1976. Econometric policy evaluation: A critique. Carnegie-Rochester Conference Series. No. 1.

————. 1977. Understanding business cycles, In *Stabilization of the Domestic and International Economy*, eds. K. Brunner and Meltzer. Carnegie-Rochester Conference Series on Public Policy No. 5. Amsterdam: North-Holland.

————. 1978. Unemployment policy. *American Economic Review.* May.

————. 1980. Two illustrations of the quantity theory of money. *American Economic Review.* December.

———. 1987. *Models of business cycles*. Oxford: Basil Blackwell.

———. 1988a. On the mechanics of economic development. *Journal of Monetary Economics*. July.

———. 1988b. Money demand in the United States: A quantitative review. *Carnegie Rochester Series in Public Policy*. Autumn.

———. 1990. Why doesn't capital flow from rich to poor countries? *AEA Papers and Proceedings*. May.

———. 1993. Making a miracle. *Econometrica*. March.

———. 2000. Some macroeconomics for the 21st Century. *Journal of Economic Perspectives*. Winter.

———. 2002. *Lectures on economic growth*. Cambridge, MA: Harvard University Press.

———. 2003. Macroeconomic priorities. *American Economic Review*. March.

Lucas, R.E., and L.A. Rapping. 1969. Real wages, employment and inflation. *Journal of Political Economy*. Sept./Oct.

Lucas, R., and T. Sargent, eds. 1981, *Rational expectations and econometric practice*. Minneapolis: University of Minnesota Press.

———. After Keynesian macroeconomics. In Miller, 1991.

MacAloon, J.J. 1992. *General education in the social sciences*. Chicago: University of Chicago Press.

Machlup, F. 1958. *An economic review of the patent system*. Study no.15 of the Subcommittee on Patents, Trademarks, and Copyrights of the Judiciary US Senate, 85th Congress.

———. ed. 1977. *Essays on Hayek*, London: Routledge & Kegan Paul.

Maler, K.-G., ed. 1992. *Nobel Lectures, 1981-1990: Economic Sciences*. London: World Scientific.

Manne, H. 1965. Mergers and the market for corporate control. *Journal of Political Economy*. April.

———. 1966. *Insider Trading and the Stock Market*. New York: Free Press.

Marcus, N. 1988. Rule of law (and economics). *The American Lawyer*. June.

Markowitz, H. 1952. Portfolio selection. *Journal of Finance*. March.

Marshall, A. 1890. *Principles of Economics*. London: Macmillan, 9th ed.1961.

———. 1923. *Money, Credit and Commerce*. London, Macmillan.

Mason, E. 1937. Monopoly in Law and Economics. *Yale Law & Policy Journal*. No.34.

———. 1939. Price and production policies of large-scale enterprises. *AEA Papers and Proceedings*. May.

Mayer, M. 1957. *Young man in a hurry: The story of William Rainey Harper*. Chicago: University of Chicago Alumni Association.

McAfee, P. 1983. American economic history and the voyage of Columbus. *American Economic Review*. September.

McCloskey, D. N. 1981. *Enterprise and trade in Victorian Britain: Essays in historical economics*. New York: Allen and Unwin.

———. 1994. *Knowledge and persuasion in economics*. Cambridge: Cambridge University Press.

———. 2003. Other things equal: Milton. *Eastern Economic Journal*. Winter.

McCormick, B. 1992. *Hayek and the Keynesian avalanche*. New York: Harvester Wheatsleaf.

McGee, J. 1958. Predatory price cutting: The Standard Oil (N.J.) Case. *Journal of Law and Economics*. October.

———. 1966. Patent exploitation: Some economic and legal problems. *Journal of Law and Economics*. October.

———. 1980. Predatory pricing revisited. *Journal of Law and Economics*. October.

McIvor, R.C. 1983. A note on the University of Chicago's "academic scribblers." *Journal of Political Economy*. October.

McLean Hardy, S. 1895. The quantity theory of money and prices, 1860-1891. *Journal of Political Economy*. March.

Meade, J. 1951. *The theory of international economic policy.* Vol. 1 of *The balance of payments.* London: Oxford University Press.

———. 1956. *The theory of customs unions.* Amsterdam: North-Holland.

———. 1957. The balance-of-payments problems of a European free-trade area. *Economic Journal.* September.

Means, G. 1972. The administered prices thesis reconfirmed. *American Economic Review.* 62 (3).

Medema, S.G. 1994. *Ronald H. Coase.* New York: St. Martin's Press.

———. 1998. Wandering the road from pluralism to Posner: The transformation of law and economics in the twentieth century. In Morgan and Rutherford 1998.

Mehra, R., and E. Prescott, E. 1985. The equity premium: A puzzle. *Journal of Monetary Economics* 15.

Meltzer, A. 1981. Comments on "Monetary Interpretation of the Great Depression." In Brunner 1981.

Meltzner, D. 1992. Mortality decline: The demographic transition and economic growth (economics), PhD diss., University of Chicago.

Menninger, K. 1966. *The crime of punishment,* New York: Viking.

Merton, R., and M.S. Scholes. 1995. Fischer Black. *Journal of Finance.* December.

Meyer, H. 1906. Railway rates as protective tariffs. *Journal of Political Economy.* January.

Miller, H.R. Jr. 1962. On the "Chicago School of Economics." *Journal of Political Economy.* February.

Miller, M.H. 1977. Debt and taxes. *Journal of Finance.* May.

———. 1991. *Financial innovations & market volatility.* Cambridge, MA: Blackwell.

———. 1992. Leverage. In Maler 1992.

———. 1993. The Modigliani-Miller propositions after thirty years. In *The new corporate finance,* ed. D. Chew, New York: McGraw-Hill.

———. 1994. Do we really need more regulation of financial derivatives? GSB Selected Paper. No. 75, Chicago: University of Chicago.

———. 1996. The social costs of some recent derivatives disasters. Draft text, Graduate School of Business, University of Chicago.

———. 1997. The Graduate School of Business of the University of Chicago: The last hundred years and the next. Talk given at the Graduate School of Business Centennial Gala, October 17, 1997: 1.

———. 1998. The history of finance: An eyewitness account. Transcript of the keynote address given at the 5th Annual Meeting of the German Finance Association, Hamburg, Germany, September 25.

Miller, M.H., and M.S. Scholes. 1978. Dividends and taxes. *Journal of Financial Economics.* December.

Miller, P.J., ed., 1994. *The rational expectations revolution.* Cambridge, MA: MIT Press.

Mincer, J. 1958. Investment in human capital and personal income distribution. *Journal of Political Economy.* August.

———. 1963. Market prices, opportunity costs, and income effects. In *Measurement in Economics,* ed. C. Christ, Stanford, CA: Stanford University Press.

Mints, L. 1945. *A history of banking theory.* Chicago: University of Chicago Press.

Mints, L. 1951. Monetary policy and stabilization. *AEA Papers and Proceedings* (May).

Mirowski, P. 2002. *Machine Dreams: Economics Becomes a Cyborg Science.* Cambridge: Cambridge University Press.

Mirowski, P., and D.W. Hands. 1998. A paradox of budgets: The postwar stabilization of American neoclassical demand theory. In Morgan and Rutherford 1998.

Mitchell, L.S. 1953. *Two lives: The story of Wesley Clair Mitchell and myself.* New York: Simon & Schuster.

Mitchell, W.C. 1896. The quantity theory of the value of money. *Journal of Political Economy.* March.

———. 1903. *A history of the greenbacks with special reference to the economic consequences of their issue: 1862-65.* Chicago: University of Chicago Press.

———. 1904. Real issues in the quantity theory controversy. *Journal of Political Economy.* June.

———. 1913. *Business cycles.* Berkeley: University of California Press.

———. 1941. J. Laurence Laughlin. *Journal of Political Economy.* December.

———. 1967. *Types of economic theory: From mercantilism to institutionalism.* Ed. Joseph Dorfman. New York: M.M. Kelley Publishers.

Mitchell, W.C., and A. Burns. 1945. *Measuring business cycles.* New York: National Bureau of Economic Research.

Modigliani, F. 1977. The monetarist controversy, or, should we forsake stabilization policy? *American Economic Review.* March.

Modigliani, F., and M.H. Miller. 1958. The cost of capital, corporation financing and the theory of investment. *American Economic Review.* June.

———. 1959. The cost of capital, corporation financing, and the theory of investment: reply. *American Economic Review.* September.

———. 1961. Dividend policy, growth, and the valuation of shares. *Journal of Business.* October.

———. 1963. Corporate income taxes and the cost of capital: A correction. *American Economic Review.* June.

Morck, R., A. Shleifer, and R. Vishny. 1990. Do managerial objectives drive bad acquisitions? *Journal of Finance.* March.

Morgan, M. and M. Rutherford, eds. 1998. *From interwar pluralism to postwar neoclassicism.* Durham, NC: Duke University Press.

———. 1998a. American economics: The character of transformation. In Morgan and Rutherford 1998.

Moulton, H.G. 1920. Banking policy and the price situation. *AEA Papers and Proceedings.* March.

Mulligan, C.B. 1997. *Parental Priorities and Economic Inequality.* Chicago: University of Chicago Press.

Mulligan, C., and X. Sala-i-Martin. 1992. *US money demand: some surprising cross-sectional estimates.* Brookings Papers on Economic Activity, No. 2. Washington, DC: The Brookings Institute.

Mundell, R.A. 1962. The appropriate use of monetary and fiscal policy for internal and external stability. *IMF Staff Papers.* March.

———. 1968a. *International economics.* New York: Macmillan.

———.1968b. *Man and economics.* New York: McGraw Hill.

———.1971. *The dollar and the policy mix: 1971.* Essays in International Finance. No. 85. Princeton, NJ: Princeton University, May.

Murphy, K., A. Shleifer, and R. Vishny. 1988. *Industrialization and the big push.* Working paper. No. 2708. Cambridge, MA: National Bureau of Economic Research.

———. 1991. The allocation of talent: implications for growth. *Quarterly Journal of Economics.* May.

———. 1993. Why is rent-seeking so costly to growth? *American Economic Review.* May.

Murphy, K., and R. Topel. 1997. Unemployment and nonemployment. *AEA Paper and Proceedings.* May.

Murphy, W.M., and D.J. Bruckner, eds. 1976. *The idea of the University of Chicago: Selections from the papers of the first eight executives of the University of Chicago from 1891 to 1975.* Chicago: University of Chicago Press.

Musgrave, R.A. 1992. Social science, ethics, and the role of the public sector. In Szenberg, 1992

Mussa, M.L. 1974. A monetary approach to the balance of payments. *Journal of Money, Credit and Banking*. August.

——. 1982. A model of exchange rate dynamics. *Journal of Political Economy*. February.

——. 1991. *Exchange rate in theory and reality*. Princeton Essays in International Finance. Princeton, NJ: Princeton University Press.

——. 1993. Making the practical case for freer trade. *AEA Papers and Proceedings*. May.

Nef, J. 1932. *The rise of the British coal industry*. London: Routledge & Sons.

——. 1967. James Laurence Laughlin. *Journal of Political Economy*. February.

——. 1973. *Searching for meaning: An autobiography of a nonconformist*. Washington, D.C.: Public Affairs Press.

Nelson, P. 1974. Advertising as information. *Journal of Political Economy*. August.

Nelson, R.H. 2001. *Economics as religion: From Samuelson to Chicago and beyond*. University Park: Pennsylvania State University Press.

Nerlove, M. 1958a. Adaptive expectations and cobweb phenomena. *Quarterly Journal of Economics*. May.

——. 1958b, *The dynamics of supply: Estimation of farmers' response to price*. Baltimore, MD: The Johns Hopkins University Press.

——. 1999. Transforming economics: Theodore W. Schultz, 1902-1998. In memoriam. *Economic Journal*. November.

Newman, P., ed. 1998. *The new Palgrave dictionary of economics and the law*. London: Macmillan.

Niehans, J. 1990. *A history of economic theory*. Baltimore, MD: Johns Hopkins University Press.

Niman, N. 1998. Marshall, Veblen, and the search for an evolutionary economics. In Rutherford 1998.

Niskanen, W. 1971. *Bureaucracy and representative government*. Chicago: Aldine.

Noll, R.,1989. Economic perspectives on the politics of regulation. In *Handbook of Industrial Organization*, ed. R. Schmalensee and R. Willig. Amsterdam, New Holland, 1254.

Okun, A. 1975. *Equality and efficiency: The big tradeoff*. Washington, DC: Brookings Institution.

Olson, M. 1965. *The logic of collective action*. Cambridge, MA: Harvard University Press.

Pashigian, P. 1985. Environmental regulation: Whose self-interests are being protected? *Economic Inquiry* October.

——. 1987. Cobweb theorem. In *The New Palgrave: A Dictionary of Economics*, eds. J. Eatwell, M. Milgate, and P. Newman. London: Macmillan.

——. 1995. *Price theory and applications*. New York: McGraw-Hill.

Patinkin, D. 1973. Frank Knight as a teacher. *American Economic Review*. December.

——. 1981. *Essays on and in the Chicago tradition*. Durham, NC: Duke University Press.

Pearson, H. 1997. *Origins of law and economics*. Cambridge: Cambridge University Press.

Peltzman, S. 1965. Entry in commercial banking. *Journal of Law and Economics*. October.

——. 1971. Pricing in public and private enterprises. *Journal of Law and Economics*. April.

——. 1973. An evaluation of consumer protection legislation: The 1962 drug amendments. *Journal of Political Economy*. October.

——. 1975. The effects of auto safety regulation. *Journal of Political Economy*. July/August.

——. 1981. The effect of FTC advertising regulation. *Journal of Law and Economics*. December.

——. 1987. Regulation and health: The case of mandatory prescriptions and an extension. *Managerial and Decision Economics*. March.

——. 1989. The economic theory of regulation after a decade of deregulation. *The Brookings Paper on Economic Activity, Microeconomics*.

Pelzman, S. 1991. The handbook of industrial organization: A review article. *Journal of Political Economy*. February.

————. 1993a. The political economy of the decline of American public education. *Journal of Law and Economics.* October.

————. 1993b. Political factors in public school debate. *The American Enterprise.* July.

————. 1998. *Political Participation and Government Regulation.* Chicago: The University of Chicago Press.

————. 2000. Prices rise faster than they fall. *Journal of Political Economy.* June.

Persson, T., ed. 1997. *Nobel lectures economic sciences: 1991-1995.* London: World Scientific.

Peterson, R., and R.J. Phillips. 1991. Lloyd Mints, 1888-1989: Pioneer monetary economist. *The American Economist.* Spring.

Phelps, E. 1967. Phillips curves, expectations of inflation and optimal employment over time. *Economica.* August.

————. 1990. *Seven Schools of macroeconomic thought.* Oxford: Clarendon Press,

Phillips, A.W. 1958. The relation between unemployment and the rate of change of money wage rates in the United Kingdom, 1861-1957. *Economica.* August.

Phillips, R.J. 1995. *The Chicago plan & New Deal banking reform.* New York: M.E. Sharpe.

Philipson, T., and J. Cawley. 1999. An empirical examination of information barriers to trade in insurance. *American Economic Review.* September.

Picker, R. 1993. Law and economics: Intellectual arbitrage. *Loyola Law Review.* November.

Pierson, F.C. 1959. *The education of American businessmen: A study of university-college programs in business administration.* New York: McGraw-Hill.

Pinera, J. 1994. Chile. In *The political economy of policy reform,* ed. J. Williamson. Washington, DC: Institute for International Economics.

Plant, A. 1934. The economic theory concerning patents for inventions. *Economica.* 1, 30.

Posner, E. 2000. *Law and social norms.* Cambridge, MA: Harvard University Press.

Posner, R.A. 1971. Taxation by regulation. *Bell Journal of Economics and Management Science.* Spring.

————. 1972. The appropriate scope of regulation in the cable television industry. *Bell Journal of Economics and Management Science.* Spring.

————. 1974. Theories of economic regulation. *Bell Journal of Economics and Management Science.* Autumn.

————. 1981. *The economics of justice.* Cambridge, MA: Harvard University Press.

————. 1992, *Economic analysis of law,* 4th ed. Boston: Little, Brown & Co.

————. 1993. Nobel Laureate: Ronald Coase and methodology. *Journal of Economic Perspective.* Fall.

————. 1994. *Overcoming law.* Cambridge, MA: Harvard University Press.

————. 1995. *Aging and old age.* Chicago: University of Chicago Press.

————. 1996. *Law and legal theory in the UK and USA.* Oxford: Clarendon Press.

————. 1997a. Community, wealth, and equality. Working paper 44. John M. Olin Program in Law & Economics, University of Chicago Law Faculty.

————. 1997b. Social norms and the law: An economic approach. *AEA Papers and Proceedings.* May.

————. 1998. Values and consequences: The introduction to economic analysis of law. Working paper 53. John M. Ohlin Program in Law & Economics.

————. 2001a. *Antitrust.* Chicago: University of Chicago Press.

————. 2001b. *Public intellectuals: A study in decline.* Cambridge, MA: Harvard University Press.

Posner, R., and C. Meyer. 1971. *Market transfers of water rights: Toward an improved market in water resources.* Washington, DC: National Water Commission.

Posner, R.A., and T. Philipson. 1993. *Private choices and public health: The AIDS epidemic in an economic perspective.* Cambridge, MA: Harvard University Press.

————. 1996. The economic epidemology of crime. *Journal of Law and Economics.* October.

Prebisch, R. 1959. Commercial policy in underdeveloped countries. *AEA Papers and Proceedings*. May.

Prescott, E. 1997. Theory ahead of business cycle measurement. In Snowdon and Vane, 1997.

Rajan, R., and L. Zingales. 2003. *Saving capitalism from the capitalists*. New York: Random House.

Reder, M.W. 1982. Chicago economics: Permanence and change. *Journal of Economic Literature*. March.

Rees, A. 1951. Wage Determination and involuntary unemployment. *Journal of Political Economy*. April.

———. 1953. The wage-price relations in the basic steel industry, 1945-48. *Industrial and Labor Relations Review*. January.

———. 1959. Do unions cause inflation? *Journal of Law and Economics*. October.

———. 1962. *The economics of trade unions*. Chicago: University of Chicago Press.

———. 1976. H. Gregg Lewis and the development of analytical labor economics. *Journal of Political Economy*. August (part II).

———. 1979. Douglas on wages and the supply of labor. *Journal of Political Economy*. October.

Rees, A., and M. Hamilton. 1963. Postwar movements of wage levels and unit labor costs. *Journal of Law and Economics*. October.

Reich, R. 1991. *The work of nations: preparing ourselves for 21st century capitalism*, New York: A.A. Knopf.

Reid, M. 1934. *Economics of household production*. New York: John Wiley & Sons.

———. 1943. *Food for people*. New York: John Wiley & Sons.

———. 1947. The economic contribution of homemakers. *Annals of the American Academy of Political and Social Science*. CCLI.

———. 1952. Effect of income concepts upon expenditure curves of farm families. National Bureau of Economic Research, Conference of Research in Income and Wealth. Cambridge, MA: Cambridge Press.

———. 1953. Savings by family units in consecutive periods. In *Savings in the modern economy*, ed. W.W. Heller, Minneapolis.

———. 1962. *Housing and income*. Chicago: University of Chicago Press.

Renshaw, E. 1958. Utility regulation: A re-examination. *The Journal of Business*. October.

Robbins, L. 1962. *The nature and significance of economic science*. London: Macmillan.

Roberts, H.V. 1959. Stock market "patterns" and financial analysis: Methodological suggestions. *Journal of Finance*. March.

Rockefeller, J.D. 1909. *Random reminiscences of men and events*. New York: Doubleday, Page & Co.

Rodriguez, C., and J. Frenkel. 1975. Portfolio equilibrium and the balance of payments: A monetary approach. *American Economic Review*. September.

Rogoff, K. 2001. Dornbusch's overshooting model after 25 years. *IMF Staff Papers*. No. 49 (special issue): 1.

Romer, P. 1986. Increasing returns and long-run growth. *Journal of Political Economy*. October.

Rosen, S. 1968. Short-run employment variations in class I railroads in the US, 1947-64. *Econometrica*. 36.

———. 1970. Trade unionism and the occupational wage structure in the US. *International Economic Review*. June.

———. 1972. Learning and experience in the labor market. *Journal of Human Resources*. Summer.

———. 1974. Hedonic prices and implicit markets: Product differentiation in pure competition. *Journal of Political Economy*. January/February.

———. 1981. The economics of superstars. *American Economic Review*. December.

————. 1983a. Specialization and human capital. *Journal of Labor Economics.* January.

————. 1983b. The economics of superstars. *The American Scholar.* Autumn.

————. 1988. Transaction costs and internal labor markets. *Journal of Economics, Law, and Organization.* Spring.

————. 1992. The market for lawyers. *Journal of Law and Economics.* October.

————. 1993. Risks and rewards: Gary Becker's contributions to economics. *Scandinavian Journal of Economics.* No. 1.

————. 1996. Public employment and the welfare state in Sweden. *Journal of Economic Literature.* June.

Rosen, S., and R. Thaler. 1976. The value of saving a life: Evidence from the labor market. In *Household Production and Consumption,* ed. N. Terleckyj. New York: Columbia University Press.

Rosett, C. 1984. Looking back on Chile, 1973-83. *National Review.* June.

Rossi, P.E. 1989. The ET interview: Professor Arnold Zellner. *Econometric Theory.* No. 5.

Rotwein, E. 1959. On the methodology of positive economics. *Quarterly Journal of Economics.* November.

————. 1983. Jacob Viner and the Chicago Tradition. *History of Political Economy.* Summer.

Rutherford, M., ed. 1998. *The Economic Mind in America. Essays in the History of American Economics.* London: Routledge.

Samuels, W.J., ed. 1993. *The Chicago School of Political Economy.* New Brunswick, NJ: Transaction Publishers.

————. 1993. Law and economics: Some early journal contributions. In *Economic Thought and Discourse in the Twentieth Century,* eds. W.J. Samuels, J. Biddle, and T. Patchak-Schuster. Aldershot, UK: Edward Elgar Publishing.

Samuelson, P. 1963. Problems of methodology: Discussion. *AEA Papers and Proceedings.* May.

————. 1965. Proof that properly anticipated prices fluctuate randomly. *Industrial Management Review.* Spring.

————. 1970. Reflections on recent Federal Reserve policy. *Journal of Money, Credit and Banking.* February.

————. 1972. Jacob Viner, 1892-1970. *Journal of Political Economy.* January.

————. 1976. An economist's non-linear model of self-generated fertility waves. *Population Studies.* No. 30.

————. 1979. Paul Douglas's measurement of production functions and marginal productivities. *Journal of Political Economy.* October.

————. 1991. Jacob Viner. In Shils 1991, 533-547.

Samuelson, P.A., and R. Solow. 1960. Analytical aspects of anti-inflation policy. *American Economic Review.* March.

Sandmo, A. 1993. Gary Becker's contributions to economics. *Scandinavian Journal of Economics.* No. 1.

Savage, L.J. 1954. *The foundations of statistics.* New York: John Wiley and Sons.

Scharfstein, D. 1994. Anatomy of financial distress: An examination of junk-bond issuers. *Quarterly Journal of Economics.* August.

Scheinkman, J., and B. LeBaron. 1989. Nonlinear dynamics and stock returns. *Journal of Business.* July.

Schiller, R. 1984. Stock prices and social dynamics. *Brookings Papers on Economics Activity.* No. 2.

Scholes, M.S. 1996. Financial infrastructure and economic growth. In *The Mosaic of Economic Growth,* eds. R. Landau, T. Taylor, and G. Wright. Stanford, Stanford University Press.

————. 1998. Derivatives in a dynamic environment. *American Economic Review.* June.

Schultz, H. 1925. The statistical law of demand as illustrated by the demand for sugar. *Journal of Political Economy.* October.

———. 1927. Mathematical economics and the quantitative method. *Journal of Political Economy.* October.

———. 1938. *The theory and measurement of demand.* Chicago: The University of Chicago Press.

Schultz, T.W. 1943. *Redirecting farm policy.* New York: Macmillan.

———. 1959a. Investment in man: An economist's view. *The Social Service Review.* June.

———. 1959b, Human wealth and economic growth. *The Humanist.* No. 2.

———. 1961. Investment in human capital. *American Economic Review.* March.

———. 1964. *Transforming traditional agriculture.* New Haven, CT: Yale University Press.

———. 1979. The economics of being poor. *Nobel Lecture Journal of Political Economy.* December.

———. 1993. *Origins of increasing returns.* Oxford: Blackwell Publishers.

Schumpeter, J. 1942. *Capitalism, socialism, and democracy.* New York: Harper.

Schwab, S. 1989. Coase defends Coase: Why lawyers listen and economists do not. *Michigan Law Review.* May.

Schwartz, A. 1981. Understanding. In Brunner 1981.

Sent, E.-M. 2002, How (not) to influence people: The contrary tale of John F. Muth. *History of Political Economy.* Summer.

Shapiro, F. 2000. The most cited legal scholars. *Journal of Legal Studies.* January.

Sharpe, W. 1963. A simplified model for portfolio analysis. *Management Science.* January.

———. 1970. *Portfolio theory and capital markets.* New York: McGraw-Hill.

Shils, E., ed. 1991a. *Remembering the University of Chicago: Teachers, scientists and scholars.* Chicago: University of Chicago Press.

———. 1991b. Robert Maynard Hutchins. In Shils 1991.

———. 1997. *Portraits: A gallery of intellectuals.* Chicago: University of Chicago Press.

Shleifer, A., and R. Vishny. 1986a. Greenmail, white knights, and shareholders' interest. *Rand Journal of Economics.* Autumn.

———. 1986b. Large shareholders and corporate control. *Journal of Political Economy.* June.

———. 1997. The Limits of Arbitrage. *Journal of Finance.* March.

———. 1998. *The Grabbing Hand: Government Pathologies and Their Cures.* Cambridge, MA: Harvard University Press.

Shultz, G.P. 1963. *The Challenge of Unemployment.* New York: U.S. Chambers of Commerce.

———. 1993. *Turmoil and triumph.* New York: Charles Scribner's Sons.

Shultz, G.P., and K. Dam. 1977. *Economic policy beyond the headlines.* New York: W.W. Norton, 1998.

Sidrauski, M. 1967. Rational choice and patterns of growth in a monetary economy. *AEA Papers and Proceedings.* May.

Silk, L. 1976. *The economists.* New York: Basic Books.

Simon, H. 1956. *Models of man.* New York: John Wiley and Sons.

———. 1996. *Models of my life.* New York: Basic Books.

Simons, H.C. 1934. *A positive program for laissez-faire: Some proposals for a liberal economic policy.* Public Policy Pamphlet No. 15. Chicago: Chicago University Press.

———. 1936a. Keynes comments on money. *The Christian Century.* July 2.

———. 1936b. Rules versus authorities in monetary policy. *Journal of Political Economy.* February.

———. 1938. *Personal income taxation.* Chicago, University of Chicago Press.

———. 1942. Hansen on fiscal policy. *Journal of Political Economy.* April.

———. 1944. Some reflections on syndicalism. *Journal of Political Economy.* March.

———. 1945. The Beveridge Report: An unsympathetic interpretation. *Journal of Political Economy.* September.

Sjaastad, L. 1962. Costs and returns of human capital. *Journal of Political Economy.* October.

———. 1966. Argentina and the five-year plan. In Wall 1972.

———. 1979. Some notes on the recent balance of payments experience in Latin America. Proceedings of the IVth Annual Paris/Dauphine Conference, Zeitschrift für Wirtschafts- und Sozialwissenschaften.

———. 1983. What went wrong in Chile. *National Review.* September.

———. 1991. The World Bank: Time for reform? In *Capital flows in the world economy,* ed. H. Siebert. Tübingen, Germany: Mohr (Siebeck).

———. 1998. On exchange rates, nominal and real. *Journal of International Money and Finance* June.

Sjaastad, L., and K. Clements. 1984. *How protection taxes exporters.* Thames Essay. London: Trade Policy Research Center.

Skaggs, N.T. 1995 The methodological roots of J. Laurence Laughlin's anti-quantity theory of money prices. *Journal of the History of Economic Thought.* Spring.

Smith, A. 1776. *An inquiry into the nature and causes of the wealth of nations.* Reprint edited by Edwin Cannan. Chicago: University of Chicago Press, 1976.

Smith, J., and F. Welch. 1989. Black economic progress after Myrdal. *Journal of Economic Literature.* June.

Snowdon, B., and H. Vane. 1997. *A macroeconomic reader.* London: Routledge.

Solomon, E. 1948. Are formula plans what they seem to be? *Journal of Business.* April.

———. 1955. Measuring a company's cost of capital. *Journal of Business.* October.

———. 1963. *The theory of financial management.* New York: Columbia University Press.

Spence, M. 1974. *Market signaling,* Cambridge, MA: Harvard University Press.

Spiegel, H.W. 1971. *The growth of economic thought.* Englewood Cliffs, NJ: Prentice-Hall.

Sraffia, P. 1926. The laws of returns under competitive conditions. *Economic Journal.* December.

Stern, N. 1978. On the economic theory of policy towards Crime. In *Economic models of criminal behavior,* ed. J.M. Heineke Amsterdam: North-Holland.

Stigler, G. 1940. *Production and distribution theories.* New York: Macmillan.

———. 1946. The economics of minimum wage legislation. In *The essence of Stigler,* edited by K. Loebe and T. Moore, Stanford, CA: Hoover Institution Press, 1986.

———. 1952. The case against big business. *Fortune.* May.

———. 1958. Ricardo and the 93% labor theory of value. *American Economic Review.* June.

———. 1962. Comment. *Journal of Political Economy.* February.

———. 1963. The government and the economy. *A dialogue on the proper economic role of the state.* Selected paper. No. 7, Graduate School of Business, University of Chicago.

———. 1965. *Essays in the history of economics.* Chicago: University of Chicago Press.

———. 1968. *The organization of industry.* Homewood, IL: Irwin.

———. 1970. Director's law of public income redistribution. *The Journal of Law and Economics.* April.

———. 1975. *The citizen and the state.* Chicago, IL: University of Chicago Press.

———. 1976. The xistence of x-efficiency. *American Economic Review.* March.

———. 1981. Economics or ethics. In *The Essence of Stigler,* edited by K. Loebe and T. Moore, Stanford, CA: Hoover Institution Press, 1986.

———. 1982a. The economists and the problem of monopoly, as reprinted as Occasional Paper. No. 10, University of Chicago.

———. 1982b. *The economist as preacher, and other essays.* Chicago: University of Chicago Press.

———. 1985. John Kenneth Galbraith's Marathon television series: A certain Galbraith in an uncertain age. In *The Essence of Stigler,* edited by K. Loebe and T. Moore, Stanford, CA: Hoover Institution Press, 1986.

———. 1987. *The Theory of Price.* New York: Macmillan.

————. ed. 1988a. *Chicago studies in political economy.* Chicago: The University of Chicago Press.

————. 1988b. *Memoirs of an unregulated economist.* New York: Basic Books.

————. 1989. Two notes on the Coase Theorem. *Yale Law & Policy Journal.* December.

————. 1992. Law or Economics? *The Journal of Law and Economics.* October.

Stigler, G., and C. Friedland. 1962. What can regulators regulate? The case of electricity. *Journal of Law and Economics.* October.

————. 1983. The literature of economics: The case of Berle and Means. *Journal of Law and Economics.* June.

Stigler, G., and J. Kindahl. 1970. *The Behavior of Industrial Prices.* New York: Columbia University Press.

————. 1973. Industrial prices as administered by Dr. Means. *American Economic Review.* September.

Stiglitz, J. 1973. The theory of "screening," education, and the distribution of income. Discussion Paper No. 354. New Haven: CT: Yale University, Cowles Foundation.

Stokey, N. 1988. Learning by doing and the introduction of new goods. *Journal of Political Economy.* August.

————. 1991. The volume and composition of trade between rich and poor countries. *Review of Economic Studies.* January.

Storr, R.J. 1966. *Harper's university: The beginnings.* Chicago: University of Chicago Press.

Street, D. 1988. Jovellanos, an antecedent to modern human capital theory. *History of Political Economy.* Summer.

Streeten, R.E. 1991. *One in spirit: A retrospective view of the University of Chicago on the occasion of its centennial.* Chicago: University of Chicago.

Summers, L. 1986. Does the stock market rationally reflect fundamental values. *Journal of Finance.* No.41.

Sumner, D.A. 1996. Agricultural economics at Chicago. In Antle and Shils 1996.

Sunstein, C. 1997. *Free markets and social justice.* New York: Oxford University Press.

————. ed. 2000. *Behavioral Law & Economics.* Cambridge: Cambridge University Press.

Swedberg, R, 1990. *Economics and sociology,* Princeton, NJ: Princeton University Press.

Sykes, A. 1989. Countervailing duty law: An economic perspective. *Columbia Law Review.* March.

————. 1991. Protectionism as a "safeguard": A positive analysis of the GATT "escape clause" with normative speculations. *The University of Chicago Law Review.* Winter.

————. 1992. The welfare economics of immigration law: A theoretical survey with an analysis of U.S. policy. Working paper 10, Law and Economics, University of Chicago Law Faculty.

————. 1999. Regulatory protectionism and the law of international trade. *The University of Chicago Law Review.* Winter.

————. 2002. New directions in law and economics. *The American Economist.* Spring.

Szenberg, M., ed. 1992. *Eminent economists: Their life philosophies.* Cambridge, MA: Cambridge University Press.

Taussig, F. 1920. *Free trade, the tariff, and reciprocity.* New York: Macmillan.

Tavlas, G.S. 1997. Chicago, Harvard, and the doctrinal foundations of monetary economics. *Journal of Political Economy.* February.

Telser, L. 1960. Why should manufacturers want fair trade? *Journal of Law and Economics.* October.

————. 1962. Advertising and cigarettes. *Journal of Political Economy.* October.

————. 1964. Advertising and competition. *Journal of Political Economy.* December.

————. 1966. Demand and supply of advertising messages. *AEA Papers and Proceedings.* May.

————. 1969a. Another look at advertising and concentration. *Journal of Industrial Economics.* No.18.

————. 1969b. On the regulation of industry: A note. *Journal of Political Economy.* November/ December.

————. 1972. *Competition, Collusion, and Game Theory.* Chicago: Aldine.

————. 1978. *Economic Theory and the Core.* Chicago: University of Chicago Press.

————. 1981. Why there are organized future markets. *Journal of Law and Economics.* April.

————. 1994. The usefulness of core theory in economics. *Journal of Economic Perspectives.* Spring.

————. 1996. Competition and the core. *Journal of Political Economy.* February.

Temin, P. 1976. *Did monetary forces cause the Great Depression?* New York: Norton.

————. 1989. *Lessons from the Great Depression.* Cambridge, MA: MIT Press.

Thaler, R. 1991. *Quasi rational economics.* New York: Russell Sage Foundation.

————. 1992. *The Winner's Curse.* Princeton, NJ: Princeton University Press.

————. ed. 1993. *Advances in Behavioral Finance.* New York: Russell Sage Foundation.

Theil, H. 1958. *Applied economic forecasting.* Amsterdam: New Holland.

————. 1971. *Principles of econometrics.* New York: John Wiley and Sons.

Theil, H., and C. Leenders. 1965. Tomorrow on the Amsterdam Stock Exchange. *Journal of Business.* July.

Theil, H., and A. Zellner. 1962. Three stages least squares: Simultaneous estimation of simultaneous equations. *Econometrica.* Vol. 30.

Theiss, E. 1932. Time and capitalistic production. *Journal of Political Economy.* August.

Thorp, W. 1971. *The reality of foreign aid.* New York: Praeger.

Tilman, R. 1987. Grace Jaffe and Richard Ely on Thorstein Veblen: An unknown chapter in American economic thought. *History of Political Economy.* Spring.

————. 1992. Thorstein Veblen. In *A Bibliographic Dictionary of Dissenting Economists.* Ed. P. Arestis and R. Ecklund, Aldershot, England: Edward Elgar Publishing.

————. 1998. John Dewey as user and critic of Thorstein Veblen's ideas. *Journal of the History of Economic Thought.* June.

Tinbergen, J. 1937. *An econometric approach to business cycle problems.* Paris: Hermann.

Tobin, J. 1978. *Harry Gordon Johnson, 1923-1977.* Proceedings of the British Academy, vol. LXIV. London: Oxford University Press.

Tolley, G. 1957. Providing for growth of the money supply. *Journal of Political Economy.* December.

Tolley, G., V. Thomas, and C. Wong. 1982. *Agricultural price policies and the developing countries.* Baltimore, MD: Johns Hopkins University.

Tommasi, M., and K. Ierulli, eds. 1995. *The New Economics of Human Behavior.* Cambridge: Cambridge University Press.

Topel, R.H. 1983. On layoffs and unemployment insurance. *American Economic Review.* September.

————. 1991. Specific capital, mobility, and wages: wages rise with job seniority. *Journal of Political Economy.* February.

Topel, R.H. 1997. Factor proportions and relative wages: The supply-side determinants of wage inequality. *Journal of Economic Perspectives.* Spring.

Topel, R., and M. Ward. 1992. Job mobility and the careers of young men. *Quarterly Journal of Economics.* May.

Tullock, G., 1983. *The Simons' Syllabus.* Fairfax, VA: George Mason University, Center for the Study of Public Choice.

Turner, R. 1958. *A History of the School of Business of the University of Chicago.* Chicago: Regenstein Library.

Valdes, J.G. 1995. *Pinochet's Economists: The Chicago School in Chile.* Cambridge: Cambridge University Press.

Veblen, T. 1899a. Preconceptions of economic science. *Quarterly Journal of Economics.* January.

———. 1899b. *The theory of the leisure class.* New York: Macmillan, 1953.

———. 1904. *The theory of business enterprise.* New York: Charles Scribner's Sons.

———. 1909. The limitations of marginal utility. *Journal of Political Economy.* November.

———. 1918. *The Higher Learning in America.* New York: Sagamore Press.

———. 1919. *The place of science in modern civilization and other essays.* New York: Russell & Russell, 1961.

Viner, J. 1923. *Dumping: A problem in international trade.* Chicago: University of Chicago Press.

———. 1924. *Canada's balance of international indebtedness: 1900-1913.* Cambridge, MA: Harvard University Press.

———. 1925a. Objective tests of competitive price applied to the cement industry. *Journal of Political Economy.* February.

———. 1925b. The utility concept in value theory and its critics. *Journal of Political Economy.* August.

———. 1927. Adam Smith and laissez faire. *Journal of Political Economy.* April.

———. 1931. Problems of international commercial and financial policy. In *Report of the round tables and general conferences at the eleventh session,* ed. A.H. Buffington. Williamstown: Institute of Politics.

———. 1932. The doctrine of comparative care. *Weltwirtschaftliches Archiv.* 36 (2).

———. 1933a. *Balanced deflation, inflation or more depression.* Day and Hour Series of the University of Minnesota, No. 2. Minneapolis: University of Minneapolis Press.

———. 1933b. Inflation as a possible remedy for the depression. In *Proceedings of the Institute of Public Affairs.* Atlanta: University of Georgia.

———. 1936. Mr. Keynes and the causes of unemployment. *The Quarterly Journal of Economics.* November.

———. 1937. *Studies in the theory of international trade.* New York: Harper.

———. 1943. Two plans for international monetary stabilization. *The Yale Review.* Autumn.

———. 1950. *The customs union issue.* New York: The Carnegie Endowment.

———. 1951. *International economics.* Glencoe, IL: The Free Press.

———. 1952. *International trade and economic development.* Glencoe, IL: The Free Press.

———. 1958. *The long and the short view.* Glencoe, IL: The Free Press.

———. 1964. Comment on my 1936 review of Keynes' *General Theory.* In *Keynes' General Theory. Reports of Three Decades,* ed. R. Lekachman. New York: MacMillan & Co.

———. 1991. *Essays on the intellectual history of economics,* ed. D.A. Irwin. Princeton, NJ: Princeton University Press.

Viner, J., et al. 1933. *Balancing the budget: Federal fiscal policy during the depression.* Public Policy Pamphlets No. 1. Chicago: University of Chicago Press.

Wali, K.C. 1991. *Chandra: A biography of S. Chandrasekhar.* Chicago: University of Chicago Press.

Wall, D., ed. 1972. *Chicago Essays in Economic Development.* Chicago: University of Chicago Press

Wallis, W.A. 1958. The functions and goals of business education and schools of business. Indiana Academy of Social Sciences. Archives of the Communications Department, University of Chicago.

———. 1980. The Statistical Research Group. *Journal of the American Statistical Association.* June.

———. 1993. George J. Stigler: In memoriam. *Journal of Political Economy.* October.

Warsh, D. 1993. *Economic principals: Masters and mavericks of modern economics.* New York: The Free Press.

Whitehead, A.N. 1954. *Dialogues of Alfred North Whitehead.* Recorded by Lucien Price. Boston: Little, Brown.

Williamson, O. 1983. Intellectual foundations of law and economics: the need for a broader view. *Journal of Legal Education*. 33.

Willis, H.P. 1896. The history and present application of the quantity theory. *Journal of Political Economy*. September.

Worcester, D. 1973. New estimates of the welfare loss to monopoly, United States: 1956-1969. *Southern Economic Journal*. October.

Wright, C.W. 1912. A trust problem — prevention or alleviation. *Journal of Political Economy*. June.

———. 1940. *An economic history of the United States*. New York: McGraw-Hill.

Yergin, D., and J. Stanislaw. 1998. *The commanding heights: The battle between government and the marketplace that is remaking the modern world*. New York: Simon and Schuster.

Yntema, T. 1928. The influence of dumping on monopoly price. *Journal of Political Economy*. December.

———. 1932. *A Mathematical Reformulation of the General Theory of International Trade*. Chicago: University of Chicago Press.

———. 1939. Henry Schultz: His contributions to economics and statistics. *Journal of Political Economy*. April.

———. 1941. The future role of large-scale enterprise. *Journal of Political Economy*. December.

———. 1944. Full employment in a private enterprise system. *AEA Papers and Proceedings*. March.

———. 1958. Transferable skills and abilities. *Journal of Business*. April.

———. 1964. The Enrichment of Man. Benjamin F. Fairless Memorial Lecture presented at the Carnegie Institute of Technology, Pittsburgh, PA.

Yoder, F. 1991. *The University of Chicago Faculty: A Centennial View*. The University of Chicago Library.

Young, A. 1913. Pigou's *Wealth and Welfare*. *Quarterly Journal of Economics*. August.

———. 1992. *A tale of two cities: Factor accumulation and technical change in Hong Kong and Singapore*. National Bureau of Economic Research, Macroeconomics Annual 1992. Cambridge, MA: MIT Press.

Zarnowitz, V. 1992. *Business cycles: Theory, history, indicators and forecasting*. Chicago: University of Chicago Press.

Zellner, A. 1997. *Bayesian analysis in econometrics and statistics: The Zellner view and papers*. Cheltenham, UK: Edward Elgar Publishing.

Zellner, A., and S. Fienberg. 1975. *Studies in Bayesian econometrics and statistics in honor of Leonard J. Savage*. Amsterdam: North-Holland.

# Notes

Introduction

1. For more on the Chicago critique of Chamberlin and monopolistic competition, see Stigler (1968) and "Monopolistic Competition in Retrospect" in Stigler (1949).

2. For more on this subject, see Hovenkamp (1986).

3. It should, however, be emphasized here that reference to the Chicago School did not become the norm in later standard books on the history of economic thought. The concept is not mentioned in such reference works as Blaug (1997) or Landreth and Colander (1989). Neither is it referred to in Greenaway, Bleaney, and Stewart (1996). It is only once referred to in a footnote in Niehans (1990).

4. Gaffney and Harrison (1994) describe Frank Knight as the man who "ruled the Chicago School for many years" (117).

5. An extreme version of the use of the Chicago School as a purely ideological product is found in Herman (1995).

6. See Friedman and Friedman (1998), especially chapter 24 and appendix A. For a more general statement about Friedman's position on the positive link between Chicago-style economics and political freedom, see Friedman (1962).

Chapter 1

7. See his 1960 paper "The Influence of Events and Policies on Economic Theory," in Stigler (1965).

8. See, for example, D.L. Kirp, *Shakespeare, Einstein, and the Bottom Line: The Marketing of Higher Education* (Cambridge, MA: Harvard University Press, 2003) especially chapter 2.

9. Joseph Dorfman referred to only one economist at the Old University of Chicago in his monumental *The Economic Mind in American Civilization*: Van Buren Denslow, who is described as an "outstanding protectionist journalist ... extremely skeptical of democratic rule and bitterly opposed to any government regulation of railroads, any check on the drift towards monopoly, any ameliorative labor legislation, and any relief to the unemployed" (1959, 75–76).

10. As University of Chicago President Lawrence Kimpton admitted in 1952, there was also an element of competition: "It must be confessed also that another motivation was to rival those heretical Methodists up in Evanston" (Murphy and Bruckner 1976, 44). Kimpton is of course referring to Northwestern University.

11. In 1907 Harper was succeeded as president of the University of Chicago by Harry P. Judson. After Harper, the "daring innovator" with respect to education, Judson, the "conservative and con-

structive builder" was probably the right man at the right time. Judson showed himself to be very skillful in stabilizing the University financially. (Ernest DeWitt Burton, quoted in Murphy and Bruckner 1976, 448).

12. See, for example, Barber (1988). Descriptions of the University of Chicago as the "Oil Trust University" and the "Standard Oil University" were circulating continuously. See Coats (1963).

13. The scientific seriousness of what economics is all about is also very much present in the graduate student body at the University of Chicago. See the survey results in Colander (1988).

14. For an analysis of the prewar period, see Bateman (1988) and Furner (1975).

15. Confirmed by Milton Friedman in an interview with the author on November 1, 1996. On this topic, see also Friedman (1953) (especially his essay "The Methodology of Positive Economics"), Friedman (1974), and Friedman (1976a). The importance attached to empirical verification in the social sciences has a long tradition at the University of Chicago.

16. Milton Friedman, interview by the author, November 1, 1996.

17. G. Stanley Hall, president of Clark University, complained bitterly that Harper's action "was like that of an eagle who robbed the fish-hawk of his prey" (Dorfman 1934, 91).

18. For more on this theme, see MacAloon (1992), especially chapter 1.

19. When Ed Levi was dean of the Law School, he proposed to give an honorary degree to the British queen, but the faculty flatly rejected the idea. See W. Mullen, "A Meeting of Minds," *Chicago Tribune,* September 29, 1985.

20. When asked what he would do first if appointed chairman of the Council of Economic Advisors, Chicago's Robert Lucas said: "I would resign" (Colander 1991, 29).

21. Robin Hogarth, interview by the author, February 17, 1996. Legendary in this respect is the case of astrophysicist Subrahmanyan Chandrasekhar, who drove several hundred miles each week to give a seminar to just two students on the Hyde Park campus. In the following decades Chandrasekhar and his students each received the Nobel Prize in Physics. See Wali (1991).

22. Although there were a lot of scholars with communist sympathies on the Chicago campus of the 1930s, certainly at the Department of Economics the suspicion of collectivist economic policies was still considerable. See for example, Gideonse (1935).

23. For the detailed story of the Cowles Commission at the University of Chicago, see Hildreth (1986).

24. For biographical notes on Marschak, see Arrow (1979).

25. Named after the French economist Leon Walras, who pioneered general equilibrium analysis.

26. The Cowles Commission moved to Yale in 1955, and not in 1953 as Reder states.

27. Milton Friedman, interview by the author, November 1, 1996.

28. In 1928, Max Mason declared: "The time is ripe to work intensively in the gaps that lie between the salients that have been established by the advance of knowledge in the special fields. After all, it is the problem that is of supreme importance; not the reputation of a department or of an individual scientific worker, but the problem as it relates to our understanding of the laws of nature and the behavior of man. As the different departments derive new knowledge, it will be found that in the gaps between departments lie many vital problems" (Murphy and Bruckner 1976, 100).

29. For more on this, see Stark (1999).

30. See also Nerlove (1999) and Emmett (1998).

31. Neumann as quoted in the *Chicago Tribune,* October 17, 1993.

32. See the remarkable analysis in Abu-Lughod (1999). Along similar lines, Chicago writer Stuart Dybek (1993) describes a specific, distinguishable Chicago Tradition in literature binding together such diverse authors as Theodore Dreiser, Studs Terkel, Mike Royko, and Saul Bellow.

33. As far the economists are concerned, George Stigler was a major exception to this rule.

34. Eli Shapiro, interview by the author, April 28, 2001.

35. Confirmed by Zvi Griliches in an interview by the author, Febraury 8, 1999.

36. Deirdre McCloskey, interview by the author, April 22, 2001.

37. The nonexhaustive list of "schools" at the University of Chicago is also taken from Friedman (1974).

Chapter 2

38. For more on the life and work of James L. Laughlin, see Bornemann (1940), Mitchell (1941), Dorfman (1959), and Nef (1967).

39. Laughlin retired from the University of Chicago in 1916. Jacob Viner was his last appointment.

40. For more on Laughlin's anti-quantity theory attitude, see also Skaggs (1995).

41. For more on Laughlin's role in the creation of the Federal Reserve System, see Bornemann (1940).

42. Among Laughlin's students, probably the one who most resembled him in terms of these personal characteristics was H. Parker Willis, who earned his bachelor's degree at the University of Chicago and stayed there until 1898. Willis had a successful career in academia and public life. For more on Willis, see Dorfman (1959, 4:314–22).

43. A list of issues on which Harper and Laughlin came into conflict can be found in Barber (1988, 422); see footnote 55.

44. For more information, see Coats (1963), Coats (1985), and Dorfman (1959, vol. III).

45. Laughlin was well aware of the fact that his original contributions to the development of economics were very limited. See Laughlin's correspondence as cited in Dorfman (1959, 3:274).

46. This point is made, for example, in Laughlin (1903). Laughlin himself was among the very first economists to make extensive use of charts.

47. The full story of this incident is told in Barber (1988, 249–55).

48. If Richard Ely had become the first head of the Department of Political Economy at the University of Chicago, it is very doubtful whether Thorstein Veblen would ever have had a position in that department. Grace Jaffe, the wife of William Jaffe, was Ely's assistant for a few years at Johns Hopkins and recalled later: "Ely hated Veblen from the bottom of his heart ... The real reason for Dr. Ely's opinion of Veblen ... [was that] ... he saw Veblen as a serious rival and, a victorious one at that, in the field of economics" (Tilman 1987, 143–44).

49. Walter Hamilton, who was at the University of Chicago in the years 1914–15, coined the term "institutionalism." See Hamilton (1919).

50. For more details on Veblen's life, see Dorfman (1934), Dorfman (1959, 3:434–47, 491–93), and Dorfman (1959, 4:352–60).

51. Typical examples are Veblen (1899b) and Veblen (1904).

52. There is some evidence that, with respect to conspicuous consumption, Veblen borrowed heavily from John Rae. See Edgell and Tilman (1991).

53. Some even argue that Veblen's work was "beyond economics and fell primarily in the realm of cultural anthropology." See Ault and Ekelund (1988, 431).

54. During his short stay at Johns Hopkins, Veblen had already met Dewey, who was also a student there at the time. For more on the interaction between Dewey and Veblen, see Tilman (1998).

55. Nevertheless, some argue that Veblen and Alfred Marshall, the founding father of neoclassical economics, stood closer to each other than is commonly assumed. See Niman (1998).

56. For more on the term "neoclassical," see Aspromourgos (1986). Veblen used the term "neoclassical" for the first time in Veblen (1899a).

57. In the essay "Why is economics not an evolutionary science?" Veblen referred to economics as the "dismal" science because it starts with the assumption that man is a "lightning calculator of pleasures and pains, who oscillates like a homogeneous global of desire and of happiness under the impulse of stimuli that shift him about the area but leave him intact" (Veblen 1919, 73).

58. Leon Marshall also played an important role in the development of the business school at the University of Chicago.

59. An extensive biography and bibliography of J.M. Clark can be found in Hickman (1975).

60. Between Columbia and Chicago an intensive two-way-traffic of scholars developed in the following decades. Major Chicago economists such as George Stigler and Gary Becker spent several years at Columbia University.

61. See Clark (1917) for more details. John M. Clark recognized the influence of Wesley Mitchell's business-cycle research on his own work. Clark's acceleration principle very much influenced Paul Douglas's thinking on the Great Depression.

62. This book led to an intense polemic between J.M. Clark and Frank Knight, who was at that time teaching at the University of Iowa, on the validity of the neoclassical theory of distribution. See the exchanges between Clark and Knight in the *Journal of Political Economy,* October 1925.

63. Wesley Mitchell's doctoral dissertation eventually became a classic: Mitchell (1903).

64. This work led Wesley Mitchell to cofound the National Bureau of Economic Research in 1920. The classic reference here is Mitchell (1913).

65. On Thorstein Veblen as a major source of inspiration for Wesley Mitchell, Homan remarked (1928, 428): "It is not a little curious that the most eminent of our economic workmen in the field of minute analysis of statistical data should be so heavily indebted to an impressionistic cosmic philosopher like Veblen, who heroically distorts facts and shows no evidence of commerce with figures."

66. This emphasis in his work makes Robert Hoxie clearly a forerunner of H. Gregg Lewis and the strong tradition at the University of Chicago in labor economics.

67. For Nef's autobiography, see Nef (1973).

68. Some argue that Frank Knight actually got kicked out of the philosophy PhD program at Cornell. See, for example, Johnson (1952).

69. *Chicago Tribune,* May 28, 1972.

70. Claire Friedland recalled that Frank Knight once even wrote "So?" in the margin of one of his own reprints. Interview by the author, October 28, 1997.

71. *Chicago Tribune,* May 28, 1972.

72. From a letter of Allen Wallis's published in the *New York Times,* June 25, 1972.

73. Rutherford, M., 2003, "Chicago Economics and Institutionalism", paper available on the website of Malcolm Rutherford at the University of Victoria, p.13 (draft of May 4, 2003).

74. Another early contributor to the analysis of uncertainty was Albert Hart, who earned a PhD at the University of Chicago in 1936. Hart spent 1932 to 1939 in Chicago as teaching assistant and instructor. In 1938 he moved to Iowa State College where Theodore W. Schultz was building a strong economics department. For Hart's contributions to the analysis of uncertainty, see Hart (1940) and Lange et al. (1942).

75. Debreu's opinion as communicated by Lester Telser, interview by the author, on March 12, 1997.

76. Price theory is the central issue in Chapters 3 and 4 of this book. On the basis of contributions such as Knight (1921) a case can be made that Knight should also be very much present in those chapters. As a matter of fact, Knight is often fiercely attacked by opponents of the Chicago School. For a rather extreme example of this, see the chapter on "The Chicago Poison" in Gaffney and Harrison (1994).

77. An excellent overview of the many papers Frank Knight wrote on the theory of capital and interest can be found in Cohen (1998).

78. See also the essay on "Interest" in Knight (1997).

79. An often neglected forerunner of Robinson's and Chamberlin's analyses is Piero Sraffa. See Sraffa (1926). Wilfried Parijs of the University of Antwerp drew my attention to Sraffa's role as forerunner.

80. Knight refers to Young's (1913) analysis in his paper.

81. James Heckman, interview by the author, October 29, 1996.

82. Sam Peltzman, interview by the author, March 6, 1998.

83. While hitchhiking through the country Director got into trouble with the police. Different stories circulate on the University of Chicago campus as to the reason, but the episode could not be verified with Director himself. At the time I began my research, Director was already 94 years old, and most of his friends at the University of Chicago advised against trying to interview him. Director died at the age of 102 on September 11, 2004.

84. Milton Friedman, interview by the author, November 1, 1996.

85. Aaron Director as quoted in a press release from the University of Chicago, March 31, 1951.

86. In 1950 Neil Jacoby, an economist at the University of Chicago, called for a vast increase in appropriations to the Antitrust Division of the Department of Justice and the Federal Trade Commission. See Jacoby (1950).

87. See, for example, Bowman (1952), Bork (1954, 1978); McGee (1958), and Telser (1960, 1964).

Chapter 3

88. A fundamental difference between the Chicago School and John Maynard Keynes has to do with the fact that Keynes claimed that neoclassical price theory was subsidiary to his theory of effective demand as developed in his General Theory. See Keynes (1936, 23–24 and 292–309).

89. Biographical data on Davenport are taken from Homan (1931) and Dorfman (1959, 3:375–89). Herbert Davenport brought Thorstein Veblen to the University of Missouri.

90. Knight attended Davenport's lectures when the latter was visiting Cornell University in 1916–17.

91. See the arguments in Davenport (1897) and Davenport (1914).

92. Arguing that it is difficult to find another candidate for the accolade "the greatest historian of economic thought," Peter Groenewegen writes that "the notable exception is Schumpeter, who at least matched Viner in his erudite knowledge of the subject in its various aspects. But Schumpeter's written contributions (perhaps partly because his major work on that subject was unfinished) never matched the accuracy, sensitivity of interpretation or historical finesse with which Viner presented his views." See Groenewegen (2003, 246).

93. As quoted in the *American Economic Review,* May 1963, 686.

94. For more on this last period of Viner's life, see Baumol (1972).

95. See Viner (1991). However, from correspondence between Frank Knight and Jacob Viner available in the University of Chicago Library, it is clear that both men were unhappy with the way in which Hutchins presided over the University. The more angry of the two seems to have been Knight. In a letter to Viner, dated October 13, 1934, he writes that Hutchins "will never be President on any other terms than being dictator or expecting to establish himself as such, and also that he really has no educational policy but flips from one utterance to another from an impossible naïve experimentalism to an equally naive absolute rationalism." But in her biography of Robert Hutchins, Dzuback (1991, 180,197) notes that Knight carried on with Hutchins "a persistent but friendly argument." Dzubeck suggests that Viner was the more aggressive.

96. The relationship between Viner and Keynes and their writings is closely examined in Davis (1971). Patinkin (1981) and Bloomfield (1992) also touch on this subject.

97. Knight's absence was certainly in accordance with his general attitude towards economists taking part in policy discussions. In a letter to Abe Harris of Howard University in Washington, Knight wrote: "I have become convinced that *one* thing absolutely necessary if economics is to play any part in affairs over any considerable period, is for some few people to keep their status as scientists, in other words, to keep absolutely aloof from current political controversy" (letter from Frank Knight to Abe Harris, dated June 30, 1934, The University of Chicago Communication Department).

98. For Keynes's counterarguments, see Keynes (1937). In this article Keynes reacted to

comments on his General Theory made by Frank Taussig, Wassily Leontief, Dennis Robertson, and Jacob Viner. Keynes describes Viner's comments as "the most important of the four comments" (210).

99. In 1944 Martin Jones, an economist from Chicago's business school, concluded that the inequalities between the propensity to save and the propensity to invest did not play a significant role in past economic fluctuations. See Jones (1944).

100. Viner's assessment of Keynes comes very close to Friedrich Hayek's. Hayek was Keynes's main opponent in England.

101. This was Lionel Robbins's description of Viner. See Hutchinson (1994, 260).

102. See the essay "The present position on the doctrine of free trade" in Taussig (1920).

103. For a detailed discussion of this issue, see Corden (1965).

104. Viner's views on cost were published in Viner (1932). Emmett (2002) contains Knight's reply to Viner's paper with comments by the latter.

105. For critical remarks on Viner's analysis, see Cairncross (1953).

106. Viner researched this topic in great detail for the cement industry. See Viner (1925a).

107. These remarks are taken from Stigler's farewell speech when Milton and Rose Friedman left Chicago for San Francisco. Stigler's speech is available in the files of the Communications Office of the University of Chicago.

108. Milton and Rose Friedman (1998, 357) quote from a letter they received from Paul Samuelson in December 1995: "I hope it will be said of us that, though we disagreed on much, we understood wherein our logical and empirical differences were based and that we were pretty good at preserving amiability, friendship and respect throughout."

109. Milton Friedman, interview by the author, November 1, 1996.

110. For more on this episode, see Wallis (1980).

111. A typical example is the essay "The Construction of Economic Knowledge" in Koopmans (1957). See also Rotwein (1959) and Samuelson (1963).

112. This was done in the context of two book reviews: Friedman (1940) and Friedman (1941). An excellent discussion of Friedman's methodology can be found in Hirsch and de Marchi (1990) and Hammond (1996).

113. Friedman, M. & Wallis, A., 1942, "The Empirical Derivation of Indifference Curves" in Lange, e.a., 1942.

114. According to Don Patinkin, Frank Knight and Jacob Viner had already made explicit reference to the Marshallian demand curve in their lectures at the University of Chicago (see Patinkin, 1981).

115. His dissertation was published as Schultz (1925).

116. Biographical notes on Henry Schultz are taken from Yntema (1939) and Heckman (1997).

117. An example of this is Schultz (1927).

118. As Milton Friedman acknowledges in the preface to the book, the largely empirical work done by his wife Rose, Dorothy Brady, and Margaret Reid also stimulated him in this project. He explicitly refers to the "original work" of "Mrs. Brady and Mrs. Reid" (Friedman 1957, ix). For more on the historical background of the permanent income hypothesis, see Chao (2003).

119. The first female recipient of a PhD in economics at the University of Chicago was Katherine Bement Davis, one of Thorstein Veblen's students, who earned her doctorate in 1900 with a dissertation on "Causes Affecting the Standard of Living and Wages." The second woman to earn a PhD in economics was Edith Abbott, who studied with Laughlin, Veblen, and Mitchell. Her 1905 dissertation was "A Statistical Study of the Wages of Unskilled Labor in the United States." For more general information on the history of women in economics, see Dimand, Dimand, and Forget (1996).

120. Mary Jean Bowman, interview by the author, March 11, 1997.

121. Ibid.

122. Claire Friedland, interview by the author, October 28, 1997. Friedland also pointed out that during the last ten years of her life Reid was working on two papers linking income, human capital and death rates. These papers remained unpublished. According to Friedland, the *Journal of Political Economy* refused them for being too long.

123. Quote from the *American Economic Review,* September 1980, opening page.

124. A third name that should be added here is Elisabeth Hoyt, a PhD from Harvard who worked her whole academic life at Iowa State College. She was a close friend of Hazel Kyrk and Margaret Reid.

125. For a good overall view of Kyrk's work, see Kyrk (1953).

126. Dorothy Brady is another woman who, mainly through empirical research, played an important role in the development of household and consumption economics. Although Brady never formally held a position at the University of Chicago, she was regularly around and was certainly not without influence on the research going on at the University of Chicago.

127. This is undoubtedly one of Friedman's most seminal papers.

128. Friedman and Friedman (1979) contains most of these points of view.

129. See also Friedman (1955).

130. See also Friedman (1967).

131. In the interviews the author conducted it was typical that economists who know the University of Chicago but are no longer there expressed much stronger opinions on this point than did economists still working at the University of Chicago.

132. Lester Telser, interview with the author, October 30, 1997.

133. According to Jim Lorie, George Shultz used to say that he wished he was as sure about one thing as Milton was about 100 things. Interview by the author, October 29, 1997.

Chapter 4

134. Milton Friedman, interview by the author, November 1, 1996.

135. Gary Becker, interview by the author, May 15, 1996.

136. D. Gale Johnson, interview by the author, May 16, 1996.

137. For more on these issues, see Schultz (1943) and Schultz (1964).

138. For the full story of this incident, see Harding (1955).

139. D. White, "Conversation with Theodore W. Schultz," text of an interview given on May 8 1985. Archives of the Communication Office of the University of Chicago.

140. Through this research T.W. Schultz became a pioneer in the relations between the University of Chicago and the *Universidad Catolica* in Chile.

141. See, for example, Johnson (1991) and Johnson (1997).

142. D. Gale Johnson, interview by the author, May 16, 1996.

143. See, for example, Johnson, D.G., 1998, "China's Rural and Agricultural Reforms in Perspective," mimeograph article (handed to the author in December 1998).

144. See, for example, Johnson (1958).

145. Zvi Griliches, interview with the author, February 8, 1999.

146. Confirmed with Zvi Griliches, interview with the author, February 8, 1999.

147. See, for example, Griliches (1961b).

148. See, for example, Griliches (1963).

149. See, for example, Griliches (1964).

150. Tolley's paper on the alternative ways in which a given growth rate in the quantity of money is achieved, has been largely forgotten. See Tolley (1957). Tolley is sure that this paper was a major source of inspiration for Milton Friedman (interview with the author, March 6, 1998).

151. See, for example, Tolley, Thomas, and Wong (1982).

152. For more about these theories, see Arrow (1973), Stiglitz (1973), and Spence (1974).

153. As a matter of fact, traces of human capital analysis go back a long way. Kiker (1966) refers to the 17th century economist Sir William Petty as an early contributor to human capital theory. Street (1988) gives a similar credit to the Spanish economist Gaspar Melchior de Jovellanos, who explicitly dealt with three major categories of investments in human capital: education, health, and migration. An excellent survey of the early literature on human capital literature is found in Kiker (1972).

154. See Friedman and Kuznets (1945) and H. Johnson (1960).

155. See Baumol and Becker (1952).

156. Almost 40 years later Becker declared: "Discrimination is the result of prejudice, and what I tried was to translate that concept into something measurable, i.e., how much is one willing to pay in order to be able to discriminate?" Interview by the author, May 15, 1996.

157. This point was already fully developed by T.W. Schultz (1961).

158. For an overview of this research, see Barro and Sala-I-Martin (1995).

159. See Marshall (1890), Arrow (1962), and Knight (1944).

160. See Becker (1981). In his 1987 presidential address to the AEA, Becker developed several links between family economics and the theory of economic growth. See Becker (1988).

161. Jeff Biddle explains the long time lag between Lewis's bachelor's degree and PhD by the war, by the fact that Lewis changed the subject of his dissertation in 1940, and by his "excessive perfectionism" (Biddle 1996, 174).

162. According to Jeff Biddle, the close relationship between H. Gregg Lewis and Henry Simons led to the initial focus on labor economics and unionism in particular. See Biddle (1996, 178–79). It is indeed undeniable that one of Lewis's major early papers was strongly influenced by Simons. See H.G. Lewis (1951).

163. The reference is, of course, to Simon Kuznets, Nobel Prize winner in 1971 and a legend in his own right for the meticulous attention he paid to data and empirical analysis.

164. Two present members of the faculty of the University of Chicago made this point explicitly. They insisted on anonymity.

165. Out of his doctoral work came articles such as Rees (1953).

166. For a survey of his earlier work on this topic, see Rees (1962).

167. See, for example, Rees (1959).

168. Sherwin Rosen, interview with the author, March 12, 1997.

169. See Rosen and Thaler (1976).

170. See, for example, Rosen (1970).

171. See, for example, Rosen (1972) and (1983a).

172. James Heckman, interview by the author, March 11, 1997.

173. Ibid.

174. Citation in the *American Economic Review*, May 1984, p.424.

175. Royal Swedish Academy of Sciences. Advanced information on the Bank of Sweden Prize in Economic Sciences in Memory of Alfred Nobel, 2000. The Scientific Contributions of James Heckman and Daniel McFadden. http://www.econ.umn.edu/graduate/nobel.pdf. This citation also gives a good overview of Heckman's contributions, which in general, are highly technical.

176. Heckman and Killingsworth (1987) gives a good survey. See also Heckman (1993).

177. For this claim see, for example, Smith and Welch (1989). The issue of the results of affirmative action opposed Heckman squarely to Richard Epstein of Chicago's Law School.

178. See, for example, Reich (1991).

179. In this context the name of Melvin Reder should also be mentioned. Reder, who was born in San Francisco in 1919, earned a master's degree in economics at the University of Chicago in 1941 and a PhD in economics at Columbia University five years later. He spent most of his career at Stanford University, but returned to Chicago in 1974 as a professor of urban and labor economics

at the GSB. In 1982 Reder published an article on aspects of the history of Chicago economics. See Reder (1982).

180. Becker was by no means the first Chicago economist to consider time explicitly as an economic factor. Frank Knight walked this route much earlier. Another interesting early contribution produced at the University of Chicago is Theiss (1932).

181. Gary Becker, interview by the author, May 15, 1996.

182. On Coleman's place in sociology, see Favell (1993).

183. See the interview with James Coleman in Swedberg (1990).

184. Daniel P. Moynihan in the New York Times Magazine, December 31, 1995.

185. Coleman et al., 1966.

186. Coleman, Kelly & Moore, 1975.

187. Coleman, Hoffner, Kilgore, 1982.

188. See, for example, the remarks made by Daniel P. Moynihan in the *New York Times Magazine*, December 31, 1995.

189. Gary Becker, interview by the author, October 28, 1997. Becker's attitude on this issue is very close to the one taken by Frank Knight.

190. In his *Business Week* columns Becker goes into specific policy matters quite often with crystal-clear ideas about and suggestions for policy. For a collection of these columns, see Becker and Becker (1997).

191. See, for example, Stern (1978).

192. See several contributions in Becker and Landes (1974).

193. Gary Becker, interview by the author, October 28, 1997.

194. For more on time preference, see Becker and Mulligan (1997).

195. AEA, 1998, Papers and Proceedings, May, p.494.

196. Gould & Lazear, 1986.

197. See, for example, Lazear, 1977, 1980, and 1983.

198. Kevin Murphy, interview with the author, May 17, 1996.

199. Ibid.

200. Topel, 1983. See also Topel & Welch, 1990.

201. See, for example, Topel, 1991.

202. Murphy, Shleifer & Vishny, 1991.

203. To be entirely correct, Shleifer graduated one year after Murphy and Vishny.

204. AEA Papers and Proceedings, May 2000, p.486.

205. Fershtman, Murphy & Weiss, 1996.

206. Interview with JVO on June 6, 2000.

207. Philipson, "Public Health and Economic Epidemiology" in Tommassi & Ierulli, eds., 1995, p.216. See also Philipson, T., "Economic Epidemiology and Infectious Disease" in Newhouse, J. & Culyer, T., eds., 2000, *Handbook of Health Economics*, New York, North Holland.

208. Posner is one of the pioneers of law and economics. See Chapter VIII.

209. Becker, Philipson & Soares, 2005.

210. Interview with JVO on March 11, 1998.

211. Ibid.

212. Levitt, S., 1998, "Juvenile Crime and Punishment", Journal of Political Economy, October.

213. Interview with JVO on March 11, 1998.

214. Interview with JVO on March 11, 1998. Together with Sala-i-Martin, Mulligan produced several interersting papers on monetary matters. See for example Mulligan, C. & Sala-i-Martin, X., 1992, "US Money Demand: Some Surprising Cross-sectional Estimates", Brookings Papers on Economic Activity, no.2.

215. Becker and Mulligan, 2003.

Chapter 5

216. For a good survey of the early contributions to quantity theory, see Hegeland (1951) and Blaug et al. (1995).

217. Fisher acknowledged that he got this equation from Simon Newcomb.

218. For the full story of this episode, see Friedman (1992).

219. This controversy over monetary policy led to passionate exchanges in which charges became highly personal. For example, Thomas Bryson, the editor of the newspaper *Farmer's Tribune* (Des Moines, Iowa), described, Laughlin as "the overzealous gold-bug teacher of the Oil Trust seat of economic ignorance" (Coats 1963, 489).

220. Although they do not seem to have had a major impact on subsequent monetary work at the University of Chicago, three of these books deserve to be mentioned here: *Principles of Money and Banking* (1916), *Commercial Banking and Capital Formation* (1918), and *Financial Organization of Society* (1921).

221. The detailed story of the Chicago Plan can be found in Phillips (1995).

222. See, for example, Mints (1945).

223. The Friedmans comment on the importance of Lloyd Mints in the development of monetary economics at the University of Chicago is in line with the conclusion reached by other researchers. See, for example, McIvor (1983).

224. See also Simons (1936b).

225. On other occasions, however, Viner showed himself more in favor of discretionary monetary policy. See, for example, Viner (1963).

226. The original paper, "The Chicago Tradition, the Quantity Theory, and Friedman," appeared in the February 1969 issue of the *Journal of Money, Credit, and Banking* and is reprinted in Patinkin (1981).

227. The Keynesian counterarguments are found in Ando and Modigliani (1965). The same issue of the *American Ecoonomic Review* contains Friedman and Meiselman's reply.

228. *Journal of Monetary Economics*, 1994, August. The page references in this paragraph are from this source.

229. Schwartz's role in her joint research efforts with Friedman has tended to be underestimated. On this topic see, for example, Bordo (1989).

230. This point is more fully developed in Hammond (1996).

231. Critics attacked the Friedman and Schwartz analysis for lacking sufficient underpinning not only on the level of economic theory, but also on the level of statistical theory. For this last aspect, see Hendry and Ericsson (1991) and the reply in Friedman and Schwartz (1991) For a full understanding of these discussions it is important to note the following sequence of events. In 1945 Wesley Mitchell and Arthur Burns published their empirical, nontheoretical work on business cycles (Mitchell and Burns 1945). This book was fiercely attacked by Tjalling Koopmans, who condemned it as "measurement without theory" (Koopmans 1947). Given the very close personal relationship between Burns and Friedman, and Friedman's huge respect for Mitchell, this incident is important for a full understanding of the personal animosity between Friedman and Koopman.

232. See Gordon (1974) for the discussion between Friedman and the Keynesians. James Tobin and Franco Modigliani were among the major exceptions among the Keynesians in the importance they attached to monetary factors.

233. Temin (1976) focused on the collapse of consumption expenditures. For Anna Schwartz's critique of Temin's analysis, see Schwartz (1981). In later work Temin emphasized the argument that the Great Depression must be seen as the ultimate result of World War I and the continuing conflicts after that war with the international monetary arrangement of that period (the gold standard) as the main mechanism in causing the economic collapse to spread internationally. See Temin (1989). This last argument of Temin's is somewhat in line with that of his MIT colleague Charles Kindleberger (1973), who presents a more international explanation of the Great Depression: that

it was, first and foremost the lack of international economic leadership that caused the widespread depression. For a modern look at the Great Depression, see Bernanke (2000).

234. For the more monetarist view of this attempt at reaching consensus, see Meltzer (1981). The more nonmonetary view can be found in Gordon and Wilcox (1981).

235. Cagan in Friedman, 1956.

236. Next he moved to Brown University and finally settled, from 1966 on, at Columbia University. Thus, Cagan was another example of the historically close links between Columbia University and the University of Chicago.

237. See, for example, Cagan (1965).

238. See, for example, Bailey (1957).

239. A summary of this dissertation can be found in Sidrauski (1967).

240. It should be noted here that already in 1933 James Angell of Columbia University had advocated constant monetary growth. See Angell (1933). This can be considered another example of the many links between Columbia and the University of Chicago.

241. This argument was fully developed in Friedman (1978).

242. DeLong's references were adjusted to match with the bibliography of this book.

243. As a matter of fact, Friedman said something more subtle than "we're all Keynesians now." In 1989 Friedman told the story as follows: "Some years ago, I remarked to a journalist from *Time* magazine 'We are all Keynesians now; no one is any longer a Keynesian.' In a regrettable journalistic fashion, *Time* quoted the first half of what I still believe to be the truth, omitting the second half. We all use many of the analytical details of the *General Theory* ... However, no one accepts the basic substantive conclusions of the book, no one regards ... its analytical core as providing a true 'general theory'" [Friedman, in the Economic Quarterly, Federal Reserve Bank of Richmond, Spring 1997, p.6].

244. Thomas Sargent, interview with the author, October 31, 1996.

245. Robert Lucas, interview with the author, October 30, 1996.

246. Ibid.

247. Muth, who holds a PhD in economics from the University of Chicago, wrote a seminal paper on rational expectations, "Rational Expectations and the Theory of Price Movements." This paper, and two of Muth's other papers on rational expectations, is included in Lucas and Sargent (1981). There is, however, earlier research than Muth's that touches on the theory of rational expectations. Keuzenkamp (1991) refers to a 1932 paper by Jan Tinbergen in which a model with rational expectations is developed. Pashigian (1987) referred to the work of Ronald Coase and Ronald Fowler on the pig cycle, published in several issues of *Economica* between 1935 and 1940, as containing the essence of what would several decades later become the rational expectations revolution in economics.

248. The way in which the new classical macroeconomists integrated Muth's analysis into their own became more controversial over time. Sent (2002, 315), a historian of economic thought, concluded that "Lucas' and Sargent's attempts to make Muth's history part of their own led them to misinterpret his intentions, misread his paper(s) and misrepresent his intentions." She also quotes Muth describing the application of his rational expectations hypothesis to macroeconomics as "a dumb idea" (305). In a lecture given one year before Sent's paper was published, Robert Lucas presented a totally different view on Muth's insights in relation to his own work. See Breit and Hirsch (2004).

249. Lucas later recalled that they were savagely attacked for this analysis, which one other economist referred to as "fascist economics" (Breit and Hirsch, 2004, 287).

250. Robert Lucas, interview by the author, October 30, 1996.

251. According to Mark Blaug (2001), the way in which Lucas uses the references to Hume's work is highly debatable.

252. Thomas Sargent, interview by the author, October 30, 1996.

253. See also the discussion in Chari (1998). Friedman (1976b), too, stressed the distinction between anticipated and unanticipated policy changes.

254. The seminal papers are Kydland and Prescott (1982), Long and Plosser (1983), and King and Plosser (1984).

255. Robert Lucas, interview by the author, October 30, 1996.

256. Ibid.

257. Friedman, M., 1951, "Comment", in Universities-National Bureau Committee for Economic Research, Conference on Business Cycles, New York.

258. Alan Blinder remarked that although Lucas's famous article on econometric policy evaluation was only published in 1976, the context of it was "well known in academic circles years before it was published" (Blinder 1988, 131).

259. See, for example, the remarks in Warsh (1993, 194). Deirdre McCloskey confirmed to the author that she remembers that Johnson and Mundell always spoke very highly of Metzler's work.

260. In an interview with the author on November 13, 2000, Paul Samuelson had the following to say on this episode: "T.W. Schultz offered me a chair in Chicago. I first accepted, not least because I thought I would have better students in Chicago. But very quickly it became clear to me that I had taken a wrong decision. The atmosphere in Chicago was one of extreme internal competition. Furthermore, it was clear to me that T.W. Schultz wanted to hire me as a counterweight to Milton Friedman, who had just come back to the University of Chicago. I feared, however, that the situation would just radicalize myself. So I called Schultz and told him that I had changed my mind."

261. Several of his earlier papers may be found in Bourneuf, Domar, and Samuelson (1973).

262. See various remarks in Frenkel and Johnson (1976).

263. Robert Aliber and Larry Sjaastad, interviews by the author, October 3, 1998 and October 4, 1998 respectively.

264. This point is more fully developed in a 1958 paper (Johnson 1976a).

265. For more on both of these approaches, see Alexander (1959).

266. Elizabeth Johnson became one of the editors of *The Collected Writings of John Maynard Keynes* during their stay in Cambridge.

267. Jagdish Bhagwati describes how, in seminars and other discussions, Harry Johnson often took sides with the isolated Dennis Robertson. See Bhagwati (1982).

268. H.G. Johnson, "Why Harry Johnson is Leaving Britain," *Times* (London), Higher Educational supplement, June 7, 1974.

269. See also remarks in Leeson (2000).

270. See, for example, H.G. Johnson (1972a).

271. Point made by Larry Sjaastad, interview by the author, October 4, 1998. See also the remarks in Laidler, (1984).

272. H.G. Johnson, "The Man Who Turned Economics into Common Sense," *Times* (London), March 9, 1976.

273. Most of these papers are collected in Mundell (1968a) and Mundell (1971b).

274. Mundell, 1962.

275. Observation made by several of the older economists at the University of Chicago, for example, Merton Miller and Larry Sjaastad.

276. The two articles are "Uncommon Arguments for Common Currencies" and "A Plan for a European Currency." See Johnson and Swoboda (1973).

277. Arthur Laffer, *Wall Street Journal*, October 18, 1999.

278. Press Release: The Sveriges Riksbank (Bank of Sweden) Prize in Economic Sciences in Memory of Alfred Nobel for 1999, http://nobelprize.org/economics/laureates/1999/press.html.

279. Ibid.

280. It cannot be overlooked that probably the most important, and in any case the most cited, paper Dornbusch ever published was an outcome of his period at the University of Chicago.

Dornbusch (1976) is a seminal analysis of the mechanisms behind exchange-rate overshooting. On the occasion of the 25th anniversary of the publication of this paper, Rogoff (2001, 1) argued that "[it] marks the birth of modern international macroeconomics."

281. Biographical data on Frenkel and Mussa were taken from the files at the Communications Office at the University of Chicago.

282. Early examples include Dornbusch and Frenkel (1973) and Frenkel (1974). See also Frenkel and Mussa (1981), Mussa (1991), and Mussa (1993).

283. For their contributions, see, for example, Mussa (1974), Rodriguez and Frenkel (1975), and Frenkel and Johnson (1976).

284. For a good survey, see Frenkel and Mussa (1985).

285. Typical examples are Robert Aliber and Anyl Kashyap.

Chapter 6

286. Most of these Chicago researchers are closely involved in the economic analysis of the law.

287. Milton Friedman, interview by the author, November 1, 1996. In this context, it is also interesting to note that there is no reference whatsoever to Coase in the memoir of Milton and Rose Friedman.

288. Coase refers to the link between the two articles as follows: "Transaction costs were used in the one case ['The Nature of the Firm'] to show that if they are not included in the analysis, the firm has no purpose, while in the other ['The Problem of Social Cost'] I showed, as I thought, that if transaction costs were not introduced into the analysis … the law had no purpose"(Medema 1994, 163).

289. That said, the fact remains that over the decades the differences between Pigou's analysis and Coase's analysis have gradually eclipsed the many parallels between the two analyses. See Aslanbeigui and Medema (1998).

290. Stigler officially "launched" the Coase Theorem in the third edition of his *Theory of Price*, which appeared in 1966. See also, for example, Stigler (1989).

291. In his memoir, Stigler points to Coleman Woodbury, one of his Northwestern teachers, as a man who played an important role in this evolution. See Stigler (1988b, 15).

292. Claire Friedland and Sam Peltzman emphasize that Stigler's lack of PhD students also had to do with the fact that he thought the best way to guide students was to let them find out everything by themselves. Milton Friedman, they claim, coached his students much more closely (Friedland and Peltzman, interviews by the author on several dates).

293. As far as the University of Chicago is concerned, typical examples are Telser (1964) and Nelson (1975).

294. Lester Telser, interview by the author, October 30, 1997.

295. Ibid.

296. Ibid.

297. From 1964 to 1965, Telser spent one additional year at the Cowles Commission after it had moved to Yale.

298. Telser himself started to use game theory early (Telser 1972).

299. Lester Telser, interview by the author, October 30, 1997.

300. Ibid.

301. Ibid.

302. Many of these papers can be found in Stigler (1965 and 1982b). On Ricardo, see Stigler (1958).

303. For the counterarguments, see Stigler and Friedland (1983).

304. Claire Friedman and James Heckman, interviews by the author on October 29 and 30, 1996, respectively.

305. Stephen Stigler, interview by the author, October 29, 1996.

306. Sam Peltzman, interview by the author, March 6, 1998.

307. Earlier in his career, Brozen produced remarkable papers on such topics as automation and the minimum wage. See Brozen (1957, 1962).

308. Clearly, a major source of inspiration for Stigler was Milton Friedman's review of Robert Triffin's book on monopolistic competition. See Friedman (1941).

309. For Leibenstein's original analysis, see Leibenstein (1966).

310. See Stigler's reply in Stigler and Kindahl (1973). See also Stigler and Kindahl (1970).

311. As a very close friend of George Stigler, Sam Peltzman realized very well that his conclusion would have been hard for his mentor to swallow. "George will probably turn around in his grave," Peltzman remarked, only half jokingly (interview by the author, December 2, 1998).

312. Actually, Stigler showed himself to be in considerable disagreement with Harberger's estimations.

313. Commenting in the mid 1960s on those who criticized his position that the minimum wage should be cut, Stigler said: "A fine thing they will say, to raise the economic status of the Negro boy by lowering his wage rate to a dollar an hour. A fine thing, indeed, I reply, to raise it from zero to one dollar" (as quoted in the *New York Times,* March 12, 1991).

314. See also the exchange of arguments between Lester Telser and Harold Demsetz in the *Journal of Political Economy,* March/April 1971.

315. Sam Peltzman told the author the story of Kessel knocking Peltzman off his feet when the latter delivered a paper on electricity pricing. The point Kessel jumped on was that one element of Peltzman's analysis was at odds with the details of the electricity bill Kessel had received that morning in his mail (interview, May 17, 1996).

316. See, for example, his 1965 article, "The Cyclical Behavior of the Term Structure of Interest Rates" (Kessel 1980).

317. A typical example is his 1967 article, "Economic Effects of Federal Regulation of Milk Markets" (Kessel 1980).

318. Several other economists at Chicago's business school also focused on empirical research on regulation. One of these was Peter Pashigian. See, for example, Pashigian (1985).

319. Sam Peltzman, interview by the author, May 17, 1996.

Chapter 7

320. In 1997 Douglas Irwin left Chicago's GSB for family reasons.

321. The intention had been to appoint Henry Schultz as director of research of the Cowles Commission. Because of Schultz's unexpected death in September 1938, Yntema was appointed to the post. Yntema was succeeded by Jacob Marshak in 1943.

322. With his remarks on large companies and monopoly power, Yntema clearly anticipated the reversal in thinking about monopoly that Chicago would undergo in the 1950s, mainly under the influence of Aaron Director. However, Evsey Domar, who was for a short time Yntema's assistant in the early 1940s, suggests that Yntema took the beneficial effects of large companies as an axiom and looked, rather selectively, for evidence to support this axiom (Domar 1992, 121–22).

323. See, for example, Yntema (1958).

324. Robert Fogel, interview by the author, October 29, 1996.

325. Ibid.

326. Fogel's conclusions were hotly contested by other economic historians. See, for example, McAfee (1983).

327. Sam Peltzman recalls: "Basically Earl Hamilton remained all his life the football coach he was during his younger days in Mississippi" (interview by the author, June 6, 2000). Rose Friedman refers to "our good friend and colleague Earl Hamilton" (Friedman and Friedman, 1998, 147).

328. See, for example, Hamilton (1934). Some historians have expressed the opinion that Hamilton's data sometimes lacked the solid basis needed for scientific inquiry. Charles Kindleberger

(1999, 157) claimed: "E.J. Hamilton collected his prices for sixteenth-century Spain from hospital records, which managers had little reason to keep accurately, and which are implausible. The numbers on silver imports for his study came from the Casa de la Contratacion in Seville whereas considerable amounts escaped official surveillance in Lisbon, at Cadiz and in smuggling."

329. Two books, both published posthumously, give an excellent overview of Kahan's work: *The Plow, the Hammer, and the Knout: An Economic History of Eighteenth-Century Russia* (1985) and *Essays in Jewish Social and Economic History* (1986).

330. In his initial plan for the University of Chicago, Harper writes about the College of Practical Arts, the curriculum of which "will be arranged with greater reference ... to the practical departments of business and of professional life" (Turner 1958, 1). In later plans and publications, Harper dropped this idea.

331. See, for example, Turner (1958, 27–28) for the letter from Rollin Salisbury, professor of geology, to president Harper on his strong opposition to business education as part of the curriculum at the University of Chicago.

332. This point is well documented in Turner (1958).

333. It was renamed the School of Commerce and Administration in 1916, and in 1959 Chicago's business school became the Graduate School of Business.

334. See Dreiser (1971). In 1929, Ursula Batchelder became the first woman in the United States to earn a PhD from a business school, and that school was Chicago.

335. For more on Hutchins, see Shils (1991a) and Dzubak (1991).

336. Jim Lorie, interview by the author, October 29, 1997.

337. For Bach's full life story, see, for example, Gleeson and Schlossman (1995, 2,41), who wrote: "of several individuals who played strategic roles in the transformation of graduate management education following World War Two, perhaps the most enduring figure was George Leland (Lee) Bach ... Bach was an educational missionary, intent on advancing scientific progress and transforming fundamental educational processes."

338. Philip Mirowski describes this Statistical Research Group as the "occasion for the consolidation of what later became known as the 'Chicago School' of economics in the postwar period" (Mirowski 2002, 203).

339. See, for example, Director, A., M. Friedman, and W.A. Wallis, W.A. 1950. *A positive program for conservatives*, Symposium, University of Chicago, archives, 1. Notice the title's resemblance to Henry Simons's tract *A Positive Program for Laissez Faire*.

340. Jim Lorie, interview by the author, October 29, 1997.

341. Jim Lorie, interview by the author, October 29, 1997.

342. Among his students was Victor Niederhoffer, the notorious speculator, with whom Lorie even published a paper (1968).

343. Jim Lorie, interview by the author, October 29, 1997.

344. Ibid.

345. Victor Zarnowitz, interview by the author, October 27, 1997.

346. Zarnowitz (1992) gives a good survey of his work.

347. Robin Hogarth, interview by the author, March 9, 1998.

348. Einhorn died of Hodgkin's disease at the young age of 45.

349. Hogarth (1990) contains a complete bibliography of Einhorn's research work.

350. Robin Hogarth, interview by the author, March 9, 1998. See also, for example, Einhorn and Hogarth (1987).

351. Robin Hogarth, interview by the author, March 9, 1998.

352. See, for example, his remarks in Arbeiter (1985, footnote 50).

353. See, for example, Davis and Hogarth (1992).

354. Robin Hogarth, interview by the author, March 9, 1998.

355. See, for example, Tinbergen (1937).

356. Typical examples of this approach are Theil (1958, 1971).

357. The original contribution here is Theil, H., 1953, "Repeated Least-Squares Applied to Complete Equations Systems", The Hague, Central Planning Bureau, mimeograph copy, from the archives at the Communications Department of the University of Chicago. See also Theil (1971).

358. See also Zellner and Fienberg (1975). Most of Zellner's papers on Bayesian econometrics can be found in Zellner (1997).

359. Several attempts by the author to get in touch with Arnold Zellner and Henri Theil failed. The quarrel between the two is common knowledge on the Chicago campus.

360. With respect to macroeconomic issues Hardy showed himself to be a solid believer in the quantity theory. See Hardy (1932).

361. Ezra Solomon, telephone interview by the author, June 1, 2000.

362. Jim Lorie, interview by the author, October 29, 1998.

363. See also Fisher and Lorie (1968).

364. Lorie, J. *The Wall Street Journal,* May 28, 1996.

365. Eugene Fama, interview by the author, January 15, 1996.

366. The seminal contributions are Alchian and Demsetz (1972) and Jensen and Meckling (1976).

367. This point was first made by Chicago's Henry Manne. See Manne (1965).

368. The classic references are Fama (1965a, 1965b). Two years earlier, he had already argued along similar lines in Fama (1963).

369. Eugene Fama made similar comments in interview by the author, January 15, 1996.

370. Jarrell, G., *Wall Street Journal,* October 1990.

371. Miller kept his good humor intact until his death. This is reflected in the e-mails the author received from Miller. The last of these, dated April 19, 2000, confirmed a meeting for the author's next trip to Chicago on June 3, 2000. Merton Miller died June 3, 2000.

372. Merton Miller, interview by the author, May 11, 1999.

373. Fama, E.F. and French, K.R., 1997, "Dividend, Debt, Investment, and Earnings", article copy presented to author by Fama.

374. See, for example, Black, Miller and Posner (1978).

375. See, for example, Miller (1991).

376. See Allen (1995). The story was confirmed by Milton Friedman in an interview with the author, November 1, 1996.

377. Paul Samuelson as quoted in the *New York Times,* August 31, 1995.

378. The Economist, September 9, 1995.

379. See, for example, Black, Jensen, and Schole (1972).

380. Dixit as quoted in the *International Herald Tribune,* October 26, 1997.

381. See, for example, Black (1995b).

382. See also Black (1982).

383. For the details of this story, see *Business Week,* August 28, 1994.

384. *Wall Street Journal,* October 15, 1997.

385. For the full story of LTCM and the role of Myron Scholes in the affair, see Lowenstein (2000).

386. At that time, Thaler and De Bondt were both at at Cornell University. De Bondt later moved to the University of Wisconsin. The papers referred to are De Bondt and Thaler (1985, 1987).

387. In several papers, it was argued that the De Bondt and Thaler analysis showed biased results because of the inadequate treatment of risk and size effects. See, for example, Fama and French (1993).

388. Richard Thaler, interview by the author, March 12, 1997.

389. This person insisted on anonymity.

390. Richard Thaler, interview by the author, March 12, 1997.

391. For more on their work, see for example, Kahneman, Slovic, and Tversky (1982).

392. Richard Thaler, interview by the author, March 12, 1997.

393. Most of these papers are to be found in Thaler (1991).

394. Richard Thaler, interview by the author, March 12, 1997.

395. In the October 21, 1996, issue, *Business Week* described how Nick Barberis was given a special visa for the United States on the grounds, argued by lawyers hired by the University of Chicago, that the British-born Barberis should be considered a genius. After earning his PhD at Harvard in 1996, Barberis joined Chicago's GSB. His research focused on issues closely related to behavioral finance such as the psychology of investors. See, for example, Barberis and Huang (2001).

396. An excellent update on the discussion of efficient markets and behavioral finance is to be found in the *Journal of Economic Perspectives,* Winter 2003. See also Barberis and Thaler (2003).

397. The original contribution is Mehra and Prescott (1985).

398. Richard Thaler, interview by the author, March 12, 1997. See also Benartzi and Thaler (1995).

399. Robert Vishny, interview by the author, December 3, 1998.

400. See also, for example, Morck, Shleifer, and Vishny (1990).

401. By the late 1960s, Michael Jensen, one of Eugene Fama's students, had come to similar conclusions with respect to mutual funds. See Jensen (1968).

402. Robert Aliber, interview by the author, January 15, 1996.

403. Ibid.

404. Ibid.

405. Anil Kashyap, interview by the author, March 11, 1998.

406. Alwyn Young was the first to make this point, but it was his former MIT colleague Paul Krugman who got most of the credit for this revelation.

407. Dennis Carlton, interview by the author, March 11, 1997.

408. First published in 1990, the book went into a fifth edition in 2005.

409. For references on these topics, see Carlton and Perloff (2005) and Carlton's website at the GSB.

410. Robert Gertner, interview by the author, October 30, 1997.

411. Ibid.

412. See, for example, Baird, Gertner, and Picker (1994) and Asquith, Gertner, and Scharfstein (1994).

413. Chicago's James Heckman was visiting Yale when Goolsbee did his undergraduate work there. Heckman played an important role in bringing Goolsbee to Chicago. Goolsbee points to James Poterba as the major influence on him while at MIT. Interview by the author, October 19, 1997.

414. For further references, see Goolsbee's website at the GSB.

415. Lars Stole, interview by the author, May 13, 1999.

416. For references to his work, see Stole's website at the GSB.

417. This senior faculty member preferred to remain anonymous.

Chapter 8

418. For a typical example of Ernest Freund's economically inspired legal reasoning, see Freund (1912).

419. For a counterargument to these allegations, see, Boulding (1958) and "The Methodology in Positive Economics" in Friedman (1953).

420. On this subject, see also Posner (1981).

421. Milton Friedman, interview by the author, November 1, 1996.

422. Edward Levi praised Katz as an innovator in legal education. See Levi (1977, 3, 23).

423. In 1950, this same W. Volker Fund would sponsor the Committee on Social Thought that brought Friedrich Hayek to the University of Chicago for a prolonged period.

424. One of the rare articles Aaron Director produced was written with Ed Levi (Director and Levi 1956).

425. "Walter was much more to the University than a professor of law," commented Howard Krane, chairman of the University of Chicago Board of Trustees in *The University of Chicago News,* December 19, 1994.

426. Arthur Okun, a leading Keynesian macroeconomist and chairman of the Council of Economic Advisors under President Kennedy, made this point in Okun (1975). For Blum's counter-arguments, see Blum (1976).

427. Lester Telser, interview by the author, October 10, 1997.

428. This meant that in those days Chicago was largely in line with the Harvard view on industrial organization, monopoly, and antitrust. For this Harvard view, see Mason (1939) and Kaysen (1959).

429. See, for example, Bork (1954).

430. See, for example, Bowman (1952) and Telser (1960).

431. Yale Brozen was an outspoken defender of the Chicago position.

432. William Landes recalled that Ronald Coase finally got tired of antitrust because "when the prices went up, the judges said it was monopoly, when the prices went down, they said it was predatory pricing, and when they stayed the same, they said it was tacit collusion" (Kitch, 1983a, 193).

433. On this issue, see also Williamson (1983).

434. Hence Karl Brunner's description of Ronald Coase as the "patriarch of the new institutional economics" (Brunner 1992, 7). For Coase's own views, see Coase (1984) and his Nobel lecture (Coase 1997). Other important members of the new institutional school include Douglass North, Oliver Williamson, and Benjamin Klein.

435. As William Landes confirmed in an interview by the author, June 5, 2000.

436. Coase, Alchian, and Demsetz, however, were not the first to develop the issue of property rights. Adam Smith, Karl Marx, and Frank Knight clearly recognized the importance of property rights in their writings. Austrian economists such as Carl Menger and Ludwig von Mises also dealt with the subject. See Chapter V in Foss (1994).

437. It should be noted that Gary Becker not only explicitly acknowledged Alchian's contribution to his textbook on economic theory (Becker 1971) but also pointed to Alchian as having inspired his work on crime and punishment (Kitch 1983a, 230).

438. John McGee's article on patenting starts with the statement that "those who know Aaron Director well may recognize how much this essay owes to him" (McGee 1966, 135).

439. Edmund Kitch, interview by the author, September 24, 1997.

440. Ibid.

441. William Landes, interview by the author, March 10, 1998.

442. William Landes, interview by the author, June 5, 2000.

443. Posner, R. 1990. 100 years of antitrust. *Wall Street Journal,* June 29.

444. The full title of the first edition was *Antitrust: An Economic Perspective.* In the 2001 edition, the second part of that title was left out because "the other perspectives have largely fallen away" since 1976 (Posner 2001a, vii).

445. This dramatic episode, in which Bork's two superiors refused to carry out Nixon's orders, came to be known as the "Saturday Night Massacre." See Russakoff, D., and A. Kamen. 1987, "The Shaping of Robert H. Bork" (three parts), *The Washington Post,* July 26, 27, and 28.

446. *Chicago Chronicles,* November 15, 1984.

447. *Washington Post,* September 10, 1995.

448. Fischel documents well his claim that U.S. Attorney General Rudolph Giuliani manipulated the Milken case to promote his own political career. Shortly afterwards Giuliani became mayor of New York City.

449. William Landes, interview by the author, March 10, 1998.

450. For references to these research papers, see Carlton's personal website at the GSB.

451. According to several commentators, the highly controversial nature of this book has cost Epstein an appointment to the U.S. Supreme Court.

452. Epstein had published on civil rights before *Forbidden Grounds*, which led to a sharp discussion with Chicago economist James Heckman. See Heckman and Verkerke (1990) and Epstein (1990).

453. A typical example of a vitriolic review was that by Clarence Page in the May 31, 1992 *Chicago Tribune*. A somewhat more balanced review by Calvin Woodward, a law teacher at the University of Virginia, appeared in the *New York Times Book Review* (May 10, 1992). One of the rare positive reviews came, somewhat ironically, from Thomas Sowell, a black scholar working at the Hoover Institution (see his comments in *Forbes*, April 30, 1992).

454. Douglas Baird as quoted in the *National Law Review*, October 14, 1996.

455. See, for example, Picker (1993).

456. Alan Sykes, interview by the author, March 12, 1997.

457. Obviously, Sunstein makes a reference here to the work of Richard Thaler, among others. In 1998 Sunstein and Thaler, together with Harvard's Christine Jolls, published a paper outlining a behavioral approach to law and economics. They depart from the standard assumptions of neoclassical economics, which are "often false" (Jolls, Sunstein, and Thaler 1998, 59). On behavioral law and economics, see Sunstein (2000).

458. For a general survey of the new directions taken in research on law and economics at the University of Chicago and elsewhere, see Sykes (2002).

459. Eric Posner, interview by the author, June 5, 2000.

460. William Landes, interview by the author, March 10, 1998.

461. Kenneth Dam, interview by the author, November 30, 1998.

462. Daniel Fischel, interview by the author, December 4, 1998.


Chapter 9

463. *New York Times*, October 28, 1982.

464. See, for example, George Shultz, "The Challenge of Unemployment," (address to the U.S. Chambers of Commerce, Washington, DC, April 30, 1963). A copy of the speech is in the Communications Department archives, University of Chicago.

465. The three quotes above are all from Dun's Review, October 1972.

466. Kenneth Dam, interview by the author, November 30, 1998.

467. Ibid.

468. See, for example, Dam (1964).

469. See also Dam (1976).

470. Kenneth Dam, interview by the author, November 30, 1998.

471. Both quotes are from John K. Gailbraith, *Chicago Tribune Magazine*, January 20, 1980.

472. In his autobiography, Douglas does not refer to his constant quarrels with Knight. George Stigler, a student of both men, covers this extensively in his memoir. See Stigler (1988b).

473. *New York Times*, September 25, 1976.

474. *Chicago Tribune*, November 14, 1976. By 1947, Paul Douglas was staunchly anti-communist. See Douglas (1947).

475. *Chicago Daily News*, September 25, 1976.

476. References to most of these critiques and replies to them can be found in Douglas (1934) and Douglas (1976).

477. See the arguments in Douglas (1976).

478. This statement comes from the 1987 edition of his *Theory of Price*. At that time economists had developed various alternatives to the CD production function such as the CES- and VES-variants.

479. For a survey, see Douglas (1934). See also Douglas and Schoenberg (1937).

480. David Broder, *Chicago Tribune,* March 29, 1992.

481. Biographical data are taken from Hayek (1994) and from the introduction in Leube and Nishiyama (1984).

482. For more on the origins of the Austrian School of Economics, see Hicks and Weber (1973).

483. The most important references with respect to Hayek's business cycle analysis are Hayek (1929 and 1931).

484. After receiving the Nobel Prize in economics in 1974, Hayek returned to these issues. See, for example, Hayek (1975).

485. For an excellent introduction to the debate between Hayek and Keynes and the Keynesians, see McCormick (1992).

486. Hayek explained why he never took issue with the Keynes of the *General Theory* as follows. Referring to the fact that his critique of Keynes's *Treatise on Money* was published in two separate issues of *Economica*, Hayek commented that "when the second part came out, Keynes told me 'Oh, never mind; I no longer believe all that.' Which is very discouraging … In retrospect I always say it was for this reason I did not return to the charge on *The General Theory*" (Hayek 1994, 90). Bruce Caldwell argues that "… in the end, Hayek did, in a manner of speaking, write a review, not of the General Theory per se, but of the whole Keynesian approach. For it turns out that in most of his accounts of why he did not review *The General Theory,* Hayek manages to slip in an assessment of Keynes' contributions." See Caldwell (1998).

487. It is remarkable how close Hayek's appreciation of Keynes comes to that offered by Jacob Viner.

488. See, for example, Finer (1946).

489. Hayek (1994) acknowledged that the financial package was very important in his transfer to Chicago. This must be seen against the background of the emotionally painful divorce Hayek was going through at the time. The financial incentive for going to the United States is also stressed in Ebenstein (2001).

490. Both insisted on not being quoted directly on this issue.

491. Milton Friedman, interview by the author, November 1, 1996.

492. Hayek wrote several articles on this issue in the early 1940s. See especially Hayek (1942 and 1974).

493. In his introduction to a volume of essays on the work of Hayek, Friedman wrote: "Friedrich Hayek's influence has been tremendous. His work is incorporated in the body of technical economic theory; has had a major influence on economic history, political philosophy and political science … I … owe him a great debt" (Machlup 1977, xxi).

494. For the detailed story of this Society, see Hartwell (1995).

495. Arnold Luhnow's Volker Fund also contributed to financing the Mont Pèlerin Society.

496. The parallels and differences between Hayek and Lucas are further explored in Foss (1994).

497. Taken from the website of The Nobel Prize for Economics: nobelprize.org/nobel_prizes/economics.

498. See, for example, Sjaastad (1983), Rosett (1984); Harberger, 1993(b); Pinera (1994), and Valdes (1995), although this last book shows a remarkable lack of knowledge about what Chicago Economics is all about.

499. For an overview of several Chicago papers on economic development, see Wall (1972).

500. See also Hoselitz (1960).

501. Simon Rottenberg was born in 1916 and earned his PhD in economics in 1950 at Harvard. He spent the period 1954–61 at the University of Chicago, during which he focused his research on labor economics.

502. Mario Zanaru, an economist strongly opposed to the Chicago approach to economics, complained: "The importance of price theory permeated everything" (Valdes 1995, 206).

503. Larry Sjaastad, interview by the author, March 6, 1998.

504. Ibid.

505. *Fortune,* November 2, 1981.

506. For the performance of the Chilean economy up to the early 1990s and the policy lessons to be drawn from it, see Bosworth, Dornbusch, and Laban (1994).

507. Milton Friedman describes this press war against him in great detail in his memoirs. Friedman's Nobel lecture was disturbed by protesters against his alleged involvement with Chile. Too often it was forgotten that on several occasions, Friedman explicitly spoke out against the brutal repression by the Chilean junta. See Friedman and Friedman (1998). Moreover, it is highly ironic that, according to Larry Sjaastad, Friedman was initially firmly opposed to the close cooperation between the University of Chicago and the UCC (Larry Sjaastad, interview by the author, March 6, 1998). This was confirmed by Deirdre McCloskey in an interview by the author, April 22, 2000. McCloskey also pointed out that sometime in the 1970s, a deal for cooperation was made between the department of economics of the University of Chicago and an Iranian university. At the last moment this deal was killed, in no small measure by Friedman, who firmly opposed cooperation with the undemocratic regime of the Shah. See also McCloskey (2003).

508. Harberger's link with his Chilean students was made closer by the fact that through two of them, Ernesto Fontaine and Luis Arturo Fuenzalida, Harberger met his wife Ana Beatriz Valjalo, who taught Spanish at Northwestern University. See del Solar (1992).

509. *Chicago Tribune,* January 13, 1997.

510. It was probably not just the traditional argument of the nice Californian climate (as opposed to the rougher weather typical of Chicago) that convinced Harberger to transfer completely to UCLA. In 1992 Harberger declared: "The orientation of the Economics Department at Chicago has changed. They are less interested in economic policy and more in the technical and mathematical aspects, which have less immediate application" (del Solar, 1992, 6).

511. The basic reference is Harberger (1972b), which brings together his major contributions in this area.

512. Three contemporaries of Stigler and Harberger confirmed the cool relationship between the two. All three insisted on anonymity.

513. For an early analysis of the economic situation in Argentina, see Sjaastad (1966).

514. Larry Sjaastad, interview by the author, June 7, 2000.

515. Ibid.

516. See, for example, Sjaastad (1998).

517. Larry Sjastaad, interview by the author, June 7, 2000.

# Index